Understanding the Emerging Contours of Power and Hegemony

Published in association with
Observer Research Foundation
New Delhi

Observer Research Foundation (ORF) is a public policy think-tank that aims to influence formulation of policies for building a strong and prosperous India. The ORF pursues these goals by providing informed and productive inputs, in-depth research and stimulating discussion. The Foundation is supported in its mission by a cross-section of India's leading public figures, academics and business leaders.

Understanding the Emerging Contours of Power and Hegemony

Contemporary Geo-political Narratives

Editors

Angira Sen Sarma
Yury Byaly

ACADEMIC FOUNDATION
NEW DELHI

www.academicfoundation.com

First published in 2014
by

ACADEMIC FOUNDATION
4772-73 / 23 Bharat Ram Road, (23 Ansari Road),
Darya Ganj, New Delhi - 110 002 (India).
Phones : 23245001 / 02 / 03 / 04.
Fax : +91-11-23245005.
E-mail : books@academicfoundation.com
www.academicfoundation.com

in association with the
Observer Research Foundation, New Delhi

Cataloging in Publication Data--DK
Courtesy: D.K. Agencies (P) Ltd. <docinfo@dkagencies.com>

Understanding the emerging contours of power and hegemony / editors, Angira Sen Sarma, Yury Byaly.
p. cm.
Contributed articles.
ISBN 9789332701373

1. National security--India. 2. National security--Russia (Federation) 3. Globalization--Economic aspects. 4. Globalization--Economic aspects--India. 5. Globalization--Economic aspects--Russia (Federation) 6. Hegemony. 7. World politics--21st century. I. Sarma, Angira Sen. II. Byaly, Yury.

DDC 355.033054 23

Typeset by Italics India, New Delhi.

Printed and bound by The Book Mint, New Delhi.
www.thebookmint.in

Contents

Part II
Global Issues: Views from India and Russia

Part III
India-Russia and the World

About the Editors/ Contributors

Editors:

Angira Sen Sarma is an Assistant Professor at the Afghanistan Studies Centre, Academy of International Studies, Jamia Millia Islamia, New Delhi. Her primary areas of research are Central Asia and Afghanistan. She has authored a book, *India and Central Asia: Redefining Energy and Trade Links (2010)* and has contributed chapters in edited volumes. Before joining the Jamia Millia Islamia, she worked with Indian Council of World Affairs (ICWA), New Delhi and Observer Research Foundation (ORF), New Delhi. She has done her PhD from Jawaharlal Nehru University, New Delhi.

Yury Byaly is the Vice-President of the International Public Foundation-"Experimental Creative Centre" (IPF-ECC), Moscow. His area of research includes problems of geoeconomy, global policy and energy.

Contributors:

Yury Bardakhchiev is the Head of Military-Political Studies Division at IPF-ECC, Moscow. His areas of research include Russia's nuclear doctrine, Russia-North Atlantic Treaty Organization (NATO) relations and non-proliferation.

Kaustav Dhar Chakrabarti was a Junior Fellow at the ORF where he researched security and politics of Pakistan and Afghanistan. After a four year stint at the ORF that culminated in August 2012, he has begun graduate study at Binghamton University, New York, where he expects to continue studying civil conflict with focus on South Asia.

Mikhail Dmitriev is a Senior Analyst at the IPF-ECC, Moscow. His area of research includes problems of drug trafficking and ways and means of fighting this threat.

Wilson John is a Senior Fellow and Vice President at the Centre for International Relations, ORF, New Delhi. He heads the Centre's South Asia Studies Programme. His interests include the South Asian geopolitics, asymmetric warfare, Islamist extremism and civil-military relations. He is recognised as one of the leading authorities on the militant group, Lashkar-e-Tayyeba. He has authored/edited 11 books on issues of security and terrorism.

Sunjoy Joshi is Director, ORF, New Delhi. Before joining the ORF, he had 25 years of experience in the Indian Administrative Service (IAS). He headed the Madhya Pradesh Energy Development Agency as its Managing Director and served as the Chairman of M.P. Windfarms. His research areas include energy, climate change and development studies.

Ajish P. Joy was an Associate Fellow at the ORF till October 2011. Presently, he is with the *The Week* magazine. He has done his PhD in International Relations from Jawaharlal Nehru University (JNU), New Delhi. His areas of interest include the US, Eurasia and the Middle East. He has a book and several articles to his credit.

Eduard Kryukov is a Senior Analyst at the IPF-ECC, Moscow. His areas of research are history of emergence and current state of radical movements and expansion of Neo-Nazi groups in Europe.

Sergey Kurginyan is President, IPF-ECC, Moscow, Academician of the National Academy for Social Technologies, Editor-in Chief of the journal *Russia XXI* and producer of the *Theatre on the Boards*. His areas of interest include development of the elite theory, research of political trends in Russia and the world at large and decision-making process.

Vladimir Novikov is a Senior Analyst at the IPF-ECC. His areas of research include inter-ethnic processes in the Caucasus and Central Asia, political trends in post-Soviet area and military-political processes in the Middle East.

Maria Podkopaeva is the Head of Information and Analysis Division at the IPF-ECC, Moscow. Her areas of research include historic religious tradition in Central Asia and contemporary manifestations of Islamic radicalism.

Rahul Prakash is a Junior Fellow at the ORF. His research interests include technology and security; chemical, biological, radiological and nuclear (CBRN) issues; and security developments in Asia. He has co-authored a report on "Chemical, Biological and Radiological Materials: An Analysis of Security Risks and Terrorist Threats in India", an outcome of a joint study conducted by the ORF and the London-based Royal United Services Institute. He has also published 'issue briefs' on China's progress in space and rise of microblogs in China.

Rajeswari Pillai Rajagopalan is a Senior Fellow at the Institute of Security Studies, ORF, New Delhi. Her areas of research include U.S. foreign and security policy, military strategies of major Asian powers including China, the US, Japan and Russia.

M. Rasgotra, a distinguished member of the Indian Foreign Service (IFS) from 1949 to 1990, was India's Foreign Secretary from 1982 to 1985. He played a significant role in the prestigious events of the period—the Seventh Non-Aligned Summit, the Commonwealth Heads of Government Meeting, the Six-Nation Appeal on Nuclear Disarmament and the Six-Nation Summit in New Delhi. He is the founder President of the International Institute of Asia-Pacific Studies. At the time of the preparation of this book, he was President, Centre for International Relations, ORF, New Delhi. In 2002, he was decorated with the Padma Bhushan.

Vivan Sharan is an Associate Fellow at the ORF, New Delhi. An economist, educated at the University of Edinburgh, and St. Stephens College, University of Delhi, his research areas include economic policy, trade, finance, energy and multilateralism. He regularly contributes to leading newspapers and journals, and is a guest lecturer at the Institute for Government Accounts and Finance, an international training and capacity building institute, run by the Ministry of Finance, India.

Vera Sorokina is a Senior Analyst at the IPF-ECC, Moscow. Her areas of research include climate change and new trends in the natural sciences.

Marina Volchkova is a Senior Analyst at the IPF-ECC, Moscow. Her area of interest includes world population trends and migration.

Editor's Note

India-Russia bilateral relations have withstood the test of time, with both remaining important partners for each other. The fall of the Soviet Union led to adjustments in the bilateral ties in keeping with the changing international milieu. Today, our strategic partnership includes a wide range of areas: economy, science and technology, energy, space and defence, indicating the continuance of strong ties between the two countries.

This volume is a joint project of the Observer Research Foundation (ORF), New Delhi, and the International Public Foundation—"Experimental Creative Centre" (IPF-ECC), Moscow. It is a compilation of papers presented at the conference held in September 2010 in Moscow and in March 2011 in New Delhi and has been published in Russian and English.

This edition is divided into three sections. The first discusses the various dimensions of security challenges and how India and Russia views these issues. Proliferation of nuclear weaponry is one of the major security challenges in the 21st century. Yury Bardakhchiev in his paper argues that there are contradictions among the members of the Treaty on the Non-Proliferation of Nuclear Weapons (NPT). He suggests that reforms in the NPT is crucial, but will not be an easy task. Rajeswari Pillai Rajagopalan, in her paper, throws light on the non-proliferation challenges facing Asia. She identifies five major threats: China-Pakistan nuclear cooperation and the nuke smuggling ring, North Korea, Iran, the Weapons of Mass Destruction (WMD) terrorism and the state of the non-proliferation regime. She also argues that the present global nuclear regime needs to be reorganised to address new challenges.

Both countries have been victims of terrorism, religious extremism and drug trafficking, which is extensively discussed in this section. Since September 11, the nature of terrorism has become more complex, argues Wilson John. Proper understanding of the changing face of terrorism is vital for effective counter-terrorism strategies. Maria Podkopaeva argues that religious extremist groups like Islamic Movement of Uzbekistan (IMU) with links with Taliban and Al Qaeda pose serious threat to the Central Asian region. She warns that these extremist groups in the region will strengthen after the international forces leave Afghanistan. Eduard Kryukov analyses the ideological factors behind terror tactics used by the extremist groups. He has outlined the long history of interactions between the Islamic radical groups and fascist groups.

The nexus between drug trafficking and crime is a well-founded fact today. Mikhail Dmitriev highlights that the problem of drug trafficking poses a serious threat not only to the main consumption destinations like Russia and Western Europe, but also for transit countries like the Central Asian Republics (CARs). He recommends that there is a need for concerted effort, such as destroying poppy fields, eradicating drug laboratories and encouraging cultivation of profitable crops to tackle the menace. Rahul Prakash argues that constant efforts by international organisations and the Afghanistan Government to curb drug trafficking have not met with much success and it is one of the major challenges thwarting development in that war ravaged country. Co-operation and consensus among various players to contain drug trafficking in Afghanistan is the need of the hour.

The second section of the volume looks into the convergence as also divergence of interests between India and Russia on various global issues. International financial crisis, climate change and migration are some of the global issues concerning the two countries. Yury Byaly in his first paper writes that the impact of the global financial crisis is visible in various sectors. There is a need for 'comprehensive monitoring' of the unfolding situation. Sunjoy Joshi discusses how resource constraints in developing countries like India and China shape their domestic energy policies. The demand for natural gas will increase, leading to global interdependence, which will redefine the global geopolitics. Vera Sorokina, in her paper, analyses the impact of climate change in international relations. The dichotomy between developed and developing countries is also highlighted in the paper. Marina Volchkova throws light on the challenges migration poses for Russia. She argues that there is need to undertake detailed studies on the impact of migration. Voluntary migration has a deep impact on a nation's security, argues Vivan Sharan. There is a need to reform immigration policies, especially in the developed world, to effectively address the issue. Multilateral cooperation is crucial, says the author.

The third section deals with the two countries' views on contemporary world order and their engagement with the world. Sergey Kurginyan in his paper argues that to find answers to the complexities of the present world order, it is essential to understand the political philosophies giving rise to negative developments and the support behind these philosophies. M. Rasgotra in his paper argues that today it is difficult for any one country or a group of states to become a hegemonic power. At the same time, with growing interdependence among states, it would not be easy for states to be in conflicts for long. States, however, will make associates and friends in their regions for greater political influence, says the author. Yury Byaly in his second paper analyses how international organisations are being used by the powerful countries to serve their own interests. He argues that a new type of international organisation has come up: 'semi-formal' international entities that deal with local conflicts on behalf of the international community.

The situation in the Middle East has far reaching consequences on both countries. Vladimir Novikov argues that differences between Israel and the US and the new policy in Turkey are clear signs of the beginning of a large-scale reconfiguration in the Middle East situation; it will deteriorate with the increase in tension in Arab-Israel, Iran-Israel and Turkey-Israel relations. Ajish P. Joy discusses the intractable nature of the Israel-Palestine conflict. The 'final status issues', Jerusalem border and settlement, status of refugees are some of the major stumbling blocks in the peace negotiation process. Peace in the region is still a distant dream.

The continuing deteriorating situation in Afghanistan is a concern for Russia and India. Kaustav Dhar Chakrabarti explores the possibilities of cooperation between India and Pakistan in Afghanistan. India-Pakistan differences on Afghanistan are confined to security issues; however, there is scope for cooperation in the economic sector. In the prevailing condition in Afghanistan, it is crucial that the regional countries play an active role in stabilising Afghanistan, argues Angira Sen Sarma. India, Russia and the CARs could jointly play a greater constructive role in this area.

It is hoped that the present volume will help in developing further understanding between the two countries. The views expressed here are individual opinions of the authors and do not necessarily reflect the views of the ORF.

For the English edition of the volume, I take this opportunity to thank a few individuals for their support, without which this volume would not have seen the light of day. I have great pleasure in expressing sincere thanks to all the contributors to the volume. I am thankful to Mr Nandan Unnikrishnan, Vice President, ORF, for his guidance and support in finalising the manuscript. I wish to thank the IPF-ECC team for their cooperation and assistance in bringing out the volume. I owe thanks also to the translators for their meticulous work. My sincere thanks to Ms Anshu John, the ORF Resident Editor, and the copy editor for their excellent editing of the manuscript. My deep appreciation to the publisher, Academic Foundation for the final publication of the volume. Last but not the least, my thanks to Ms Sadhavi Chauhan, Associate Fellow, ORF, for helping to prepare the manuscript for publication.

— Angira Sen Sarma

Part I

Security Dynamics: Indian and Russian Perspectives

1

Non-Proliferation or Proliferation?

What are the Global Nuclear Trends of the 21st Century?

Yury Bardakhchiev

Today, it is universally acknowledged that there is no alternative but to enforce non-proliferation of nuclear weapons. The world is unified in the belief that there should in no case be an increase in the number of countries possessing nuclear weapons, as there would then be the risk of a global nuclear war, which is guaranteed to destroy the world. The primary mechanism of deterrence against spread of nuclear weapons is the Treaty on the Non-proliferation of Nuclear Weapons (NPT), to which all of the countries in the world belong, with the exception of four.

However, is this mechanism working on the ground? Even a cursory look at the world scenario shows that among the parties to the Treaty, there are irreconcilable contradictions—that different countries interpret the NPT articles in different ways. The Treaty, *per se,* is incapable of solving the major problems of disarmament, and the very idea of non-proliferation, which has long been imposed on the world, is resisted by many nations. The countries that had signed the Treaty in 1968 did so in the fond hope that doing so would bring the nuclear arms race to a halt and all such weapons would be destroyed in the foreseeable future. Time has belied this hope: the number of nuclear powers has not reduced but increased and, for the time being, no one intends to destroy their nuclear weapons.

There are no indications that the 'nuclear five' (USA, Russia, Britain, France and China) intend to abandon their nuclear weapons, which violates the spirit and letter of the NPT. Just the same, countries not wishing to join the NPT (India, Pakistan, North Korea and Israel) also do not intend to abandon their nuclear weapons, and the given situation calls into question the very existence of the NPT. Assistance in building a peaceful nuclear energy programme, promised by the Treaty to all the other countries—the condition being that they abstain from acquiring nuclear weapons—has either been intentionally slowed or is carried out selectively, and this is again a violation of the substantive provisions of the Treaty.

As a result, the majority of these countries are irritated by the limitations of the NPT and would like to withdraw from it, since only the 'nuclear five' benefit from the Treaty (especially the USA and countries close to it) by using the non-proliferation regime as a tool for political pressure and manipulation. It is for this reason that the Review Conferences on Non-Proliferation held every 5 years have failed to adopt resolutions on a consensus basis. This raises the fundamental question of whether the chosen path in the fight against non-proliferation of nuclear weapons is the correct one.

In this paper, we will attempt to analyse the *status quo*, consider the main areas of conflict and present alternatives to break the deadlock over proliferation.

Principal Problematic Areas in the Non-proliferation Regime

If we summarise the basic conflicts between nuclear and non-nuclear countries that have virtually paralysed the non-proliferation regime today, it would be seen that the majority of these conflicts have been inherent in the NPT from the beginning.

First, the Treaty distinguishes five countries that have the right to possess and develop nuclear weapons and strictly prohibits this for other states (Article 1 and Article 2 of the NPT).[1] The consent of all other states

1. "Each nuclear-weapon State Party to the Treaty undertakes not to transfer to any recipient whatsoever nuclear weapons or other nuclear explosive devices or control over such weapons or explosive devices directly, or indirectly..." (Article 1); "Each non-nuclear-weapon State Party to the Treaty undertakes not to receive the transfer from any transferor whatsoever of nuclear weapons or other nuclear explosive devices or of control over such weapons or explosive devices directly, or indirectly..." (Article 2); Treaty on the Non-proliferation of Nuclear Weapons, UN Website (Conventions and Agreements), *<http://www.un.org/ru/documents/decl_conv/conventions/npt.shtml>*.

to such a clearly discriminatory provision was based on the fact that the official nuclear weapons countries had promised to eventually destroy their nuclear weapons completely (Article VI of the NPT).[2] However, no movement towards the complete disarmament of the 'nuclear five' has occurred over the years. It is clear that only two countries have carried out this process: the USSR (Russia) and the USA, but they too destroyed only their surplus weapons. The other nuclear countries have signed no other multilateral or bilateral agreements to reduce their nuclear stockpiles. Moreover, nuclear weapon countries (both formally and informally recognised ones) have not abandoned the use of nuclear weapons at all—on the contrary, the military doctrines of the majority of them presume that they could be used even in the case of local threats.

First, since it was assumed that the outcome of the non-proliferation process would be the full nuclear disarmament of the world, the NPT did not provide a mechanism for expanding the list of countries that would possess nuclear weapons in the future. However, the process has taken a different route—the nuclear weapons countries have not destroyed their arsenals and the non-nuclear weapons countries have begun to manufacture (or buy) them.

Second, the NPT does not specify the date for the complete destruction of nuclear arsenals; i.e., this obligation is entirely dependent upon the goodwill of the countries. They have not shown any such 'goodwill' and, on the contrary, are developing and improving their nuclear prowess. Realising this, many countries have begun at different times to create nuclear weapons (including Israel, South Africa, Pakistan, India, North Korea, South Korea, etc.). As a result, the 'nuclear five' (above all, the USA) have increasingly and all the more strictly begun to control non-nuclear states, which in response have shut themselves off from any supervision.

Third, the Treaty has also not accounted for the process of developing nuclear technology. If immediately after the Second World War, the

2. "Each of the Parties to the Treaty undertakes to pursue negotiations in good faith on effective measures relating to cessation of the nuclear arms race at an early date and to nuclear disarmament, and on a Treaty on General and Complete Disarmament under strict and effective international control," Treaty on the Non-proliferation of Nuclear Weapons, UN website (Conventions and Agreements), <*http://www.un.org/ru/documents/decl_conv/conventions/npt.shtml*>.

creation of nuclear weapons was indeed within the power of only the most industrially and technologically advanced countries, then by the end of the 20th century, with a certain concentration of effort and the active technological support of nuclear countries, even poor countries were able to obtain nuclear weapons (e.g. Pakistan, which was helped by China). The situation has changed even more so today—the basic provision of the NPT that nuclear weapons cannot be obtained without the assistance of nuclear states is no longer functional. Access to technical information, including information about the construction of various types of nuclear devices, as well as the rapid development of electronic triggering and control systems, makes the creation of nuclear weapons accessible today for almost every interested state.

Fourth, the NPT has established the right of non-nuclear states to develop peaceful atomic energy programmes,[3] however, this right was limited by a stringent condition—the mandatory acceptance of the International Atomic Energy Agency (IAEA) safeguards. This organisation had the right to control the production of fissile materials (beginning with the amount necessary for the creation of a simple explosive device) in order to prevent the transition of a peaceful or research nuclear programme into a military one. Any programme related to fissile material essentially fell under the IAEA control. By 1975, the Nuclear Suppliers Group (NSG) had also been formed, monopolising the export of nuclear materials and delivering them only under certain stringent conditions.

Thus, countries that chose to create a peaceful nuclear power programme were obliged to abide by the principles and technologies of the IAEA and the procurement of fissile materials could take place only with the approval of the NSG. Countries that decided, for example, to build a

---

3. "1. Nothing in this Treaty shall be interpreted as affecting the inalienable right of all the Parties to the Treaty to develop research, production and use of nuclear energy for peaceful purposes..."

2. All the Parties to the Treaty undertake to facilitate, and have the right to participate in, the fullest possible exchange of equipment, materials and scientific and technological information for the peaceful use of nuclear energy, especially in the territories of non-nuclear-weapon State Party to the Treaty..., Treaty on the Non-proliferation of Nuclear Weapons, UN Website (Conventions and Agreements), <*http://www.un.org/ru/documents/decl_conv/conventions/npt.shtml*>.

nuclear power plant on their own, could at any time be accused of trying to develop nuclear weapons.

Fifth, there are already three non-NPT countries openly testing nuclear explosive devices—India, Pakistan and North Korea—and have no desire to join 'the club'. This means that the Treaty no longer exists even as a formality. But that is not the least of it. Two of these three countries have signed certain agreements that essentially imply their recognition as nuclear weapons states.

The first of these countries, India, signed the Civil Nuclear Cooperation or the Indo-US Nuclear Deal on 10 October 2008. Also, the 123 Agreement removes the prohibition on export of civil nuclear equipment and technologies from the USA to India, allows unlimited supplies of fuel for the 14 Indian civil nuclear reactors and also opens up the Indian market for American companies working in this field. To circumvent the restrictions in place, India has agreed to divide its nuclear programme into a military and civilian one, placing the latter under the IAEA safeguards. Following the example of the USA, other nuclear countries (e.g., France) are also ready to conclude nuclear agreements with India.

The second country, Pakistan, has already been helped financially and technologically for several years by the USA to establish a security system for its nuclear facilities. Another member of the 'nuclear five,' China, which originally in the early 1980s supported the transformation of Pakistan into a nuclear power,[4] today has concluded a major agreement on nuclear energy with the country. For a start—the construction of two new reactors.

North Korea has not yet been recognised as a nuclear partner by any agreement; however, its patron China is quite capable of taking such a step. In this context, nuclear-armed Israel, which is absolutely free from control by the IAEA, thanks to the patronage of the USA, also cannot be left out of the equation. Thus, the members of the 'nuclear five' themselves undermine the NPT for tactical and even commercial gains.

Sixth, a big, separate problem connected with the non-proliferation regime is international terrorism, which has proven itself to be a powerful

4. Zimmermann, T. and B. Chellaney (2012). "Nuclear Ambitions", *US News & World Report 1996*. February. p.44.

destructive force. Large-scale terrorist attacks in recent years (beginning with the attack on the Twin Towers on 11 September 2001) show the assumption that extremists want to gain access to weapons of mass destruction (WMD), including nuclear weapons, is not unfounded.

Some experts and politicians are convinced that this is a real problem and that it poses a direct threat to international peace and stability. Others think that the threat of possible nuclear terrorism is not sufficiently realistic. Even, if we can assume the possibility of a theft of a ready-made nuclear explosive by terrorists, then triggering it would present them with an almost impossible task. Modern warheads are highly secure systems, protected by a wide range of physics-based, engineering and structural measures. If we talk about creating a so-called primitive nuclear device, the very complexity of the acquisition of fissile materials, the technology for its creation, the need for testing and, most importantly, the delivery of the nuclear warhead to the future attack target would also be essentially insurmountable obstacles for terrorists, especially given that these materials are constantly monitored by international intelligence structures. It is not hard to guess that the representatives of countries interested in a tightening of the non-proliferation regime insist on the first version, and developing countries who need to prove that they can be trusted with nuclear weapons, primarily insist on the second. One way or another, the reality of this threat has become conventional wisdom which, as a result, has allowed the 'nuclear five' to obtain the consent of the state parties in 1995 to make the term of the NPT indefinite. As a result, it turned out that all the existing contradictions, anachronisms and controversial provisions in the Treaty have now been given a permanent status.

Finally, among the problems that are not directly related to the NPT, the following should also be distinguished:

1. the spread of nuclear technology due to competition in the market between suppliers of equipment, fissile materials and technology;
2. the existence of a 'black market' of fissile materials and technology;
3. the presence of a tense political situation in a number of regions and the geopolitical threats perceived by some countries from

their neighbours and the world's largest states, as well as the example of the impunity with which India, Pakistan and North Korea have developed nuclear weapons despite the NPT ban, encouraging several other countries to seek nuclear weapons.

Options for the Solution of the Problem of Non-proliferation

Thus, a picture in which there is the gradual destruction of the non-proliferation regime is becoming increasingly clear. Meanwhile, it seems the USA and the 'nuclear five' countries have not noticed this and are continuing to tighten control mechanisms (the IAEA safeguards, the 1997 Additional Protocol) and exerting pressure on countries at the first suspicion of intent to acquire nuclear weapons.

This increase in pressure is occurring for the third time in the last 10 years. The second war against Iraq (2003) took place precisely because of suspicions that the country was secretly producing nuclear weapons (later the accusation was expressed differently—as the production of WMD). When these suspicions were not confirmed, the new reason offered for the war was changed to the despotic regime of Saddam Hussein's government committing crimes against the Iraqi people.

Quite illustrative is the example of North Korea, which withdrew from the NPT and created its own nuclear weapons. North Korean scientists began to engage in nuclear physics back in 1951. The country had its own scientific-industrial complex, as well as reserves of uranium. North Korea's aim was the independent creation of a peaceful nuclear energy programme, which was feasible and reasonable for a country requiring energy resources. Since the country was a member of the NPT, it had agreed to come under the supervision of the IAEA in exchange for the delivery of three VVER-440 reactors from Russia and two Pressurised Water Reactors (PWR) from the USA. However, neither the USA nor Russia (under US pressure) fulfilled their obligations, pushing North Korea to withdraw from the NPT and to create a nuclear power plant outside of the IAEA safeguards. There followed further threats and North Korea, fearing not wanting to undergo aggression on the Iraqi model, quickly acquired nuclear weapons, detonating its first nuclear device on 9 October 2006.

Finally, there is the spectre of a third case of pressure tactics leading to military aggression against Iran. After all, Iran signed and began to voluntarily abide by the Additional Protocol to the IAEA safeguard agreement by Parliamentary ratification in 2003, but as a result of pressure and threats against it, the process of ratification is now virtually frozen and voluntary compliance was suspended in 2006. Now, Iran is hurriedly creating a full nuclear fuel cycle, though denying the military component of its nuclear programme.

Tough sanctions and military threats from the USA against Iran caused resentment on the part of most developing countries (Brazil, Turkey, etc.). Iran's right to develop nuclear energy and self-enrichment of uranium had consistently been supported by the Non-Aligned Movement—an international organisation that includes over 100 countries in Asia, Africa, Europe and Latin America. This once again shows that it is this very eagerness of the USA to use military force against weaker countries with regard to non-proliferation that increases the latter's desire to acquire the means for strategic deterrence to be prepared for aggression.

Can we find a way out of the current situation, leaving intact the NPT and the regime that has been formed around it? It appears not. The greater the severity of the control from the 'nuclear five,' the more the countries will want to acquire nuclear weapons to rid themselves of this pressure. The result may be a situation in which extreme pressure, i.e., inflicting a nuclear attack, could be used against the dissenting country. A tragic paradox would take place—a nuclear war would begin as a result of the struggle for non-proliferation.

A number of ways have been proposed to end this impasse. They could be brought down to three main options. Two of them are poles apart from each other—first being the repeal of the non-proliferation regime and the second complete renunciation of nuclear weapons. The third is an intermediate variant—a modernisation of the NPT (i.e., adding significant amendments to the Treaty).

Repeal of the Non-proliferation Regime

The option of eliminating the non-proliferation regime and the denunciation of the NPT seems intimidating at first glance. With the rejection of the familiar Treaty, it seems to many that a new nuclear arms race would begin at the risk of a global nuclear war, increasing the chances of mutual destruction. However, as has been shown by many years of experience with the erstwhile USSR's and the USA's containment strategy, it is the risk of global nuclear war that is an extremely effective and powerful constraint on aggression by nuclear states. After all, it was out of the fear of destroying each other and all mankind that the USA and the USSR arrived at treaties for the reduction of offensive strategic arms, the limitation on tests of nuclear weapons, a ban on nuclear weapons deployment in space, etc.

The idea that from non-proliferation we should move towards proliferation has quite a lot of supporters among Western and Russian specialists. One of the founders of the proliferation idea was the recently deceased French geopolitics and military strategist, the late General Pierre-Marie Gallois. As early as in 1960, Gallois formulated the main positive points that follow from the concept of nuclear proliferation in his book: *The Balance of Terror: Strategy for the Nuclear Age*.

He argued, firstly, that countries possessing nuclear weapons would be bound to maintain the *status quo* because the risk of retaliation is much higher than the benefit obtained through aggression. Secondly, the possession of nuclear weapons removes the division of countries into the 'strong' and the 'weak' categories. Thirdly, the containment strategy is applicable not only to major conflicts, but also to regional and local ones. Fourthly, even precision-guided weapons for the first strike are not a complete guarantee for a potential aggressor, because the defender can hide part of its nuclear arsenal in a very secure place (underground, in caves, etc.) and strike back.[5]

Gallois used the following logic: the more the number of nuclear weapons states, the more responsible would they be, for fear of unleashing a nuclear war and, less likely it would be for a more powerful state to dare to attack even a weaker nuclear country. We note that this logic was confirmed in practice, in particular during the acute Cuban missile crisis of 1962, and later during the 2002 crisis between India and Pakistan. In

5. Quote from Mikhailov, V.N. and S.T. Brezkun (2002). *Good or Evil? A Philosophy for Stable Peace*. Book 1. Moscow: Sarov.

both cases, the countries very responsibly refused to allow the conflict to go nuclear, and even abstained from indulging in conventional warfare. It turns out that to achieve global stability (or at least the elimination of large-scale conflicts), nuclear weapons are the most rational political and military means to deter aggression. In 2010, in one of his last interviews to the *Krasnaya zvezda*, the official newspaper of the Russian Ministry of Defence, Gallois offered a concrete plan, "to ensure nuclear weapons for a number of Asian countries. North Korea, India, and Pakistan already have nuclear weapons. Soon Iran will have them. These are factors for stability in Asia. It is also important for Japan to acquire nuclear weapons... Russia, I believe, should not prevent the spread of nuclear weapons in Asia and the Far East. American hegemony can be stopped only if major Asian powers possess a strong national security system with a reliance on nuclear weapons."[6]

The resort to a containment strategy (this is precisely what we are speaking of, though on a larger scale) was recognised as highly effective in the USA. Two former secretaries of Defence, James Schlesinger and Robert McNamara, believed that mutual nuclear 'restraint' was achieved only through this strategy. The patriarch of Soviet rocketry, Boris Chertok, writes, "According to the strategy proposed by McNamara, if both sides have huge nuclear arsenals, in the case of global nuclear war it would be impossible to reduce damage to an acceptable level. So the doctrine of "containment" of nuclear weapons was recognised as a threat that could inflict damage on an overwhelming scale. US military theorists proposed mutual assured destruction to be the main guarantor of peace."[7]

Of course, psychologically it is very difficult to get used to the idea that the world must learn to live in constant fear of nuclear war. Nevertheless, a number of Russian experts, in particular the long-term Russian Minister of Atomic Energy, Vladimir Mikhailov, also see no alternative to the strategy of containment. Speaking of the opposition of Russia and the USA, he said: "Even ten of our strategic warheads (SW) actually reaching the US in a retaliatory strike guarantees us peace. If we can guarantee ourselves with

6. "It is most important for Russia to preserve and build up its nuclear potential." Interview with General Gallios, *Newspaper Krasnaya Zvezda*, 5 November 2004.

7. Chertok, B.E. (1999). *Rockets and People*. 2nd Edition. Moscow: Mashinostroenie. p.71.

at least this ten, then let the USA have thousands of SWs. Nonetheless they will not risk using them. Leave the heavy 'Satan,' that is, the ICBM R-36M2, even with expired components in the silos—the USA will fear all the same that they might still activate and reach their target."[8]

Yet another option for abolishing the non-proliferation regime would be to expand the list of countries that have acquired nuclear weapons in circumvention of the Treaty. If India, Pakistan, Israel and North Korea are recognised as nuclear weapons countries, it would essentially mean rejection of the NPT and give a 'green light' to any country to build or acquire nuclear weapons.

Global Zero

The second option—the idea of a complete rejection of nuclear weapons—has existed for rather a long time. Among states, the Soviet Union first proposed it in 1946 to the UN Commission for Atomic Energy and then repeated its offer several times subsequently. As is known, the Indian Prime Minister, Rajiv Gandhi came forward with a similar initiative in 1988.

Today, this idea called 'Global Zero' has again been taken up, now by the USA, which had previously always rejected it. In 2007, the manifesto 'A World Free of Nuclear Weapons' appeared, sponsored by former Secretaries of State, Henry Kissinger and George Shultz, former Defence Secretary, William Perry, and former Senator, Sam Nunn.[9] President Barack Obama made this initiative by authoritative American politicians, one of the main planks in his Presidential platform.

The essence of this idea, as the name implies, is the complete elimination of nuclear weapons by all countries that hold them, the rejection of their acquisition by all non-nuclear countries and the establishment of a nuclear-free world.

The road map for its implementation can be summarised as follows: the NPT should be revised and an article introduced for the obligatory elimination of nuclear weapons in all states by a certain date. Then

8. *op cit.* no.5: chapter 22.

9. *Wall Street Journal*, 4 January 2007.

the 'nuclear club' should be disbanded. Nuclear power is recognised by default as a peaceful branch of industry and the freedom to produce fissile materials and develop nuclear energy is proclaimed for all countries desiring to do so. IAEA control remains only to prevent the production of nuclear weapons and nuclear explosive devices. In this case, the non-proliferation regime would indeed be a mechanism guaranteeing the non-use of nuclear weapons. It would not be discriminatory and it would not give any country unilateral privileges.

At first glance, the idea is wonderful and very humane. Mankind will rid itself of the fear of the dire consequences in even the local use of nuclear weapons, let alone the nightmare of global nuclear war, which is capable of destroying all life on Earth. However, on closer examination, a whole series of unanswered questions arise.

Firstly, the destruction of nuclear weapons in general without the destruction of strategic weapons (above all, high-precision weapons) would bring the world not into the post-nuclear era, but simply return it to the pre-nuclear era. This was the era in which the masters of the world were the countries with the most sophisticated and technologically advanced weapons. Secondly, the world would be hostage to the sense of responsibility and honesty of disarmed nuclear states, having to take it for granted that one of them is not hiding two or three nuclear warheads. In the context of 'global zero', such a country would be the ruler of the world. Thirdly, even having given up nuclear weapons, the world would be unlikely to give up the atom for peace. But insofar as every nuclear power plant in any country in the world is essentially a very powerful bomb, an attack on it even with a non-nuclear missile or sabotage would be tantamount to a strike with a nuclear weapon. Fourthly, the Anti-Ballistic Missile (ABM) system today can be considered a very real factor that was previously absent. Moreover, it can work effectively against all means of delivering not only nuclear but also conventional weapons, as well as destroy spacecraft, which would make a country with such an ABM system 'master' of the outer space. Today, to own space is to own the world. Fifthly, if we consider all means of non-nuclear war as a whole, one thing becomes clear: a state with the most powerful conventional and precision weapons under a defensive umbrella of an ABM system and capable of employing integrated informational and command system via satellites would be sorely tempted to strike at its enemy first with a lightning-fast pre-emptive attack. It is clear that we are speaking above all of the USA and North Atlantic Treaty Organization (NATO) countries. This could very likely occur precisely as a direct result of the fact that nuclear weapons would be completely destroyed in all countries and there would be nothing to confront the aggressor with.

It is worth turning our attention to the fact that the idea of 'nuclear zero' gained new impetus when precision weapons, no less effective and capable of meeting the challenges of major regional conflicts, were created as an alternative to nuclear weapons. Everyone remembers the CNN (Cable News Network) footage in which a smart, high-precision cruise missile flies into the bunker of the dictator. Of course, one cannot compare this 'surgically precise' strike with the terrible and inhumane nuclear explosions at Hiroshima and Nagasaki. But the difference here is only that the world offers a transition from a ruthless nuclear club to a conventional scalpel, but still held in the same hands.

So, what positive consequences of nuclear disarmament are advocates of the 'global zero' talking about? Something else is more likely—that all nuclear countries would be forced into a 'race for nuclear disarmament' instead of the former nuclear arms race. Thereby, it turns out that countries possessing both nuclear weapons and the complete nuclear cycle should disarm (receiving nothing in return, except for moral satisfaction), and countries that do not possess them should forgo nuclear weapons and the production of nuclear materials.

Modernisation of the NPT

Finally, the option of solving the problem of non-proliferation by means of introducing a number of amendments to the Treaty is under discussion, although the amendments occasionally contradict one another. Reform of the NPT is suggested by both non-nuclear countries and unrecognised nuclear states.

One of the main issues discussed is the question of respecting the right of non-nuclear countries to implement their national nuclear programmes (e.g., the conflict with Iran). In particular, a transition to importing the relevant nuclear components is proposed. Among others, there is an idea, also supported by Vladimir Putin, to establish a network of international centres for uranium enrichment on the territory of nuclear powers. This would meet the demands of non-nuclear countries for nuclear fuel for their peaceful nuclear energy programmes without undermining the legal foundations of the non-proliferation regime.

Another issue under discussion, inspired by the exit of North Korea from the NPT, is what to do with a country that has received the ability to legally develop nuclear technology under the Treaty provisions and then withdraws from the NPT to build nuclear weapons? One of the proposals is a ban on withdrawal from the Treaty, which of course is a violation of state sovereignty. Another way is to oblige countries leaving the Treaty to return nuclear equipment, materials and technology to the suppliers. It is obvious that to do this by peaceful means would be extremely difficult.

The so-called 'unrecognised nuclear countries' (India, Pakistan and Israel) represent another acute problem. India acts as the leader among these countries. Its position is that the non-proliferation regime established by the NPT is discriminatory and India will never agree to give up the status of a nuclear power. (to a large extent Pakistan's position is similar.) India's proposal to reform the NPT is to accept countries that have nuclear weapons today (India, Pakistan and Israel) as members of the NPT with the rights of a nuclear power. At the same time, India underlines its commitment to "a voluntary, unilateral moratorium on nuclear testing" the rejection of a nuclear first strike and declares that it "does not support any arms race, including the nuclear arms race."[10]

Israel's position has been that its nuclear weapons will never be used, except to repel aggression. However, Israel will be ready to join *de jure* nuclear weapons states if India and Pakistan gain formal membership in the 'nuclear club.'

This demand of the three countries has not yet met with the understanding of the parties to the NPT, specially the 'nuclear five,' as the induction of the three countries would immediately give rise to a number of problems. After all, it is obvious that upon recognition of the nuclear status of these countries, the expansion of the 'nuclear five' would not stop there. As soon as the decision would be made, all countries capable of developing nuclear weapons (according to various estimates, there are about 40) would

10. RIA Novosti, 24 September 2009.

quickly launch their own programmes. Then the 'nuclear five' would quickly become 'ten', 'twenty' and so on.

Thus, we see that, to date, no fundamental ideas have come up with the capability of bringing about a broad international consensus on the problems of nuclear non-proliferation and thus create a sustainable peace and safe (nuclear or nuclear-free) world.

Conclusion

Not so surprisingly, the era of nuclear confrontation between the two global blocs led by the USA and the former USSR was one of stability. In those days, the common belief was that 'the world stood on the brink of nuclear war.' And yet, not once was there an exchange of even limited nuclear strikes. On the contrary, realising their great responsibility, all nuclear countries have learned to consult with one another, develop regulations for the mutual control of nuclear arsenals and establish multiple backup systems for the technical inspection of nuclear weapons.

Today, nuclear proliferation spreads across the planet in the form of precise knowledge of nuclear military technologies, in the form of nuclear materials for 'military' purposes obtained from reactors, in the form of nuclear explosive devices, and in the legal form, i.e., demands by non-nuclear countries to give them access to nuclear dual-use technology. We must admit that the NPT, as any international treaty, guarantees nothing by itself if a concerted policy by powerful states is not behind it to ensure its implementation. World history teaches us that as soon as the balance of power between states changes, all international treaties become vulnerable to violation.

Today, the global balance of power is changing swiftly. It is obvious that members of the 'nuclear five' cannot ensure the absolute adherence of non-nuclear countries to the Treaty (especially while they themselves do not abide by the direct requirements of the NPT). At the same time, the significance of the NPT and the non-proliferation regime for a global peace remains great and simply to discard them would be extremely unwise. Therefore, it seems that the most acceptable solution to this problem would be a well thought-out reform of the NPT, with the prospect of signing a new comprehensive treaty on non-proliferation of nuclear weapons. However, this is a very difficult and time-intensive task and positive results can be achieved only given one irrevocable condition—the political leaders of all countries of the world must agree not only to a balanced consideration of their mutual interests, but also to abandon the desire to achieve unilateral gains.

2 Non-Proliferation Challenges in Asia

An Indian Perspective

Rajeswari Pillai Rajagopalan

While nuclear proliferation has been a major challenge for more than 60 years, the enormity of the challenge has grown manifold since the end of the Cold War. In the past, there was one major nuclear threat—US-Soviet rivalry and the threat of nuclear war—but today, the world is faced with other challenges, such as Weapons of Mass Destruction (WMD) proliferation, terrorism and, of course, nuclear terrorism. The number of countries pursuing nuclear weapons has multiplied. It is particularly in this context that the proliferation of WMD along with their delivery systems has become a major issue of concern. The threat is particularly loud and clear in India's neighbourhood. Issues of China-Pakistan nuclear and missile cooperation, nuclear and missile activities of North Korea and Iran are of specific concern from an Indian perspective. Chinese proliferation of nuclear weapons and technology, including delivery mechanisms to North Korea, Pakistan and Iran, has altered the military balance in South Asia and beyond.

The paper analyses the emerging challenges to nuclear non-proliferation in Asia, from an Indian perspective. The paper is divided into three broad sections. The first section provides a contextualisation to the developments taking place in Asia, wherein there is a major emphasis on military power, conventional or otherwise. This section in particular will deal with the changing security environment that is feeding into these developments. The second section outlines four major non-proliferation challenges in Asia: China-Pakistan nuclear cooperation; North Korea's intransigence; Iran's intentions; and the state of the non-proliferation regime itself. The final section examines the Indian approach to proliferation in each of these cases.

Contextualisation of Asian Securitisation

At the end of the Cold War, there was a general euphoria that the world was moving towards a phase of peace and tranquillity, ushered in by a wave of democracy around the world. Those expectations were short-lived, for the world witnessed the beginning of a new wave of conflicts based on ethnicity, identity and the emergence of virulent nationalism, particularly in Asia and Europe. In fact, the democracy movements around the world sprung up new demands that further triggered conflicts in several parts of Asia. Additionally, resource hunger has sharpened the security debate in Asia—with state's responses to secure themselves against these challenges only contributing to more insecurity. Asia is a classic case of this new phenomenon. Four of the major rising powers are in Asia—China, Japan, Russia and India. Asia is also home to five of the world's nine nuclear powers (six if Israel is counted as part of Asia). There are serious historical differences among all these major Asian powers, contributing to a huge trust-deficit among them. Unresolved boundary and territorial issues further complicate the situation. Given this background, there has been increasing focus, at least in Asia, on increasing security by strengthening military forces.

A second contributing factor to Asian securitisation has been the increasingly unilateral policies of the USA in the post-Cold War era. This was particularly evident during the Bush Administration, which had generated a huge sense of insecurity among the Asian countries. Sidestepping the UN and other multilateral processes to attack Iraq in 2003 was watched with wariness by countries like China, Iran and North Korea. Meanwhile, there is a general sense of the US power being on the decline, even in relative terms, which is shaping up the motivations of several new candidates in Asia to become, at the least, major regional powers, a development, which cannot be disregarded. Iran is a case in point. Non-conventional warfare and terrorism too have been contributing factors to increased securitisation.

Moreover, the rise of China as a major economic and military power has forced other Asian powers to review and upgrade their security preparedness. There have been several debates as to what kind of a power China will turn out to be as it grows even stronger in the coming years.

Chinese military modernisation along with the country's opaqueness about its military programmes and objectives has clearly upped the ante in Asia, creating insecurities and contributing to a new arms race. Much of the military modernisation in India, Japan and Russia has been triggered by the Chinese action.

In conclusion, one can broadly agree that, today, hardly any country is interested in waging a full-fledged war—conventional or nuclear—but occurrence of limited conflicts and the possibility of these conflicts escalating into regional conflicts, with potential use of tactical nuclear weapons, cannot be ruled out. Asia, in fact, appears ripe for such conflicts, even under a nuclear umbrella, given the unsettled boundary and territorial issues and mutual distrust among major powers. The Kargil conflict is a case in point. These conflicts may be termed as limited conflicts for two reasons: they may be limited by geography and limited by the type of weaponry used in the conflict. For instance, the most likely scene of action in an India-China conflict may be around the border region; it would be fought essentially by the land forces, but use of air power as a supplementary force cannot be ruled out as it has the potential to alter the outcome of the conflict.

Therefore, given these contextual factors, there is an increasing tendency on the part of states to beef up their security as well as strengthen their deterrence postures by the accumulation of new weapons including nuclear weapons. Such an approach could give rise to the mushrooming of new actors in the nuclear arena. Explaining the utility of nuclear weapons, the late K. Subrahmanyam wrote in 1970 (words that are still relevant): "Today, the role of the nuclear weapons is not military but essentially political. No country which has developed the nuclear weapons contemplates with equanimity its offensive use in war. On the other hand, there is very clear evidence that the possession of nuclear weapons has served to develop a sense of caution and responsibility among the decision-makers."[1] Michael Mandelbaum, writing on the subject, said: "Anarchy is the root of the problem of nuclear weapons. Countries will worry that

1. Subrahmanyam, K. (2010). "The Role of Nuclear Weapons in International Relations", *Strategic Analysis* 34(2): 328, March. (The article was originally published in the *IDSA Journal* 3(1), July 1970).

their neighbours will attack them as long as there is nothing to prevent the neighbours from doing so. They will feel the need to be prepared for attacks and to discourage them if possible, by having armaments."[2] As long as this urge exists, there is no stopping states from pursuing nuclear weapons. The rationale for the pursuit of nuclear weapons by Iran and North Korea fits into the category of countries that develop nuclear weapons as a deterrence, as also a tool of power and strength. This was aptly illustrated by K. Subrahmanyam, who pointed out how in the 1960s China was more than willing to negotiate with the USA and the USSR, but had refused to negotiate with India.[3] He explained the Chinese rationale thus: "the reasoning underlying the Chinese posture is that the only form of struggle or conflict they could rationally engage in with a nuclear power is at the conference table."

Major Non-proliferation Challenges in Asia

China-Pakistan Nuclear Cooperation and the Nuke Smuggling Ring

This probably remains a continuing threat even if Abdul Qadeer Khan (father of Pakistan's nuclear programme, popularly known as AQ Khan) has been stopped in his tracks. China's initial role in providing an impetus to Islamabad's nuclear ambitions cannot be overlooked. China poses a challenge to India by its past and continuing activities of proliferation in India's near and far neighbourhood. Its proliferation of nuclear and missile technologies and material have been well-documented.[4] Given below is not a comprehensive listing of items and technologies transferred by China to Pakistan, it is, however, indicative of the kind of transfers made, allowing one to come to conclusions about the impact on the Asian strategic balance.

Beijing's transfer of ring magnets to Pakistan in February 1995 was one of the first instances that became particularly well-known in the ever-

2. Mandelbaum, Michael (1983). *The Nuclear Future*. Ithaca: Cornell University Press. p.19.
3. *op. cit.* no.1: 329.
4. One of the best documentation of Chinese proliferation of nuclear technology and items has been done by the Center for Nonproliferation Studies, Monterey Institute of International Studies, <*http://cns.miis.edu/archive/country_india/china/npakpos.htm*> (24 January 2011).

growing China-Pakistan proliferation partnership.[5] *The Washington Times* reported that China had sold 5000 ring magnets to the AQ Khan Research Laboratory in Kahuta, Pakistan.[6] Ring magnets are used for extracting weapons-grade enriched uranium from uranium gas. Earlier in 1986, China is reported to have sold Pakistan tritium that is used for fusion in hydrogen bombs, as also to strengthen the yield of atomic bombs. The tritium supplied in this transaction was enough to produce 10 nuclear weapons. Also supplied was heavy water (D2O), an important component needed to run particular reactors, which can also be used for developing plutonium for nuclear weapons. Despite the repetitive transfers, China continued to maintain that it had supplied heavy water only for the safeguarded Kanupp facility and not the Khushab facility, which is not safeguarded. Additionally, there have been Chinese transfers of Highly Enriched Uranium (HEU), as also nuclear weapon designs, among other items.

Pakistan developing nuclear weapons and delivery systems with the help of China was worrisome enough; what made it more dangerous was Islamabad's engagement in further proliferation of these technologies and items to other countries of concern.[7] In 2004, reports of AQ Khan being engaged in the supply of uranium enrichment equipment to Libya, Iran and North Korea had come up. There were several intelligence reports in the 1990s voicing suspicions about Pakistan's proliferation activities; among them was the UK Joint Intelligence Committee Report in April 2000, claiming the unearthing of "an evolving, and as yet incomplete, picture of the supply of uranium enrichment equipment to at least one customer in

5. Pressler, Larry (1996). "Chinese Nuclear Exports to Pakistan", Senate Hearing, 7 February, <*http://www.fas.org/irp/congress/1996_cr/s960207b.htm*> (23 January 2011).

6. Gertz, Bill (1996). "China Nuclear Transfer Exposed", *The Washington Times*, 5 February <*http://www.fas.org/irp/congress/1996_cr/s960207b.htm*> (14 February 2011). While there was no firm information about the supplier firm in China, a Congressional source had reportedly said the ring magnets were sold by the China National Nuclear Co., a government-owned firm that makes nuclear-related products.

7. Countries of concern can be subjective in nature but here it is used as countries where there are unstable regimes, where civil-military relations are not clearly defined or where there is already a serious issue of insurgents and terrorists or where there are no adequate safeguarding mechanisms.

the Middle East, thought to be Libya, and evidence linking this activity to Khan."[8]

Much later in a televised confession, AQ Khan stated he had sold nuclear technology to Iran, Libya and North Korea in the period between 1989 and 2000, although he maintained that he was acting on his own and that the Pakistani government had nothing to do with these transactions. AQ Khan was reportedly part of a global network involving Dubai, Germany, China and included several middlemen and suppliers.[9] Similarly, the letter that *The Sunday Times*, UK, found with AQ Khan's niece had clearly detailed the proliferation activities *vis-à-vis* Iran, Libya and North Korea. On Iran, the letter said: "Probably with the blessings of BB [Benazir Bhutto, who became prime minister in 1988] and [a now-retired general]... General Imtiaz [Benazir's defence adviser, now dead] asked... me to give a set of drawings and some components to the Iranians... The names and addresses of suppliers were also given to the Iranians."[10] Similarly, about North Korea, it said, "[A now-retired general] took $3 million through me from the N. Koreans and asked me to give some drawings and machines."[11]

Although the Pakistan government tried to distance itself from the AQ Khan affair, some reports indubitably point out the role of the Pakistan Army. Even before the scandal broke out, Li Chew, senior Chinese Minister in charge of China's Nuclear Weapons Programme, had warned AQ Khan about the Pakistan Army, saying: "As long as they need the bomb, they will lick your balls. As soon as you have delivered the bomb, they will kick your balls."[12]

---

8. Khan, A.Q., *GlobalSecurity*, <*http://www.globalsecurity.org/wmd/world/pakistan/khan.htm*> (23 January 2011). For more details on A.Q Khan and his links to the west in the area of nuclear weapons, read the note available at GlobalSecurity.
9. Ibid.
10. Henderson, Simon (2009). "Investigation: Nuclear Scandal—Dr. Abdul Qadeer Khan", *The Sunday Times (UK)*, 20 September, <*http://www.timesonline.co.uk/tol/news/world/asia/article6839044.ece*> (23 January 2011).
11. Ibid.
12. Ibid.

Therefore, the danger of Pakistan acquiring nuclear weapons is not just about the command and control mechanism within the Pakistani establishment but of greater concern is the possibility of Pakistan proliferating these materials to other nations or even terrorists getting hold of some of these units or materials. There is an additional worry in the case of Pakistan. Although it is difficult to put a number, there is a sense that today many officers below Brigadier level are extremists by faith, having had the Sharia law imposed on them by General Zia-ul Haq in the mid-1980s. The so-called professional army is quickly transforming itself into an Islamised body, not willing to fight against their fellow brethren, be it in Swat or elsewhere in the Pakistan-Afghanistan tribal region. Seymour Hersh, writing for *The New Yorker*, cites two Research and Analysis Wings (R&AW) officials saying what was worrying was not so much the prospects of nuclear weapons falling into the hands of the mullahs, but into the hands of "those senior officers in the Pakistan Army who are Caliphates. ....We've been watching colonels who are now brigadiers. These are the guys who could blackmail the whole world." Hersh also quotes Pakistani nuclear physicist Pervez Hoodbhoy's address. At a Nation and Lawyers Committee on Nuclear Policy Forum in New York, he said: "Nuclear weapons are only as safe as the people who handle them. For more than two decades, the Pakistan Army has been recruiting on the basis of faithfulness to Islam. As a consequence, there is now a different character present among Army officers and ordinary soldiers. There are half a dozen scenarios that one can imagine. There was no proof either that the most dire scenarios would be realised or that the arsenal was safe."[13]

China's proliferation of nuclear weapons, thus, constitutes one of the biggest challenges to non-proliferation, extending from South Asia to conflict-prone Middle East and beyond.

13. Hersh, Seymour (2009). "Defending the Arsenal: In an Unstable Pakistan, Can Nuclear Warheads Be Kept Safe?", *The New Yorker*, 16 November, <*http://www.newyorker.com/reporting/2009/11/16/091116fa_fact_hersh?printable=true*> (23 January 2011). On the Pakistan army recruitment pattern, see also Shuja Nawaz (2008). *Crossed Swords: Pakistan, its Army, and the Wars Within*. Karachi: Oxford University Press. pp.570-72.

North Korea

North Korea has been a problem for many countries for quite some time. Japan and the USA have been particularly concerned about North Korea's development of nuclear weapons and advanced missile delivery systems.

The 'military first' politics of Kim Jong Il, advancement of military capabilities and the increasing defence budget continue to be an area of concern. Under the new leadership of Kim Jong-Un, there seems to be more continuity than change. The North Korean Supreme People's Assembly in April 2008 stated that its defence expenditure is 15.8 per cent of its total national expenditure.[14] It has the world's fourth largest army and yet continues to train and prepare its forces for a war, in addition to developing robust missile capabilities. According to General B.B. Bell, North Korea remains "the single most dangerous threat to regional security in East Asia."[15]

Several events over the last two decades have brought the world's attention on North Korea: the 1994 crisis; North Korea's testing of a medium-range ballistic missile that flew over Japan en route to a landing in the Pacific Ocean in 1998; its disclosure in 2002 of its covert nuclear programme; testing of nuclear device in October 2006; rocket launch in April 2009; and repeated attacks on South Korea in 2010.

Assisted by the former Soviet Union and China, Pyongyang has been building up its nuclear capability since the 1950s.[16] Upon setting up a nuclear reactor fueled with natural uranium, it was urged to join the Nuclear Non-Proliferation Treaty (NPT), which it did finally in 1985, but

---

14. Japan Ministry of Defense (n.d.). "Chapter 2: Section 2–Korean Peninsula", *Defense of Japan 2008 (Annual White Paper)*, <*http://www.mod.go.jp/e/publ/w_paper/pdf/2008/10Part1_Chapter2_Sec2.pdf*> (23 February 2011).
15. Statement of General Burwell B. Bell III, U.S. Army, Commander, United Nations Command and Republic of Korea/United States Combined Forces Command; Commander, United States Forces Korea, at the Senate Armed Forces Committee Hearing, 11 March 2008, <*http://armed-services.senate.gov/Transcripts/2008/03%20March/A%20Full%20Committee/08-20%20-%203-11-08.pdf*> (25 February 2011).
16. For details on the origins of the North Korean nuclear programme, see Charnysh, Volha (2009). "North Korea's Nuclear Program", Nuclear Age Peace Foundation, 3 September, <*http://www.nuclearfiles.org/menu/key-issues/nuclear-weapons/issues/proliferation/north-korea/charnysh_dprk_analysis.pdf*> (25 February 2011).

never signed the International Atomic Energy Agency (IAEA) Safeguard Agreements that would allow the agency to inspect its facilities. In 1992, after much pressure from the NPT regime and the South Korean admission that there were no US nuclear weapons on its territory, Pyongyang agreed to the IAEA agreement. Thereafter, the inspections that followed from 1992 onwards found several discrepancies in North Korean claim that it was not doing any reprocessing on any of its facilities. Several disagreements between North Korea, IAEA and the USA continued. Pyongyang withdrew from the NPT in 2003 and conducted nuclear tests in October 2006.

The apprehension of the concerned countries is "North Korea's possession of nuclear weapons might lead to a potential tsunami of nuclear proliferation in Asia that would engulf Japan and force it to shift its position on nuclear armament."[17] Its secret deals prove that other states with nuclear ambitions can also smuggle in technologies and materials from countries like Japan.[18] The threat is real: a North Korean defector admitted in the US Congress in 2003 that 90 per cent of North Korea's missile components were smuggled in using cargo ships from Japan's Niigata port to Wonsan.[19] What makes it easy is that several items are dual-use items that have both civilian and military utilities. For instance, sodium cyanide is used in the agricultural and mining sectors, but it is also used to manufacture nerve gas tabun.

Far more alarming are Pyongyang's attempts to transfer nuclear weapon technologies to Iran and Syria and, possibly, even Myanmar.[20]

---

17. Izumi, Hajime and Katsuhisa Furukawa (2007). "Not Going Nuclear: Japan's Response to North Korea's Nuclear Test", *Arms Control Today*, June, <*http://www.armscontrol.org/act/2007_06/CoverStory*> (25 February 2011).

18. This reflects also the weak security measures within Japan.

19. Smith, Hazel (2009). "North Korean Shipping: A Potential for WMD Proliferation", *Asia Pacific Issues* No. 87, Analysis from the East-West Center, February, <*http://www.eastwestcenter.org/sites/defaultfiles/private/api087.pdf*> (17 February 2011).

20. Charnysh, Volha (2009). *North Korea's Nuclear Program*. Nuclear Age Peace Foundation. 3 September, <*http://www.nuclearfiles.org/menu/key-issues/nuclear-weapons/issues/proliferation/north-korea/charnysh_dprk_analysis.pdf*> (17 February 2011).

Iran

Iran's desire to become a nuclear weapons power can be traced back to the 1970s when Tehran showed interest in procuring sensitive technologies. Also, the late Shah of Iran had been firm in stating that it was imperative that his country possessed nuclear weapons. He is reported to have said, "...if ever a country [of this region] comes out and wants to acquire atomic weapons, Iran must also possess atomic bombs."[21]

After the Iranian Revolution, it has been the Russian-Chinese assistance that has made the Iranian bomb tick. The Chinese assistance in this regard has been significant. It started technical training for Iran way back in the 1980s and also supplied Tehran with sub-critical or zero yield nuclear reactors. More importantly, it helped Iran to set up a primary nuclear research facility in Isfahan through a secret nuclear cooperation agreement.[22] Although it was then claimed that the assistance was for Iran's civil nuclear energy programme, there was little doubt in western minds that the aid was intended for Tehran's clandestine nuclear weapons programme. China denied all the western reports, calling them 'groundless' and claimed that there were no major agreements with Iran in the nuclear arena. China reportedly stopped nuclear transactions with Iran in the mid-1990s. However, reports in the late 1990s noted that China was assisting Iran in uranium enrichment and conversion facilities, notably a Uranium Hexafluoride (UF6) plant. Beijing and Tehran yet again denied these reports. The western countries and the USA, in particular, were certain that the Chinese assistance had brought Iran "close to acquiring a uranium enrichment facility."[23] Coming under severe US pressure, China made several pledges to Washington in the late 1990s that it would halt all nuclear transactions with Tehran. Towards the end of 1998, the US National Security Agency (NSA) intercepted communications between Iranian officials (of the Isfahan Nuclear Research Center) and mid-level

21. "Monarch Sees Persian Gulf as Center of Big Power Rivalry", *Journal of Tehran*, 16 September 1975, cited in Dunn, Lewis A, (1982). *Controlling the Bomb: Nuclear Proliferation in the 1980s*. New Haven: Yale University Press. p.63.

22. "China's Nuclear Exports and Assistance to Iran", Nuclear Threat Initiative, <*http://www.nti.org/db/china/niranpos.htm*>(22 February 2011).

23. Ibid.

officials from China regarding the sale of hundreds of tons of Anhydrous Hydrogen Fluoride (AHF), a chemical used to enrich uranium. It took Washington two years to confront Beijing about this sale. The latter backed down, promising to halt the sale, but not without pointing out that AHF was not on the list of controlled substances prohibited for sale.

WMD Terrorism

WMD terrorism, which had by and large remained an academic or theoretical exercise for a considerable time, assumed significance particularly after the September 11 attacks on the USA. Despite the renewed attention, the spectre of terrorists getting hold of nuclear weapons and using them against states still remains somewhat theoretical.

But, this fear is very real in Asia—South Asia and East Asia. Concerns regarding the Pakistani possession of nuclear weapons have intensified manifold post-September 11 attacks.[24] The safety of Pakistan's nuclear arsenal has been added to existing American concerns about its ally in South Asia.[25] What is of particular concern is the linkages between some of Pakistan's nuclear scientists and the Taliban/Al Qaeda.[26] Revelations in 2004 about AQ Khan's international proliferation network added a new dimension to the issue and confirmed American fears of Pakistan's indulgent outlook on proliferation activities. Several analysts believe that other states or terrorist organisations could get hold of nuclear technology, expertise and even materials from Pakistan.[27] Earlier revelations about AQ Khan having assisted Libya, North Korea and Iran with uranium enrichment materials have neither been forgotten nor can clandestine nuclear

---

24. This section on the safety of Pakistan's nuclear weapons has been dealt with in great detail in Rajagopalan, Rajeswari Pillai (2010). "Drivers of Obama's AfPak Policy: An Indian View", *Indian Foreign Affairs Journal* 5(3): 353-54, July-September.
25. Sanger, David (2001). "Nuclear Experts in Pakistan May Have Links to Al Qaeda", *The New York Times*, 9 December.
26. "Pakistan Holds Two Amid US Fears of Nuclear Terrorism: Top Weapons Scientists Suspected of Links with bin Laden's Al Qaeda Group," MSNBC News, <*www.msnbc.com/news/652309.asp*> (22 February 2011); "US Fears Bin Laden Gain in the Nuclear Front", *The New York Times*, 4 December 2001.
27. Although not openly stated, the possibility of nukes falling into the hands of terrorist groups in places like Pakistan was undeclared themes of the just concluded Nuclear Security Summit in Washington.

supplies from Pakistan be ruled out in the future.[28] Pakistan scientists' flirtations with al Qaeda, among others, raise the spectre of n-materials and technology falling into terrorist hands, and this very real threat has come under the scanner.[29] The 2005 report by the Commission on the Intelligence Capabilities of the United States regarding WMD had also brought out this aspect.[30] The then CIA Director, George Tenet, noted that these Pakistani scientists were affiliated to an organisation not associated with the AQ network. While Pakistan is believed to have taken several steps

---

28. Libya obtained uranium enrichment technology and nuclear weapons designs that could support a nuclear weapons programme. North Korea currently has a plutonium-based nuclear weapons programme, but it is not clear whether it also has uranium-based one. Iran is suspected of pursuing both plutonium- and uranium-based nuclear weapons programmes. See, Kerr, Paul and Mary Beth Nikitin (2008). "Pakistan's Nuclear Weapons: Proliferation and Security Issues", *CRS Report for Congress*, Updated 14 January, *<http://ftp.fas.org/sgp/crs/nuke/RL34248.pdf>* (22 February 2011).

29. While it is generally believed that Pakistan nuclear scientist A.Q. Khan has avoided doing nuclear commerce or transfer of nuclear technology or material to Al Qaeda or Osama bin Laden, these are murky issues that cannot be verified one way or the other entirely. In addition to suspicion of linkages between Pakistan nuclear scientists and bin Laden network around September 2001, in October 2001, on US request, Pakistani authorities arrested Bashiruddin Mahmood and Abdul Majeed, two retired Pakistan Atomic Energy Commission (PAEC) officials, who, since retirement, were working in Afghanistan with a non-governmental organisation that they had set up called the Ummah Tameer-e-Nau (UTN). In November 2001, the coalition forces found documents in Afghanistan relating to UTN's interest in biological weapons. This led the Pakistani security forces to arrest seven members of UTN's board, most of whom were retired Pakistani Army officials or nuclear scientists. See, Zahid Hussain (2007). *Frontline Pakistan: The Struggle with Militant Islam*. New York: Columbia University Press. pp.154-55, cited in Curtis, Lisa (2007). "Keeping Pakistan's Nuclear Weapons Out of the Hands of Terrorists", *Heritage Lectures* No. 1043, 27 June (published on 18 September 2007), *<http://www.policyarchive.org/handle/10207/bitstreams/12884.pdf>* (22 February 2011).

30. Commission on the Intelligence Capabilities of the United States Regarding Weapons of Mass Destruction, Report to the President of the United States, 31 March 2005, *<http://www.wmd.gov/report/wmd_report.pdf>* (25 February 2011). The report noted that al Qaeda was in touch with Pakistani nuclear scientists, discussing the development of nuclear devices.

to cap this threat,[31] the effectiveness of these measures is questionable. The Director of US National Intelligence, John D. Negroponte, in a statement to the Senate Select Committee on Intelligence in January 2007, asserted that the AQ Khan network was dismantled.[32] Then Under Secretary of State for Political Affairs, Nicholas Burns, however, was not certain about this assertion. During a July 2007 Senate Foreign Relations Committee hearing, he said: "I cannot assert that no part of that network exists, but it's my understanding based on our conversations with the Pakistanis that the network has been fundamentally dismantled. But to say that there are no elements in Pakistan, I'm not sure I could say that."[33] The London-based International Institute for Strategic Studies had similarly found that "at least some of Khan's associates appear to have escaped law enforcement attention and could ... resume their black-market business."[34]

---

31. Steps taken include: strengthened export control laws, improved personnel security, and international security cooperation programmes. Pakistan adopted new national export controls legislation in September 2004. This legislation requires the government to issue control lists for goods, technologies, material, and equipment which may contribute to designing, development, stockpiling, and use of nuclear weapons and related delivery systems. International cooperation could include Pakistan becoming part of Container Security Initiative (CSI) and the Secure Freight Initiative, under which the USA and Pakistan work together to install screening and radiation detection equipment to scan US-bound cargo, as also its participation in the Global Initiative to Combat Nuclear Terrorism. For details, see IAEA, Information Circular, Pakistan's National Legislation Entitled "Export Control on Goods, Technologies, Material and Equipment Related to Nuclear and Biological Weapons and Their Delivery Systems Act, 2004," 23 November 2004, *<http://www.iaea.org/Publications/Documents/Infcircs/2004/infcirc636.pdf>* (22 February 2011); Kerr, Paul and Mary Beth Nikitin (2008). "Pakistan's Nuclear Weapons: Proliferation and Security Issues", *CRS Report for Congress*, Updated 14 January, *<http://ftp.fas.org/sgp/crs/nuke/RL34248.pdf>* (22 February 2011).

32. Negroponte, John D. (2007). "Annual Threat Assessment", *Hearing of the Senate Select Committee on Intelligence*, 11 January, *<http://www.dni.gov/testimonies/20070111_transcript.pdf>* (22 February 2011), cited in Kerr, Paul and Mary Beth Nikitin (2008). "Pakistan's Nuclear Weapons: Proliferation and Security Issues", *CRS Report for Congress*, Updated 14 January, *<http://ftp.fas.org/sgp/crs/nuke/RL34248.pdf>* (22 February 2011).

33. Kerr, Paul and Mary Beth Nikitin (2010). "Pakistan's Nuclear Weapons: Proliferation and Security Challenges", *CRS Report for Congress*, 23 February, p.15.

34. A.Q. Khan and the Rise of Proliferation Networks (2007). *Nuclear Black Markets: Pakistan*, London: The International Institute for Strategic Studies, p.159, as cited in Kerr, Paul and Mary Beth Nikitin (2010). "Pakistan's Nuclear Weapons: Proliferation and Security Challenges", *CRS Report for Congress*, 23 February, p.16.

Traditionally, the west has characterised Russia as "the most likely source from which terrorists might acquire nuclear material or a complete warhead" due to "inadequate or nonexistent security."[35] In fact, in January 2001, the US Department of Energy in a report stated, "[t]he most urgent unmet national security threat to the United States today is the danger that weapons of mass destruction or weapons-usable material in Russia could be stolen and sold to terrorists or hostile nation states and used against American troops abroad and citizens at home."[36] For instance, the National Intelligence Council in its report said, "quite sufficient material to produce an atomic bomb" was stolen from the Chelyabinsk region in 1998."[37] But on the other hand, the statement by Victor Yerastov, Head of the Russian Ministry of Atomic Energy's Nuclear Materials Accounting and Control Department, denied the theft of any material. But he did admit that, if such a quantity of material had been stolen, it would have been quite sufficient to produce an atomic weapon.[38]

In its own territory, Russia could not but be concerned about nuclear weapons falling into the hands of Chechen terrorists. Russian and Western concerns about nuclear terrorism are quite different. The former's concern is over the Chechens or other terrorists getting hold of nuclear material, a radiological dispersion weapon (what is popularly called the dirty bomb), low-level radioactive wastes or, worse, a nuclear warhead itself,

35. Collina, Tom Z. and Jon B. Wolfsthal (2002). "Nuclear Terrorism and Warhead Control in Russia", *Arms Control Today*, April. *<http://www.armscontrol.org/act/2002_04/colwolfapril02>* (24 February 2011).

36. For details see US Department of Energy, Secretary of Energy Advisory Board, A Report Card on the Department of Energy's Non-Proliferation Programs with Russia, 10 January 2001, cited in Collina, Tom Z. and Jon B. Wolfsthal (2002). "Nuclear Terrorism and Warhead Control in Russia", *Arms Control Today*, April, *<http://www.armscontrol.org/act/2002_04/colwolfapril02>* (24 February 2011). The report was prepared by a bipartisan commission chaired by Howard Baker, former Senate Republican majority leader, and Lloyd Cutler, former Clinton White House counsel.

37. National Intelligence Council, Annual Report to Congress on the Safety and Security of Russian Nuclear Facilities and Military Forces, February 2002, p.2, cited in Collina, Tom Z and Jon B Wolfsthal (2002). "Nuclear Terrorism and Warhead Control in Russia," *Arms Control Today*, April, *<http://www.armscontrol.org/act/2002_04/colwolfapril02>* (12 February 2011).

38. However, a Russian source citing the statement of Viktor Yerastov has a different meaning and interpretation. The Russian report says, "had such a quantity of material been stolen, it would have been quite sufficient to produce an atomic weapon." For details, see the link *<http://npc.sarov.ru/digest/202006/appendix5.html>*.

whereas the US concern is over Russia being too relaxed in controlling and safeguarding these materials and weapons. The US expression of concern over Russia's casual attitude has not helped much, even though they share the same threat. In all fairness, it must be acknowledged that recognising the intensity of the threat, Russia has taken steps to cooperate with the USA and Europe. At the G-8 Summit hosted by Moscow in 1996, nuclear security was the focus. Russia made special effort to display its safety and security mechanisms for nuclear weapons and fissile materials. Additionally, Summit agreements were signed on nuclear security issues; on the effort to address illicit circulation of nuclear materials; on ensuring safety and security of excess weapon-grade fissile materials no longer needed; and on nuclear material protection, control and accounting. The Summit also adopted two declarations, one on the 'Program of Addressing Illicit Circulation of Nuclear Materials' and a 'Statement on the Comprehensive Test Ban Treaty.'[39]

Many argue that in the case of terrorism, it is difficult to put a fix on a state-actor, although there are different patrons within a particular region, or around the world, as in the case of Al Qaeda. What needs to be done to tackle the issue of WMD terrorism is to increase the safety and security of installations, prohibit transfer of fissile or any radiological material and place sanctions on states/entities that engage in proliferation. It is often the failure of implementing these punitive measures for the sake of making quick gains that heightens the threat. The USA, for instance, has a tendency to sideline important goals for minor, but quicker gains *vis-à-vis* certain other national security objectives. The best example of this is Pakistan: in the 1980s, although the USA clearly knew that Pakistan was developing nuclear weapons (with the Chinese help), it chose to ignore the matter as Pakistan was supporting it against the Soviets at the time.

State of the Non-Proliferation Regime

Are the existing non-proliferation regimes capable of tackling the above-mentioned challenges? There have been differing views on their successes and failures. The inability of the West, the USA in particular, and

39. Mikhailov, V.N. (2003). "The Nonproliferation Regime and Nuclear Threat Reduction", in S. Rajagopal and Sridhar K Chari (eds.), *Prospects for Stability in a Nuclear Subcontinent*. Bangalore: National Institute of Advanced Studies, p.20.

the existing non-proliferation regimes to take punitive measures against states like North Korea demonstrates the weakness of the regimes. This demonstrated that weakness has important consequences. This inability can force other regional powers to aspire towards nuclear capability. Japan is a case in point. During times of crises in the past, Japan has contemplated going nuclear; there have been several debates even within political parties on the need to do so. It is possible that Japan has been compelled to consider options along these lines on two accounts.[40] First, the worry that North Korea's nuclear-and-missile issues cannot be sorted out through international arms control agreements. There is a sense that these arrangements are not effective in tackling the nuclear programmes of Iran and North Korea. Given the increasing North Korean threat, Tokyo is far from sure that these agreements can curb North Korea. Some Japanese scholars believe that Japan should acquire nuclear weapons whenever the situation so warrants, because as they argue, "credibility of the US commitment to Japan would inevitably erode, China would develop a blue water naval presence in Japanese strategic sea lanes, and the international community would acquiesce to North Korea's nuclear weapons and allow the NPT regime to collapse."[41]

Second, when there are "hard-core proliferants,"[42] can the regimes be effective and stop them from weaponising their nuclear technologies? Iran, North Korea and Pakistan are states that fall in this category.

---

40. Some of these aspects have been dealt with in great details in Pinkston, Daniel A. and Kazutaka Sakurai (2006). "Japan Debates Preparing for Future Preemptive Strikes against North Korea", *The Korean Journal of Defense Analysis* XVIII(4): 95-121 (Winter). <*http://cns.miis.edu/north_korea/Pinkston_Sakurai_KIDA_Winter_2006.pdf*> (16 February 2011).

41. In fact, Terumasa Nakanishi argues that with Japan going nuclear, it will improve Japan's diplomatic position vis a vis China than weaken and isolate it. See, Nakanishi, Terumasa, Nihonkoku Kakubushouheno Ketsudan (2003). (Japan's Decision to be Armed with Nuclear Weapons), Shokun!, August, pp.14-58, cited in Green, Michael, J. and Katsuhisa Furukawa (2008). "Japan: New Nuclear Realism", in Muthiah Alagappa (ed.), *The Long Shadow: Nuclear Weapons and Security in 21st Century Asia*. Stanford, CA: Stanford University Press. p.357.

42. Stephen Meyer defines "hard-core proliferants" as states "that have already made decisions to become nuclear weapons powers. ..., no matter how many technology barriers are thrown up in their paths, they will continue to pursue a nuclear weapons capability." See Meyer, Stephen M, (1984). *The Dynamics of Nuclear Proliferation*. Chicago: The University of Chicago Press. p.160.

Dealing with the technology suppliers and the supply side of the equation are important aspects that need to be addressed to give a boost to non-proliferation efforts. The lacuna in the concerned regimes and sanctions is that they allow the hard-core proliferants to buy time and invest in domestic and dedicated talent aiding weaponisation. These measures do little to halt the programmes of the "hard-core" countries.

It may also be naive to assume that stopping horizontal proliferation is most critical. States need to get realistic and also address the demand side of the equation for, as long as nuclear weapons remain legitimate for some, others are bound to seek it for them. And this is not just for reasons of prestige, as it has been made out in the case of India. The Cold War rivalry drove the USA and the Soviet Union to build their arsenals and, thereafter, Chinese insecurities about the USA and subsequently the Soviet power drove the China to develop its arsenal. This same chain reaction also led to the Indian and Pakistani nuclear weapons programmes. This quest is likely to continue in the foreseeable future. Even if overwhelming American military power manages to stem the tide of proliferation for the next several years, the inevitable (relative) waning of American power can be counted upon to start off a new round of WMD proliferation. Indeed, the disparity in power between the USA and the other powers itself is likely to spur nations to seek nuclear weapons. For example, North Korea appears to have decided that the main lesson of the decade-long crisis in Iraq is that one cannot challenge the USA without first acquiring nuclear weapons.

The non-proliferation fundamentalists in Washington have found it very convenient to assume and even conclude that possessing nuclear weapons is a matter of prestige for states, for it then allows them to turn their attention away from the real reasons for acquiring these weapons, which is the security and integrity of their country. If Washington shifts its focus to security, then it would come to the reasonably correct conclusion that the process of proliferation is inevitable unless there is some serious drive towards nuclear disarmament, which is rarely paid the attention it requires. Instead, the global (particularly Washington's) focus has almost entirely been on the supply side of the question: how and why states acquire these capabilities and what capabilities they acquire. But there are other issues that need attention too.

First and foremost, questions should be asked as to how the policies of the great powers have encouraged such acquisition; Pakistan's acquisition/ development of nuclear weapons is a good point to start with. Without American and Chinese acquiescence or assistance, neither Pakistan nor Israel could have acquired nuclear weapons. The logic of such actions suggests that a significant source of future proliferation could be the imperatives of great power politics. The US policy approaches tend to be very short-sighted. In order to make some quick, tactical gains, these critical issues are often ignored.

Second, NPT has been instrumental in ensuring that there is no horizontal proliferation, i.e., states other than the five 'haves' do not become nuclear weapon states. There has been hardly any mention of nuclear disarmament. This mismatch has to be looked into and until then, there cannot be any genuine progress towards disarmament. This issue needs to be addressed even if regional weapon free zones become a reality. Although there has been significant reduction in American and Russian nuclear arsenals, they still have thousands of warheads each and, of course, the other three nuclear powers are not yet part of this nuclear arms control process.

Therefore, the P-5 members have to get realistic that there are not going to be any 'rollbacks'. One cannot predict with certainty also that more countries will not go nuclear in the near future, before the next NPT Review Conference in 2015. As long as the P-5 members are not able to agree on a timeframe for nuclear disarmament, countries around the world are going to pursue these weapons. In such a scenario, global disarmament would remain a pipe dream for the near future.

Role of Nuclear Weapons in Asian Security

The role of nuclear weapons in Asian security thinking is going to be one factor that will determine the number of nuclear actors in Asia. As long as the role of nuclear weapons in Asia remains undiminished, more and more countries will seek these weapons and the non-proliferation regimes dominated by the West will hardly be able to do anything. This is not to suggest that countries in Asia are going to be irresponsible, but the deterrence value of these weapons in the security calculus cannot be negated.

What is the role of nuclear weapons in the emerging Asian strategic landscape? In the nuclear arena, the USA remains the only country that is capable enough to "disarm the long-range nuclear arsenals of Russia or China with a nuclear first strike."[43] Scholars like Lieber and Press believe that a pre-emptive strike by the USA on Russia during a 'peacetime alert' and on China even during a 'crisis time alert' can be reasonably successful.[44] These scholars argue that China and Russia cannot claim to have a "survivable nuclear deterrent."[45] It should, however, be noted that, despite major technological gap, Russia and China in the last few years have been forced to improve their capabilities for two reasons. First, they want to eliminate their existing vulnerabilities and second, because the USA has continued with a policy of maintaining nuclear primacy.[46]

Of course, China's nuclear capabilities have been expanding also because it is not limited by any international arms control agreements, unlike the USA and Russia. This could lead to a nuclear arms race, potentially reducing US security and increasing regional insecurities, particularly that of Japan.[47] China and Russia could improve their nuclear

---

43. There has been considerable reduction of US strategic nuclear forces too, although they are considered much more 'lethal' today. The USA has also been regularly updating and beefing up the 'old' triad. While the MX Peacekeeper Intercontinental Ballistic Missile (ICBM) was dismantled in 2005, some of the critical components that gave it that lethality have been retained. In fact, the US plans to use re-entry vehicles and warheads from the MX missiles to upgrade about 200 Minuteman ICBMs. These will significantly improve the precision and accuracy of the ICBMs while increasing the warhead yield. See, Lieber, Kier A. and Daryl G. Press (2006). "The End of Mad? The Nuclear Dimension of US Primacy", *International Security* 30(4): 13 and 29, Spring.

44. Lieber, Kier A. and Daryl G. Press (2006). "The End of Mad? The Nuclear Dimension of US Primacy," *International Security* 30(4): 7-8, Spring.

45. Ibid.: 9; Russia's economic difficulties have had serious impact on its strategic nuclear programme. Russia is estimated to be having 58 per cent fewer ICBMs, 39 per cent fewer bombers, and 80 per cent fewer SSBNs, as compared to the Soviet arsenal of 1990. Also, the overall life cycle and maintenance of Russia's triad is considered to be in bad shape. On the size of the Russian nuclear arsenals, see, Natural Resources Defense Council, "USSR/Russian Strategic Offensive Force Loadings, 1956–2002," *<http://www.nrdc.org/nuclear/nudb/datainx.asp>;* and Norris and Kristensen, "Russian Nuclear Forces, 2006," p.65 cited in Lieber, Kier A. and Daryl G. Press (2006). "The End of Mad?: The Nuclear Dimension of US Primacy", *International Security* 30(4): 12, Spring.

46. Lieber and Press note that several analysts disagree with them about US nuclear primacy. See, Lieber, Kier A. and Daryl G. Press (2006). "The End of Mad? The Nuclear Dimension of US Primacy", *International Security* 30(4): 30-31, Spring.

47. See, *op. cit.* no. 44: 10 and 31.

capabilities by expanding their nuclear arsenals, dispersing their nuclear forces and pre-delegating the launch authority to local commanders, thus avoiding delay in decision-making, besides possibly also adopting hair-trigger nuclear retaliatory doctrines. Japan also believes that China could move away from its current nuclear posture of minimum deterrence to developing a "robust second-strike capability, perhaps with Japan as a primary target."[48] However, the more worrying aspect for Japan is that US nuclear primacy could be eroding with projected reduction in US nuclear capability and an increase in the Chinese capabilities. In such a scenario, the US might enter into a bilateral arms control agreement with China that "endorses protection of a Chinese limited nuclear strike capability against the United States, with a decoupling effect that would be devastating for Japan."[49] Also, if a nuclear arms race recurs, the chances for an accidental nuclear war cannot be ruled out. For instance, an accident involving the USA and China during a Taiwan crisis cannot be overlooked. The impact on Japan in any of these situations can be nightmarish. Therefore, China's approach of finding techno-military solutions to geopolitical issues has led to an arms race in the race.

The asymmetry created by the presence of nuclear weapons in China cannot be neglected. China's possession of nuclear weapons and a triad of delivery mechanisms have created an asymmetry and tilted the balance in its favour. Despite the existence of a no-first-use policy, it feels that it can use nuclear weapons under extreme circumstances (Taiwan being one case), "without fearing a large scale retaliatory strike on its territory."[50]

---

48. Green, Michael J and Katsuhisa Furukawa (2008). "Japan: New Nuclear Realism", in Muthiah Alagappa (ed.), *The Long Shadow: Nuclear Weapons and Security in 21st Century Asia*. Stanford, California: Stanford University Press. p.354.

49. Ibid.: 355; Furukawa, Katsuhisa (2007). "Japanese Perspectives on Nuclear Weapons, Disarmament and Nonproliferation", Research Institute of Science and Technology for Society, Powerpoint Presentation, 29 November, cited in Chanlett-Avery, Emma and Mary Beth Nikitin (2009). "Japan's Nuclear Future: Policy Debate, Prospects and US Interests", *CRS Report for Congress*, 19 February, <*http://www.fas.org/sgp/crs/nuke/RL34487.pdf*>.

50. Dutta, Sujit (1998). "China's Emerging Power and Military Role: Implications for South Asia", in Jonathan D. Pollack and Richard H. Yang (eds.), In *China's Shadow: Regional Perspectives on Chinese Foreign Policy and Military Development*. Santa Monica, CA: RAND, p.97. <*http://www.rand.org/pubs/conf_proceedings/CF137/CF137.chap5.pdf*> (26 February 2011).

As long as Asia continues in this vicious cycle of security and insecurity, the salience of nuclear weapons in the overall security calculus cannot diminish, which in a way indicates that nuclear weapons will continue to play a major role in the coming decades and disarmament remains a talk shop topic and nowhere close to reality.

Indian Approach to Dealing with Non-Proliferation Challenges

Since the collapse of the Soviet Union, preventing WMD proliferation has been the single most important global strategic objective. Some of the related concerns include: the safety of Russian and Pakistani WMD technologies and weapons; the lack of information about Chinese capabilities in general, but particularly about its command and control procedures; and about the general trend in the development of these weapons.

India's commitment to non-proliferation is well known. In 1956, India proposed the international control of military reactors and then co-sponsored the non-proliferation proposal in the United Nations. Indian sensitiveness to non-proliferation in a sense predates the NPT. Nonetheless, India did not become a party to the NPT due to the inherent discriminatory nature of the regime. Finally, the indefinite extension of NPT in 1995 and the enactment of the Comprehensive Nuclear-Test-Ban Treaty (CTBT) forced India to go overtly nuclear. Despite India being a nuclear state or a state with nuclear weapons, it remains committed to global disarmament and complete elimination of nuclear weapons. But there has to be an agreement on a broad timeline for global disarmament before India can shed its nuclear weapons.

Today, there is a need for reorganising the global nuclear regime taking into account a whole range of new challenges. India cannot accept as legitimate the clandestine activities that went on between China and Pakistan[51] and thereafter from Pakistan to Iran and North Korea. India's security interests have been put to risk through such clandestine activities.

51. The latest Chinese attempt to sell more nuclear reactors grandfathering the clauses in an earlier agreement is a concern too. The USA and the international community appear unable or unwilling to pressure China not to carry on with the deal. This again brings out the weakness of the current non-proliferation regime.

The Sino-Pakistani nuclear weapons collaboration, which was a clear violation of the NPT, made it abundantly clear that the NPT regime was a failure at least in the South Asian context.

The other challenges include Iran and North Korea. Regarding the Iran nuclear issue, India welcomes Iran's cooperation with the IAEA. Every state has a right to pursue civilian nuclear technology. While India acknowledges this right, it still has reservations about Iran's nuclear weapons programme, and therefore, it voted against Iran at the IAEA meeting. What now remains to be done is to sort out the issue relating to AQ Khan network and its links to Iran and North Korea. The other point is that though Iran is a member of the NPT, it continues to flout the regime rules. India's position has been that if a country is party to a treaty/mechanism, it is bound by the rules that govern it. India's stand on North Korea is also the same.

On the non-proliferation issue, North Korea has been cooperating as well. In this case, China has played a critical role in convincing Pyongyang to cooperate with the international community and shut down its nuclear reactors. Even so, Beijing plays by different rules when it relates to developments closer home. While the Chinese interests seem congruent with those of the USA and other regional powers, they are actually different. For instance, the Chinese and American perspectives about North Korea's stability are very different. What the regional powers and the USA want is a denuclearised North Korea at peace with its neighbours, whereas Chinese interests are to ensure that there is no crisis that might prompt the influx of large number of refugees into China and that there are no US troops on Chinese borders, which would be the case if South Korea takes over the North after a collapse. Therefore, the Chinese interests are driven by narrower perceptions of North Korea's stability.[52]

It has also become evident that the USA is beginning to lean on China far more heavily when dealing with issues related to North Korea or Myanmar. First, it appears that China has not put any serious pressure on North Korea because it sees it as a buffer state between itself and the US allies in its neighbourhood. Second, with the USA having been preoccupied with Iraq and Afghanistan, China has managed to create a vital strategic

52. Rajagopalan, Rajeswari Pillai (2010). "North Korean Crisis and China", Analysis, ORF Website, <*http://www.orfonline.org/cms/sites/orfonline/modules/analysis/AnalysisDetail.html?cmaid=20681&mmacmaid=20682*> (22 February 2011).

space for itself in Asia wherein the West, and the USA in particular, is forced to route itself through China for any dialogue, be it on democracy, human rights or WMD issues. This has limited India's manoeuverability and marginalised New Delhi's role on important strategic issues. Relying on China on a tactical basis is important, but countries like the USA must also recognise the limitations, given that there is divergence in the US and Chinese approach towards many issues, North Korea being a prime example.

What has been the Indian strategy on all these challenges? Being outside the formal non-proliferation mechanisms, India is constrained from doing anything significant even though New Delhi has taken some tactical steps against Iran at the IAEA. The international community has to recognise the fact that India is now exempted from the Nuclear Suppliers Group (NSG), and therefore, there is a greater need to bring India into some of the global non-proliferation mechanisms.

What is the biggest non-proliferation challenge that India perceives in this arena? It is, indubitably, the lack of great power consensus. Such a consensus is essential even for instituting Confidence Building Measures (CBMs)—the establishment of Nuclear Weapons Free Zones being one such measure. The lack of consensus among the P-5 nuclear weapon countries, for instance, on the question of Iran has created a situation wherein Tehran is able to exploit the loopholes to its advantage, thereby weakening the effectiveness of the non-proliferation regime.

This is not to suggest that there have been no crises or failures in the past. There were crises from time to time—India's nuclear tests in 1974 and discoveries about the Iraqi nuclear weapons programme are examples. However, the great powers were unanimous on the need to tighten the measures to strengthen the regime and the result was the establishment of the NSG after the Indian nuclear tests and then the formulation of Additional Protocol after the Iraqi revelations. Similarly, Pyongyang's decision to withdraw from the NPT to conduct nuclear tests has led to some proposals that would eliminate the right of withdrawal clause for any NPT member state, although an agreement is yet to be reached. Thus, there have been steps taken in the past by great powers through consensus—from identifying the challenge to instituting mechanisms to strengthen the regime. However, today the political differences between the USA and other power centres have spilled over into the non-proliferation issue, and this has given the violators the perfect opportunity to exploit and weaken the regime. This breakdown of consensus is posing the greatest challenge to the non-proliferation regime.

3 Mapping Terrorism Post 9/11

Key Trends and Challenges

Wilson John

There have been dramatic changes in the nature and character of terrorism since the Twin Towers in Manhattan, New York, fell to Al Qaeda's suicide squad hijackers on September 11, 2001. These changes have been evident in the diverse nature of terrorist acts and threats, the operational capability, reach and objectives of various terrorist groups and their networking dynamics—all of which have combined to make today's terrorist landscape more complex than before.

This paper broadly outlines the contours of the new landscape of terror and the myriad challenges this changing dynamics pose to the counter-terrorism strategies as currently understood and practiced, especially in South Asia, which has emerged as the epicentre of terror.

New Landscape of Terror

The new challenges come from the manner in which terrorism has evolved in the past decade, the nature of support the terrorist groups draw from the state and no less as the consequences of flawed counter-terrorism policies that the international community as a whole followed in the wake of the US-led 'global war on terror'.

The most critical flaw stemmed from a deliberately naive and dangerous interpretation of terrorism as a religious phenomenon spearheaded by a single entity called Al Qaeda. Millions of dollars were expended and thousands of lives were taken in the pursuit of Al Qaeda and its leadership. The most common belief projected across the world was that if Al Qaeda and its leadership were to be decimated, the world would be rid of the scourge of terrorism.

In that sense, this 'global war on terror' could claim to have had its share of tangible and visible successes. Al Qaeda today is a depleted force—its ideologue and Head Osama bin Laden hunted down in his hideout in Pakistan, other leaders decimated over the years, its funding sources contained and its ideology made at least less attractive to millions of impressionable minds.

What went unnoticed in the heat and dust of the global war and invasions were the unintended consequences of running a unilateral, military-centric counter-terrorism war against a movement driven in part by extreme ideology, and in part by hatred and fear. Al Qaeda as a group might be in the throes of death, but it has already spawned countless proxies, allies, clones, 'lone wolves' and associates in different parts of the world. They do not share a common language or a lineage as most of the Arab leadership of Al Qaeda had but a sense of perceived or real injustice, access to dangerous technology and materials and some level of overt or covert (often both in different measures) state support. In addition, an over-estimated sense of power and a deep anchorage in the society give at least some of these groups both autonomy and security, magnifying the complexities of dealing with terrorist groups, post-Osama.

Key Features

A better understanding of this landscape requires a closer study of some of its key features. For the sake of brevity, some key features are being listed:

1. *Eclipse of Al Qaeda and diffusion of terrorism:* The killing of Osama bin Laden in May 2011 was a defining moment in the life of Al Qaeda. It was the single biggest blow to the global terrorist group. In the last decade, several of its senior commanders had been killed or arrested, degrading the group's overall capability. But it would be premature to write Al Qaeda's obituary. In fact, since 2001, Al Qaeda and its ideology has spawned and sustained several old and new terrorist groups in different parts of the world. Al Qaeda allies have grown in number since 9/11. They may not have posed as serious a threat as the Al Qaeda itself till now, but their presence in different parts of the world has made

the job of neutralising the global terrorist movement even more difficult. They have been facilitating recruitment and training of new sets of recruits from different parts of the world who are now quite capable of carrying out terrorist attacks. Today, we have groups which may not owe their origin and ideology to Al Qaeda, but have benefited from its vast resources of knowledge and experience in carrying out attacks against more organised and resourceful militaries.

2. *Home-grown terror*: Home-grown terrorism poses one of the most imminent threats to the affected countries. Since 2001, there has been spurt of local terrorist groups, some of which today pose grave threats to the host countries as well as the world. The growth of these groups, small in size but equally adept, has created a virtual string of modules across South Asia, sharing resources, training capacities, funds, weapons and ideologies to create a complex threat. These groups are geographically dispersed, ideologically unconnected, mobile, tech savvy and young in age—factors which create an adversary, which is amorphous, difficult to label and identify. The operational capabilities of some of these groups, especially those operating in Pakistan, have been improving over the years. They are now capable of infiltrating heavily guarded military and government installations and engage in armed assaults and fire fights with conventional security forces. These groups have now moved guerrilla tactics honed in the wilds of the tribal areas and Afghanistan to urban centres. They are also adept at making bombs of various intensity, Improvised Explosive Devices (IEDs) and launch suicide attacks.

3. *State support of terrorism:* The most pressing challenge, however, stems from the fact that a large part of terrorism in South Asia is state sponsored. Although there is relatively a wider awareness about the unintended consequences of Afghan Jihad today, there are not many positive signs from the two key actors, the USA and Pakistan, of having learnt any sobering lessons from history. Even after nearly 11 years of fighting its '9/11 wars,' the US policy makers are ambivalent about dealing with terrorist groups. Its policy of 'cherry picking', when it comes to these groups, has

spawned a whole generation of terrorist groups since 9/11. The significant increase in the number of terrorist groups poses, more than ever, a serious threat to global order and peace.

A primary reason for this is the role played by Pakistan, a strategic ally of the USA in its 'global war on terror.' It is now well known that Pakistan has been creating, sponsoring and supporting various kinds of terrorist groups ever since it became a sovereign country. First it was the 'tribal lashkars,' which the Pakistan Army dispatched to lay claim on Kashmir in 1947. Then, it was a set of terrorist groups launched in East Pakistan by the Pakistan Army, with the help of radical religious party, Jamaat-e-Islami, to terrorise and subdue the rebellion against Islamabad launched by the Bengali Muslims. Then, with the beginning of the Afghan Jihad, Pakistan became the fulcrum of a terrorist movement planned, armed and funded by the West.

Then, as the West and everyone else looked the other way, Pakistan launched its own version of jihad, sweeping the terrorists who fought in Afghanistan into India to carry out terrorist attacks. This proxy war has so far killed over 40,000 people and is far from over. The international community chose to remain a mute spectator, calling the acts of terrorism a 'bilateral issue.' What the world did not know, or chose to ignore, was that Pakistan Army had, along the way, created a vast terrorist infrastructure, raised a reserve force of terrorists and extremists and facilitated the radicalisation of state agencies and structures.

This is one of the biggest challenges, which the world, not India alone, must address if it has to deal with global terrorism. How do you deal with a state, which sponsors terrorism so openly while at the same time is considered by the West as part of the 'solution'? How do you persuade a state, which calls itself a 'victim of terrorism' to neutralise terrorist groups, which its Army believes to be its 'strategic asset'?

In short, dealing with Pakistan is today's biggest counter-terrorism challenge for India as well as the international community.

4. *Expanding terrorist sanctuaries*: Terrorist sanctuaries have expanded many times ever since 9/11. The most obvious (and well documented) sanctuary for terrorists has been the large expanse of mountainous area straddling the Durand Line. Here several thousand terrorists have been living, training and launching terrorist attacks since 2002. The emergence of this sanctuary was not unknown to the USA. There were enough indications in 2002 itself that different terrorist groups, allied to Al Qaeda, were regrouping in these areas. It was also known that Pakistan Army was quietly allowing them to settle down in these areas. Instead of neutralising these groups, Pakistan President and Army Chief Pervez Musharraf in fact signed peace deals with them to avoid a direct military confrontation.

   But there are other sanctuaries inside Pakistan that cannot be so easily defined in terms of geographical boundaries, but are in a way far more dangerous. These sanctuaries exist inside crowded cities and hence remain impregnable in many senses. Quetta, for instance, has been a sanctuary for the Taliban leadership for over 10 years now. Karachi has been a sanctuary for various extremist, sectarian and terrorist groups since the Afghan Jihad days. Peshawar has been a sanctuary for Al Qaeda and Taliban since the early 1990s. Lahore, Jhelum, Sargodha, Faislabad and Bahawalpur have been sanctuaries for Lashkar-e-Tayyeba (LeT) and Jaish-e-Mohammad (JeM) for over two decades now. Pakistan occupied Kashmir (PoK) has been a sanctuary for Hizbul Mujahideen and other groups since the mid-1990s.

   In all likelihood, the sanctuary comprising Pakistan's tribal areas and Khyber Pakhtunkhwa and south-eastern provinces of Afghanistan will expand to include northern areas, including Gilgit and Baltistan. The presence of Taliban and terrorist groups like LeT and JeM in these areas has been noticed in the past. The result would be a sweeping arc of terrorist sanctuaries connecting the border areas of Pakistan, Afghanistan, India and China.

5. *Cyber warfare*: Terrorist groups and their patrons in the region have been eager to adopt hi-tech communication tools including

the social media to propagate their ideology, attract recruits and funds besides planning and executing terrorist attacks. Use of these tools has enabled them to dodge sanctions and extend their reach at the same time. These groups are aware of the multiplier effects of social media exploitation in psychological warfare (PSYWAR) operations. Although there is no evidence of any of these groups acquiring capabilities to launch direct cyber attacks, the recent case of Stuxnet attack on the Iranian nuclear establishment raises the possibility of these groups attempting to acquire such a capability in the near future. It is also quite likely that states sponsoring such groups can enable such a technology transfer.

6. *Operational capability*: Operational capabilities of almost all the terrorist groups have grown in the past decade. Local groups have become global threats and smaller groups have networked with other groups to magnify the threats. The groups today are capable of carrying out suicide attacks, armed assaults and bombings not only in less guarded places but highly secure places. The groups have not only trained their cadres in using sophisticated weapons but also developed their capabilities in intelligence, cyber and maritime domains. As seen in Pakistan recently, some of them have effectively infiltrated security establishments and are capable of launching multi-pronged attacks with smaller teams, exploiting often the element of surprise and heavy offensive in the first few minutes to overwhelm the security forces.

7. *Nuclear terrorism threat*: The threat of nuclear terrorism has never been as real as at present. Today, there is a greater likelihood of individuals or groups of malcontents getting access to nuclear materials and weapons. Such a possibility certainly exists in Pakistan today. This was not the case in 2001. There are several reasons for such an assessment. First, Pakistan is a country that has over 100 nuclear weapons and one of the fastest growing nuclear development programmes. It is also a country with the biggest number of home-grown and foreign terrorists. It is a country with one of the biggest terrorist infrastructures. It is a country with the largest number of sympathisers of terrorist

causes, many of them in the security forces, including the Pakistan Army. It is also a country where some of the top nuclear scientists are not averse to helping the cause of Islamic Jihad. It is a country, finally, that is unwilling and incapable of countering terrorism.

But these facts are more or less known. A deeper scrutiny of the situation in Pakistan will bring to light the contours of world's worst nightmare. Most of Pakistan's nuclear establishment is located in Punjab. It is also likely that most of its weapons too would be located in Punjab, since the other provinces are in perpetual state of conflict. It is from Punjab that most of the troops and officers in the Pakistan Army, Inter-Services Intelligence (ISI) and other security forces are enlisted. About 60 per cent of the soldiers and officers are Punjabis from central and south Punjab. The troops come from rural, semi-urban areas and from the farm lands of Jhelum, Sargodha, Lahore, Bahawalpur, Faislabad and Multan. The officers come from urban middle class families of Lahore, Rawalpindi, Jhelum and other comparatively prosperous regions of Punjab. These are also the recruitment grounds for terrorist groups like LeT and JeM. LeT has its headquarters in Lahore and its nearby suburb, Muridke. JeM is headquartered in Bawahalpur, a city closer to the Indian border where Zia-ul Haq had encouraged retired soldiers and officers to settle down to create a 'military buffer zone'. Majority of the LeT cadres and leadership come from rural Punjab. The group also has considerable presence and support in the urban areas where it runs over 180 English-medium schools, over 100 madrasas and several technical, medical and engineering institutes. It has one of the most extensive charity networks in Pakistan with a large fleet of ambulances, social welfare centres and hospitals, most of them located in Punjab. The Punjab government had even given about $1 million as grants to LeT institutions.

What should worry us all is the fact that at least a certain percentage of officers and men in bureaucracy, politics, police and armed forces will come from schools and colleges run by the terrorist group. In all likelihood, the LeT educational institutions might also be a recruitment base for the nuclear establishment. Since there is no empirical data to prove these points, we are forced to rely on anecdotal evidence to understand the nature of threats. AQ Khan, often called the father of nuclear bomb in Pakistan, is a LeT sympathiser. He used to attend the LeT annual congregations at Muridke every year till such meetings were banned after 9/11. Khan used to be accompanied by his other colleagues. At least two of them were later found to be associated with Al Qaeda.

And, what multiplies these dangers is the fact that Pakistan is a highly unstable country and will continue to be so for the near future. Clearly, a strong and deterrent counter-terrorism policy needs to factor in threats in the CRBN (Chemical, Radiological, Biological and Nuclear) domain.

Conclusion

It is apparent from the above discussion that the security and intelligence agencies must first note the changing dynamics of terrorist groups, their attitudes and second, review the current counter-terrorism strategies that primarily focus on single or few groups and individuals and not on an amorphous and nebulous network of individuals, groups and alliances.

4 The Radical Islamic Militant Groups of Central Asia as Intermediaries between the Central Asian and Afghanistan-Pakistan Regions

The Islamic Movement of Uzbekistan and the Islamic Jihad Union

Maria Podkopaeva

The military and ideological ties between radical Islamism's epicentre in the Afghanistan-Pakistan region and the centre in Central Asia began to grow from the very beginning of the Taliban's activities. Over the past years, many fighters from these areas in Central Asia and the Caucasus have undergone military and religious training in Afghan and Pakistani camps. However, there is a Central Asian military and religious organisation that has transformed this support and the strong ties into a foundation for its growth and an instrument for achieving its goals. This organization is the Islamic Movement of Uzbekistan (IMU).

This paper looks into the development of the IMU both as a centre of radical Islamic militancy in Central Asia and as a link between Islamic radicals in the Central Asian and Afghanistan-Pakistan regions.

The Formation of Militant Groups with Radical Islamic Objectives and their Activities in Central Asia

The IMU is one of the most powerful and stable radical organisations in Central Asia. From its inception, it has been multinational/international in its makeup comprising Uzbeks, Tajiks, Kazakhs, Kyrgyz, Uyghur, Turkmen, and representatives of the people of the Northern Caucasus, as well as Tatars.

The founders of the IMU had previously been members of other parties and underground groups both in the Ferghana Valley and throughout the former Soviet Union that had operated in Central Asia since the late 1980s (such as the Islamic Renaissance Party).[1] The radical nature of these initial groups can be adequately characterised by the presence of the Islamic Renaissance Party among them. In the early 1990s, the Tajik branch of the Party (the Islamic Renaissance Party of Tajikistan—IRPT) drew the government into a civil war so brutal that even many years later Tajikistan has still not recovered from its consequences. In 1992-93, many radical groups were banned and their activists were forced to change their tactics in Uzbekistan. Thus, during the civil war in Tajikistan, members of the future IMU participated on the side of radical Islam in the fighting against the forces of President Emomali Rahmon, as a part of the United Tajik Opposition (UTO) in conjunction with the IRPT.

Formally, the IMU was founded in 1996. Its political Head was Tahir Yuldashev and its military leader Juma Namangani. However, as much as a year before the formal establishment of the IMU, Tahir Yuldashev enlisted the support of organisations that had already been formed abroad. Information leaked to the press that in November 1995, he travelled to Peshawar, where through the mediation of Pakistan's Inter-Services Intelligence (ISI) officers, he held talks on assistance for Uzbek radical Islamic organisations with representatives of similar organisations in Pakistan, Turkey and Saudi Arabia. During this period, a network of military bases and training camps for the movement were formed in northern Tajikistan.

Upon the creation of the IMU, its main objective was proclaimed to be the establishment of an Islamic state in the Ferghana Valley.[2] This objective itself takes the activities of the movement beyond that of a single state, as the Ferghana Valley is divided among several Central Asian states.

1. Shustov, A. (2010). "Central Asia: Syndrome of the Spring Escalation", *stoletie.ru*
2. Roschupkin, V.T. (2004). "The Bombings in Tashkent: The Suicide Bomber's Belt as a Political Argument", *Nezavisimaya Gazeta*, 13 August.

Figure 4.1

Central Asia

It is the Uzbek part of Ferghana Valley that remains the movement's central zone of interest. It is no accident that the first two leaders of the IMU—the military leader Juma Namangani and the political leader Tahir Yuldashev—came from the Valley. It is noteworthy that since the end of Soviet era, Namangan has been considered the unofficial Islamic capital of Uzbekistan.

In the summer of 1997, after the end of the civil war in Tajikistan, in accordance with the Peace Accords, the UTO obtained a third of the seats in the government. After this, the IMU, refusing to compromise its positions, was forced to dissociate itself from its allies. The response of the IMU leadership to inter-Tajik peace talks in the second half of the 1990s was to construct new international ties, as well as to enhance military training. In June 1997, an IMU representative held talks with the then-famous Jordanian Wahhabi instructor Amir Khattab on the territory of the Russian Federation in Chechnya. With Khattab's assistance, a training camp was set up especially for the IMU in Chechnya, where at least 300 Uzbek militants were trained.

Subsequently, the IMU continued its policy of armed resistance against the authorities of Central Asian governments. It was obvious that in the given political environment there was no place in Central Asia for the IMU's irreconcilable factions, all the more so because they had already gained considerable military experience in the Tajik war. It became more and more difficult for them to remain in Tajikistan after the peace agreement between the authorities and the opposition was concluded. The IMU began to search for a new area for its activities.

In the summer of 1999, IMU bands from Tajikistan invaded the territory of the Batken region of Kyrgyzstan that borders Uzbekistan.

Figure 4.2

Batken Region of Kyrgyzstan

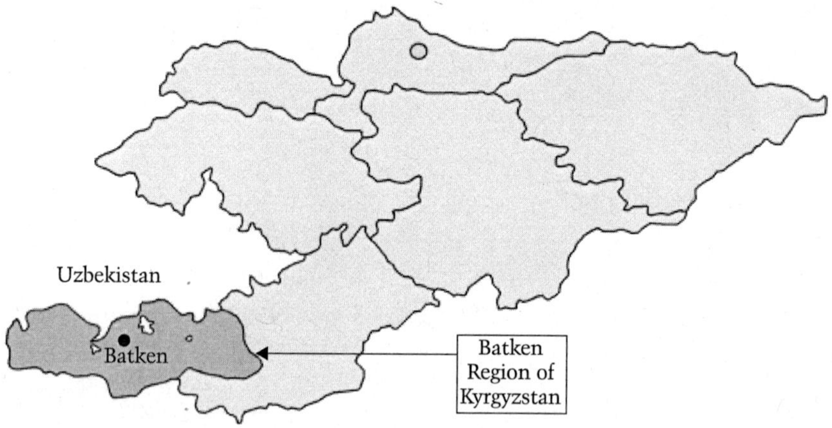

It is not possible to treat this action as just one of the usual forays by armed gangs that create trouble in Central Asian region. In August 1999, the Commander of the Interior Ministry Forces of Kyrgyzstan, Major-General Anarbek Shamkeev, ended up among the hostages held by the IMU in the Batken region of Kyrgyzstan. The situation was so serious that to repel the IMU invasion, Kyrgyzstan was forced to declare a partial mobilisation and seek the assistance of the Uzbek Air Force.[3] Clashes between the Kyrgyz army and the IMU lasted for more than two months, after which in October 1999, the bands of militants returned to Tajikistan. However, the IMU's field of activities in Tajikistan in that period continued to narrow, forcing it to relocate its fighters to the south.

Relocation of the IMU to the Afghanistan-Pakistan Region

At the end of the 1990s, the IMU had already gained support in Afghan militant training camps. In 1999, up to 400 IMU fighters received training in four camps near Kabul with the goodwill of Mullah Omar and Osama bin Laden. In addition, the Afghans trained another 2,750 IMU fighters during this period. Of the people trained, 200 participated directly in the Taliban's fight against the Northern Alliance.[4]

A year later, in the August of 2000, IMU militants again invaded Kyrgyzstan. This time they came to Uzbekistan, so the fighting of IMU bands took place 80 km from Tashkent. It was only towards the end of September 2000 that the militants were driven out of Uzbekistan and in October from Kyrgyzstan. During this period, the IMU militants suffered heavy casualties.

The IMU's bases continued to be located in Tajikistan. At the same time, the positions of the troops that had fought in Afghanistan for the Taliban were greatly strengthened. In late 2000, the Head of the IMU was acknowledged as 'Afghan guest number 2' by the leadership of the Taliban—the first being none other than Osama bin Laden.[5]

3. Bibikova, O. "Batken: the Advent of Muslim Extremism", *ca-c.org*, also *stoletie.ru*.
4. Landa, R.G. "Political Islam: Preliminary Results", Chapter III, Institute of Religion and Policy, *www.i-r-p.ru*.
5. Ibid.

In 2001, a new phase began for the IMU. Under pressure from the Central Asian states, it was forced to relocate from Tajikistan to Afghanistan. It is worth noting that the gradual transfer of militants and their families was carried out with the support of law enforcement agencies in Tajikistan.

Figure 4.3

Central Asia

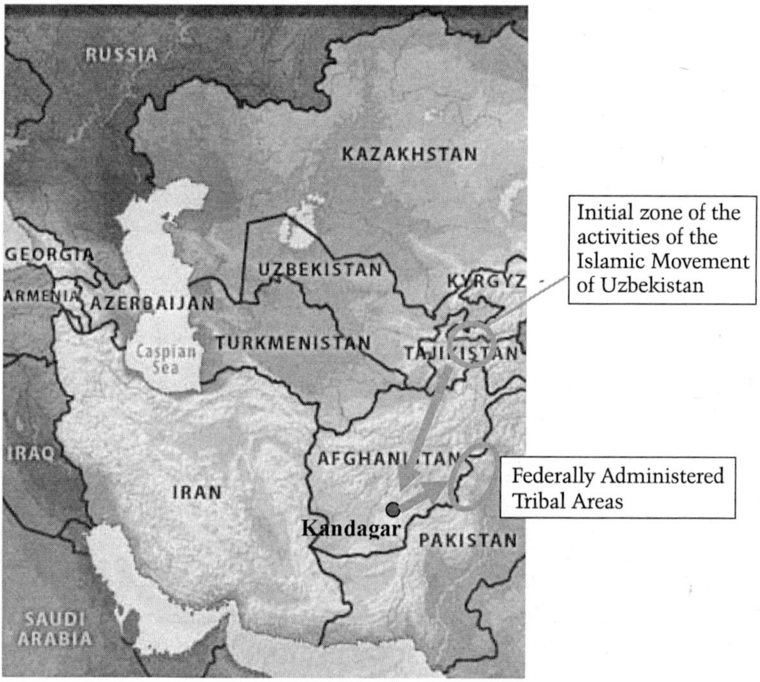

After the relocation, the IMU initially set up its headquarters in Kandahar.[6] Subsequently, along with a segment of the Afghan Taliban, the IMU fighters moved to the tribal areas in north-western Pakistan. In mid-2001, the IMU leadership took the initiative to create a new association: the Party of the Islamic Movement of Turkmenistan. The new organisation, according to the Ministry of Defense of Kyrgyzstan, included movements and parties from Kazakhstan, Tajikistan, Uzbekistan, Chechen and Uyghur

6. *op. cit.* no. 1.

separatists, as well as Arab and Pakistani representatives. The objective of the alliance was the Islamisation of Central Asia, as well as the Xinjiang Uygur Autonomous Region of China. The newly named alliance was created in the Afghan province of Balkh, south of Mazar-i-Sharif.

Experts on the region have repeatedly remarked about the IMU's close links with Islamic groups in the Xinjiang Uygur Autonomous Region of China—such as the Lop Nor Tigers and the East Turkistan Islamic Movement. This provided the IMU the opportunity to raise slogans for the creation of a greater Turkistan, if necessary. Simultaneously, a process for further radicalisation was taking place within the movement itself.

Division of the IMU and Split of the Most Extreme Faction into an Independent Group, the Islamic Jihad Union

The Uzbek organisation, the Islamic Jihad Union (IJU), was spawned out of the split within the IMU. The split occurred as a result of long-standing disagreement about the aims of the movement. The IMU leadership initially aimed to overthrow the secular regime of Islam Karimov in Uzbekistan forcibly. The radical wing of the IMU that was formed in 2001 extended its objective to the spread of 'jihadist activity' throughout Central Asia and, subsequently, even in Western countries.

Discord in the IMU began to appear in Afghanistan as far back as in the autumn of 2001 after the start of the anti-terrorist operation of the Western coalition. Then a group of militants expressed dissatisfaction with the passivity of their leaders in regard to the tactics used in the *jihad* and wanted it to be carried out specifically on the territory of Uzbekistan. The fact is that many of the militants were Uzbeks who, after the Western allies began active operations in Afghanistan in 2001 and later in 2002-03, said they wanted to die in Uzbekistan, not in Afghanistan. As one of the fighters said emotively, "...at home the kindled flame of *jihad*, declared for the victory for Islam and the declaration of the caliph, would burn brighter—it's our home..."[7]

7. Gudarzi, A. (2004). "*Hizb-uh-Tahrir: Myths and Reality*", *centrasia.ru, 24* November.

The supporters of the IMU's radical wing could not impose their new, broader goals on the entire movement. The conflict ended with the departure of the breakaway group, calling on the main group to follow their example. In 2002, the rebel group proclaimed the creation of the IJU. The leadership of the new organisation, like the leadership of the IMU, was based in Mir Ali town (Pakistan's North Waziristan).

Figure 4.4

Mir Ali Town (Pakistan's North Waziristan)

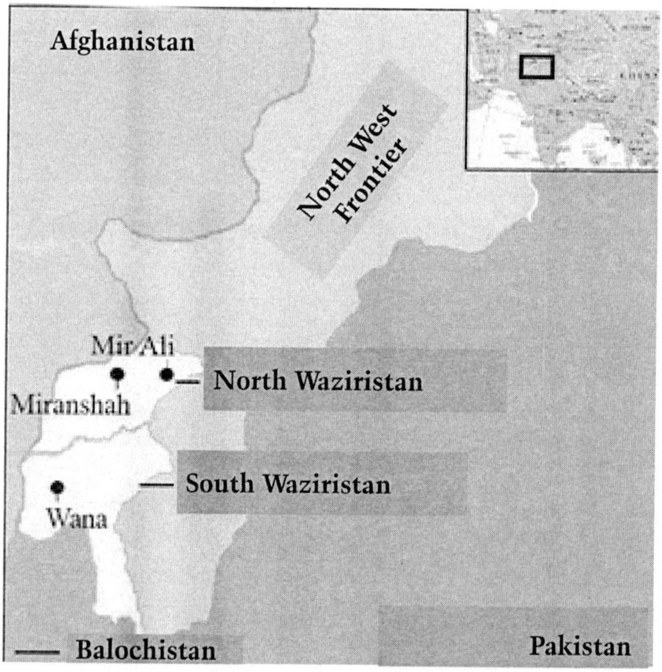

In the first years of its existence, the breakaway organisation was known as the IJU. It announced itself under this name in the spring of 2004, when it owned responsibility for the explosions at the embassies of the USA and Israel, as well as in the lobby of the office of the Prosecutor General of Uzbekistan by suicide bombers. In 2007, the IJU declared Afghanistan to be the primary zone of its activities and continued to assist the Taliban.

Thus, during the early and mid-2000s, the IMU and the IJU developed a plan of parallel action in the Afghanistan-Pakistan region and their native Central Asian region.

Figure 4.5

Central Asia

Assessments of the IJU as an organisation vary widely. It is even assumed to exist only in virtual space—an opinion based on its small size and relative youth. However, the German Federal Bureau of Investigation stated in autumn 2008 that the IJU proved its combat capability in 2004, after the aforementioned terrorist acts committed in Uzbekistan (in Tashkent and Bukhara) against Uzbek, the USA and Israeli targets.

Following these events, the US State Department included IJU in its list of international terrorist organisations. To paint a comprehensive picture of the IJU's activities is difficult, as the information is in the top secret files of Central Asian states such as Kazakhstan.

Nonetheless, it is known that the creation of the IJU during the IMU split was connected with the activities of three faction leaders—Ahmad Bekmirzaev, Zhakshibek Biymarzaev and Najmiddin Jalolov. The last, a native of the Andijan region of Uzbekistan, was wanted in his own country after the bombings in Tashkent in February 1999. In November 2000, Jalolov was convicted of premeditated murder, terrorism, incitement to feud and attempting to overthrow the President of Uzbekistan and was sentenced in absentia by the Supreme Court of Uzbekistan to 18 years imprisonment. It is believed that it was he who was the initiator of the radical group's departure from the IMU.

At the same time, the soft attitude of the main organisation IMU towards the breakaway group under war conditions is telling. The leader of the IMU, Tahir Yuldashev, turned to Arab militants in connection with the split.[8] After negotiations with them and under a guarantee of personal safety, the group initially returned to the IMU camp with the help of the security services of the parent organisation. Subsequently, Jalolov managed to convince the leaders of the IMU that the best way out was to give him the right to form his own group in South Kazakhstan and Uzbekistan.[9] Among the reasons were also his plans to intensify *jihad* in Uzbekistan by means of organising training for Kazakhstan's militants "prepared to risk their lives to contribute to the *jihad*." After negotiations, Jalolov and his supporters were released from the camp (the core of the group consisted of 15 persons).

Some information exists about further movement of the group members. In Pakistan, they were under the tutelage of a famous figure, Hassan Ghul, a Saudi citizen, and a representative of Al Qaeda in charge of the city of Karachi (a so-called *mas'ul shaxs*). Hassan Ghul was subordinate to the Al Qaeda's *mas'ul shaxs* in Pakistan, Abu Musab Baluchi. Ghul first organised the placement and maintenance of the new militant group in

8. Ibid.
9. Ibid.

Afghanistan. Back in early 2002, on the orders of Baluchi, several members of the group (Bekmirzaev, Iskandarov and Matyakubov) were provided with documents and air tickets and flown to Kazakhstan.[10] It is known that they reached Shymkent (near the Kazakhstan-Kyrgyzstan border). However, for a long time, they failed to get into Kazakhstan. Bekmirzaev's group moved to the Iranian city of Zahedan.

Figure 4.6

Central Asia

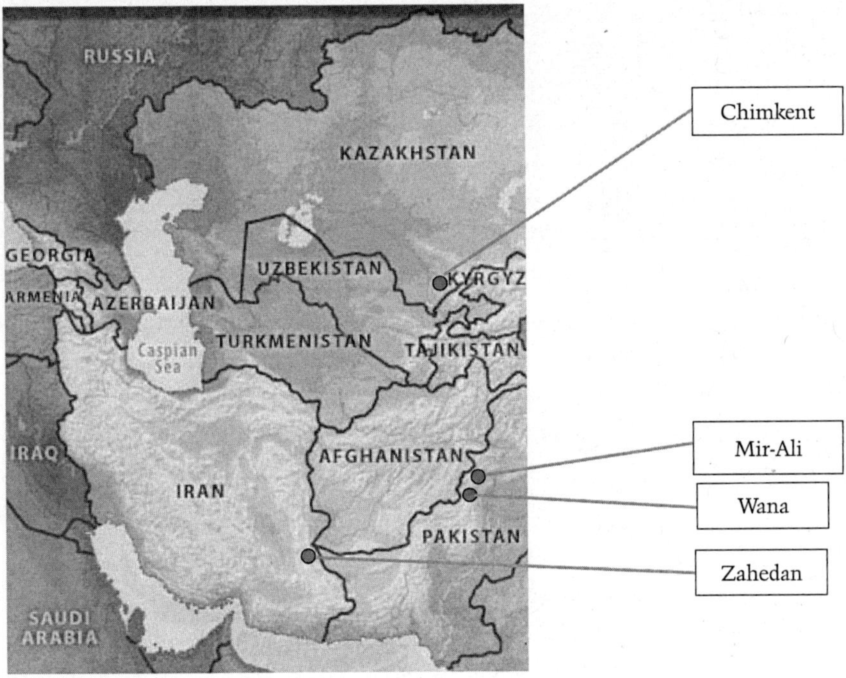

Simultaneously, the new group began to develop its own connections. The IJU's closest contact was with Libyan Abu Laith al-Libi, who was very close to Osama bin Laden. According to some reports, al-Libi acted as a link between Al Qaeda and the IJU until 2008. It must be stressed that a

10. Ibid.

group of IJU militants was already located in Zahedan under the tutelage of al-Libi. Subsequently, this tutelage was preserved, as al-Libi was the Head of a subdivision of the radical group, Libyan Jamaat, located in Pakistan in the village of Wana. It is important to note that one of the goals of the Libyan Jamaat is the creation of an Islamic *caliphate* in the Middle East and Central Asia. In addition, among al-Libi's contacts was the aforementioned Baluchi, with whose help IJU began to organise its activities.

After the stormy beginning of the so-called 'Arab spring' in the Middle East and North Africa in early 2011, the Libyan Jamaat's tutelage of the Uzbek IJU took on an entirely different significance. In the light of the hostilities that unfolded in Libya in the spring of 2011, as well as the strengthening and increased activities of the Libyan Jamaat there, a small group of the IJU men received new positions and prospects in the world of radical Islam. The group is becoming a ward of one of the two strongest modern radical Islamic organisations (the Muslim Brotherhood and the Libyan Jamaat) that are actively participating in the 'Arab tsunami.'

In the spring of 2003, a new attempt to organise a south-Kazakhstan base for *jihad* began. The members of the IJU group (Bekmirzaev and Biymurzaev) were once again moved from Pakistan to Kazakhstan. There the organisation of bases for the initial training and ferrying of militants began in settlements on the Uzbek border, Shymkent and Taraz, as well as in Aksukent and Saryagash.

At the same time, the Amir of the group, Najmiddin Jalolov, did not leave Pakistan. He channelled funds to Biymurzaev, the Amir of the 'southern Kazakh subdivision, from where the funds moved on to the Amirs of Jamaats in the 'Uzbek subdivision.' The year 2003 witnessed the most intensive organisational activity of the IJU in Uzbekistan. The Jamaats were organised in the major regions of the country and supervised from southern Kazakhstan.

Figure 4.7

Central Asia

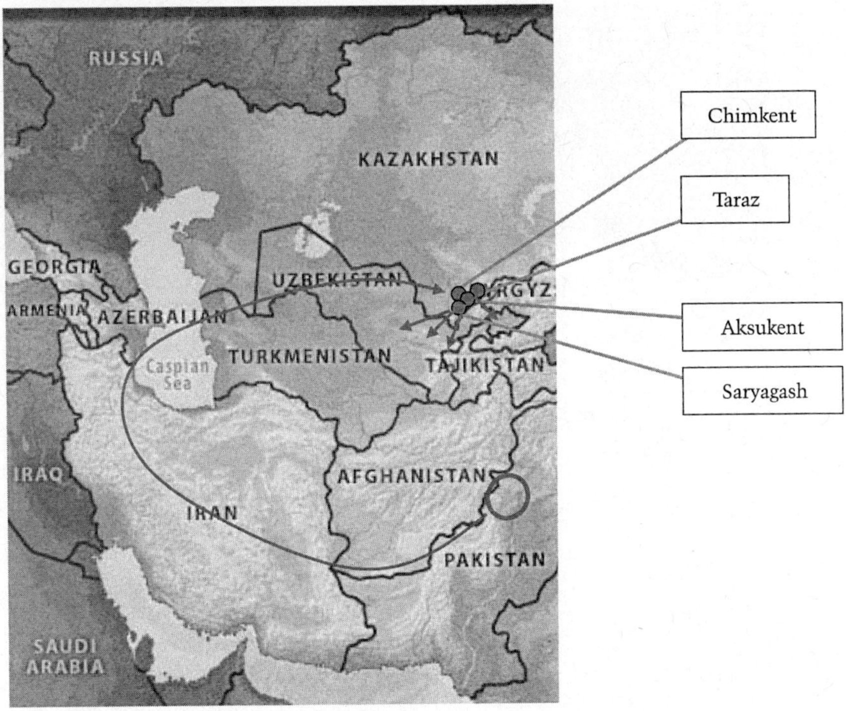

Selected recruits were sent for special training in Pakistan. Thus, in mid-2003, the most radical cadre of the Bukhara Jamaat were trained in Quetta in Pakistan. Moreover, a route that had already been tested by the main group of the IJU was used for ferrying—Shymkent—Taraz—Baku—Tehran and Zahedan—Quetta and Peshawar. At the end of the route, there were training camps for militants in south Waziristan (including Wana), where they were sent for a period of up to one and a half months.

The aforementioned activists of the IJU, Bekmurzaev and Biymurzaev, were quickly neutralised. However, this did not abort the tasks that the Union had taken upon itself—gaining footholds for carrying out jihad in Central Asian countries, primarily in Uzbekistan.

Figure 4.8

Central Asia

The third participant in the creation of the IJU, Jalolov, initially took the course of building relationships with Al Qaeda. But, his initial sponsor, al-Libi, was killed in January 2008 by the US troops during an operation in Mir Ali. At the same time, it was reported that several militants of Najmiddin Jalolov were killed. But Jalolov remained alive then. In 2007, a major scandal erupted when it emerged that an Islamist group from Germany (partly of Turkish origin), dubbed the Sauerland cell, was recruited under the aegis of the IJU. It was reported that members of the cell were trained in the IJU's training centres (i.e., essentially in Pakistani international training camps for *mujahideen*).

In September 2007, members of the Sauerland cell were arrested. At the trial in Düsseldorf, they were accused of plotting terrorist attacks in Germany. Moreover, the leader of the group, the German Fritz Gelowicz, told the court that he acted on the behalf of the IJU. It is obvious that the apparent lack of numerical strength of the group, as well as their mode of action, speaks not so much of the intention of their leaders to organise a truly broad front of *jihad* in Europe, but to conduct Public Relation (PR) campaigns for widening the sphere of political influence of *jihadism*. This is the professed trademark of the IJU.

In court, the members of the Sauerland cell testified that the planned activity of followers of the IJU included attacks on either the Pakistani army or US soldiers. From the outset, it was assumed that the IJU was oriented towards representatives of Turkic-speaking people. In 2008, a suicide bomber, Cüneyt Ciftc, a German born of Turkish origin and recruited by the IJU, launched a terrorist attack in Khost province on the US military base. As a result of the attack, two US soldiers and two Afghans were killed. The IJU took responsibility for the terrorist attack, releasing videos that show the suicide bomber preparing for the terrorist attack and then carrying it out. It was after these events that the Western media (mostly in Germany) began to talk about the IJU. At the same time, it was stressed that the IJU was a small organisation, numbering only 100-200 people and consisting primarily of Uzbeks, but also having Tajiks, Kyrgyz and Kazakhs in its ranks.

In June 2008, the US Treasury Department announced sanctions against Najmiddin Jalolov and another of the IJU's activists, Suhayl Buranov, due to their association with Al Qaeda. Buranov had joined the radical wing of the IMU at the time of the split. He studied explosives at the Al Qaeda camp in Afghanistan (Khost province) and participated in the Taliban's fighting in Afghanistan and Pakistan. In addition, both Jalolov and Buranov were in the lists of the UN Security Council's Committee on sanctions against Al Qaeda, the Taliban, and associated individuals and entities.

According to some reports, Najmiddin Jalolov was killed on 14 September 2009, at Mir Ali in an American drone attack. Nonetheless, Mir Ali remains the centre of concentration of Uzbek militants, primarily from the IMU, but also from the IJU, which had played a role in the radicalisation of militants of Central Asian origin. In September 2009, the Pakistani newspaper *Daily Times* reported that at least 5,000 Uzbek militants were based in Waziristan, many of whom joined the Taliban in Helmand.

Moreover, according to a Pakistani senator from the Jamaat-e-Islami Party, Muhammad Ibrahim Khan, the IMU is the largest group of foreign fighters operating in Pakistan. After the IJU broke away, the IMU continued its build up in the Afghanistan-Pakistan region, but without giving up their earlier goals. Thus, according to Ibrahim Khan, it was initially thought that the goal of the IMU was only to establish an Islamic state in its homeland. But after one of the video messages of the IMU leader Tahir Yuldashev calling for an attack on Pakistani security forces, it became clear that "the movement is guided by the goals of Al Qaeda."[11]

Complications in the IMU Factions in Afghanistan and Pakistan: Beginning of their Ouster to their Native Region

On 6 April 2007, the Pakistani newspaper *Dawn* published an article covering a story that had long remained secret to experts and observers—the development of relations between Uzbek militants and tribesmen in south Waziristan.[12] It was specifically about IMU fighters, natives of Uzbekistan, Turkmenistan and Kazakhstan. In Pakistan, the group was accepted by the Ahmadzai Wazir tribe in Wana. Moreover, the leader of the IMU, Tahir Yuldashev, acquired religious authority in the mosques of Wana. It must be stressed that the concerns of the Pakistani authorities about the presence of foreign militants on its territory manifested itself in 2001, even before the attacks in New York. As early as June 2001, Pakistan began one of its first military operations in the tribal areas, encountering fierce resistance and suffering casualties.

On 7 October 2001, the military operation against the Taliban in Afghanistan was launched. In November 2001, the first Head of the IMU, Juma Namangani, was killed in northern Afghanistan in a US air strike. Tahir Yuldashev then led the movement. A new Pakistani military

11. Rotar, I. (2009). "Terrorist Enclave in Pakistan", 8 October, <*russianews.ru.*>

12. "The game is up for Uzbeks", 4 April 2007, <*DAWN.com*>

operation against foreign militants in South Waziristan was conducted in March 2004. Uzbek militants are said to have responded to this operation with a series of terrorist bombings, ambushes and attacks using explosive devices. As a result of these actions, over the next two years, about 200 people were killed, including tribal elders, journalists and officials. Uzbek militants were accused of most of these killings.

This policy of terror has changed the attitude of Waziristan to the natives of Central Asia, not just among the tribes, but also among Taliban commanders. In 2006, the commander of militants of the Ahmadzai Wazir tribe, Maulvi Omar, who was known for protecting Uzbek militants, was dismissed from his post. Loyal field commanders remained with him and they were joined by Uzbek groups, uncompromising in respect to the new commander appointed in place of the displaced Maulvi Omar. Thus, the militant groups of IMU became a factor in the conflicts within the Taliban. In addition, according to some estimates, the groups collectively known as Uzbek clearly showed a greater tendency to fight for their influence in Waziristan than to engage in the Taliban's war with the US in Afghanistan.

By late 2006, the partially mended relations between Uzbek groups and the new leadership of the Ahmadzai's troops were brought to naught by a series of murders. At the same time, one tribal elder who had survived several attempts on his life by the Uzbeks initiated fighting against the Uzbek militants. He was backed by military commanders and tribal troops loyal to the new leadership of the tribe. In 2007, the main pillar of the IMU among the Taliban was Baitullah Mehsud, leader of the Taliban in Pakistan.[13] Overall, however, the Uzbek groups were the cause of conflict in intra-tribe strife, and this was a hurdle to their plans for a long stay in Waziristan.

The Updated Goals of the IMU and Reverse Movement into Central Asia from Afghanistan and Pakistan

It is believed that the second leader of the IMU, Tahir Yuldashev, died in a US drone attack in Waziristan on 27 August 2009, as announced by the Pakistani Intelligence Services. Nonetheless, it is necessary to take into consideration how often such information about the death of notorious

13. Steinberg, G. (2008). "Islamic Jihad Union", SWP-Aktuel, 23 March, <*germania-online.ru*>

warlords or major terrorists is false or unsubstantiated. According to one version, the IMU leader has taped several interviews in response to information about his death that refute these rumours.

In an interview[14] that was reportedly conducted with Tahir Yuldashev after the official reports of his death, he set forth his vision of their goals on a grand scale and updated the movement's objectives. He stated:

> By 2001, the IMU was able to move from a small political stage to a large political arena. The goal of the IMU in Mawarannahr (i.e., Central Asia) is to protect Muslims. But while located in Afghanistan, we are obliged to protect and defend the Sharia system here. After the initiation of a 'crusade' here in 2001 against the Muslims of Afghanistan, organised by the damned Bush, the IMU has decided to defend the Sharia government and Muslim lands, and today this objective is our priority, rather than our goals in Mawarannahr.

Moreover, the initial aims of the movement were also confirmed in this interview:

> The IMU has temporarily suspended its large-scale operations in Mawarannahr. But our activities have not stopped and with time they will increase. In the future, we will certainly return to our homeland, and we have vowed to do this and to make our goals a reality. We will return home with glory, holding the Koran in one hand and a weapon in the other.
>
> The Muslims of Mawarannahr and especially the Muslims of Tajikistan should not consider themselves to be forgotten. Soon we will enter Central Asia as victors, and circumstances are developing precisely for this. But our goals do not end with just the creation of a caliphate in Mawarannahr; we endeavor to restore the Islamic caliphate and the supremacy of the Koran in Afghanistan, Pakistan, and other countries. Our forces are capable of fighting NATO and US forces, as well as the SCO forces, and therefore it will not be difficult for us to deal with the 'dirty puppet'-states that have been left in Central Asia after the collapse of communism. That our efforts in Central Asia have become less visible is not because of our weakness or lack of strength. Today, the IMU is busy fighting the forces of the great enemy that has invaded Afghanistan.[15]

Characterising this change, some observers said: "The old guard gave way to a younger, more aggressive group of commanders."[16] The reason for

---

14. According to a number of experts in the audio resources provided on the website: <*www.furgon.com*>, (Ozbekiston Islomi Harakatining rasmiy saity) the actual voice of T. Yuldashev is recorded, <*www.easttime.ru*>.

15. Askarov, Aset and Said Amin (2009). "Interview with the 'deceased' Tahir Yuldashev...", 5 November, <*www.easttime.ru*>.

16. Tynan, Deirdre (2009). "Central Asia: The Islamic Movement of Uzbekistan undergoing Dangerous Transformation", *EurasiaNet.org*, 19 October, *www.eurasianet.org/departments/insightb/articles/eav102009b.shtml*>

these conclusions was the increased activity of the IMU in Central Asia since the fall of 2009, after the news of the death of Yuldashev. Even before this, the IMU was suspected in the summer of 2009 of involvement in a number of assassination attempts on religious and security organisations in Uzbekistan.[17] This increased activity indicated that the expected return of IMU militants to Central Asia had already begun.

In the second half of October 2009, it was reported that on the Tajik territory of the Ferghana Valley, in the town of Isfara near the Uzbek and Kyrgyz borders, four militants suspected in the recent murder of the Head of Isfara Crime Detection Centre were killed in a gun battle. Immediately thereafter, the Border Service of Kyrgyzstan announced that Tajik security forces had arrested several IMU militants in the Vorukh enclave (a Tajik autonomous area, surrounded by the Batken region of Kyrgyzstan).

In addition, a number of clashes with militants took place along the northern border of Afghanistan in 2009, which also marks the beginning of their movement to the north from Pakistan. According to the Deputy Interior Minister of Kyrgyzstan, no less than 20 members of the IMU infiltrated into the Batken district in October 2009 alone. In this regard, in the fall of 2010, *The Wall Street Journal* referred to the statement of one of the commanders of the Afghan Taliban in North Waziristan. He said, the number of mujahids from the IMU in Waziristan had risen in late 2008 and early 2009, and an outflux of Central Asian militants was recorded at the end of 2009, when some of them were sent to help the Afghan Taliban in the northern Afghanistan provinces of Kunduz and Baghlan.

At the same time, the authorities in Afghanistan reported the capture of another 15 IMU militants on 11 October 2009, by US troops in Kunduz.[18] Data from the Ministry of Defence of Afghanistan were cited, according to which not less than 4,000 IMU fighters were in northern Afghanistan during this period.[19] If we compare this with the information that 5,000 Uzbek militants were stationed in Waziristan, migrating in part to the north of Afghanistan, then it becomes clear that these are well-

---

17. "The Islamic Movement of Uzbekistan Attempts to Return to Central Asia", <*azattyk.org*>.
18. *op. cit.* no. 16.
19. Ibid.

trained, combat-capable forces able to cause massive outbreaks of violence in Central Asia, leading to further destabilisation for many years.

Figure 4.9

Central Asia

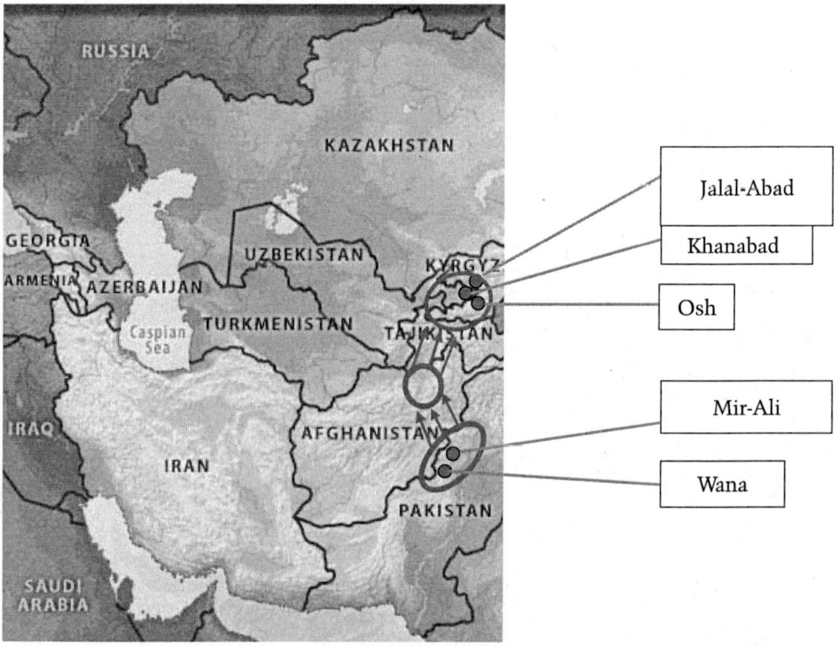

In addition, an important place in the leadership of the IMU was occupied by a well-known functionary of the movement, Abdur Rahman, an ethnic Tatar, formerly the Deputy Leader and Head of the IMU Press Centre. Abdur Rahman is described as a representative of the interests of not only supporters fighting the *jihad*, but also those carrying out a pan-Turkic policy, and as possessing contacts with adherents of the movement in Central Asia.[20] This change in leadership also leads to the conclusion that the movement is radicalising and preparing for new operations in Central Asian countries, bolstered by its Afghan military experience and Pakistani ties.

20. <*stoletie.ru*>, 19 March 2010.

It is no accident that in early 2010, material from the British magazine, *Jane* received wide resonance in the electronic media of Central Asia. It contained a rather definite conclusion to the effect that the IMU is actively attempting to return to Central Asia. According to British estimates, about one-third of IMU personnel are entrenched in Waziristan, raising families. The rest "associate their future with the return to Central Asia" and the main object of their attention is the Ferghana Valley.[21] *Jane* pointed out that even the presence of a few hundred veterans would have a very serious impact on the situation in the region, especially upon the movement's return to its initial objective: enthronement of a *caliphate* somewhere in Central Asia.

By examining the phases of the IMU's activities, it is possible to conclude that it is a developing, flexible organisation ready for quick alterations. Depending on its current objectives, it can be built up into a small army or turned into an extensive network (as has been shown with the Sauerland cell incident). In addition, there is yet another function within the capabilities of the IMU that has been used to the utmost in recent years. The IMU is a kind of explosive charge that periodically engages a chain of centres of instability in Central Asia. This is particularly manifested in the new and rapid growth of instability in all three countries of the Ferghana Valley—Tajikistan, Uzbekistan and Kyrgyzstan.

Region-wide Instability in Central Asia

The Beginning: Tajikistan

According to data published in the Western media quoting a high-ranking source in the Taliban, small groups of Tajik and Uzbek militants began to move into Tajikistan late in the winter of 2009.[22] The number of militants who have crossed the border since the end of 2009 is more than a hundred and most of them belong to the IMU. In addition, in spring 2009, information was spread in Tajikistan about the return to the country of the group's field commander, Mullah Abdullah (Abdullah Rakhimov), who had become famous for his uncompromising attitude during the civil

21. <*www.azattyk.org*>, 2 March 2010.

22. *Rosbalt*, 5 October 2010, citing Newsweek.

war in Tajikistan in the early 1990s. (This field commander for the UTO refused to accept the ceasefire agreement in 1994 and after signing a Peace Treaty in 1997, he continued terrorist activities. In 2000, he relocated to Afghanistan.) Rumours spread in Tajikistan that he was travelling from village to village talking with elders and that the strength of his unit was growing. Shortly after his alleged return, gang shoot-outs began to occur more often on the Tajik-Kyrgyz and Uzbek-Kyrgyz borders. Kyrgyz authorities have emphasised in this case that the bandits were citizens of other states and members of the IMU.[23]

A series of incidents took place in Tajikistan in late summer 2010. The intensity of these events was much more severe than ever before. It all began in late August with the escape of 25 prisoners accused of attempting a coup. Later, one of the leaders of the Afghan province of Kunduz said that some of the fugitives had taken refuge in northern Afghanistan. However, the IMU distributed a statement saying that the fugitives had been transferred to a safe haven.[24] On 3 September, a terrorist act involving a suicide bomber took place in Tajikistan for the first time. On 8 September, 40 armed militants were prevented from crossing the border from the Afghan side. But the most serious act was without a doubt the attack which took place on 19 September on a military convoy that was ambushed in the Rasht Valley in eastern Tajikistan, about 50 miles from the Afghan border. Out of a column of 70 soldiers, only 15 survived.[25]

The Tajik authorities have blamed the attack on the group of the aforementioned Mullah Abdullah. But a Kabul political expert, Waheed Muzhda, a former functionary of the Taliban, stated that a group associated with the IMU was behind the sabotage.[26] The reason for these findings is the high professional training and modern equipment of the saboteurs. However, the deteriorating situation in Tajikistan was just one piece of the overall picture of the situation in Central Asia during this period.

23. Myasnikov, V. (2009). "Islamists are Pushed into Post-Soviet Space", *Independent Military Review*, 3 July.

24. *Rosbalt*, 5 October 2010, citing *Newsweek*.

25. Davlat, Nurali (2010). "Ambush", Charkhi Gardun (gazeta.tj), 22 September.

26. *Rosbalt*, 5 October 2010, citing *Newsweek*.

Background of the Instability

Parallel to the Tajik incidents, clashes broke out in neighbouring Uzbekistan. At the end of May 2009, there was an attack on a branch of the security forces in the border town of Khanabad. Then in Andijan, a series of explosions took place, causing casualties. The Uzbek authorities, claiming the attackers came from Kyrgyzstan, deployed armoured vehicles in Andijan and sealed the border between the Andijan region of Uzbekistan and the Jalal-Abad region of Kyrgyzstan.[27] Early that June, Uzbekistan started constructing a security barrier on the border with Kyrgyzstan and began to resettle its citizens away from the border strip. Exactly one year later, Uzbek refugees began to stream in from Kyrgyzstan after the riots in Osh and Jalal-Abad in June 2010.

Meanwhile, the wave of incidents in 2009 did not end with the clashes in Uzbekistan. In late June, a counter-terrorist operation was launched against militant groups in the Osh and Jalal-Abad regions. According to Kyrgyz Law Enforcement agencies, the militants in the Jalal-Abad region belonged to the IMU.

Alexander Shustov (2009), a researcher of Central Asian developments, evaluates the situation thus:

> The operation to eliminate militants in Kyrgyzstan once again confirmed the assumption expressed by analysts after the events in Khanabad and Andijan that participants in the attack came from Pakistan's 'tribal area' on the border with Afghanistan. In addition, the close relationship between events in Pakistan, Afghanistan, and the newly independent states of Central Asia showed that the destabilization of the situation in one of them can cause a chain reaction throughout the region.[28]

True to Shustov's prediction, there were major clashes between the Uyghurs and Han in Urumqi and Kashgar in Xinjiang Uygur Autonomous Region of China in July 2009. The density and intensity of these outbreaks from May to July 2009 in the four neighbouring countries in the region belie any notion that these were isolated incidents insulated from one another.

---

27. Shustov, A. (2009). "Eurasian Arc of Instability: The Process of 'Balkanization' in Central Asia", <*www.russians.kz*>, 24 September.

28. Ibid.

The Osh Riots in the Summer of 2010

The well-known, June 2010's tragic events in Kyrgyzstan (in Osh and Jalal-Abad) certainly demand a separate consideration, but for this paper, it is all the more necessary to present the events in detail as they point to a significant jump in the temperature of the Central Asian cauldron. On the evening of 10 June 2010, there was a massive brawl between Uzbeks and Kyrgyz in the centre of Osh, which erupted into riots. The next morning, the Kyrgyz and Uzbeks from suburban villages swarmed in to gather in the city. Large-scale clashes began on the streets and innumerable houses were burnt down in the Uzbek enclaves of the city. One of the enclaves was razed to the ground. By evening, clashes started in the Kyrgyz capital, Bishkek. Troops were deployed in Osh. Casualties on both sides rose. The arson and the massacre of Uzbeks continued the next day and clashes spread to Jalal-Abad and surrounding areas. Witnesses said the militants were young men who fired both at Kyrgyz and Uzbeks.

Later, when the peak of unrest passed, the Special Services of Kyrgyzstan released a statement about the involvement of the radicalised branch of the IMU—the IJU in the clashes. The statement said that shortly before the beginning of the riot, a small Uzbek band of the IJU was redeployed from Pakistan to the riot area in Osh to add fuel to the fire of arson and massacre. The band allegedly consisted of snipers and demolition experts.

According to unofficial data, over 2,000 people were killed in the riots. The clashes and fires had yet another result. On the third day of the riots, 13 June, Uzbekistan opened its borders with Kyrgyzstan and admitted nearly 75,000 Uzbek refugees. They were given shelter in camps in the Andijan, Namangan and Ferghana regions—the most significant Islamised centres of the Ferghana Valley.

Later, when the riots subsided, many Uzbek refugees chose to go back to their burnt out homes in Kyrgyzstan. With this mass migration of embittered people, a wide channel of communication was established between the Uzbek and Kyrgyz parts of the Ferghana Valley. The channel is sure to play an important role in escalating tension in Central Asia, spreading the ethnic clashes to other states.

There exists a clear danger that what began as ethnic conflicts will, in the future, be given a religious colouring. The trans-regional radical-Islamic alliances of Ferghana origin (which have been analysed in this paper) are ever ready to give a religious twist to any events and happenings. In the middle of the summer, a statement made on behalf of the IJU in connection with the riots in Kyrgyzstan received great response from the Central Asian and North Caucasus electronic media. The statement said:

> We, the Mujahedeen of the IMU, express our deep condolences to the oppressed Muslim peoples in south Kyrgyzstan who suffered casualties during the bloody tragedies. ...The IMU calls on all Muslims of the Mawarannahr, regardless of their nationalities, to turn away from worldly concerns and to embark on Jihad against the enemies of Islam! It continues: If you ignore the jihad, Allah will punish you with unparalleled torment and banish you from your land and lead another tribe here.[29]

This is an obvious call for war throughout the region in the name of the IMU, as well as a call to overcome ethnic hatred through Islam, since other regulatory norms for inter-ethnic relations in Kyrgyzstan have not helped to avoid bloodshed. In the context of the political disaster in Kyrgyzstan, such appeals cannot but win favour with the people seeking protection from violence.

A few months after the Osh events, in September 2010, Kyrgyz law enforcement agencies stated that they were deeply concerned over the Uzbeks, who had left for the mountains and attended militant training camps in Afghanistan and Pakistan after the Osh events, returning to Kyrgyzstan areas with dense Uzbek population. Conflicting rumours about the number of militants capable of breaking through to Kyrgyzstan—up to 3,000—added to the worry because, according to a widespread expert opinion, Kyrgyzstan was just a stopover for the militants, whose main goal was Uzbekistan.[30]

In the autumn of 2010, *The Wall Street Journal* published an opinion by the Kabul political analyst, Waheed Muzhda, on the movement of militants among the countries of Central Asia and the Afghanistan-Pakistan area. Waheed Muzhda, who until 2001 worked in the Taliban's Foreign Ministry and maintains contacts with the movement, stated that

---

29. *Emiratkavkaz.hiblogger.net*, 18 July 2010.
30. Panfilova, V. (2010). "Kyrgyz fear retaliation from local Uzbeks", *Nezavisimaya Gazeta*, 17 September.

insurgents connected with the Taliban are now intensifying their activities in Central Asia. The objective of this intensification, according to the expert, is to interrupt supplies along the northern channel to the US-led coalition in Afghanistan.[31]

Esteemed Kyrgyz expert and theologian, Kadyr Malikov (2011) assessed the situation as follows:

> Perhaps in the spring and summer of 2011 the next target of destabilisation will be Tajikistan, and then the whole Ferghana Valley. If the theory of 'controlled chaos' is to be tested in the valley, then there is danger for the south of Kyrgyzstan. ...The process of reshuffling the various factions and their consolidation on the basis of a common ideology of struggle against the 'secular' regimes in Central Asia is intensifying. ...In the short term, the situation in the Ferghana Valley will become much worse.[32]

Conclusion

1. IMU and allied groups have strengthened and expanded their influence over Central Asia. These groups have benefited considerably from the growing consolidation of Islamists in the region, which has offered new opportunities of alliances and pathways.
2. IMU and its allies have established alliances with major Islamic forces—Taliban and Al Qaeda. This has given the groups a global outreach and access to a wider network of funding sources, training capacities and safe houses.
3. The expected drawdown of the North Atlantic Treaty Organization (NATO) forces from Afghanistan is likely to further boost the cadre strength and morale of terrorist groups like the IMU.
4. The events in Middle East will shape and accelerate the growth of the sweeping arc of extremism in the region. For long, the Afghanistan-Pakistan region has been the dynamic centre of this arc. But the events of early 2011 have added a number of Arab

31. Trofimov, Ya. and A. Cullinson (2010). "Islamists Hit Central Asia in New Strikes", *The Wall Street Journal* (from the website of the Central Asian News Agency, Bishkek, 22 September).

32. Malikov, Kadyr (2011). "If the theory of controlled chaos is tested in the Ferghana Valley, then a threat exists for the south of Kyrgyzstan", 25 January, <*www.24kg.org*>.

countries—Tunisia, Morocco, Egypt and Bahrain—to the most radical part of the 'Greater Islamic Arc' that had earlier been relatively peaceful. In the context of an entirely new phenomenon called the 'Arab tsunami', the entire 'Greater Islamic Arc' will inevitably take on a new importance. The clear description of composition of the Islamic Arc is clearly described by none other than Zbigniew Brzezinski in his book *The Grand Chessboard*, calling this area the 'Eurasian Balkans'. Brzezinski writes: "... the Eurasian Balkans (...) are located within that large geographic oblong that demarcates the central zone of global instability (...) that embraces portions of southeastern Europe, Central Asia and parts of South Asia, the Persian Gulf area, and the Middle East." In Brzezinski's definition, 'Central Asia and part of South Asia' (i.e., the Afghanistan-Pakistan region, as well as a part of India, and other countries) play an important role in the designation of 'the zone of global instability'.

What needs to be emphasised is the fundamental view that Middle and Central Asia had become central to the 'Greater Islamic Arc' even before the collapse of the USSR. It is clearly expressed in the language used by the prominent ideologue of Islamic fundamentalism, Alija Izetbegovic, in his Islamic Declaration (written in the 1970s and published in 1990):

> In the modern context, the natural objective for the establishment of an Islamic order is the convergence of all Muslims and all Muslim communities around the world. This trend means that it is necessary to fight for the creation of a great Islamic Federation from Morocco to Indonesia and from tropical Africa to Central Asia.

5. The 'Greater Islamic Arc' of today demonstrates the ability to simultaneously create pockets of instability in various parts of its sweep. Thus, the tension in each of these hotbeds is further intensified by the overall mood in these regions. This cannot fail to affect the situation both in the Afghanistan-Pakistan region and in Central Asia.

At the same time, as a result of the 'Arab spring' in the western part of the arc, the Muslim Brotherhood is gaining considerable political success towards the re-creation of the caliphate. We can expect other *caliphate*-oriented organisations in Central Asia to respond to its success, the first among them being the Hizb-ut-Tahrir and the IMU, to the study of which this work is devoted.

The speed with which destabilisation of parts of the Central Asian region has occurred over the past two years is a clear signal that the region is dangerously close to flaring up, which will further strengthen and accelerate the developments in the Middle East.

5 Radical Islam and Neo-Nazism

Temporary Alliance or Strategic Partnership?

Eduard Kryukov

Over the last decade, the fight against international terrorism has been understood, above all, as a fight against a certain type of Islamic groups. The ruthless terrorist methods employed by them raises a fundamental question: What are the origins of the ideological basis that legitimises such terror? For the majority of researchers, it is obvious that these origins cannot be found within the great world religion of Islam itself. What, then, fuels radical Islamism?

A study of the period of Islamists' prolonged interaction first with the Nazis and then neo-fascist movements in Europe and the United States might bring us closer to an answer. After all, they have in fact interacted for about 80 years. This interaction began in the 1930s, became much stronger during the Second World War, and later played an important role in the development of terrorism as a destabilising political factor in the world. In order to assess the scale and significance of this kind of neo-Nazi-Islamist alliance, the history of its origin and its further development in the post-war period should be examined.

Middle Eastern Allies of Hitler

The main reason for the rapprochement between some Middle Eastern Muslim leaders and the Nazis in the 1930s was that they found common enemies in the Jewish population of Palestine and in the British and French 'colonialists' of that period. By the time Hitler came to power, the Nazis had already gained many admirers in Arab countries. Moreover, the main ally of Hitler in Palestine was the Grand Mufti of Jerusalem, Haj Amin al-Husseini. He had obtained his religious position in 1921 through the approval of British authorities, who were trying to enlist the support of the influential local family clan. Later, the young Mufti actively used his position to fight British imperialism and the Jewish population in the British-controlled territory of Palestine, winning high regard in the Muslim world.[1]

In 1926, Haj Amin al-Husseini became one of the founders (and later President) of the World Islamic Congress, formed to integrate Muslim communities around the world.[2] By 1933, al-Husseini had established his first contact with the Nazis. A secret trip to Palestine by a senior functionary of the *Schutzstaffel* (SS), the Head of the Department for Jewish Affairs, Adolf Eichmann, played a significant role in establishing Nazi-Islamic ties. During his visit in 1937, he met with the leaders of the Arab movement, including the Mufti of Jerusalem.[3] Between 1936-1939, a wave of violent activities was launched against Jews resulting in a substantial number of casualties. Known as the Great Arab Revolt, it had been funded by the Military Intelligence Service in Germany with the personal approval of the Department Head, Admiral Wilhelm Canaris. Under the leadership of the Mufti of Jerusalem al-Husseini, representatives of the Arab Higher Committee (established in 1936) actively participated in these events. During the Second World War, they collaborated to carry out other such Nazi 'Arab projects.'[4]

Until the spring of 1945, al-Husseini took part in the formation of the Muslim sections of the Wehrmacht and the SS, consisting of volunteers and prisoners of war—Arabs, Bosnians, Croats, Albanians, Indians and citizens of the Soviet Union. For example, among them there were the highland *Jaeger* SS division's Handschar and Skanderbeg of Balkan Muslims, who 'found glory' through their brutal actions against Yugoslav partisans. Al-Husseini was involved in sending Islamic clerics for the German army,

1. Kontorer, Dov (2004). "Arabic Nazism", *Historical Journalistic Project, Israeli Newspaper Vesti*, 10 June, *http://base.ijc.ru/basesite/site.aspx?SECTIONID=48582&IID=231203*
2. *http://www.pravenc.ru/text/155510.html*
3. Grim, William (2004). "Neo-Nazi al Kaide", 4 March, *TheJewishPress.com*
4. *op. cit.* no.1.

presided over the Arab Institute for the study of the Jewish Question and was also engaged in radio propaganda of Nazi ideology in Arab countries.[5]

After the war, the Mufti escaped the Nuremberg Tribunal with the assistance of French authorities, who did not want to come into conflict with the Arab world. He turned up in Egypt in 1946, where he was greeted as a national hero. al-Husseini maintained quite a significant authority here since the 1930s; his Palestinian terrorist groups received a lot of support from the radical Muslim Brotherhood, which originated in Egypt.[6]

In Cairo, Haj Amin al-Husseini continued his anti-Zionist propaganda and became one of the organisers of the Arab-Israeli war of 1948. As head of the World Islamic Congress, whose headquarters had been moved to Karachi (Pakistan) since 1949, he was actively involved in efforts to 'unify the Muslim world.' In this position, the Grand Mufti played an important role in "shaping the ideology of the new Islamic state of Pakistan."[7]

In addition, al-Husseini was an important element in the clandestine network formed in participation with the US intelligence agencies for 'evacuating' Nazis and their collaborators from Europe. He participated in ferrying Nazis to Arab countries and their integration with the local elite. It needs to be kept in mind that this process had reached a huge scale, playing a crucial role in the development of Nazi-Islamist relations and the emergence of terrorist organisations in the post-war period.

The Post-War Nazi-Islamist Alliance: Former Nazis in the Service of Arab Regimes

In November 2010, *The New York Times* published excerpts from a secret US Department of Justice report showing that during and after the Second World War, American intelligence services actively cooperated with the Nazis. In a highly abridged 'version for the press,' evidence was provided that the US granted asylum to many Nazi war criminals and their associates and that the Central Intelligence Agency (CIA) provided

5. Kontorer, Dov (2010). "Haj Amin al-Husseini: Jihad in the Service of the Third Reich", 29 April, *http://www.kurginyan.ru/clubs.shtml?cat=60&id=481*.

6. Glick, Caroline (2005). "Starting Point", *Jerusalem Post*, June, *<http://www.evrey.com/sitep/object/print.php?menu=371>*.

7. *<http://orien.byethost13.com/nazi4.htm>*.

them with assistance in exchange for information about their associates. These war criminals were also made to agree that they would continue to cooperate with the CIA within the framework of the Cold War.[8]

Some experts were quick to label the report a belated official recognition of the US-Nazi collaboration, pointing out that just after the war, there had appeared a large amount of investigative journalism and literature on this subject that had examined the enormous role of the CIA in shaping the Nazi-Islamist alliance. But in any case, the report prepared by the Office of Special Investigations (Agency of Ministry of Justice) and published on the site of the US National Archives added even greater weight to facts on this subject that had already been previously known to many.

Thus, in the early post-war years, the American intelligence services were actively engaged in the evacuation of high-ranking Nazis from Germany. Organisations created under the cover of the Vatican by Croatian fascists took part in this special operation, which was supervised by Allen Dulles, the Head of the Office of Strategic Services (OSS—the predecessor of the CIA) in Bern. But this was only part of the 'evacuation network' through which many high-ranking Nazis fled.

After the defeat of Nazi Germany, several clandestine organisations were formed to smuggle out SS and Wehrmacht officers, mainly to Latin America, South Africa and the Middle East. The largest among these were from the Organisation of Former SS Members (ODESSA) and The Spider (*Die Spinne*).[9] Subsequently, these organisations were actively involved in shaping the neo-Nazi parties and movements in Europe.

A significant role in these evacuation networks was played by a former commander of the Nazi special forces' sabotage division, Otto Skorzeny (1908-1975), who had been acquitted by the American military tribunal at Dachau and had worked closely with the CIA, as well as by Leon Degrelle (1906-1993), leader of the Belgian Nazis who fought in the 28th SS Volunteer Grendier Division Wallonien. Degrelle and Skorzeny took

8. "A Long-Concealed Report: the CIA Created a 'Safe Harbor' in the USA for Nazis", 15 November 2010, <*http://mixednews.ru/?p=2005*>.

9. Polmar, Norman and Thomas B. Allen (1999). *Encyclopedia of Espionage*. Moscow: Kron-press. pp.447-48.

part in ferrying Nazis along the so-called 'Roman route' to Spain under the protection of the Franco regime and financed by clandestine Nazi organisations, such as HIAG (Mutual Help Association of Former Waffen-SS Members).[10]

It should be noted that during the restoration of the Nazi intelligence network of cells that had been created during the war, Skorzeny visited many countries in Europe, where he met with his former colleagues. In Italy, he established contact with a former naval officer and a master of maritime sabotage, Prince Valerio Borghese (1906-1974), who at that time was heading the neo-fascist Italian Social Movement Party.[11] The infiltration of Nazis into the Arab world took place through clandestine organisations instigated by Skorzeny and his team. The major Arab countries that sheltered the fugitives were Egypt, Syria and Saudi Arabia. By 1946-47, the Nazis had linked up with a lot of their old contacts in Egypt, such as with King Farouk and the headquarters of the Jerusalem Mufti Haj Amin al-Husseini in Cairo.

Through the ODESSA organisation, the Mufti himself maintained contact with many high-ranking Nazis who ended up in the Arab world. Among them was one of Eichmann's assistants, the SS Hauptsturmführer Alois Brunner, the Chief Gestapo Inspector in Nazi death camps who had found refuge in Damascus as a senior advisor to the Syrian general staff, and Major General Otto Ernst Remer, a former commander of Hitler's guard battalion who became military adviser to Egyptian President Abdel Nasser in 1953-54 (Remer is considered one of the founding fathers of the neo-fascist movement in Europe). For many years, this Nazi duo operated the Orient Trading Company out of Damascus, which participated in the illegal arms trade.[12]

In 1951, an unofficial German mission of 60 officers (the majority of them were SS) led by General Fahrmbacher began operations in Egypt. The mission supplied training instructors for pilots, tank men and saboteurs, besides setting up the amphibious unit of the Egyptian army. At the same

10. Mader, Julius (1964). "Following the Man with the Scars", Documentary about the former SS Secret Service Chief, Otto Skorzeny, Moscow: Politliteratura. pp.131 & 146.

11. Ibid.: 124.

12. *op. cit.* no.3.

time, former SS officer Tiefenbacher led the training of the Cairo police and former Head of the SS Special Forces in Ukraine, Dirlewanger formed a commando unit "to fight Israel".[13]

Most of the Nazi emigrants converted to Islam, took Arabic names, and studied Arabic for their covert objectives. In the early 1950s, the Arab-German Immigration Centre was created under the leadership of Lieutenant-Colonel Hans Muller who converted to Islam, and became a Syrian citizen, changing his name to Hassan Bey. The Centre was involved in the recruitment of former Wehrmacht officers to serve in the armies of Arab countries. With the help of the Centre, about 1,500 people were recruited.[14] From 1953, the former SS Colonel Otto Skorzeny also participated in the recruitment of ex-Nazis to be advisers to the Egyptian Intelligence Services, with financial support from the CIA. In addition, Nasser's government engaged him to work in the State Security Services and to train Special Forces for operations in the Suez Canal zone.

At the same time, Skorzeny trained an Arab foreign legion consisting of more than 400 former SS men at the Bilbays military base. In addition, it was under Skorzeny's leadership where training of the first Palestinian terrorists and the planning for their anti-Israel actions in 1953-1954 took place, as well as the trafficking of weapons from Europe to the Middle East.[15] In August 1957, the Swiss newspaper *Neue Zürcher Zeitung* published an article on the activities of Nazi war criminals in the Arab world. According to the information presented, general coordination of Nazi actions in the Middle East was taken over from the autumn of 1956 by Johann von Leers, a former associate of Goebbels and Rosenberg and a promoter of the racist theories. After the war, he resided in Argentina under the protection of the dictator Juan Domingo Peron and then he moved to Egypt, where he converted to Islam and changed his name to Omar Amin. During his tenure as adviser to the Ministry of State for Administrative Development of Egypt, Leers was engaged in anti-Jewish propaganda and

13. Etinger, J. "Metastasis of Nazism: Hitler's Criminals Laid the Foundation of Middle EasternTerrorism", *<http://nvo.ng.ru/printed/history/1999-12-03/5_meta.html>*.

14. Ibid.

15. "From Hitler to the "Arab Reich", *<http://www.freerepublic.com/focus/f-bloggers/2238002/posts>*.

'employment' of fugitive Nazis in Arab countries. He was assisted in the organisation of new fascist networks in the Islamic world by another prominent Nazi, Hans Appler, who took the name of Salab Gough and became the Secretary of the World Islamic Congress (led, as mentioned above, by the Mufti of Jerusalem al-Husseini).[16]

According to Western media, a total of around 8,000 German army officers had fled to Arab countries by the end of 1950, including about 2,000 former members of the SS and Security Service of the Third Reich (most of them settled in Egypt).[17] It should be noted that in the 1950s, Egypt became a sort of 'Mecca' for neo-Nazis. Thus, in the spring of 1957, von Leers was visited by a fervent admirer of Hitler and the future cult figure for American and European neo-fascists, Savitri Devi (1905-1982). A Frenchwoman by birth (her real name was Maximiani Portas), she had spent a significant part of her life in India, where she married Asit Krishna Mukherjee, Editor of the National Socialist Magazine *The New Mercury*. In her writings, Savitri Devi promoted 'pagan Aryan heritage' in an attempt to combine National Socialism with the Vedic cults of India. Starting from the first half of the 1950s, she became an active participant in the international Nazi underground, which provided her with the opportunity to communicate with a number of fugitive Nazis in Europe and the Middle East, including Otto Skorzeny, whom Devi met in 1961 in Madrid.[18]

In the second half of the 1940s, large-scale Nazi infiltration of military institutions took place not only in Egypt, but also in other countries of the Arab world. In Syria, the German military mission overseeing the training of the army was headed by Kribl, a former Colonel in Hitler's general staff; Rapp, a former Gestapo officer, undertook the reorganisation of the Army Intelligence. The Nazis, deeply rooted in Syria's military structures, actively participated in several coups that shook the country from 1949 to 1951.[19]

Nazis also influenced the Saudi Wahhabis. In the early 1960s, the Cairo newspaper *Al-Ahram* stated: "Former German officers are of great

16. *op. cit.* no. 13.

17. Ibid.

18. Goodrick-Clarke, Nicholas (2002). *Black Sun, Aryan Cults, Esoteric Nazism and Politics of Identity*. New York: New York University Press.

19. *op. cit.* no. 13.

interest to Saudi Arabia. They consider Wahhabism to be one of the most promising trends in Islam. SS officers have established military training camps in the country, where training of young Wahhabis is carried out."[20] This 'new personnel' brought up by the Nazis in the Islamic countries of the region subsequently took an active part in a number of military coups and terrorist activities in Palestine, Syria, Iraq and Algeria. For example, led by Otto Skorzeny, his students participated in the organisation of the Algerian coup in April 1961 with the support of former SS men who served in the First Foreign Parachute Regiment. After collapse of the coup, many of Skorzeny's teammates from the clandestine military organisation fled to Spain.[21]

It must be stressed that in all cases, it was those radical Islamists who clearly had terrorist leanings and were virulently anti-Semitic who turned out to be the most natural allies of fugitive Nazis. Moreover, the infiltration of former SS members took place both in key military and special services institutions in Arab countries, as well as in the command centres of Islamic terrorism.

'Nazi Bankers' and Sponsors of Terrorism

An active role in the formation of a Nazi-Islamist alliance in the post-war period was played by major financiers who collaborated with the Nazis. One of the key figures was Swiss banker Francois Genoud who, on the one hand, has been called the manager of the Third Reich's Swiss accounts and, on the other hand, was the financial adviser for the Grand Mufti of Jerusalem. The career of this young financier began to grow rapidly after he joined the pro-Nazi National Front of Switzerland in 1934. In the second half of the 1930s, Genoud was already working for German Intelligence and visiting the Middle East. In Palestine, he established friendship with al-Husseini, with whom he was in constant contact both during and after the war. British author and journalist Gitta Sereny claims that the Mufti "authorised Genoud to conduct his extensive financial affairs".[22]

---

20. Briman, Shimon, "Muslims in the SS", *<http://gazeta.rjews.net/Lib/briman/5-briman.shtml>*.
21. *op. cit.* no.10: 168 & 175.
22. Preston, David Lee (1997a). "Swiss Man of Hitler", Philadelphia Inquirer, 5 January.

As part of his commercial activities of a special kind, Francois Genoud was engaged in currency and diamonds deals and gold trade. One of his friends and companions was the Abwehr agent and SS officer Paul Dickopf, who had joined the Swiss underground during the war and who headed Interpol from 1968 to 1972. At the end of the war, Genoud was a representative of the Swiss Red Cross, thanks to which he not only escaped punishment, but also helped many fugitive Nazis. He participated in the creation of the above-mentioned ODESSA and the management of Nazi accounts in Swiss banks.[23]

In the post-war years, Genoud promoted National Socialism, publishing the works of the leaders of the Third Reich, and participated as a consultant and banker in various special projects related, among other things, to the development of Nazi-Islamist communications and financing terrorist organisations. In the mid-1950s, together with the former SS officer Reichenberg, he created the import-export company *AraboAfrika* in Tangier (Morocco) and Cairo, which was a front for the supply of weapons to Algeria's National Liberation Front (FLN) and for anti-Israeli propaganda.[24]

Genoud participated in several business projects of Hjalmar Schacht, former Nazi Reich Minister of Economics, President of the Reichsbank and one of the major post-war intermediaries between the Germans and Arabs. In the fall of 1956, the Swiss banker acted as a representative of Schacht in negotiating of a major investment project in Morocco. Genoud opened Swiss bank accounts for the 'liberation armies' of Morocco, Tunisia and Algeria. In 1958, with the participation of Schacht (as a consultant), Genoud founded the Arab Commercial Bank in Geneva to manage the accounts of the Algerian FLN that was fighting against 'the French colonialists.' Genoud headed the local Arab National Bank from 1962 when Algeria was declared independent and continued to cooperate with Schacht. He held this position for almost two years until a scandal broke out in connection with irregularities in the transfer of funds into the Swiss bank.[25]

23. Ibid.

24. Ibid.

25. Ibid.

Genoud's biography in part related to Algeria and cooperation with Schacht has clear intersections with the post-war activities of the aforementioned Nazi Otto Skorzeny, who was a relative of the former Reich Minister and his representative for business projects in Spain. In addition to the training of terrorists and participation in the Algerian events, Skorzeny was engaged in brokering an arms trade in Africa, Southeast Asia and Latin America.[26] Genoud, in turn, being one of Schacht's representatives in the Arab world, was also involved in the arms trade. The Swiss banker was simultaneously engaged in financing Arab terrorist groups. In addition, he financed the defence of Nazi war criminals, such as Adolf Eichmann (1961) and Klaus Barbie (1987).

American journalist Kevin Coogan claimed that Genoud established some 'foundation for the Nazis' to support those serving long sentences for their crimes.[27] In November 1969, Genoud as advisor and his lawyer, Jacques Verger, defended three terrorists from the Popular Front for the Liberation of Palestine (PFLP) in a Swiss court, who in February of that year had blown up an Israeli plane in Zurich. The defence was financed by Arab Commerical Bank previously created by Genoud.[28]

But all was not limited to this. On 21 February 1972, terrorists from the PFLP hijacked a Lufthansa aircraft. The next day, representatives from the airlines in Cologne received a letter with a ransom demand for US$ 5 million. In the end, the money was paid and the hostages released. This operation was organised by one of the leaders of the PFLP, Wadie Haddad, with the assistance of Genoud, who wrote and sent the letter of ultimatum.[29] Genoud was also associated with the Palestinian terrorist group, 'Black September,' which organised the massacre of nine Israeli

26. Teplitsyn, V. (2000). "Otto Skorzeny or Commando—A Dangerous Trade", Smolensk, "Rusich". p.431.

27. *op. cit.* no.22.

28. "Francois Genoud, a Virulent Swiss Nazi not only looked after the stolen millions of the Nazis in post-war Switzerland.doc", *<http://www.jihadwatch.org/2004/12/report-canada-security-net-full-of-holes.html>*.

29. *op. cit.* no. 22.

athletes at the Munich Olympics in 1972.[30] Subsequently, it was Genoud who provided treatment in a private Swiss clinic for the leader of the 'Black September,' Hassan Salameh.[31]

In the 1980s, the international press fairly often reported on the links between fundamentalist Islamic groups and traditionalist ultra-right European organisations. The name of Francois Genoud also appeared in these publications. For example, in August 1987, *The Herald Tribune* reported that "Francois Genoud, pro-Nazi Swiss banker residing in Lausanne... who has been named several times in the French press as the trustee of the 'Nazi war chest,' had been a contact of Wahid Gordji, an official in the Iranian embassy in Paris, who was implicated by a French court in bombing attacks that killed 13 persons in Paris in 1986." It was assumed that the attacks were carried out by "a pro-Iranian Islamic fundamentalist terrorist network."[32]

After the trial of Klaus Barbie in 1987, the accusations against Genoud of harbouring Nazi gold stolen from Holocaust victims were heard increasingly in the Western press. At the end of May 1996, in the midst of an investigation concerning the cooperation of Swiss banks with Nazi Germany, Genoud, fearing imminent trial, committed suicide.[33] However, the neo-Nazi-Islamist network that Francois Genoud participated in organising and financing remained. For example, a large part of this network was an alliance of European neo-Nazi organisations.

'Black Internationale' and the Islamic Jihad

In May 1951, the European National Congress was held in Malmo (Sweden). It was attended by representatives of several neo-Nazi parties and movements,[34] prominent among them being: leader of the Swedish neo-Nazis, Per Engdahl; Head of the Italian Social Movement (ISM), Giorgio

30. *op. cit.* no. 3.
31. Lee, Martin A. (2002). "The Swastika and the Crescent", 2 May, <*http://www.aijac.org.au/review/2002/275/essay275.html*>.
32. Preston, David Lee (1997b). "Hitler's Swiss Connection", *Philadelphia Inquirer*, 5 January.
33. Ibid.
34. Pustogarov, V.V. (1989). *Neo-Nazism and International Security*. Moscow: Nauka. p.157.

Almirante; 'Fuhrer' of the British Union of Fascists, Oswald Mosley; and representative of the Austrian ultra-right, former SS officer William Landig.[35] The establishment of the European Social Movement (ESM) with branches in 12 countries in Western Europe was declared at the Congress. This organisation, also called the 'Malmo Internationale' and the 'Black Internationale,' became the largest post-war ultra-right organisation.[36] Subsequently, it grew due to associations of former Nazis and neo-Nazi and right-wing extremist groups. Funding came from various 'SS funds'—Francisco Franco's Spain, Antonio de Oliveira Salazar's Portugal and from the CIA, which had opened special accounts in dozens of European banks.[37]

With this organisation as its base, an extensive terrorist network came into being, elements of which were used for the realisation of the 'Strategy of Tension' in Italy in the late 1960s and early 1970s. Former Nazis and their young followers interacted with leaders of Arab countries and Islamic terrorist organisations within this network. Investigations conducted by Italian parliamentary and judicial commissions identified links between the European ultra-right and Libya. It was argued that the Libyan embassy in Rome had provided financial support for the terrorist Mario Tutti who was hiding from persecution and who was suspected in the bombing of an express train near Florence in 1974.[38]

It is also known from various sources that German neo-Nazis had ties with Islamists. On 14 September 1982, the *Journal of the Jewish Institute for National Security* published the article 'Operation PLO,' which said:

> Contacts between the Palestine Liberation Organization (PLO) and the neo-Nazi groups (blacks) had already begun in the 1960s. At that time, the German officers who had found refuge in Arab countries were advisors and instructors of these nascent groups. One of the first congresses of neo-fascist movements was held in the Swedish city of Malmo. In April 1969, a World Congress of neo-Nazi groups was held in Barcelona with the participation of about 100 delegates from Europe and Latin America. The Algerian delegate, who proposed a resolution condemning the

---

35. Anderson, Scott and John Lee Anderson (1990). *Secrets of the "Black League"*. Moscow: Political Literature. pp.106-07.

36. Ibid.

37. Veselitsky, A.A. (1976). *Top Secret: Conspiracy against the Republic, Italian Neo-Fascism*. Moscow: Political Literature. pp.203-04.

38. *op. cit.* no.31.

> Zionist imperialism, obtained promises to help the PLO with weapons and manpower from the organisations represented. The first evidence of this was an SS officer, who served as commander of a training camp of the Popular Front in the Iraqi city of Basra... In 1973, several European newspapers reported that two well-known neo-Nazis, the Belgian Carl van der Peet and the German Johann Schuler, recruited volunteers for the Fatah (Movement for National Liberation of Palestine). In January 1978, the German prosecutor in Karlsruhe initiated an investigation to identify ties between neo-Nazi organisations and the PLO. The investigation began after the arrest of four Germans, members of the Freikorps Adolf Hitler involved in smuggling arms to the PLO from Arab countries.[39]

It should be noted that many former Nazis and their young followers took part in the terrorist acts of Palestinian military groups. For example, among them was the veteran of the Belgian SS troops, Robert Kurdrua, who died in 1968.[40] One of the German ultra-right organisations well known for its terrorist acts of the 1970s-1980s in Europe was known as the Wehrsportgruppe Hoffman. Its leader maintained close ties with the PLO, with whose help it organised a training camp in Lebanon in 1980.[41]

The PFLP enjoyed the support of European neo-Nazis. The neo-Nazi Odfried Hepp who committed four terrorist attacks on US military bases in West Germany in 1982 is suspected of having ties to this organisation.[42] The Gulf War in 1991 gave new impetus to the relations between right-wing radicals from Europe and the USA and Islamic countries. At that time, the famous German neo-Nazi Michael Kuenen sent volunteers to Iraq from the military group he had set up, the Antisionistische Legion (a.k.a. *Antisionistische Aktion*).[43]

Although the Freedom Corps, formed out of 500 mercenaries from several European countries to fight against international Zionism, had little impact and soon left Iraq, this action had a considerable propaganda effect

---

39. "The PLO/NeoNazi connection",13 January 2010, *http://webcache.googleusercontent.com/search?q=cache:lopq75FeHQMJ:islamo nazism.blogspot.com/2010/01/ploneo-nazi-connection.html+%22Probably+the+best+clue+[to+the+identity+and+motivation+of+the+terrorists]+came+from+the+%22&cd=1&hl=en&ct=clnk*
40. *op. cit.* no.15.
41. *op cit.* no.3.
42. *op cit.* no.15.
43. Aralov, S., "The Brown Reconquista", <*http://www.agentura.ru/press/aralov/*>.

and resulted in strengthening the neo-Nazi-Islamist alliance. Moreover, some researchers see a 'historical continuity' in this act. For example, in 1980s, the previously mentioned Nazi Otto Roemer, who at that time had already returned to Germany, was one of the consultants of Kuenen, a striking representative of the younger generation of Europe's ultra-rightists. It should be noted that even before his flight to Egypt, Roemer was one of the originators of the neo-Nazi movement. In 1949, he created the *Sozialistische Reichspartei* in Lower Saxony, which was banned in 1952.[44] Despite its short history, the organisation, calling for 'restoration of the Reich,' also managed to participate in the elections and helped promote the formation of new right-wing radical organisation in Germany.[45]

The history of the development of the neo-Nazi-Islamist alliance is not limited to the events of the twentieth century. Information about the existence of these relations appeared after the attacks of 11 September 2001. The terrorist attack on the 'twin towers' in New York provoked numerous journalistic investigations into the sponsors of terror. This list also featured the organisations created by Francois Genoud, who participated in the financing of the 'Black Internationale.'

The Fascist-Islamic Financial Network of Francois Genoud and the Terrorist Attack of September 11

In early November 2001, the Swiss authorities froze the accounts of the financial consulting firm Nada Management, which was based in Lugano. This firm, a member of the International Banking Group, *Al Taqwa* (or 'Fear of God') was suspected of laundering money to finance the Al Qaeda. One of the founders of *Al Taqwa* (which the US Office of the Coordinator for Counterterrorism included in the list of organisations connected with financing of terrorism) was no other than the former banker of the ODESSA organisation, Francois Genoud.[46]

On 12 March 2002, the *San Francisco Chronicle* reported that Swiss police "believe that Genoud founded the Al Taqwa Bank and through

44. *op. cit.* no.3.

45. Pustogarov, V.V. (1989). *Neo-Nazism and International Security*. Moscow: Nauka, pp. 127-8.

46. Constantine, Alex, "Adnan Khashoggi Linked to 9/11 Terrorists." <*http://www.american-buddha.com/lit.khashoggiconstantine.1.htm*>

it financially supported such international terrorists as Vladimir Ilich Ramirez (Carlos 'the Jackal') and Osama bin Laden." A few days later Salon added that "among the shareholders of Al-Taqwa there are prominent Arab figures from various Middle Eastern countries, including the Grand Mufti of the United Arab Emirates and members of prominent families from the Emirates and Kuwait".[47]

Thus, the financial network built by the 'Nazi banker' in the post-war years, continued to operate and work for 'Islamic Jihad.' The activities of several major figures of this international banking group, which was considered a key financial organisation for the radical Muslim brothers, attracted attention of the Swiss law enforcement agencies. One of them was the President of *Al Taqwa* Bank Group, Youssef Moustafa Nada, who joined the militant branch of Muslim brothers in 1940, worked for the German Military Intelligence and took part in a plot against King Farouk after the war. Nada was also a member of the Egyptian terrorist organisation al-Jamaa al-Islamiya, which is associated with Al Qaeda. Since 1970, Nada has lived in Saudi Arabia. Thanks to his contacts with members of the Royal family, he established a civil engineering firm in Riyadh and Faisal Bank, the first Islamic bank in Egypt.[48]

One of the directors of the *Al Taqwa* banking group, Ali Ghaleb Himmat, is a member of the Muslim Brotherhood. Until 2002, he headed the Islamic Society of Germany, based in Bavaria and created by the Muslim Brotherhood. One more major figure is the President of *Al Taqwa*'s Advisory Board on religion, Yusuf al-Qaradawi, who lives in Qatar. He is considered one of the main spiritual leaders of the Muslim Brotherhood.[49] It is claimed that in 1988, Youssef Nada, having received approval from the Muslim Brothers, took part in the establishment of the bank *Al Taqwa*, together with two Swiss nationals—Francois Genoud and Ahmed Huber. Nada met the latter in Iran in the second half of the 1980s.[50]

---

47. Ibid.
48. Ibid.
49. Coogan, Kevin (2002). "Mysterious Achmed Huber: Friend to Hitler, Allah... and Ben Laden". April/May, <*http://ftrsupplemental.blogspot.com/2002/05/mysterious-achmed-huber-friend-to.html*>.
50. Morgan, Adrian (2009). "The Muslim Brotherhood: Islam, Anti-Semitism and Totalitarianism," Part No. 2, 11 December <*http://www.familysecuritymatters.org/publications/id.4976/pub_detail.asp*>

Ahmed (formerly Albert) Huber, a board member of Nada Management, is a former Swiss journalist, who had helped Algerian separatists in the late 1950s. Following these contacts, he twice officially converted to Islam after having become Ahmed Huber—first in the Geneva Islamic Centre founded by the Muslim Brotherhood and then in Cairo's Al-Azhar University. In the early 1960s, while in Egypt, according to the revelations of Huber himself, he "took up the views of the Grand Mufti of Jerusalem Amin al-Husseini" and "became close to a former employee of the Nazi Ministry of Propaganda, Johann von Leers." At the same time, Huber "met the banker Francois Genoud in pro-Arab associations" and came into close contact with him after returning to Switzerland.[51]

According to the German Office for the Protection of the Constitution, Huber is widely known in European neo-Nazi circles and "considers himself an intermediary between Islam and right-wing groups."[52] This is confirmed by the results of investigation of the Al Taqwa banking group that was undertaken after the terrorist attacks of September 11. For example, during a search of Huber's house, a photo was found showing the owner of the house together with Genoud visiting the SS General, Leon Degrelle in Spain, one of the leaders of the neo-Nazi movements in Europe.

Huber assisted the Swiss far-right group Avalon Gemeinschaft, which consisted of former SS volunteers.[53] He collaborated with the neo-Nazi National Democratic Party of Germany (NDP), lecturing at its events on "the alliance of Islam and the rightists." He visited Islamic and neo-Nazi organisations in Europe and the USA giving sermons and building bridges between the "deniers and revisionists of the Holocaust" in the West and the Arab world. By his own acknowledgement, he communicated with representatives of Al Qaeda at Muslim conferences in Beirut, London and Brussels more than once.[54]

Lectures and international conferences on Holocaust revisionism have long been a platform where the Nazi-Islamist cooperation received further impetus for development. They are attended by the radical Islamists

---

51. *op. cit.* no 49.
52. *op. cit* no.31.
53. *op. cit.* no 49.
54. *op. cit.* no.31.

of Hezbollah and Hamas, as well as leaders of American and European neo-Nazis. The Californian Institute for Historical Review, one of the key academic institutions in the world that questions the existence of the Holocaust, participates in sponsoring such international events.[55]

Conclusion

In sum, the initial alliance between Islamic radicals and the Nazis originated about 80 years ago on the basis of anti-Semitism, anti-Communism and hatred of the liberal West. After the war, this alliance developed on the basis of 'terror training' among other things, where teachers were aces of sabotage operations of the Nazi Germany.

Subsequently, radical Islam has been used by the USA to destroy the USSR, as well as to destabilise the political and economic situation in many regions of the world that are important for the Americans. The Islamists and the CIA have actively used the experience of Nazi experts in information warfare and various special operations, including terrorist activities. But in parallel with these developments, the representatives of radical Islam have talked about the fight against the 'two Satans,' the big (American) and the small (Soviet), while neo-Nazies spoke about the 'two predators of Yalta'—the USSR and the USA. And as some results of the investigation of the September 11 terrorist attacks have shown, such seemingly American 'instrument' as 'Islamic terrorism' has already begun to work against the USA using the capabilities of neo-Nazi networks.

And, not only in the USA. In May 2007, several German politicians made statements, the essence of which was that Islamists and right-wing radicals are cooperating in Germany and in the future they could unite in an effort to overthrow the constitutional order. Thus, according to the opinion of Bavarian Interior Minister, Gunther Beckstein, expressed to the German TV channel *Südwestrundfunk* (SWR), "such dangerous cases of cooperation are not unique. Especially for groups which are prone to violence. There is no need to panic yet, but you have to constantly be on guard." This position is shared by both the Vice-Chairman of the Christian

55. *op. cit.* no.49.

Democratic Union/Christian Social Union of Bavaria (CDU/CSU) Party, Wolfgang Bosbach, and Social Democrat, Dieter Wiefelspülz.[56]

What we have possibly talked about is a neo-Nazi-Islamist alliance aimed at the realisation of large political projects, where terror is only one of the means of achieving their objective. But, if some researchers still have doubts regarding the preparedness of Neo-Nazis for the tasks on such a scale, then they should have much less doubt in the capabilities of Islamic groups, especially after the series of so-called 'Arab revolutions' in the Middle East and North Africa, which have already led to major changes in this region.

56. Shelemba, Vitaly (2007). "An Alliance of Islamists and Neo-Nazis is Possible in Germany", 21 May, <*http://www.baznica.info/newsid-4718.html*>.

6 The Drug Trade as a Factor in Global Destabilisation

Mikhail Dmitriev

The increasing transnationalisation of drug trafficking is one of the greatest threats to the world today. This process is of particular concern to Russia, which has been embroiled in the international system of production, distribution and consumption of drugs after the collapse of the USSR. According to the official data of the Federal Service for Drug Control (FSKN), there are about 6 million drug addicts in Russia, of whom 62.4 per cent are under the age of 30.[1] Up to 100,000 people die from drug use in this country every year[2] and 80-86 per cent of the addicts use drugs produced in Afghanistan.

This paper examines the processes and problems associated with the drug trade from the perspective of this nefarious trafficking activity emanating from Afghanistan. The operations specific to this region do not reflect all the current trends in the spread of the international drug trade. Therefore, to begin with, we will indicate the global trends.

Trends in the Transnationalisation of the Drug Trade

There are two main drug centres—or 'corporate capitals' to coin a phrase—operating on a transnational level in the world.[3] The first is the cocaine trade working out of Colombia in Latin America. The second is the heroin trade, with its roots in Central Asia, in which the bulk of the product's flow in the past decade has been coming from Afghanistan.

1. See <*http://www.upfo.fskn.ru/ru/advanced/65/308/*>.
2. Ivanov, V. (2010). "Global Octopus", *www.izvestia.ru* No. 226 (28241), 2 December.
3. Ibid.

Both cocaine and heroin trafficking have long histories with well-established routes. What have been the main trends in recent years?

1. The menace is actively expanding its trade routes, involving more and more new regions of the world into the cocaine and heroin business. For example, drug cartels have responded to the reduced demand for Latin American drugs in the USA—mainly brought about through the implementation of the new US National Drug Control Strategy—by increasing the supply of Latin American cocaine to the European continent. According to data from the UN, the European cocaine market ($34 billion a year) is worth almost as much as the North American market ($37 billion).[4] Since 2004, Colombian drug cartels have also been using West Africa as an initial trans-shipment point for deliveries to Europe.

East African countries have for some time been connected to the Afghan drug trade. The annual flow of heroin through the region is estimated at 30-35 tonnes.[5] According to experts, the drugs mainly flow through Sahel, a vast arid region south of the Sahara, where the real authorities are not the governments, but various militant groups.

In 2009, the UN Security Council urged the international community to combat the relatively new African drug trade, since, according to UN Secretary General Ban Ki-moon, the continent already "has become a world center for drug trafficking"[6] and a major independent producer of narcotics.

2. The number of people involved in various aspects of the business (production, transportation, trade and consumption of drugs) is increasing. According to the UN, 250 million people (5.7% of the world population) aged 15-64 years are drug users today. Moreover, the scale of the problem still cannot be fully appreciated on account of the lack of data for many countries, particularly for Africa, parts of Asia and the Pacific Islands.[7]

3. The trade generates pockets of instability, extremism, organised crime and terrorism.[8] Experts studying drug-related issues have no doubts

4. World Drug Report 2010, Summary,13, <*www.unodc.org/unodc*>.

5. Ibid.

6. "The UN: Africa has Become a 'Transhipment Base' for World Drug Trafficking", (2009), 10 December, <*www.nr2.ru/inworld/260922.html/print/*>.

7. *op. cit.* no.2.

8. Ibid.

about the relationship between the drug trade, terrorism, arms trafficking and local conflicts. The rapid growth of drug production in countries where civil war has been waged for decades supports the conclusion that internal 'armed conflicts' are not only a powerful stimulus for narcotics and weapons mafias, but are often the direct result of their activities.

This process is spreading both in drug-producing regions (Central America, Afghanistan, South-East Asia) and in territories far from the epicentres of production (Kosovo, Russia's North Caucasus, republics of Central Asia, Xinjiang Uygur Autonomous Region of China, etc.).

The former Canadian diplomat and researcher, Peter Dale Scott gave an accurate description of this process. He said: "Terrorism creates the kind of anarchy that favours drug production and trafficking, while drug trafficking provides the most convenient and local source of funds for terrorism."[9]

4. The drug trade is increasing its influence over global economic processes. It is fast integrating with the global economy and gaining control of many industrial branches and sectors, thereby garbing itself in the guise of legitimate business, as well as strengthening its political and social base. The process occurs most acutely and painfully in countries and regions with a poor socioeconomic situation and weak political authority (Central and South America, Central Asia).

According to the UN and the International Monetary Fund (IMF), the annual profit of drug mafias is around $600 billion, or 7.6 per cent of world trade. This is comparable to the income of the international steel market and the automotive industry (2.8 per cent and 5.3 per cent respectively, of the volume of international trade), or oil and gas incomes (8.6 percent). Each year, up to $1.5 trillion received from the drug trade is legalised, which corresponds to 5 per cent of Gross World Product (GWP).[10]

The role played by this menace in the 2007 global economic crisis is all too evident. According to former UN Under Secretary General and

9. Scott, P.D. (2010). "Kyrgyztan, America, and the Global Drug Trade: Subsurface Forces, Coup d'Etats, Narcotics and Terror", 14 July.

10. "International Life", 31January 2009, <*http://www.rian.ru/spravka/20100609/244280867.html?*>, "Global Drug Trade", <*http://www.interaffairs.ru/arpg.php?pg=149*>.

Executive Director of the UN Office on Drugs and Crime (UNODC), Antonio Maria Costa, in the midst of the global financial crisis, approximately 352 million drug dollars were chanelled into the banking systems of a number of leading countries in order to compensate for their financial losses. Costa said: "In many instances, the money from drugs was the only liquid capital. In the second half of 2008, liquidity was the banking system's main problem and hence liquid capital became an important factor."[11]

5. This trade is resolved to improving its technological and organisational standards. Drug cartels invest considerable resources into the financing of laboratories engaged in the search for new drugs and improved technologies for their manufacture. The latest scientific advances are used in the manufacture of synthetic drugs and precursors (substances needed to produce the final drugs). Moreover, some of these chemicals are not subject to international control and not all countries have mechanisms for the legal regulation of activities related to the use of these substances.

Furthermore, the traffickers actively use telecommunication technology and the internet network. A powerful computer connected to an electronic international banking network facilitates the international flow and legalisation of drug revenues. Also, the direct sale of drugs to consumers through numerous online retailers is rapidly growing and the drug industry itself is not only expanding but upgrading means to ensure its own safety. The inventories of today's multinational drug cartels contain the most modern weapons and ammunition, electronic tracking systems, satellite communications, private aviation and a submarine fleet.

6. Attempts to liberalise attitudes to drug-related issues are being undertaken. In some countries, a consolidation of forces has been observed, which advocates the revision of the UN 'anti-drug' conventions, drug legalisation and liberalisation of government and society standpoints with regard to the control of drug production and consumption. This trend is observed in both European countries and in Russia, as well as in Central and North America.

11. From the interview with A. Costa, *Observer Magazine*, <*http://stratgap.ru/pages/strategy/3662/3887/4139/index.shtml*, Adapted from *www.ifx.ru*>.

Proponents of drug legalisation are taking action to change international public opinion on the issue of combating the menace. Arguments in support of drugs legalisation have also popped up in the media on a regular basis. An article by Mick Moore, an expert at the British Institute of Development Studies, "Drugs: Towards a Global Tolerance Regime," deserves special attention. It is worth noting that Moore, a supporter of the legalisation of drugs, specialises in management issues in poor countries. Sharply criticising the UN for 'militant prohibitionism', Moore calls for lifting "the curse of the illegal international drug trade." We will then, he adds,"...really have made our contribution to the well-being of the world's poor, and done ourselves a large favour in the process."[12]

In turn, the famous American financier and billionaire, George Soros, initiated the legalisation of marijuana. A referendum for the legalisation of marijuana was passed in autumn 2010 in California (USA). Although the idea was not approved, the voting results make us pause and think: 46.5 per cent of legislators voted for the proposal and just 53.5 per cent said 'nay.' During late 2010 to early 2011, representatives of the highest Mexican and Brazilian elite repeatedly announced their readiness to legalise drugs. In February 2011, Colombian President Jose Manuel Santos spoke on a similar note: "If the world decides to legalise and believes that this would reduce violence and crime, I could accompany it."[13] Such statements may be interpreted as a sign of readiness of these countries' governments 'to give in' to the criminal and political pressure of drug cartels.

On 2 June 2011, the UN Global Commission for Drug Policies[14] admitted: "The global war on drugs has failed, with devastating consequences for individuals and societies around the world."[15] The

12. Moore, M. (2010). "Narcotics: on the Path to a Global Regime of Tolerance", 11 March, *<http://www.polit.ru/institutes/2010/03/11/drugs.html>*.

13. "Columbia in Despair is Prepared to Legalize Drugs", 2011, 14 February, *<http://evrazia.org/news/16922>*.

14. The commission includes former UN Secretary General, Kofi Annan, as well as the former Presidents of Brazil, Mexico and Colombia. Among the members of the Commission are former US Federal Reserve Chairman, Paul Volcker, and the former Prime Minister of Greece, George Papandreou. It also includes the well-known Latin American writers, Carlos Fuentes and Mario Vargas Llosa, the former EU Commissioner for Foreign Policy, Javier Solana, and the former US Secretary of State, George Shultz.

15. For example, see *<inopressa.ru/article/.../drug.html>*.

Commission called for radical reforms and proposed "experiments in the legal regulation/experimentation by governments with models of legal regulation of drugs...."

Now, we come to the issue under study in this paper: the drug situation in Afghanistan. The export of Afghan drugs (and this is up to 90 per cent of the world's production of opiates) represents a serious threat to the national security of transit countries, especially Afghanistan's neighbours, such as the republics of Central Asia. But this is no less serious a threat for the primary countries of consumption: Russia and Western Europe. According to the UN, Russia and Europe are the world's largest markets for Afghan heroin (70 and 88 tonnes respectively, or 21 and 26 per cent of the heroin produced in the world).[16]

Trends and Dynamics of the Drug Trade in Afghanistan: The Main Actors and Groups

Beginning in 1970, three sharp rises occurred in Afghan drug production, as a result of which Afghanistan became the world leader in opium and heroin production. Moreover, from 1970 to the present day, drug production in Afghanistan has been an important component of all military conflicts that have taken place in the country.

The first sharp rise in opium and heroin production occurred in the late 1970s and early 1980s, after the entry of Soviet troops into Afghanistan. At the time, it coincided with a sharp drop in opium and heroin production in other major regions of the world. After the success of the 1979 Islamic Revolution in Iran (the largest traditional producer of opium in the region), a ban on poppy cultivation was introduced by Tehran. In a parallel occurence, a two-year drought resulted in a temporary sharp drop in opium production in Southeast Asia's 'Golden Triangle,' situated where the borders of Myanmar, Laos and Thailand meet.

Although Middle East production was resumed in the 1980s, by then, Lebanon's Beqaa Valley had become the centre of opium-heroin production. It was Afghanistan and Pakistan that became the largest producers of opium, capable of compensating for the 'deficit' that had arisen on the global drug market. In the early 1980s, areas of Afghanistan—where opium

16. *op. cit.* no. 4.

poppy cultivation was already flourishing—came under the control of Islamic fundamentalists and traditionalist factions that waged war against the government of the People's Democratic Party of Afghanistan and the Soviet troops. By 1985, under pressure from the USA and Pakistan, these factions formed a political and military alliance of the leaders of the Afghan *mujahedeen* or the so-called 'Peshawar Seven'. In March 1985, President Reagan signed National Security Decision Directive No. 166, authorising an increase in clandestine military assistance to the *mujahedeen*. The aim was to defeat and chase out Soviet troops from Afghanistan.[17]

According to experts, the Central Intelligence Agency (CIA) spent up to 80 per cent of its budget earmarked for covert operations around the world on special operations in Afghanistan.[18] Over the 10 years of war (1979-1990), US aid to the *mujahedeen* amounted to about $4 billion.[19] Saudi Arabia spent almost as much on the war against Soviet troops. In addition, the *mujahedeen* received generous financial aid from various Western non-governmental organisations (NGOs). However, with the active encouragement of the USA, the main source of finance for the *mujahedeen* became the dramatic expansion of drug production in Afghanistan and Pakistan.

A theory exists that a special CIA programme code-named 'White Jihad' was developed, the essence of which was to use Afghanistan as a base for the production of raw opium and its movement into the Soviet republics of Central Asia.[20] Pakistan's Inter-Services Intelligence (ISI) acted as a facilitator and coordinator of this foreign military and financial assistance, as well as for covert special operations. "Across the border in Pakistan," said the well-known researcher, Alfred McCoy, "Afghan leaders and local syndicates under the protection of Pakistani intelligence operated hundreds of heroin laboratories".[21] What is noteworthy in this respect is that

17. Coll, Steve (1992). "Anatomy of a Victory: CIA's Covert Afghan War", *Washington Post*, 19 July.
18. Stepanova, E.A. (2005). *The Role of the Drug Trade in the Political Economy of Conflicts and Terrorism*. Moscow: Ves Mir.
19. Ibid.
20. Mukashev, A.K. (2010). "Reasons for Drug Abuse and the Current Drug Situation in Kazakhstan", AkMU KHABARSHYSY, zan fylymdary seriyasy, No. 4 (45).
21. McCoy, A. (1997). "Drug Fallout: the CIA's Forty Year Complicity in the Narcotics Trade", *The Progressive*, 1 August.

during the 10 years of the Soviet-Afghan war, the US Drug Enforcement Administration in Islamabad did not undertake even one major seizure or arrest and there was not even a single investigation into charges of heroin trafficking against leaders of the Afghan *mujahedeen*. The explanation is that the US policy towards drugs in Afghanistan was subordinated to the need to counter the Soviet influence.

After the Soviet withdrawal from Afghanistan in May 1990, *The Washington Post* accused the US State Department of supporting the *mujahedeen* "who do not carry out military operations, but poison the population of other countries with drugs."[22] In mid-1995, the former head of CIA operations in Afghanistan, Charles Cogan, admitted "the US sacrificed the drug war to fight the Cold War".[23]

During the 1980s, the focus of drug trafficking from Afghanistan to Europe was the 'Balkan route'. Afghan drugs arrived in Turkey through Pakistan and Iran, where they were processed in local laboratories. Then the narcotics were shipped to Europe and the USA through the Balkans.

In addition, large shipments of drugs were transported along the 'southern route'—Peshawar–Karachi and further on (by sea or by air) to Europe, the Middle East and the Asia-Pacific region.

Less popular, but quite significant in terms of the quantity of drug trafficking, was the route across India, with a trans-shipment point in Pakistan's Sukkur.[24]

At the same time, attempts to open up routes across the Afghan-Soviet border to the border regions of the Uzbekistan and Tajikistan did not cease. However, the well-guarded Soviet-Afghan border and the absence of a well-functioning, large-scale drug market in the Soviet Union prevented any large inflow into the USSR. During these years, storehouses of weapons, drugs and pro-Islamic propaganda literature were already being set up in the border areas of the USSR Central Asian Republics.[25] In the decade

22. Senchenko, N.I., "The Albanian and Afghan Drug Trade in Participation with the US Intelligence Services", <*http://rusmir.in.ua*>.

23. *op. cit.* no.21.

24. Khokhlov, I.I., "This History of the Drug Trade in Countries of the 'Golden Crescent'", <*http://www.nationalsecurity.ru/research-5976.html*>.

25. *op. cit.* no.20.

from 1980 to 1990, opium production in Afghanistan increased almost eightfold—from 200 tonnes to 1,570 tonnes per year. Afghanistan's share in the world production increased from 19 per cent in 1980 to 42 per cent in 1990.[26]

The second rise in Afghan drug production occurred in the second half of the 1990s with the Taliban's ascent to power in Kabul in 1996. According to experts, a particularly important factor in the expansion of the Afghan production was the close relationship between the Taliban and Osama bin Laden's Al Qaeda international terrorist network (the Global Salafi Jihad).

By the mid-1990s, Al Qaeda had established connections with criminal terrorist, and separatist groups in virtually all developed countries, connecting the geographically disparate zone of heroin production and its consumption. Moreover, according to experts, the mode of building an international terrorist network proved to be very similar to the scheme of international opium trafficking.[27] Under the Taliban, Al Qaeda actively used bases and training camps in Afghanistan as well as in the north-western provinces of Pakistan. While the Taliban and Al Qaeda built up a major drug cartel and the Kabul authorities looked after the cultivation of opium poppy and heroin production, Osama bin Laden's and Ayman al-Zawahiri's factions took care of transportation, sale of drugs and money laundering in Yemen, Sudan and Pakistan.[28]

The Head of the American Drug Enforcement Administration (DEA), Asa Hutchinson, calculated that the income derived from drug trafficking was distributed by Al Qaeda's international network among terrorist organisations like the Taliban, the terrorist group Revolutionary Armed Forces of Colombia and the Egypt Islamic Jihad.[29] A Federal Bureau of Investigation (FBI) report published following an investigation of the explosions at the US embassies in Nairobi (Kenya) and Dar-es-Salaam (Tanzania) on 7 August 1998, indicates that Osama bin Laden laid a stake

26. *op. cit.* no.18: 57.
27. Khokhlov, I.I., "The Production of Opiate Narcotics (Heroin) in Afghanistan: The Infrastructure of the Drug Trade", Chapter II, *<http://www.narkotiki.ru/research_5988.html>*.
28. Ibid.
29. *<www.washprofile.org/ru/node/2502>*.

on the mass production of heroin with two goals: first, as a means for financing terrorist activities and, second, for politically influencing the *kafir* (infidel).[30]

The same report says that in the mid-1990s, bin Laden organised supply chains of Afghan heroin to Russia's North Caucasus in order to build a financial base for Chechen terrorists. Former employees of Pakistan's ISI acted as facilitators. Revenues from drug trafficking went to finance Chechen extremist groups conducting terrorist operations against the Russian army in Chechnya.[31] At the same time, Chechens were transporting heroin to Kosovo Albanians and, under their control, it was spread to a number of European countries (Switzerland, Germany and Denmark) and the USA.

After the collapse of the USSR in late 1991 and the subsequent weakening of border controls along all the former Soviet borders, the 'northern route' running through Central Asian countries proved to be the safest and cheapest way to transport drugs from Afghanistan. According to experts, in 1999, a record-breaking amount of about 4,500 tonnes of opium (or 79 per cent of world production) was produced in Taliban-controlled areas.

However, in February 1999, the spiritual leader of the Taliban, Mullah Omar, issued a decree on the reduction of poppy cultivation by a third, and on 27 July 2000, a decree on the total ban of poppy cultivation as an activity 'forbidden by Allah.' According to the most widespread point of view, the ban on poppy cultivation might become a bargaining chip in the Taliban leadership's negotiations with the international community, especially the USA.[32] Some experts point out that the ban imposed by Mullah Omar on the production of heroin coincided with a sharp drop in prices from $700 to $450 per kilogram.

There is another interpretation of the events: the destruction of poppy fields and several drug laboratories by the Taliban leadership was purely for show. In reality, the fields had been destroyed only after harvesting

30. Khokhlov, I.I., "The Increase in Heroin Production after the Beginning of US and UK Operations", <*http://www.narkotiki.ru/research_6216.html*>.

31. For example, see <*http://nvo.ng.ru/wars/2002-11-22/2_moscow.html*>.

32. *op. cit.* no.18.

and the unprocessed poppies and raw opium were stockpiled until a 'more favourable' time. In a sense, this explains the near-explosive growth in opium production since 2001.

The third rise in drug production in Afghanistan coincided with the beginning of the North Atlantic Treaty Organisation (NATO) anti-terrorist operation and the entrance of the International Security Assistance Force (ISAF) into the country in October 2001. Mullah Omar responded to this military operation with the repeal of the previously mentioned 'anti-heroin' *fatwa* and called for "flooding the West with drugs." As early as 2002, the growth of opium and heroin production was 1,400 per cent (after repeal of 'anti-heroin' *fatwa,* production rose from 185 tonnes to about 2,700 tonnes, which is 1400%). In 2001 (before the anti-terrorist operation), 185 tonnes of opium were gathered, in 2002, about 1900-2700 tonnes and in 2009, about 8000 tonnes (98 per cent of world production).[33]

By 2005, a closed industrial cycle from opium poppy cultivation to processing of the final product 'heroin hydrochloride' had essentially been set up on the territory of Afghanistan—in provinces like Nangarhar, Paktia, Helmand, Kunar and Balkh and the cities Kunduz and Fayzabad. Its storage and wholesale trade took place in the heroin markets in Afghan Kandahar and the Pakistani Chitral.

One of the leading Russian experts on Afghan-Pakistani issues, Igor Khokhlov, says that since 2001 (with the beginning of the anti-terrorist operations by NATO troops), the international drug mafia has created a full-fledged production, transit, credit and financial drug infrastructure in Afghanistan. Moreover, many of the major lending institutions are involved in servicing the Afghan drug trade, including those active in the countries of the anti-terrorist coalition.[34]

Experts explain the 2010 reduction of opium production to half (to 3,600 metric tonnes) was caused by climatic conditions and a fungal disease that infected the opium poppy. However, the threat is that heroin is produced in Afghanistan not only for current consumption, in the course

33. Khokhlov, I.I., "How will the NATO Operation in Southern Afghanistan End", *Lenta.ru.*

34. Khokhlov, I.I., "The Transportation of Heroin through the Countries of Central Asia", <*http://www.narkotiki.ru/research_6284.html*>.

of which not more than 10-15 per cent is sold, but also for the creation of strategic reserves, which amount to about 3-7 thousand tonnes of pure heroin; from this amount, more than a trillion single doses can be manufactured. In fact, it is this 'strategic drug fund' that would allow huge amounts of high-quality heroin to be tossed into international markets for many years, even in the event of a complete cessation of opium cultivation.

Afghan Drug Trafficking: Routes and Zones of Instability

According to experts, the transportation of Afghan drugs currently takes place along three main routes: the 'southern,' the 'Balkan' and the 'northern.' Russia is especially concerned about the 'Balkan' and the 'northern' routes. Most of Afghan drug trafficking along the 'Balkan' route goes through Turkey. Up to 80 per cent of Afghan heroin is transported via this route. In the 1990s, the central Balkan station along this route was Bosnian Sarajevo. In the late 1990s, the main transit station became the autonomous province of Kosovo. The drug situation in Kosovo, where for decades, the drug trade has played a key role in destabilising the region, remains one of the most serious security challenges for both the Balkans and Europe at large.

Experts stress the role of drug mafia networks in Kosovo (Albanian) separatist movements in Yugoslavia since the 1980s. However, at that time, Kosovo Albanians primarily played only the role of couriers for the Turkish drug mafia and Bulgarian criminal networks. Since the early 1990s, with the growth of Albanian separatism, independent Albanian mafia groups have begun to form; they are involved in the 'Greater Albania' project. Drugs were used to finance and arm the Kosovo Liberation Army (KLA). In 1994-95, evidence appeared that Afghan mujahedeen mercenaries were fighting in the ranks of the terrorist Albanian National Liberation Army of Kosovo and Macedonia (KLA-NLA).[35]

In 1997, Interpol prepared a special report, in which all national Interpol Bureaus were asked to pay close attention to the criminal organisations linked to the Kosovo Albanian mafia. In 2005, Europol acknowledged that the Albanian mafia was the most dangerous for European Union (EU)

35. Subramanyam, K. (1995). "Pakistan Seeks Asian goals", *India Abroad*, 3 November.

countries.[36] According to experts, 30 Albanian mafia groups engaged in trafficking operate in Kosovo, Albania and Macedonia. Their annual income is about $2 billion. The Albanian drug mafia controls 75 per cent of the heroin supply in Western Europe and about 50 per cent of deliveries to the USA. Revenues are laundered in restaurants, shops and beauty salons that belong to emigrants from Albania and Kosovo in England, Germany, Italy and Spain.[37]

In western Macedonia, which has become a major trans-shipment centre for the drug trafficking route between Turkey and Kosovo, the trade is controlled by the Menduh Thaci's group (a relative of the current Prime Minister of Kosovo, Hashim Thaci). The leaders of the Kosovo separatists—Thaci, Haradinaj and Ceku—are at the same time leaders of drug-related crime communities.[38]

All these activities take place before the eyes of the US intelligence service. It is in Kosovo that Europe's largest US military base camp Bondsteel is located. Construction of the base was carried out by the company Halliburton (its CEO, from 1995 to 2000, was the future US Vice President, Dick Cheney). More than 7,000 servicemen are based at Bondsteel (the total number of the military personnel stationed in the province is 16,000).[39] In addition, another base was built in Kosovo, Camp Monteith (also with 7,000 soldiers). The US Air Force military transport aircraft regularly use these bases. It is worth noting that these aircraft are not subject to any customs inspection either on arrival or departure.[40]

It should be noted that the appearance of Camp Bondsteel in Kosovo and its special status is of great concern to many European countries and to Russia. Some experts believe that the tough US support for the Kosovo

36. Ovchinsky, V.S. (Head of the Russian Interpol Office, 1997-1999) "'War of the Worlds'": The 'Independence' of Kosovo as Reflected in Shady Politics", *<http://www.contrtv.ru/common/2651/>*.

37. Kuznetsov, A. (2009). "The Geopolitics of Drugs". Baltinfo, 30 June.

38. Ibid.

39. Ibid.

40. Ibid.

Albanians is motivated by Washington's plans to turn 'an independent Kosovo' into its centre of influence over south-eastern Europe.[41]

It cannot be ruled out that if Kosovo unites with Albania (and such plans exist and are pronounced openly), it will become a centre around which the 'awakening European Muslims' may consolidate. This essentially refers to the formation of a 'hot Islamic arc' (Bosnia-Kosovo-Albania-Macedonia) in the south-eastern Europe.

From Russia's perspective, the following 'branches' of the Balkan route pose the primary drug threat.

- Iran-Azerbaijan-Dagestan: This border area between Azerbaijan and Russian Dagestan is called the 'golden gate' or 'golden bridge' in the drug dealers jargon. In addition, there are three more routes that zero in on Russia:
- The Tran-Caspian route: Iranian port of Noushahr-Dagestan-Astrakhan.
- The Turkmen route: Iranian Mashhad-Sarahs-Kushka (Turkmenistan): Kushka is a trans-shipment point for the port of Turkmenbashi on the east coast of the Caspian Sea, from which heroin enters Azerbaijan and then into Russia by overland transport.
- The Black Sea route: Iran-Azerbaijan-Georgia-Black Sea-Russia's North Caucasus: According to experts, this route is becoming more important due to the increasing terrorism and political instability in the North Caucasus republics. Since the 1990s, the drug trade has played a key role in financing terrorism and extremism in North Caucasus.

The 'northern route' for the transit of Afghan drugs is completely oriented to Russia. Today, it includes several heroin transport paths that run through Central Asia (Uzbekistan, Tajikistan, Kyrgyzstan and Turkmenistan), and then the drugs are delivered to Russia after transiting through Kazakhstan.

---

41. Ponomareva, E. MGIMO MID RF, "Why does Washington Need Kosovo?", *<http://www.mgimo.ru/news/experts/>*.

The key route here is Gorno-Badakhshan (Tajikistan)-Osh (Kyrgyzstan). The main flow of narcotics is along three roads: Khujand-Osh, Khorog-Osh and Dzhergital-Osh. In summer, drugs are ferried from Tajikistan to Kyrgyzstan by hundreds of mountain pedestrian and equestrian passages that are impossible to control.[42]

An analysis of the developments in Central Asia reveals that funds from Afghan drug trade were well-nigh the plod line for the major incidents and turmoils in the region, they being—the civil war in Tajikistan (which many experts fear, has simmered down only temporarily), the tragic events of 14-15 May 2005 in Andijan (Uzbekistan), the Tulip Revolution of 2005 and the April 2010 revolution in Kyrgyzstan. From the early 1990s, the warlords of the Northern Alliance and militants of the United Tajik Opposition (UTO) controlled drug trafficking in the area. Then the baton was taken up by the terrorist organisation Islamic Movement of Uzbekistan (IMU) and the cells of the Hizb-ut-Tahrir group, which control the traffic through Fergana Valley region.[43] Due to the criticality of the issue, it is necessary to briefly describe the role of drug trafficking in the conflict in Kyrgyzstan.

Drugs in the Kyrgyz Events of 2010

Even before 2001, Kyrgyzstan's geopolitical position (close to the main Afghan routes through Tajikistan) had made it a vital zone for transnational drug trafficking and extremist groups. It needs to be noted here that the people from Osh region (Kyrgyzstan's main drug region) did not play any active role in the 2005 Tulip Revolution, when President Askar Akaev was ousted and replaced by Kurmanbek Bakiyev.[44]

In 2010, new evidence came to light about the involvement of the drug mafia and narco-terrorist groups in the political events in Kyrgyzstan. On 6 April 2010, mass opposition protests began in Kyrgyzstan and ended in the ousting of President Bakiyev from Bishkek. By 10-12 June, armed incidents broke out in Osh and Jalalabad (southern Kyrgyzstan), the hub of

42. *op. cit.* no.34.

43. Ivanov, V. (2009). *Report at the Meeting of the State Anti-Drug Committee*, 26 June.

44. *op. cit.* no.34.

Afghan drug trafficking, and several hundred people were killed (unofficial estimates were as high as 2,000).

According to analysts of the Chatham House,[45] one of the reasons for the June clashes in southern Kyrgyzstan was the competition between different drug factions. According to this version, before the April Revolution, the family of former President Bakiyev became enriched by illegal means linked to drugs. The fall of his regime meant that the balance of interests in this highly profitable sector skewed.[46]

A number of researchers believe that the massacre in Osh was an attempt by Bakiyev's clan to restore and even expand its lost position. The main suspect in instigating the carnage in Osh was Janish Bakiyev, the ousted President's brother. Kygyz Deputy Security Council Secretary, Alik Orozov, has drawn attention to the fact that as early as in 2009, Janish Bakiyev initiated the liquidation of the Kyrgyz Drug Control Agency. Orozov does not exclude the possibility that Janish had planned to take control of all drug trafficking along the 'northern route' on the Kyrgyz land.[47]

On 24 June 2010, Keneshbek Duishebayev (appointed to Chair the Kyrgyz National Security Agency in December 2010) announced that it was "through the Bakiyev clan [that] international terrorist organisations have become involved in the drug barons-mediation by proxy..." adding that they "...instigated bloodshed in the south, where local nationalist leaders worked for them." He also noted that the inner circle of Kurmanbek Bakiyev had ordered international terrorist organisations (the Islamic Movement of Uzbekistan and the Islamic Jihad Union) to create a destabilising situation in the country.[48] This same interpretation has also been offered repeatedly by the Director of the Federal Drug Control Service of the Russian Federation, Victor Ivanov.

Indirect confirmation of this version of events appeared in summer 2010, when several internet sites spread the news of the death of one of the

---

45. The Royal Institute of International Affairs, London.

46. Shustov, A. (2011). "Kyrgystan: the State and Narcotics", Strategic Culture Foundation, 26 February, *<http://www.fondsk.ru/news/2011/02/26/kirgizija-gosudarstvo-i-narkotiki.html>*.

47. *<http://www.easttime.ru/allanalitic/127.html 24.08.2010>*.

48. *<http://www.dn.kz/>*.

leaders of the IMU, Tahir Yuldashev, as well as the appointment of the new leader of the IMU, Usman Adil, known for his ties with the Taliban and Al Qaeda. On 17 August 2010, Adil commented on the events in southern Kyrgyzstan in a radio address to his supporters, saying: "May Allah make way for Muslims to make the right conclusion and be able to follow the path of jihad".[49] This statement was seen by many experts as a declaration of jihad against 'non-Bakiyev' Kyrgyzstan.

In February 2011, the Deputy Chief of Staff of the Kyrgyz State Service for Drug Control, Urmat Abrybekov, said that Kyrgyzstan "is in the process of changing from a large number of small criminal groups once divided along patriotic, national, or kinship lines into several well-organised drug cartels with a clear hierarchy and connections in the neighboring countries and beyond."[50] This raises the concern that these changes are threatening not only the loss of Kyrgyzstan's southern regions, but also instigating a new round of destabilisation in all of post-Soviet Central Asia.

Paradox of the Afghan Drug Situation: Existence of the Major Drug Threat and the Absence of a Real Fight Against It

Russia has repeatedly drawn international attention to the menace of the Afghan drug issue. Over several years, it has urged the UN Security Council to recognise Afghan drug production as a threat to international peace and security. Russia also insists that the destruction of poppy fields, along with the fight against drug trafficking, the destruction of drug laboratories and assisting Afghanistan to reorientate peasant agriculture towards growing of crops, was one of the priorities in the fight against "the evil of the 21st century." In this context, Russia offered to immediately implement the so-called 'Raduga-2' plan.

In June 2010, the then Russian President Dmitry Medvedev and the Russian Federal Drug Control Service Director, Victor Ivanov appealed the 'Moscow International Forum: Drug Production in Afghanistan—a Challenge to the International Community' to mobilise countries to support Russia in resolving the Afghan drug problem. In autumn 2010,

49. *<http://www.centrasia.ru/newsA.php>*, 30 August 2010.

50. *op. cit.* no.46.

Russia won a diplomatic victory. On 13 October 2010, the UN Security Council, in Resolution No. 1943, declared Afghan drug production "a threat to international peace and stability". However, on the question of the destruction of poppy fields, Russia does not find support from its Western counterparts, primarily the Americans.

The USA has been emphatic that the combined contingent of the anti-terrorist coalition should be used "only to fight terrorists and not to touch the issues of combating drugs".[51] This was said repeatedly by former US Secretary of Defense Donald Rumsfeld. The same position was voiced in 2009 by the late Special Representative of the US President for Afghanistan and Pakistan, Richard Holbrooke.

In early March 2010 at the briefing on the 2010 International Narcotics Control Strategy Report, David Johnson (Assistant Secretary of State) said: "Certainly, there should be no destruction of plantations by external forces, including us".[52] In mid-March 2010 at the NATO-Russia Council meeting in Brussels, the NATO spokesman, James Appathurai, confirmed the position of the US State Department.

The official US explanation for this policy lies in the fact that drug production is the foundation of the Afghan economy and the only competitive export item for this extremely poor country. Despite the fact that Afghan drug production and trafficking threatens the security of European and Asian countries in an obvious way, US officials have regularly voiced the argument that they are "unwilling to deprive Afghan farmers of their only source of income".

This position cannot but evoke bewilderment. Indeed, according to various estimates, up to 3 million Afghan farmers are involved in various aspects of the drug trade. However, in the analogous situation of Latin American (Colombia, Mexico), the United States demands that national governments wage an increasingly tough fight against drug production. It would appear that when the addiction menace hits its soft under belly, the Americans could not care less about how their neighbours, common Mexicans and Colombians, are to earn their living.

---

51. For example, see <*http://www.nationalsecurity.ru/library/00021/00021opium5.htm*>.
52. Johnson, D. (2010). "US Assistant Secretary of State, Washington, District of Columbia", 1 March, <*stratgap.ru/page/strategy/3662/3885/4368/print.shtml*>.

But what does the USA offer as a plan to combat the Afghan drug problem? The US strategy is limited to military operations against the rebels (supporting the Taliban in the southern provinces of Helmand and Kandahar), the destruction of drug laboratories and the suppression of drug trafficking. But, unfortunately, such actions may well produce the opposite effect on the drug mafia-terrorist combine, as was experienced by coalition forces in February 2010. They conducted Operation Moshtarak to free Helmand province (which produces more than 65 per cent of the world's opiates) from armed rebels. As early as in the spring, NATO Secretary General, Anders Rasmussen, praised the operation as a great success.

What followed was the rebels' backlash. In late 2010, the commander of NATO forces in Afghanistan, General David Petraeus, officially announced that the number of combat clashes in Afghanistan had more than doubled. Experts estimate that 2010 was the bloodiest year for coalition forces in the history of the anti-terrorist operations. Moreover, the intensity of armed clashes is growing at an alarming rate, not only in the south, but also in the northern provinces of Afghanistan: Kunduz, Balkh, Samangan, Takhar and Jowzjan. For example, in Balkh Province in October-November 2010, 56 combat operations against Taliban militants were conducted by the Afghan National Army with support from Bundeswehr army units.[53]

At the same time, according to experts, the intensification of hostilities in southern Afghanistan was provoking a rise in drug production in the northern and northeastern provinces (Herat, Badghis and Badakhshan). Here, the growth of the number of drug laboratories has also been noted. This whole process was evolving on the border between Afghanistan and Central Asian states.

It may be that the US policy is linked to Washington's desire to shift the costs of the main activities in Afghanistan to Europe, Asia and Russia, which are the main markets for Afghan drugs. However, the current 'colour revolutions' in the Maghreb suggest that the aim of a particular segment of the American elite is more global and long-term. Its aim is to exploit the drug situation in order to create more profound political, military,

53. Khalekyar, S.A., "Afghanistan-2010: The Failure of Washington's Strategy", *<www.centrasia.ru/newsAphp?st=1295682780>*.

humanitarian, and terrorist problems not only for countries that will come under the throes of 'controlled chaos,'[54] but will also hit America's potential competitors like China, India, EU and, quite naturally, its only real nuclear competitor, Russia, even if substantially weakened after the collapse of the USSSR and post-Soviet reforms.

According to the Federal Drug Control Service, Director Victor Ivanov, "the unabating actions of terrorists and international crime in Russia's North Caucasus are funded by Afghan drug trafficking. It is this Afghan drug trafficking that has created tensions, clashes, and unrest in the Ferghana Valley. There is no doubt that Afghan drug production is the main investor in the organisation of the destructive manifestations in the Xinjiang Uygur Autonomous Region of China."[55] The same processes are observed in Europe in the newly independent state of Kosovo.

Meanwhile, in the dialogue between the Afghan government and Western countries, the provision of financial and economic assistance rides on President Hamid Karzai's genuine commitment to fight the menace of drugs. Commenting on Karzai's address at the Ninth International Conference of donor countries for Afghanistan in Kabul in July 2010, Alexander Mikhailov (the former Head of the Information Department of Russia's Anti-Terror Agency) said that it all comes down to a simple formula: "Give money, so we will not flood the world with drugs".[56]

The Western media have in the past reported on the role of Karzai's close associates in drug trafficking. Back in 2004, *The New York Times*, citing intelligence reports from American Special Services, published the names of senior Afghan officials who were involved in drug production. Among these were Minister of Tribal and Border Affairs, Mohammad Arif Noorzai, Helmand Province Governor, Sher Muhammad Akhundzada, and

54. Byaly, Yury (1999). "Fight for the African Resource and Its Projections", Almanach School of Comprehensive Analysis, Issue No. 5, M.

55. *op. cit.* no.2.

56. See: "Heroin Contorls Policy: The President of the Islamic Republic of Afghanistan Announces His Plan to Control the Situation in the Country", 20 July 2010, <*http://er-portal.ru/*>.

the brother and Campaign Manager of President Hamid Karzai, late Ahmed Wali Karzai.[57]

According to Julien Marseille (an expert on foreign policy and geopolitical issues in Dublin), in Afghanistan, "more than 75 per cent of funds are embezzled by government officials, the police, local and regional brokers, and drug lords—many of these groups are supported (or recognised) by the USA and NATO and are very important players in the drug trade."[58] Drug deals expert, Said Amin Khalekyar, citing the *Financial Times*, has said that the Afghan elites transfer $10 billion annually to their bank accounts in Dubai, which "is the product of corruption, extortion, and shady business schemes including drug trafficking".[59]

It seems that the revelation about the involvement of the President's associates is no accident. According to experts, in both the USA and EU, there is a growing realisation that it is neither possible to bear the exhorbitant cost of the ongoing war, nor to continue to provide the Karzai regime with unequivocal support; this reluctance does not exclude the possibility of removing Karzai from power. There is also talk of the possibility of introducing a programme for 'reconciliation with the Taliban.' On 20 December 2010, the UN Secretary General, Ban Ki-moon, spoke about the possibility of beginning negotiations with the armed opposition. However, many experts, among them are Indian analysts, Vikram Sood and Wilson John, warned that given the current developments in Afghanistan, a positive change in this country should not be expected in the foreseeable future.

Conclusion

Given the developments described above, a number of questions come to mind. Are not the events in Afghanistan and Latin America a reflection of a trend of 'global drug addiction', which is advocated in effect by promoters of drug trade legalisation, such as Mick Moore and George Soros? Ultimately, will not this fast spreading addiction, apart from provoking

57. "Karzai's Brother Ahmed Wali Involved in Drug Production", *The New York Times*, 29 November 2004, <*Farsi.ru*>.

58. Marseille, Julien (2009). "Foreign Policy in Focus", 5 November, <*http://stratgap.ru/pages/strategy/*>.

59. *op. cit.* no.53.

outbreaks of extremism, separatism and terrorism, become another tool for the redistribution of world income in favour of the drug cartels and, at the same time, an instrument of 'global population correction'?

It is not just that this 'global menace of addiction,' especially among the younger generation, will cause an irreparable blow to the gene pool of nations and the people of the world. In itself, this development requires the international community to take urgent action. It could also be that 'global drug addiction' is an instrument in the hands of forces that want to "freeze development in isolated areas"[60] because countries in these areas are, according to them, a "threat to continental and global stability for military reasons, [besides being the] breeding grounds for incurable diseases" and need to be turned into isolated compounds under international control (of course, 'in the name of humanity').

Such extremist ideas and notions have found takers in the American and European press. Though, primarily, it is aimed at the underdeveloped states in Africa, it also targets developing countries in Latin America and Asia that can, in the long run, pose a challenge to US domination. Is not the world today taking into account such proposals and facing specific threats, sliding into an era of 'controlled chaos' where—given the increasing local conflicts, population correction and rising crime rates—drugs will first become one of the main tools 'to stop development,' and in the end, a tool for a secondary archaisation of huge regions of the planet? And will not Russia and India be among those 'practice grounds' on which the narcotic, terrorist and criminal processes being exploited for 'secondary archaisation' will be tested?

---

60. Byaly, Yury (1999). "The Fight for Afghanistan's Resources and its Prospects", *Almanac of the School of Holistic Analysis*, Issue No. 5.

7 Narcotics Trafficking in Afghanistan

Prospects and Challenges for India and Russia

Rahul Prakash

Narcotics trafficking has become a major challenge for the sustenance of peace and stability in Afghanistan. Since the beginning of the US-led 'Operation Enduring Freedom' (OEF) in 2001, illicit opium trade has reached new heights. Today, Afghanistan produces 80 per cent of the world's total opium.[1] The Taliban is earning millions of dollars from opium trade, which it uses to recruit and train fighters, purchase arms and ammunition. The insurgency plays a huge role in supporting the trade by providing protection to farmlands against eradication efforts, providing credit to the farmers and transiting drugs across borders. This nexus is an enormous problem that the USA and its allies are facing in Afghanistan. Apart from fuelling insurgency, the illicit trade means huge sums of bribe money for Afghan politicians, bureaucrats, the police and the military. The US-NATO forces have been trying to crack down on the narcotics insurgency and various Counter Narcotics (CN) policies have been put in place, but a comprehensive solution to the problem is yet to be found.

The impact of the opium trade has spread wide around Afghanistan. Neighbouring countries like Russia, Pakistan, Iran, India, Central Asia and Europe are being severely affected by the surge in opium smuggled in from Afghanistan, substantially increasing the rate of drug abuse in these countries. Each country has its different strategic interests, but the narcotics industry has become a common problem for all the players.

1. United Nations Office on Drugs and Crime (2010). *Afghanistan Opium Survey 2010*. Vienna.

Russia is amongst the worst affected; its proximity to Afghanistan and the porous borders have made it the largest opium market in the region, resulting in huge health care problems. India, again because of geographical position, has become the transit point for the opiates. It has also become one of the largest markets for precursor chemicals that are required to manufacture drugs and are marketed illegally with the help of the Internet.

This paper will study the role of the USA, NATO, Pakistan, India, Russia and the government of Afghanistan in containing the growth of the narcotics-trafficking industry. The CN strategies that are being implemented in Afghanistan are also examined in the paper. An attempt has been made to identify the challenges that India and Russia would face in the coming years and how both countries can cooperate to contain the illicit opium trade and the consequent security concerns it raises.

Current Situation

Despite the efforts made by international organisations and the Afghan government, narcotics trafficking stands like an impregnable wall between Afghanistan and its development. Opiates remain its largest export commodity, accounting for 80 per cent of the world's opium product in 2010. According to the 'Afghanistan-Opium Survey' conducted by the UNODC in 2010, the farm-gate value of opium was estimated to be US$ 605 million, 38 per cent more than in 2009; 1.6 per cent of the country's total agricultural land was used to produce opium. The survey revealed that there had been no decrease in the total area used for cultivating opium from 2009 to 2010 despite eradication efforts by authorities. Interestingly, the total yield of opium fell by 48 per cent as compared to the previous year. The survey report noted that the main cause was the unfavourable climatic conditions and crop diseases and not the anti-narcotics or eradication efforts. In fact, due to the fall in yield, the prices of opium saw an increase of 164 per cent. Adding to the problem, the prices of alternate crops like wheat had fallen, keeping opium cultivation the first choice of farmers. In 2010, 14 provinces involving 248,700 households went in for poppy cultivation, accounting for 6 per cent of the total population. It is worth noting that most of the cultivation took place in areas which were most affected by insurgency.[2]

Role of the Afghan Government

Afghanistan's Government has formulated various laws and established departments to counter the menace. A Drug Regulation Committee was established comprising members from the Ministries of Public Health, Counter-Narcotics and Finance. Under the Constitution, a narcotics tribunal was set up within the Kabul Primary Provincial Court. The Ministry responsible for conducting CN operations is the Ministry of Counter Narcotics (MCN). The agencies responsible for seizure of illegal drugs, related materials and equipment are the Afghan Counter Narcotics Police (CNP-A), the Afghan Special Narcotics Force, the National Police, the Border Police and the Afghan Customs Staff. The CNP-A has been operating an Operational Drugs laboratory since September 2006. Governor-led eradication campaigns have also been fairly successful. According to the UNODC's 'Afghanistan Opium Survey,' a total of 1,602 ha were made poppy-free in these campaigns. These agencies receive large amount of aid and training from the USA, NATO, UN and other countries to fight narcotics trafficking.

However, the tentacles of the narcotics trade have penetrated so deep into government departments that Afghanistan has been given the unenviable label of a Narco-State. Corruption is rampant among officials in the narcotics-related departments. They earn millions of dollars, with the beneficiaries ranging from lowest to the highest levels of the administration. The US State Department's 2009 'International Narcotics Control Strategy Report' (INCSR) on Afghanistan stated that "profit from the drug trade and narcotics related corruption is pervasive in provincial and district levels of the government".[3] According to another US Report leaked to ABC News, Ahmed Wali Karzai, half brother of President Hamid

2. Estimates are based on a population of 24.5 million for 2010 and an average household size of 6.2 persons (Government of Afghanistan, Central Statistical Office). United Nations Office on Drugs and Crime (2010). *Afghanistan Opium Survey 2010.*

3. United States Department of State (2009). *International Narcotics Control Strategy Report.* Bureau of International Narcotics and Law Enforcement Affairs.

Karzai and representative of Kandahar province, earned huge profits from illicit drug trafficking to Iran. He allegedly prevented his supporters' crops from eradication.[4] He was killed in July 2011 in Kandahar by one of his close associates. Bribing is considered an easy way to avoid eradication and seizures of stockpiles by drug lords.

All round corruption is one of the biggest threats facing the Afghan national security apparatus. People entrusted to uphold the law are violating it. What is particularly reprehensible is that corruption is undermining counter insurgency, CN and nation-building efforts in Afghanistan. It has eroded the trust and faith of the people in the administration and the government they had elected. As for the international community, it looks on helplessly, merely mouthing words of concern.

Pakistan

The role of Pakistan is a crucial factor in determining the future of Afghanistan. Its dual role is no longer a secret. On one hand, it is the most important ally of the USA in its war against terror in Afghanistan and, on the other, it has been providing support to Taliban and promoting insurgency in the region. There is enough evidence to prove that Pakistan's Inter-Services Intelligence (ISI) Agency is supporting Taliban to gain influence in the region. WikiLeaks documents underline the fact that the crucial element behind Taliban's success against the USA is the support it gets from ISI.[5] There had been allegations that ISI agents had attended meetings of Taliban's top leadership council, the Quetta Shura.[6] In 2010, US Secretary of State, Hilary Clinton claimed that some elements in the Pakistani Government were aware of Osama bin Laden's whereabouts. The dilemma facing the USA is that it has to depend on a double dealing ally who is also supporting the enemy, the Taliban. On its side, it is understandable that Islamabad finds US proclivity to treat Afghanistan-

4. BBC News (2009). "Envoy Damns US Afghan Drug Effort", 21 March, <*http://news.bbc.co.uk/2/hi/south_asia/7957237.stm*> (5 March 2011).
5. Galbraith, Peter (2010). "WikiLeaks and the Taliban-ISI Nexus", *The Guardian*, 26 July, <*http://www.guardian.co.uk/commentisfree/2010/jul/26/wikileaks-isi-taliban-nexus*> (5 March 2011).
6. BBC News (2010). "Pakistani Agents 'Funding and Training Afghan Taliban," 13 June. <*http://www.bbc.co.uk/news/10302946*> (5 March 2011).

Pakistan as one region irritating, if not insulting. Its national pride demands that Pakistan be treated as an individual, separate nation that it is.

Be that as it may, Pakistan also plays the role of a transit country for Afghan opiates, its work facilitated by inefficient governance in its tribal areas bordering Afghanistan. Much of the opium is also smuggled across the border into India with assistance from the ISI.[7] Pakistan itself as can be expected, is a large opium consumer.

India's efforts for Afghanistan's development are undermined by Pakistan supported terrorist groups. A number of attacks have taken place targeting developmental efforts in Afghanistan. According to Indian and US intelligence agencies, the July 2008 suicide attack on the Indian Embassy in Kabul was planned and supported by the ISI.[8] Pakistan has been uncomfortable with India's increasing role in Afghanistan. It had also raised objections to the setting up of Indian consulates in Jalalabad and Kandahar, claiming that this was a move to support terrorism inside Pakistan.[9] Pakistan's longstanding conflict with India and suspicion of its regional engagement, especially in Afghanistan, have adversely affected the security situation. International efforts to liberate Afghanistan from the clutches of insurgents, terrorist groups and drug traffickers cannot be successful until Pakistan gets on the same side as the international community.

India

As noted earlier, geographically, India is positioned to play a key role in the international drug trafficking racket. Its strategic location between the Golden Triangle and the Golden Crescent makes it an important transit point.[10] Opium produced in Afghanistan is smuggled into India from areas

7. IBN Live (2009). "ISI smuggling opium into India from Pakistan: Report," 19 February, *<http://ibnlive.in.com/news/isi-smuggling-opium-into-india-from-pakistan-report/85808-3.html>* (7 March 2011).

8. Mazzetti, Mark and Eric Schmitt (2008). "Pakistanis Aided Attack in Kabul, US Officials Say", *The New York Times*. 1 August, *<http://www.nytimes.com/2008/08/01/world/asia/01pstan.html>* (26 February 2011).

9. Ramachandran, Sudha (2008). "Now its war against India in Afghanistan," *Asia Times Online*, 9 July, *<http://www.atimes.com/atimes/South_Asia/JG09Df02.html>* (26 February 2011).

10. Golden Triangle comprises Myanmar, Thailand and Laos, while the Golden Crescent is formed by Afghanistan, Pakistan and Iran.

falling on the India-Pakistan border like Punjab, Gujarat and Rajasthan. Local carriers and suppliers move in to transport drugs into different parts of the country.[11] Indian port cities like Kochi and Mumbai are the traffickers' favourite transit points to various countries of the world.[12] The postal and courier service of India is also being exploited by drug traffickers to smuggle drugs.[13] A number of incidents have been reported wherein foreign nationals were involved with illegal drug trafficking in India. They use well-knit human networks to transit drugs via India. The recent case in which two Nigerian nationals were arrested in India for possession of Afghan heroin is just one example out of many such cases that have become a common story in the Indian media.[14]

India has been listed amongst the hotspots for manufacturing precursor chemicals[15] and psychotropic substances. Such chemicals are manufactured by criminal networks in different parts of India and are being smuggled to other countries where they are used to produce drugs. Such chemicals are marketed through the Internet which mostly goes undetected. The Internet is becoming a major threat for anti-narcotics officials, as it provides easy access to both buyers and sellers and has low probability of detection. The link between terrorism and drugs trafficking became apparent after the terrorist attack in Mumbai in 2008, when Dawood Ibrahim's name was highlighted by the Russian intelligence agencies for his alleged role in the massacre. In an interview to Russian Government daily *Rossiskaya Gazeta*, Federal Anti-Narcotics Service Director, Viktor Ivanov said: "The gathered inputs testify that regional drug baron Dawood Ibrahim had provided his logistics network for preparing and carrying out the Mumbai terror

---

11. Singh, Divyesh (2010). "A Contraband 'Trip' from India to Around the World", *Daily News and Analysis*, 10 September, <*http://www.dnaindia.com/mumbai/report_a-contraband-trip-from-india-to-around-the-world_1436041*> (27 February 2011).

12. Kanth, Ajay (2011). "Kochi One of Top 5 Drug-Transit Points in India", *Express News Service*, 22 January, <*http://expressbuzz.com/cities/kochi/kochi-one-of-top-5-drug-transit-points-in-india/241415.html*> (27 February 2011).

13. United Nations (2011). *Annual Report 2010*. International Narcotics Control Board.

14. Nigerian Compass (2011). "Two Nigerians Held for Drug Trafficking, Fraud in India," 24 February, <*http://www.compassnewspaper.com/NG/index.php?option=com_content&view=article&id=75878:two-nigerians-held-for-drug-trafficking-fraud-in-india&catid=40:crime-a-security&Itemid=696*> (27 February 2011).

15. Precursor chemicals are required to produce synthetic and semi-synthetic drugs of abuse. For example, precursors are used to make heroin from opium.

attacks". Dawood's network is actively involved in the smuggling of drugs from Afghanistan into India via Pakistan. Ivanov observed that Dawood's involvement in the Mumbai attack was a 'burning example' of how funds from narcotics trafficking were used for terrorist activities.[16]

Insurgency and terrorism in different parts of India is also being financed by 'narco barons.' Drug money, for instance, is used by Jammu and Kashmir (J&K) terrorists for financing their operations. Opium produced in Afghanistan, which finds its way into India across the J&K Line of Control (LOC) is smuggled in with the help of Pakistan's state/non-state elements.[17]

Afghanistan's territory under Taliban's control was used by the Harkat-ul-Mujahideen terrorist outfit to carry out the hijacking of an Air India flight in 1999. Taliban's close ties with the ISI, Al Qaeda and the sympathy towards the terrorist groups fighting against India in Kashmir clearly make it necessary from India's security perspective that the Taliban is effectively defeated. Since Taliban insurgency in Afghanistan is being supported by narcotics trade, it is very much in India's interest to help in the dismantling of the opium industry in Afghanistan.

India provides the crucial second tier of the counter-terrorism strategy of "clear, hold, build and transfer,"[18] by providing support for the last two processes. India has been making these efforts without being a part of any international consortium. It has contributed more than $1.3 billion for development in Afghanistan since 2001, which includes programmes to support the Afghan agricultural staff with scholarships, university exchanges and internships to work with Indian agricultural institutions.[19] India's contribution in the development of agriculture in Afghanistan is

---

16. For details see, "Dawoods Network Finance Mumbai Attacks: Russia", Express News Service, 18 December 2008, *<http://www.indianexpress.com/news/dawoods-network-financed-mumbai-attacks-ru/400124/>* (28 February 2011).

17. Islah, Mufti (2007). "J&K's Drugs, Terror Links Snapped," CNN-IBN, 20 June *<http://ibnlive.in.com/news/jk-customs-snaps-terrors-lifeline/40053-3.html>* (27 February 2011).

18. In 2010, US administration launched a new strategy known as the "Clear, Hold, Build, Transfer" for Afghanistan, wherein it envisaged to dismantle terrorist networks, transferring responsibility to the Afghan government while providing economic assistance and military training for Afghans.

19. Office of the Press Secretary (2010). "Fact Sheet: U.S, India Supporting Afghanistan's Development," The White House, 8 November, *<http://www.america.gov/st/texttrans-english/2010/November/20101108155635su0.1023327.html>*.

significant as it helps the farmers to shift from opium cultivation to other legal alternatives.

The Narcotics Control Bureau (NCB) of India, the apex agency, coordinates activities to check the illicit trade of narcotics. The NCB is mandated to extend possible support to international agencies and organisations to curb narco trafficking. It has entered into several bilateral agreements on narcotics-related matters with 22 countries and has signed Memorandum of Understanding (MOU) with four countries in 2010. Drug issues having a bearing on terrorism were discussed in several working groups established for counter-terrorism with 27 countries. Abiding by international conventions, the NCB submits quarterly, half-yearly and annual reports to the International Narcotics Control Board (INCB), Vienna.[20] There is, however, scope for greater engagement between the NCB and its counterparts in the region to curb narcotics trafficking.

United States of America

Since the beginning of the OEF, the US Congress has appropriated billions of dollars for providing support to counternarcotics programmes in Afghanistan, such as interdiction, poppy eradication, economic development, demand reduction, public information and judicial reform. Despite the amount of money being pumped in, Afghanistan still remains the largest opium producer in the world. The late Richard Holbrooke, the then Obama Administration's Special Representative for Afghanistan and Pakistan, commented in March 2009 that the poppy eradication funds spent by the US in Afghanistan were the most wasteful and ineffective expenses he could think of.[21]

Under the Bush administration, the US followed the Five Pillar Counter Narcotics policy: public information, judicial reform, alternate livelihood development, interdiction and eradication. This strategy was revised in 2007 and the focus shifted from eradication to agricultural development and intensification of interdiction efforts. The US-led interdiction effort named 'Operation Containment' focused on depriving drug trafficking actors of their access to markets, cutting the funding of international terrorist organisations from narco-trade, precursor chemicals,

---

20. Ministry of Home Affairs (2010). *Annual Report 2010.* New Delhi: Government of India.
21. *op. cit.* no.4.

weapons and currency. The US Drug Enforcement Agency (DEA) has played a significant role in implementing 'Operation Containment'.

The Obama Administration's 'US Counternarcotics Strategy for Afghanistan 2010' gives priority to demolishing the link between narcotics and insurgency, reducing the support that insurgency receives from narcotics-trafficking, tackling narcotics-corruption and reinforcing the Afghan government. The main change that can be seen in the US CN policy of 2010 is the reduction in funding for eradication programmes. However, it is clarified in the policy document that the USA has no objections to Afghan-led local eradication campaigns. To achieve these goals, the USA plans to strengthen the CNP-A by creating an operational concept and a comprehensive development plan for the force. The new policy also aims to make the Afghan CN forces self-reliant, capable, accountable and effective.[22] To achieve ground level efficiency, the USA has deployed its DEA agents to Afghanistan to assist the Afghan CN forces.[23] The shift in the policy has drawn criticism specially from Russia because it gives less importance to eradication. Russian experts believe that the cut in the funding for eradication would lead to a surge in the opium products that are smuggled into Russia.

North Atlantic Treaty Organisation (NATO)

After the beginning of the OEF, the United Nations set up the International Security Assistance Force (ISAF) to support the operations. The ISAF, in addition to providing combat support, was also responsible for nation building and security assistance. In 2003, NATO took charge of the ISAF and in 2005-2007, took command of all operations in Afghanistan. Initially, ISAF's mandate did not authorise direct military action against narcotic targets. But, in October 2008, the ISAF was given the authority to take such action against narcotics linked insurgents, traffickers and production facilities, etc.[24] NATO's current CN operations follow the US strategy of specifically striking the nexus between narcotics and

22. Bureau of South and Central Asian Affairs (2010). *US Counternarcotics Strategy for Afghanistan Report*. Washington, DC: US Department of State.
23. US Department of State (2010). *US Counternarcotics Strategy for Afghanistan*. Washington DC: US Department of State, March.
24. Morelli, Vincent and Paul Belkin (2009). "NATO in Afghanistan: A Test of the Transatlantic Alliance", 3 December, <*http://www.fas.org/sgp/crs/row/RL33627.pdf*> (15 February 2011).

insurgency.[25] Various large-scale operations have been conducted by the US-NATO-Afghan Forces, targeting insurgents who use the profits from opium trade to destabilise Afghanistan. Large amounts of drugs, laboratories and precursor chemicals have been seized and destroyed by the troops.

NATO has also struggled to effectively contain the narco menace in Afghanistan. The alliance has come under strong criticism from the member countries, which are not sure about the extent they are willing to dedicate their resources for a war, to which there currently seems to be no end. Besides, the strategies followed till now have not yielded the commensurate results and Afghanistan still remains the world's largest opium producer.

Russia

According to Russia's Federal Drug Control Service, Afghan heroin causes death of 70,000 Russians each year. Its concern is understandable; an estimated 90 per cent of heroin consumed in Russia is smuggled in from Afghanistan. At an international conference in Moscow, Russian President, Dmitry Medvedev commented: "We consider drug addiction as one of the biggest and most serious threats to our country's development and our people's health".[26] Afghan drug production increased dramatically after the fall of the Taliban regime in 2001, affecting Russia the most. Nikolai Tsvetkov, the Deputy Director of the Federal Service to Control Drug Trade, while responding to a question about the current situation of narcotics trade in Afghanistan, stated: "...if you compare it with what it was a decade ago, then it looks much worse, and for Russia, more tragic. Since fall 2001, when the Operation Enduring Freedom began and an international contingent of security forces went into Afghanistan under the UN flag, the production of narcotics there, mainly of the opiate group, has multiplied by a factor of 40."[27]

---

25. Allied Command Operations (2009). "ISAF Counter Narcotic Activities: The Facts", 19 March, <*http://www.aco.nato.int/page29620395.aspx*> (20 February 2011).

26. Stack, Graham (2010). "Russia puts Anti-Narcotics in Afghanistan at Top of International Agenda", *Russia Beyond The Headlines*, 11 June, <*http://rbth.ru/articles/2010/06/11/russia_puts_anti-narcotics_in_afghanistan_at_top_of_international_agenda.html*> (25 February 2011).

27. Yavlyansky, Izvestia Igor (2010). "The Silk Route of Afghan Poppy", *Russia and India Report*, 15 June, <*http://indrus.in/articles/2010/06/15/silk_route_afghan_poppy.html*> (20 February 2011).

This flow of opium is a source of tension between Moscow and USA-NATO, with Russia unsparing in its criticism of the latter's counter-narcotics strategy in Afghanistan. Its envoy to NATO, Dmitry Rogozin expressing dissatisfaction over the on-going CN efforts by USA and NATO, said in an interview: "In the case of the heroin which goes to Russia, they are doing practically nothing [and] this is not how you treat your friends and partners." He added, "...today, we are helping them [the US] fight the same fanatics whom they supported against us 20 years ago."[28]

Moscow has been trying to attract international attention on the issue for some time now. Russian officials have been trying to get the allied forces to engage in more eradication campaigns in Afghanistan, as it helps in decreasing production output. NATO appears reluctant to meet Russia's demands to eradicate the opium crops through aerial spraying of poppy or other actions against individual Afghan farmers.[29] They argue that eradication of crops would in turn strengthen the Taliban, as the poor farmer would think eradication was aimed at destroying his livelihood, it could also make him turn to insurgents for support.

Russia has been taking part in joint CN operations with the US, NATO and Afghan Anti-Drug forces. It has been holding talks with NATO to enhance cooperation in Afghanistan and has offered to provide helicopters, crews to train Afghan pilots, assistance in training Afghan National Security Forces, cooperation with CN and help in border security work.[30] Russia and the USA had created a working group in 2009 to reconcile disagreements regarding the CN policy in Afghanistan. In October 2010, Russian CN agents took part in a joint operation with the US and Afghan anti-drug forces. The operation, in which opium laboratories and over 2000 pounds of opium were destroyed, was the first in which Russian

---

28. *USA Today* (2010). "Russia Criticizes US, NATO over Afghan Drug Trafficking Fight", 3 December, <*http://www.usatoday.com/news/world/afghanistan/2010-03-12-russia-us-nato_N.htm*> (25 February 2011).

29. DuPee, Mathew C. and Sara Kauffman (2010). "In Afghanistan, Poppy Eradication Pits Russia vs. NATO", *OffNews*, 21 April, <*www.offnews.info/verArticulo.php?contentidoID+21603*> (25 February 2011).

30. Tisdall, Simon (2010). "Russian Military Could be Drawn Back into Afghanistan," *The Guardian*, 26 October, <*www.guardian.co.uk/world/2010/oct/26/nato-afghanistan-russia-military*> (25 February 2011).

agents were involved.[31] In a recent development, the Russian Parliament has ratified an agreement with the USA on air transit of military cargoes to Afghanistan. The agreement would allow the USA to fly weapons, military property and personnel to Afghanistan using the Russian air space free of navigation charges. This agreement has helped in the ongoing CN efforts in Afghanistan.[32]

Opium Trade in 2011

According to the UNODC Winter Assessment that covered the central, eastern, southern and western provinces of Afghanistan, a slight overall cultivation decrease in these areas has been predicted. Many reasons have been given for this welcome situation. In some areas in Hilmand and Kandahar, farmers said that cold and dry climatic condition was hampering the sowing of poppy crop. The UNODC Report believes that the Governor had partially succeeded in his efforts to convince the farmers and elders in the region not to grow poppy. It is also possible that the presence of counter-insurgency forces in the region, although not directed against the farmers, could well have discouraged them. The Report confirmed the findings of the Afghanistan Opium Survey of 2010 regarding the link between insecurity and poppy cultivation. Even though a declining trend was observed by the Report, it would be premature to expect a big impact from the current CN strategy in Afghanistan. Awareness campaigns have covered only 33 per cent villages surveyed. Notably, the average farm-gate value of opium in December 2010 crossed the highest price recorded since the war in Afghanistan began in 2001.[33]

---

31. Schwirtz, Michael (2010). "Russia Joins Drug Raid in Afghanistan, Marking Advance in Relations with US", *The Newyork Times*, 29 October, <*www.nytimes.com/2010/10/30/world/asia/30opium.html?_r=1*> (25 February 2011).
32. Radyuhin, Vladimir (2011). "US-Russia Air Transit Deal", *The Hindu*, 26 February, <*www.thehindu.com/news/international/article1490399.ece*> (28 February 2011).
33. United Nations Office on Drugs and Crime (2011). "Afghanistan Opium Survey 2011: Winter Rapid Assessment for the Central, Eastern, Southern and Western Regions", *Afghanistan Opium Survey 2011*. January. Vienna.

Challenges

Insurgency

The common problem for all stake holders is the resurgence of Taliban insurgency. 'Narco-Insurgency,' a term used to describe the narcotics-funded insurgency, is the key facilitator of the destabilisation process. During the 1990s, the Taliban government banned cultivation of *hashish* as it was consumed by Afghans, who are predominantly Muslim. However, opium production was allowed as it was mainly consumed by the Western *kafirs* (the heretics), besides being the source of finance for the Taliban and Al Qaeda activities. After the Taliban took over the administration of Afghanistan, it is believed that Al Qaeda, with Mullah Omar's assistance, turned the state into the largest opium production region in the world. According to US and British intelligence, Osama bin Laden, with the blessings of Mullah Omar, had turned the state-owned Ariana Airlines into a 'Narco-Terror charter service,' transporting militants, drugs, weapons and cash to United Arab Emirates and Pakistan. The United Nations countered by imposing flight sanctions in late 2000, grounding the airline's international flights. With OEF, the link between narcotics trafficking and insurgency has only strengthened. The ousted Taliban took control of the opium fields after the war, began to generate funds for their movement and ran the trade with great efficiency. It put in place the system of credit, opened access to markets and secured the fields from the threat of eradication. The trade routes used for trafficking of opium were also secured by insurgents.[34] Today, the insurgency in Afghanistan is better funded than ever. The drug money is being used to purchase weapons, ammunition, for recruitment and paying salaries to the fighters. Counter-narcotics efforts like eradication on the ground face heavy resistance from the well-paid insurgents protecting the farmlands. As can be expected, most of the drug-producing areas (mainly the southern and western regions) are the most affected by the insurgency, according to the UNODC 'Afghan Opium Survey' Report of 2010.

---

34. The corruption in the security forces indulged in border management and counter-narcotics operations also helped in the trafficking of opium products across borders.

Afghan Economy

Narcotics trade forms a significant part of the Afghan economy. The data from the UNODC annual reports show that a significant number of households are involved in poppy cultivation. The high price that the harvest fetches is the biggest attraction for the farmers and, by comparison, crops like wheat fetch a pittance. There exists a guaranteed global market for opium, which maintains high demand. The trade routes for trafficking are well established and are well protected by insurgents in all sectors. Corruption in the local security forces engaged in border management and CN operations also exacerbates the problem. The dependency of the Afghan society and economy on narcotics trafficking is a major challenge that needs to be addressed in order to build a stable Afghanistan.

Radicalism

The spread of Taliban and its radical ideology throughout the large Afghanistan-Pakistan region, including the new republics of Central Asia, is a threat to the modern civil society of the world. The reaction that followed the assassination of the Governor of Pakistan's Punjab clearly indicates the spread of fundamentalism in the society. The resurgence of Taliban would promote the Islamic radicalisation process throughout the region since the Taliban already has connections with insurgent groups in Central Asia. It is suspected that there are radical elements within the military and Government of Pakistan. To contain the spread of radicalism in the world, it must be ensured that Taliban never regains power in Afghanistan.

Pakistan's Role in Afghanistan

Pakistan is crucial for peace and stability in the region. The ISI-Taliban nexus greatly debilitates the efforts being made for stabilising the country. The exaggerated worries of Pakistan about India's role in Afghanistan is also an issue that needs to be addressed. We need, therefore, to reorient our regional policies to the prevailing conditions.

US Exit from Afghanistan

It becomes an imperative for regional players like India and Russia to form a strategy that should help sustain the sovereignty of Afghanistan after the international forces leave and to ensure that Afghanistan continues to develop as a modern state and stays free from the control of radical elements.

Recommendations: Prospects for Cooperation

The nexus between insurgency, terrorism and narcotics trafficking has to be broken in order to sustain peace and stability in Afghanistan. Since the narcotics industry has become the financial bloodline of Taliban, it is vital that the CN strategies succeed and effective eradication steps are taken to bring down the production. Drug-related addiction and deaths affect the region far more than they do the distant USA, where the immediate threat is from Colombia and Mexico to the south.

Pakistan should be pressurised to take a tougher stand and action against the Taliban. Reducing Pakistan's support for insurgency movements would play a big role in defeating the drug menace, as well as terrorism. Pakistan's worries about India's influence in Afghanistan are exaggerated, but confidence-building measures should be taken so that both the nations can join hands for the development work in Afghanistan.

The middlemen, precursor chemicals and trade routes should be targeted so that the market is starved of the commodity. There is a need to substantially check the transit of drugs via Pakistan, India and Central Asia to the rest of the world.

India could play an exemplary role in curbing the availability of precursor chemicals of which it is one of the largest producers. Measures should be taken to crack down on fake pharmaceutical companies and controlling the use of Internet for trafficking could prove to be a tough but highly gainful task.

Post US exit from Afghanistan, neighbouring countries with stakes in Afghanistan like India, Pakistan and Russia must step up cooperation and formulate a strategy to deal with a post American Afghanistan.

Enhanced intelligence sharing with Russia can be of great value. The latter's Anti-Drug Agencies, constantly at war with the Afghan drug nexus, can offer a lot to agencies of our country in terms of expertise and strategies.

The two countries have already taken a few steps to enhance cooperation in this area. During Prime Minister Manmohan Singh's visit to Russia in December 2009, the two sides expressed the same views about enhancing the role of the ISAF in Afghanistan.[35] Similar views were highlighted in the joint statement issued after the visit of the Russian President, Dmitry Medvedev, to New Delhi, which stated that both the countries fully appreciate the importance of stability in Afghanistan, recognise the need to control narcotics trafficking, which funds the extremist forces and underscored the need for stepping up efforts by the ISAF in combating production and trafficking of narcotics.[36]

It would require a global effort to solve the menace and it is an imperative that policies implemented for containing narcotics trafficking should have a global consensus. The recent enhancement in the cooperation between Russia and US-NATO is a welcome progress in this direction.

35. Government of India (2009). *Joint Declaration between the Republic of India and the Russian Federation on Deepening the Strategic Partnership to Meet Global Challenges*. 7 December, <*http://pmindia.nic.in/lprel.asp?id=1043*>.

36. Ministry of External Affairs (2010). *Joint Statement: Celebrating a Decade of the India-Russian Federation Strategic Partnership and Looking Ahead*. 21 December, <*http://www.mea.gov.in/mystart.php?id=530516902*> (24 February 2011).

Part II

Global Issues: Views from India and Russia

8 Economic Globalisation and the Crisis

Yury Byaly

Globalisation is a multidimensional process in which the economic, social, political, scientific, technological, cultural and, as Club of Rome ideologue, Ervin Laszlo put it, the 'internal human' dimensions are inextricably interrelated.[1] This is because even when discussing the purely economic aspects of globalisation (finance, investment, industry, commerce, etc.), their connection with other processes—including political and socio-psychological processes—comes into play.[2]

Contemporary Globalisation as an Economic Phenomenon

The current cycle of economic globalisation is not the first in history. Large empires in ancient and medieval times created unified monetary systems and trade relations over vast areas covering the entire 'civilised world' of their era.[3] In modern times, the globalisation cycle developed very fast in the first decade of the 20th century, when there were virtually no restrictions on foreign financial transactions and international cross-flows of labour for the countries that were the economic leaders; yet their share of foreign trade in the Gross Domestic Product (GDP) was not much less than their present share.[4] The stability of the global economic system at that

1. Laszlo, E. (1998). *Globalization and the Future of the Nation State.* Proceedings of the Roundtable. Sardinia Cagliari, Italy. 25-27 May, 31 October. Moscow: Gorbachev Foundation.
2. Berger, P. and S. Huntington (eds.) (2004). *The Many Faces of Globalization.* Moscow: Aspekt-Press; Bauman, Z. (2004). *Globalization: The Consequences for Individuals and Society.* Moscow: Ves Mir; Held, D., D. Goldblatt, E. McGrew and J. Perraton (2004). *Global Transformations.* Moscow: Praxis.
3. Minkova, K.V. (2006). *International Multilateral Trade: From Antiquity to the WTO.* SPb:SPbGU.
4. Chernoy, L.S. (2003). *Globalization: Past or Future: Transformations of the Market Economy and Economic Systems.* Moscow: IKC Akademkniga. pp.315-17.

time was upheld by a single monetary system, the gold standard, which guaranteed the parity of national currencies for international investments and trade.[5]

In the further transformation of the global economy, the two World Wars had a decisive influence, causing an abrupt weakening of the economies of most countries at war and an acute global credit crunch associated with the need for investment in accelerated post-war reconstruction. The outcome of a search mechanism for investment lending to weakened economies was the Bretton Woods agreements of 1944. In addition to gold, these agreements established the US dollar as a basis for monetary systems (as the country had been made rich by the war and had accumulated the largest gold reserves) and gave the right to exchange dollars for gold only to the Central Banks of countries emitting a national currency. The Bretton Woods agreements also set up two new international organisations: the International Monetary Fund (IMF)—to financially support the macroeconomic stability of countries in need of assistance—and the International Bank for Reconstruction and Development [later the World Bank (WB)]—to support specific development projects in such countries.[6]

The Bretton Woods monetary system, as well as the IMF and WB, truly contributed to the restoration of the war-torn economies of most developed countries as well as to a relatively high growth rate of the world GDP. However, by the early 1970s, it became clear that, using a dollar-based monetary system, the USA was abusing its actual function as a 'lender of last resort' and emitting dollars in excess gold reserves and other national assets.[7] After a series of international scandals involving the unsuccessful attempts of a number of countries to trade accumulated US dollars for gold, the USA undertook several devaluations of the dollar (reducing its gold content). For example, on 17 December 1971, it devalued the dollar

5. Zinglas, L. and R. Rajan (2004). *Saving Capitalism from the Capitalists*. Moscow: TEIS. pp.281-83.

6. Egorov, A.V. (2009). *International Financial Infrastructure*. Moscow: Linor.

7. In 1965, French President Charles de Gaulle demanded that the USA should exchange US$ 1.5 billion for gold at the established price of US$ 35 per ounce in accordance with the Bretton Woods Agreements, and if the US refused, France threatened to withdraw from NATO and to eliminate the alliance's bases and contingents from the territory of the republic. The USA fulfilled the demand only by half on account of its inability to cover that quantity of dollars with free gold reserves.

against gold by 7.9 per cent (from US$ 35 to US$ 38 per troy ounce). On 13 February 1973, it devalued the dollar to US$ 42.2 per troy ounce. By 1980, the exchange price of gold rose to US$ 750 per troy ounce. Due to this, the USA devalued its external debt several times, which, likening it to the reduction of gold content in their coinage by medieval lords, the analysts have called it "spoilage of the coins".[8]

At a conference in Jamaica in 1976, the format of the world monetary system was fundamentally changed, while nominally maintaining the status of the Bretton Woods agreements. Since then, every country acquired the right to issue a national currency without being formally pegged to gold reserves and the availability of assets denominated by the dollar. The value of domestic currency in domestic and international calculations began to be determined by the foreign currency supply and the demand on the world market.[9]

The freeing of currencies from any universal value equivalent has fundamentally changed the structure of the global economy. Firstly, the commodity market itself has become a currency. Secondly, since the currency exchange rates and the market value of goods on world markets have become more volatile (the amplitude of oscillations has increased), all investment risks, especially long-term risks, have sharply increased. The need arose for a multilevel system of insurance (hedging) of such risks and thus derivative financial instruments (derivatives) that provide investment insurance. Thirdly, the opportunities increased for playing upon the volatility of commodity and financial markets in the stock market, and, as a result, there arose diverse derivatives that allowed for speculations, futures and forward contracts, options, etc.

As a result, the financial market grew more sophisticated and the share of derivative instruments in it increased exponentially.[10] Most importantly, there was a gradual lessening of differences between, on the one hand, the actual money that was generated by the economy as added value on account of producing goods and services and, on the other hand, 'virtual money'—derivative financial instruments that were generated

8. *<http://www.kredit-moskva.ru/kritika08.html>*.

9. *<http://www.xserver.ru/user/mvsivk/2.shtml>*.

10. Between 1989 and 1995, the total price of derivative contracts doubled yearly, reaching US $41 trillion, *Reuters*, 25 January 1996.

by financial markets and very weakly linked to the real economy. The emergence of huge amounts of virtual money on financial markets sharply increased the total money supply, part of which was invested in the real economy, increasing its investment potential and thus contributing to economic growth.

In the context of the globalisation of financial markets, this new investment potential was seen as a general positive phenomenon by the economic authorities, regulators and the business communities of most countries. Moreover, this positive effect 'multiplied' in 1990s, when the huge economic potential of the countries of the former Soviet bloc, which had previously been significantly isolated from the world market, became involved in the global economy. Thus, it increased public optimism in regard to large-scale 'virtual finance'. The new 'virtual' investment potential has one major drawback: the vast majority of investments and loans based on financial derivatives are relatively short-term, due to the specifics of the corresponding derivatives markets.

Prominent American economists, including Nobel laureates Robert Merton, Myron Scholes and Harry Markowitz, took on the task of attracting 'long-term' investment money to financial markets. They turned their attention to the 'longest' mortgage capital money, building a mathematical model of the risks associated with the release of derivatives based on mortgages. Their models showed that given a 'mixed' package of mortgages with a varying reliability of return, derivatives could be created that guarantee minimum risk.[11] Accordingly, they would enable the huge financial resources of mortgage and insurance companies to be attracted to the markets.

The US credit rating agencies Moody's, Standart & Poors and Fitch revised their risk assessment techniques and began to assign mortgage derivatives the highest 'AAA' rating. This sparked confidence in the new financial instruments and high interest from investors, significantly increasing the total volume of the financial markets. Moreover, the holders of mortgage derivatives often released 'tertiary,' etc., securities based on them, further increasing the amount of credit issue.[12]

---

11. *<http://www.polit.nnov.ru/2009/06/20/gistderivative19/>*.

12. Based on primary mortgage derivatives intended to cover the corresponding risks (Credit Default Swaps, CDS), secondary 'derivatives of derivatives' were issued (Collateralized Debt Obligation, CDO), and even tertiary 'derivatives from derivatives' (Collateralized Loan Obligation, CLO).

The crisis of 1997-98 required increases in the scale of lending to the US economy. In 1999, the Glass-Steagall Act, adopted in the USA in 1933, was abolished once and for all on the initiative of the Head of the Federal Reserve, Alan Greenspan. This law differentiated between, on the one hand, commercial banks and finance companies under supervision by the state and entitled to its financial assistance, yet without the right to speculate on the stock exchanges, and on the other hand, investment banks that could carry out risky speculation on the exchanges, but could not rely on government assistance.[13] Commercial banks, insurance and mortgage companies, etc., followed behind investment banks and joined in the speculation with huge amounts of derivatives of different origin. Moreover, this process engulfed almost the entire world due to the substantial trans-nationalisation of capital that had already taken place (especially with financial capital).

As a result, the volume of derivative trading on world financial markets rose hundreds of times higher than the volume of trade in actual goods and services by just the middle of the first decade of the 21st century. According to the Basel Bank for International Settlements, the average daily turnover in the derivatives market in April 2004 was US$ 5.541 trillion, including US$ 1.025 trillion worth of over-the-counter (OTC) derivatives.[14] According to the same bank, the volume of OTC derivatives in the middle of 2008 (the peak of the crisis) amounted to US$ 595 trillion (11 times more the global GDP), while the volume of issues of OTC derivatives (options and futures) reached US$ 2,300 trillion (43% per annum of the world GDP).[15]

There was a gradual liberalisation of world trade after the World War II, associated with the creation of yet another international economic institution in 1947, the General Agreement on Tariffs and Trade (GATT), which was renamed the World Trade Organization (WTO) in 1995, on the basis of the Bretton Woods agreements.[16] The objective of the GATT and then the WTO was to conclude international agreements that reduce tariff protection in national markets and, consequently, the costs of global trade.

13. Yu Samonov, President of Delus Corp, USA, *Zh. Ekspert* 4 (690), 1 February 2010.

14. Bank for International Settlements (2004). *Triennial Survey of Foreign Exchange and Derivatives Market Activity.* April.

15. *<http://www.bis.org/forum/research.htm>*.

16. *<http://www.wto.ru/chto.asp?f=history&t=8>*.

Unlike the preceding era, when trade tariffs were set by countries through bilateral agreements, the GATT-WTO agreements were binding for all member states. As a result, the average international tariffs successively dropped from 40 per cent in the mid-1940s to 5 per cent by the beginning of the 21st century.[17] Many WTO member states, having lost the opportunity for tariff protection of their markets, began to use an undervalued parity exchange rate for their national currency (instead of sticking to its purchasing power) to compensate for non-tariff protection—the result of the Jamaica agreements on the determination of market exchange rates. This ensured an increase in the competitiveness of the country's products and services in domestic and international markets.[18]

Nevertheless, the lifting of tariffs in the majority of national markets has led to a process of trade globalisation synchronous with financial globalisation. Moreover, experts stress that these processes are interdependent when financial globalisation spurs on trade and *vice versa*. Prominent economists grounded these processes theoretically to a greater or lesser degree on the ideologies of the maximum liberalisation of global finance and trade and the maximum deregulation of markets, including the markets for goods and capital, minimal involvement of state capital in the economy, and the maximum openness of national economies to world markets.[19] The only means of economic regulation recognised as sufficient was the regulation of the Central Bank's discount rate.

These theoretical concepts, known as the Washington Consensus, gave rise to a phenomenon that seemed to be a single universal optimal (and therefore universally obligatory) global economic policy, a kind of global "liberalising [of the] economic mainstream".[20] In particular, the WB and the IMF have demanded mandatory compliance with the rules of this 'liberalising mainstream' in recent decades when issuing stabilisation loans and loans for development programmes.

---

17. *<http://www.wto.org/english/res_e/statis_e/statis_e.htm#worldtrade>*.
18. Dolotenkova, L.P. (2001). *Exchange Rate and Purchasing Power Parity: Statistical Analysis.* Novosibirsk: Nauka.
19. *<http://www.itinvest.ru/analytics/archive/360/48148/>*.
20. Stiglitz, Joseph (2003). *Globalization and Its Discontents.* New York: W.W. Norton & Company. pp.34-36.

Financial Globalisation and the Sources of the Current Crisis

The sharp rise in trading volumes in stock and derivatives markets, the steady rise in complexity of these markets and the increasing speed of transactions due to the advent of global Internet communication created a kind of 'wall' between the market speculators and the great mass of potential investors. The mass investor, due to initial misunderstanding of the structure and behaviour of new financial markets, could afford to carry out credit operations and stock market speculations only on relatively simple stock and bond markets of the real sector enterprises. Professional speculators, as well as banks and large financial firms who understood the specifics of the organisation, the operations of the highly complex, 'fast' currency market and the numerous derivative markets became more and more concentrated in these markets.

But as the real money of economy from the production of goods and services was inseparable and indistinguishable in the new global economy from the 'virtual' money of 'financial structuring,' a swelling segment of financial structures began to have an increasingly significant impact on the functioning of the real economy. This was through the mechanism of 'inflating' and 'bursting' small and large market 'bubbles'. The fact is that, for the stock speculator, there is no fundamental difference in what to play upon in the volatile markets: with their market savvy, they could 'make money' irrespective of whether the market was growing or declining. Profit in this game is almost independent of the state of the national and global economy.

At the same time, in the current wave of globalisation of 'financial and speculative' market-focused structuring, there has arisen a huge, concentrated mass of real and virtual money, almost instantly able to leave one market and enter another. The ability to manipulate markets and make profits both from their 'inflation' and on their collapse has increased dramatically. The space for this kind of manipulation in the late 20th and early 21st century increased rapidly with the expansion of the scope of financial transactions through offshore jurisdictions[21] that are essentially exempted from control, as well as through the growth of the virtually uncontrolled segment of OTC derivatives trading.[22]

As a result, the financial and speculative segment of the global markets covers virtually the entire world at the current stage of globalisation and, from a supporting "superstructure" over the real economy, they have become simply by fact of the scale of the virtual and real money supply controlled the actual "owner" of the economy, able to dictate its own rules and special interests. Former Commercial Director of Deutsche Bank, Thomas Fischer said that, from the start of derivatives trading, "the financial world has been emancipated from the real sphere".[23] This process was marked among other things by the rapid increase in the share of financial companies in the capitalisation of the domestic markets of developed countries (primarily the USA), as well as by the growing share of the financial segment of the economy in national GDP.[24]

At the same time, the financial basis of the new "economics of ultrafast electronic trading of derivatives" turned out to be decisively subordinate to the speculative environment and all the more dependent on it. In a scenario where the annual trading volume of derivatives was 10 times more than the entire annual GDP of all countries, the financial basis of the global economy could not but fail to maintain stability. In an open global economy, based on the principles of the aforementioned 'liberalising

21. For high returns and tax evasion purposes, banks and hedge funds issue and sell mortgage-backed securities through special companies (SPV) located in offshore zones and trading these securities combined in a 'baskets' of their own derivatives. In all developed countries, including the US and Europe, there are rules in the financial legislation requiring disclosure of the content of 'baskets' of securities bought and sold. In the majority of offshore jurisdictions, there is no such rule. Market agents acting through SPV in offshore zones never know for sure what exactly they are buying and selling, i.e. they cannot reliably assess the risks.

22. On the OTC market, the exchange of derivatives took place among a narrow circle of participants, between which a direct relationship was established. This market is characterised by poorly standardised trading conditions and the wide range of instruments traded, <*http://www.derivatus.ru/14.html*>.

23. Martin, G.P. and H. Shuman (2001). *Western Globalisation*. Moscow: Alpina. p.82.

24. From 1978 to 2008, the share of manufacturing in US GDP fell from 25 per cent to 12 per cent and the share of financial services in GDP for the same period rose from 12 per cent to 20-21 per cent. In 2008, the share of the financial sector in total corporate profits in the USA and UK reached 35 per cent; IMF (2009). *World Economic Outlook*. Washington D.C.

mainstream', the volume of market fluctuations and insider transactions on speculative financial markets is much higher than the cash flow that generates the real economy. This 'virtual financing' has an inexorable influence on the state of the real sector and acquires the ability to create (both accidentally and intentionally) geographic and sector-wide 'zones of chaos' in the world economy.

However, the influence of 'financial and speculative' structuring on the real economy was not the only factor. First, under the influence of the obvious success of financial speculators in the production of income, more and more market agents are beginning to try their hand at risky speculative games, thereby diverting the financial resources of the market from capital investments in the real economy, reducing its investment potential and thus undermining its development potential. Second, in the course of the increasing complexity of the aggregate economy a 'managerial revolution' has taken place, especially in large public companies. This has meant the passing of the control of firms from shareholders, who do not understand market games, to professional salaried managers. This, in turn, has led to a significant change in the managements' priority motivations.

A significant portion of shareholders, fascinated by the stock market game, went from being strategic investors to investors in portfolios, ready at any moment to sell their company shares and to shift their money elsewhere, guided by market forces. As a result, strategic investors interested in the long-term development of companies have steadily lost influence in boards of directors. But hired managers, whose earnings are determined by current market capitalisation and company profitability, are also becoming less and less interested in investing profits in long-term development programmes. Both strategic investors and the hired managers now seek to attract the maximum amount of money from the financial market into the stocks and bonds of their companies, that is, they indirectly support the growth of the speculative financial segment, which is able to quickly generate this kind of money.

Professor Fredmund Malik of the Swiss University St. Gallen says: "The achievements of each company are evaluated only on its financial performance... As a result, a self-destructive system arises. It is easy to obtain a quick profit if you do not have to think about the future. It is sufficient to reduce expenditures on innovation, marketing, and training; and the exchange rate will go up rapidly. Today there are no shareholders in the classic sense of the word, leaving only share turners. Most of them... are not at all interested in the fate of the company. They come to the general meeting of shareholders and vote for their own kind. After a couple of weeks, they sell their shares."[25]

Calling for the utmost privatisation of state property and accusing managers of state companies of mismanagement, the ideologues of the 'liberalising mainstream' explain their position thus: if there is no specific owner then the state would be the owner, but since in principle, the state cannot be a specific owner, it is no one's property. However, the erosion of equity shares in public companies and the dominance of speculative investment capital interested only in current capitalisation and profits have given rise to the same phenomenon of 'no one's property' and resulted in a lack of strategic management.

The outcome of the processes described above is the increasing investment risks associated with a high probability of an instantaneous withdrawal of portfolio investments from assets and a high volatility and unpredictability of all markets, including markets for goods and services and, as a consequence: the massive reduction of a 'planning horizon' in company development; a steady decline in the share of profit allocated to development and; the growth of the share of profits allocated for payment of dividends to shareholders and manager bonuses.

For these reasons, in developed countries, the physical volume of the issue of real goods, as well as the share of investment in the renewal of assets of the real economy, scientific research and development activity, has been steadily declining. But their GDP has from all outward appearances grown steadily, reflecting, among other things, price increase and the 'inflated' capitalisation of companies. In addition, due to the 'superfast' manipulation of capital, the 'inflated' speculative financial segment of the economy has given an unwelcome boost allowed not only to the 'inflation' of capitalisation bubbles in different segments of the global economy, but also their strategic 'deflation,' by transferring virtual capital to other segments and other 'bubbles.' It is through this mechanism, associated with

25. Interview with Professor F. Malik, Handelsblatt, 17 July 2009.

the management of 'virtual financial innovation' that developed countries were able to relatively safely pass through the major crisis of 1997-98 (we recall that it had a very painful effect on the developing countries of Asia and the former USSR).

These circumstances provided the grounds for one of the ideologists of the 'liberalising mainstream,' Nobel laureate Robert Lucas, to declare in 2003: "The central problem, depression-prevention, has been solved from a practical point of view, but in theory it was resolved decades ago".[26] This 'baggage' of economic and motivational transformations, as well as the conceptual and ideological illusions—associated with the inflation and globalisation of the 'speculative financial' structure of a liberalised market economy—sent the world into crisis in 2007.

The Underlying Causes of the New Crisis

It must be noted that the current crisis was predicted repeatedly. For example, back in 1995, a major US banker, Felix Rohatyn, said: "The deadly potential of the combination of new financial instruments and high-tech methods of trade may contribute to the initiation of a destructive chain reaction. Today, the world's financial markets are more dangerous to stability than atomic weapons."[27] In 2006, George Soros wrote: "Currently, the inflation of a giant bubble is taking place in the US housing market... Mortgage organisations... have lowered lending standards and brought new products to the market... stimulating interest of borrowers. All this has triggered a speculative rise in housing prices... a consumer boom broke out ensuring sustainable economic growth for the last two years...."[28]

However, neither Rohatyn nor Soros predicted that at the centre of this resulting mortgage bubble was either a gross theoretical error by the Nobel Prize-winning creators of mortgage derivatives or a conscious effort to ensure a global financial scam, because it became clear as early as the beginning of the crisis that the authors of the valuation models of mortgage

26. Cited from newspaper *Vedomosti*, 9 June 2009. *<http://www.vedomosti.ru/newspaper/article/2009/06/09/199580#ixzz0uKWMXVSg>*

27. America in the year 2000, Vortrag beim Kreisky Forum, 8 November 1995, Wien.

28. Soros, George (2008). *The Age of Fallibility: The World on the Threshold of a Global Crisis*. Moscow: Alpina Business Books. pp.49-50; Soros, George (2006). *The Age of Fallibility*. Public Affairs.

derivatives (quickly dubbed 'trash paper') had advised the investment banks issuing these securities; the investment banks then paid the rating agencies, which awarded this 'trash paper' an 'AAA' rating. This is what the magazine *Finance* writes on this topic: "A risqué feature... was that the rating agencies for assigning bonds a credit rating were paid by the investment banks issuing the same bonds, which largely explains both the overestimation of the true credit quality of the securities and devil-may-care attitude of banks to the actual solvency of borrowers".[29]

During an investigation into the mortgage crisis conducted in 2007-08, the US Securities and Exchange Commission (SEC) identified that approximately 400 people were involved in the crisis, including members of the rating agencies Fitch, Moody's and Standard & Poor's. For example, in 2006, more than half of the issue of Collateralised Debt Obligation (CDO) derivatives, amounting to more than US$ 1.3 trillion, received a rating of 'AAA' from the rating agencies.[30] In 2010, it became clear that major US and multinational banks—Goldman Sachs, Citigroup, JP Morgan and others—had played upon the drop in the markets with the derivatives they themselves released[31]—i.e., they were the insiders who manipulated the market to the detriment of other market players and the global economy. In 2011, most of these banks avoided prosecution for this insider fraud by paying a small penalty (compared to the scale of the fraud).

Why were these destructive processes beyond the control of national regulators? And why were there no attempts to avert the impending crisis, even though the US financial authorities could not have failed to recognise the risk of a crisis? The answer lies in the overall status and trends of the US economy in recent decades. Figures 8.1 and 8.2 show graphs of the trade balance and the share of domestic and foreign investment in the US economy as the percentage of GDP, taken from a report by the former

29. *Finance*, 20 August 2007, *<http://www.buhsmi.ru/lenta/161903/>*.

30. *<http://fundmarket.ua/digest/491aac87726a1/>*.

31. "In the field of vision of the Securities and Exchange Commission (SEC) were already six major financial institutions that were suspected of foul play on the derivative market, notification of the beginning of investigation was sent to Goldman Sachs, Morgan Stanley, JP Morgan Chase, Citigroup, Deutsche Bank, and UBS. All of them sold a variety of structured financial instruments to market participants, knowing of the imminent decline of their retail price and moreover, making a stake on it" (*Wall Street Journal*, 13 May 2010).

Director of Economics and Business Policy for the Mayor of London, Professor John Ross. It was presented at the Experimental Creative Centre in Moscow in early 2010.[32]

Figure 8.1

US Balance of Trade (% of GDP)

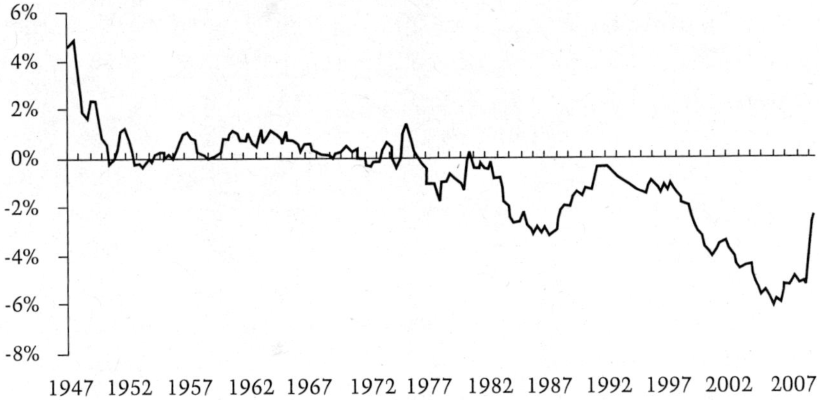

Source: Ross.

Figure 8.2

Balance of US International Portfolio Investment (% of GDP)

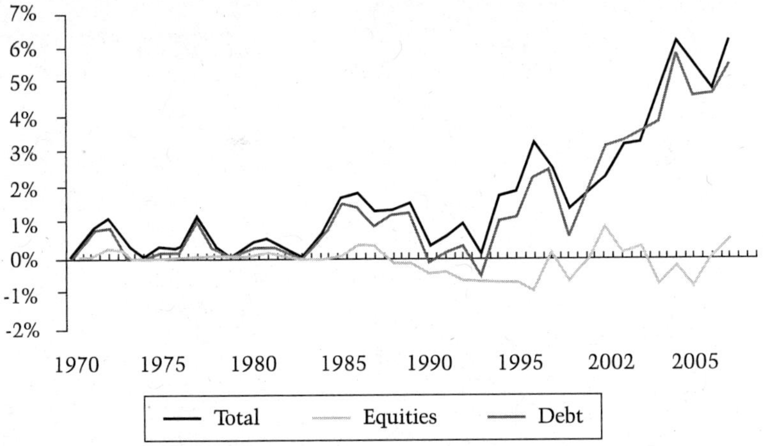

Source: Ross.

32. Ross, John, "The International Economic Crisis and the Rise of China", <*http://kurg.rtcomm.ru/clubs.shtml?cat=41&id=509*>.

The graphs show that since the early 1990s, the US economy has become persistently unprofitable, according to the balance of both foreign trade and investment (which are financed entirely by debt). Moreover, these deficits are growing. In other words, the US has been losing competitiveness in the open markets of the global economy for 20 years.

At the same time, the total US debt is also steadily increasing; it includes all debts: the federal, state, municipality, corporate and household. As of August 2008, the total debt amounted to US$ 47 trillion, and the national debt (the debt of the Federal Government) amounted to US$ 8.7 trillion.[33] As of the beginning of 2011, total US debt exceeded US$ 55 trillion and the national debt had reached US$ 13.9 trillion.[34] On 6 January 2011, the US Secretary of Treasury, Timothy Geithner spoke in an open letter to Congress of the urgent need for a law to increase the US national debt ceiling (it was US$ 14.3 trillion at that time).[35] In May 2011, both Geithner and President Barack Obama announced to Congress that if a law to raise the national debt ceiling to US$ 2 trillion was not adopted by 2 August, the US could well be in technical default.[36]

To eliminate these debts and deficits in investment and trade, balance four basic mechanisms were opened to the political and financial elite of the US. The first was a sharp reduction in public expenditure, including military spending. But since even after the decline of America's economic power, its main 'global asset' continues to be its military power, the option was not acceptable and the allocation for the military continues to grow in US budgets.

The second mechanism is a smooth (inflation) or severe (devaluation) depreciation of the dollar (and, consequently, the price of US dollar-denominated securities, including US Treasuries). This policy of 'spoiling the coin' (which the US financial authorities had tried out in the 1970s-80s) softens the impact of US debts and reduces the cost of their maintenance; simultaneously, it increases the competitiveness of American products in

---

33. Report Z.1 US Federal Reserve, "Flow of Funds Accounts of the USA" from 18 September 2008, p.8.

34. *<http://www.ustreas.gov/tic/debtad09.html>*.

35. *<http://www.treasury.gov/connect/blog/Pages/letter.aspx>*.

36. PRAIM-TASS, 16 May 2011.

world markets, thus improving the trade balance. But the flip side is that this policy robs not only the American holders of dollar assets (and they are a substantial part of the US population), but also those of other countries—the big holders being China and Japan, followed by the European Union (EU), Russia and a number of other countries. This would cause a surge of mistrust in the USA and the dollar, which could torpedo both the US and world economy. Therefore, the US financial authorities do not undertake targeted actions that would either mean inflation or the devaluation of the dollar.

The third mechanism would be to bridge the gap between American production and American consumption by investing in new productive assets, thereby restoring the global competitiveness of the US economy. However, for this, it would be necessary to restore investor confidence in the markets and large-scale lending to the real sector by raising taxes and using public finance. But the crisis and the financial fraud revealed during the Madoff scam and a number of others[37] have undermined public confidence to such an extent that pushing credit through the financial clots to the real economy is as yet unthinkable.

The fourth method would be to drastically reduce social spending in both the private and public sector (wages, pensions, medical insurance, etc.). However, Obama's medical reforms and the bailout of corporations with high employment, such as General Motors (GM), clearly indicate that the US authorities are not prepared to take this route either. The reason is that all of the above, except for reductions in military spending, lead to a massive reduction in living standards. Even accounting for the official exchange rates (which state the GDP in developing countries), according to various estimates, the US produced only 18-23 per cent of world GDP in 2007, while consuming 35-40 per cent of global GDP.[38] That is, any 'correct' measures aimed at balancing US income and expenditure would

37. On 11 December 2008, the largest Ponzi scheme was uncovered, created by Bernard Madoff, the former Chairman of the Board of Directors of NASDAQ and the founder of the investment company, Bernard L. Madoff Investment Securities LLC. The collapse of the pyramid brought losses to depositors of more than US$ 50 billion. After this, it was reported in the American press that several dozen more large-scale pyramid schemes and fraudulent transactions had been exposed. On 16 June 2010, the Miami Herald reported that fraud charges were brought against 94 suspects in the theft of US$ 251 million from the trust fund of Medicare Health Insurance.

38. For example, see: <*http://www.newsland.ru/News/Detail/id/83626/*>.

mean a fundamental decline in the average standard of living of Americans (at least initially), which is something no government in the USA can afford if it intends to stay in power.

In these circumstances, building 'virtual finance' pyramids, a huge part of which was realised outside the USA and thereby fuelling the US economy with credit, was one of the most affordable ways to put off a radical solution to the deficits and debt crisis. A second method was to ensure the attractiveness of the USA as a safe harbour for capital by bringing about a situation of an increased risk of crisis in some troubled region of the world i.e., fomenting 'controlled economic chaos' in other countries. This would entail, through manipulation, exacerbating both the political and economic situation of the chosen country, the former by the use of the US 'military and special services machine' and the latter with the assistance of US rating agencies and interested US corporations.

Thus, after the overthrow of Saddam Hussein in Iraq, a terrorist war developed in the country, significantly worsening the investment climate in the region. And then, the US announcement of withdrawal of its troops from Iraq was quickly followed up by a new surge of terrorist activity in the Middle East.[39] Immediately, the political risk apprehensions of the business world intensified not only in the Middle East region, but beyond, starting off the outflow of investment money (both speculative and long-term) into the USA. An even more powerful burst of political risks in investments in the Greater Middle East was caused by the wave of revolutions in 2011, in which the USA again took an active part, providing unconditional political and even military support to the revolutionary opposition in Egypt, Syria, Libya, Yemen, Sudan and Côte d'Ivoire.[40] German analyst William Engdahl vividly explains how it was all done:

> When the world came to realise that the sale of US government bonds had decreased because customers were concerned about the scale of the US budget deficit, the agency Moody's unexpectedly lowered the rating of Greece in November 2009, which caused... the flight of capital from the euro to the dollar... now... the US rating agencies have downgraded Greece to the level of "junk bonds" and thereby set in motion a new crisis for the euro. At the same

---

39. Kurginyan, S. (ed.) (2011). *Political Tsunami*. Moscow: IPF ECC. p.218.
40. Ibid.: 274-75.

> time... debt securities of countries far less at risk, such as Portugal and Spain, have also been reduced.[41]

The Wall Street Journal reports that, in early February 2010, Heads of 18 US hedge funds held a secret meeting in New York to coordinate their actions in the currency markets against the euro (apparently modelled after the attack of George Soros' hedge funds against the British pound in 1992). The US Department of Justice launched an investigation and sent a letter to the participants at the meeting 'urging' not to destroy any documents and electronic communications concerning their transactions with the euro.[42] However, according to the American press, there were no sanctions by the US Department of Justice against the hedge funds as a result of this investigation.

Consequences of the Crisis

The most debated issue is the economic consequences. Direct losses from the global economic crisis are estimated to have already reached many tens of trillions of dollars. No one has managed to determine the precise sum, as vast majority of the corporate houses have kept their losses well hidden as their revelation would lead to a further fall in market capitalisation. Other macroeconomic parameters lend themselves to a more realistic accounting.

According to analysts of the UN Conference on Trade and Development (UNCTAD), the volume of Foreign Direct Investment (FDI) in 2009 decreased by 39 per cent after the reduction in 2008 by 14 per cent,[43] i.e., foreign investment in the real sector of the global economy in its 'liberalised part' fell by nearly half over the two years of the crisis. (This excludes countries like China or India, as they implement an active policy of government investment and lending.) From 2010 to the beginning of 2011, contrary to the predictions of the UNCTAD, the recovery of FDI to the pre-crisis level did not occur. In addition, amid the increased scale of operations in mergers and acquisitions, the share of investment in FDI associated with the creation of new industries declined sharply.

41. Engdahl, William (2010). *Finanzielle Kriegsführung: Verdächtiges Timing der US-Rating-Agenturen*. Germany: KOPP-Verlag, 30 April.

42. *The Wall Street Journal*, 26 February 2010.

43. *<www.unctad.org>*.

According to the WTO, the decline in the volume of world trade amounted to 10.3 per cent in 2008 and 12 per cent in 2009.[44] The WTO Director General, Pascal Lamy, stated it was the worst figure since 1945. The total loss over the two years of crisis was 21 per cent. From 2010 to the beginning of 2011, contrary to Lamy's prediction,[45] a 10 per cent growth in trading volume compared to 2009 did not occur. Moreover, according to analysts at Global Trade Alert, in the G 20 countries alone, the number of direct discriminatory and protectionist measures that restrict freedom of trade is growing every month. In February 2010, this number was 367.[46] By early 2011, according to some estimates, it had already exceeded 420 and continues to grow.

According to the International Labor Organisation, from 2007 to January 2010, global unemployment rose by 16 per cent[47] and continued to rise, albeit at a slower pace. In November 2010, Federal Chairman, Ben Bernanke, expressed apprehension that the unemployment rate for quite some time will remain at the same high level.[48] In April 2011, Barack Obama admitted that it was not possible to significantly lower unemployment in the USA. There is an even worse (and it continues to worsen) unemployment situation in the three crisis hit European countries—Greece, Portugal and Spain.

The debt situation in the world is not improving. According to the Bank for International Settlements, in the middle of 2010, the total debt of banks to bondholders and other creditors meant to be repaid by 2012 was about US$ 5 trillion[49]; US$ 2.6 trillion of which was in Europe and US$ 1.3 trillion in the US till the middle of 2011, the debt of banks had not declined and, as would be obvious, the cumulative debt of the world's non-financial sector had significantly increased.

Meanwhile, these problems are being solved primarily by 'pumping' money from the Central Banks into the global financial system. According

44. <*http://www.wto.ru/*; see also *Bloomberg*, 24 February 2010>.

45. WTO Director-General, Pascal Lamy says he forecasts a growth in worldwide trade in 2010 by 10% in comparison with 2009, *Reuters*, 21 July 2010.

46. <*http://www. globaltradealert.org*>.

47. *RBC-Daily*, 27 January 2010.

48. *Bloomberg*, 26 November 2010.

49. *Bloomberg*, 13 July 2010.

to the Bank of England, in the middle of 2010, the total amount of 'anti-crisis' emissions in the world exceeded US$ 9 trillion and, by mid-2011, rose to US$ 11.8 trillion. At the same time, during the meetings of the G-7 Ministers of Finance, US Treasury Secretary, Timothy Geithner, opposing the resolve of the financial leadership of European countries to carry out cuts in budget deficits, insisted on extending the policy of 'stimulating domestic demand,' i.e., to continue emissions.[50] This 'financial pumping' of the world economy alleviates part of the ongoing problems, which allows many analysts (as also the representatives of economic and political power interested in 'pacifying' investors) to say that the crisis as a whole had ended or was close to the end.

However, the following results ensue: reduction in consumer and investment demand; unemployment that won't decrease; a huge overhang of debt and credit contraction: falling production in the real sector; and almost a total lack of confidence among the majority of market agents. There is an atmosphere of distrust among the economic regulators. There is distrust of the market economy model (and its creators) that until recently was considered almost the highest achievement of human genius. A particularly high 'degree of distrust' at all levels has appeared in regard to the transnational financial elites of the leading countries, who had essentially imposed their model of a 'virtual financial turbo-capitalism' upon the world, specially the USA, the main schemer and 'beneficiary' of the model.

All this intensifies the crisis of economic globalisation delineated above. The macro-regional economic centres—the USA, EU, the Association of Southeast Asian Nations (ASEAN), and China—are beginning to pursue their own economic policies, not looking much at other centres. For example, in December 2009, the member countries of ASEAN plus China, Japan, South Korea and Hong Kong signed an agreement establishing a joint reserve fund worth US$ 120 billion to resolve the participating countries' short-term liquidity problems.[51] Recent G-7 and G-20 summits indicate that the macroeconomic policy differences between the USA and leading European countries (notably Germany and France) are intensifying over the issues of budget deficit management, questions of

50. *Reuters*, 5 June 2010.

51. *Reuters*, 29 December 2009.

trust in the estimated standings of countries and corporations, as well as financial institutions' tax policies and foreign exchange transactions.[52]

On 10 March 2010, the US Secretary of Treasury, Timothy Geithner warned the European Commission that its plan to restrict the activities of hedge funds and private investment groups "may cause tensions in the relations between Washington and Brussels".[53] At the G-20 summit that ended on 5 June 2010, in South Korea, there arose a fierce debate among finance leaders of the USA, Germany, Japan and China on the issue of stimulating domestic demand outside the USA.[54] In 2011, the conflict intensified between the USA and the EU over the uncontrolled growth of the US budget deficit and national debt.

The idea of a multi-currency economic world in which the dollar would lose its role as the main unit of account and the world's reserve currency was now being more actively discussed. At the G-20 summit in early 2009, a proposal was mooted for transferring the function of the world reserve currency to special IMF drawing rights. In December 2009, member countries of the Bolivarian Alliance for the Peoples of the Americas (ALBA) decided to abandon the dollar in mutual settlements and to introduce a non-cash currency, the '*sucre,*' for this purpose.[55] In that very month at a meeting of leaders of the Cooperation Council of Arab Gulf states, the creation of the Monetary Union of Saudi Arabia, Bahrain, Qatar and Kuwait was announced.[56] In Southeast Asia, the debate launched in 1998 by the Malaysian Prime Minister, Mahathir Mohamad, was resumed on the establishment of a Monetary Union of the ASEAN countries, which could be joined by China, Japan and South Korea.[57] In November 2010, the WB President, Robert Zoellick admitted that the global financial system would have to return to the era of the 'gold standard.'[58]

52. *BBC News*, 10 December 2009.
53. *The Financial Times*, 10 March 2010.
54. *Bloomberg*, 5 June 2010.
55. *newsru.com*, 14 December 2009.
56. *BBC News*, 16 December 2009.
57. *<http://www.nbrb.by/bv/narch/>*.
58. *Financial Times*, 8 December 2010.

Many experts see as a foregone conclusion the failure of the Doha Round of negotiations for the transformation of the WTO regime to be followed by the replacement of the WTO regime with a system of macro-regional economic blocs and bilateral trade agreements.[59] Since 1 January 2010, the 'Free Trade Area, ASEAN–China' has been officially operative.[60] Negotiations to expand free trade zones in Latin America have intensified. Already, many analysts now speak about a final crisis of or even the death of the globalisation process.[61]

What does this means in totality? It means a simultaneous crises of finance, credit and trust as the foundation of a market economy, plus a crisis (or at least a very strong inhibition) of the globalisation process; it also means a growing uncertainty associated with the aggregate of these crises and a general distrust among market entities in regard to further transformations of local economic systems, as also loss of faith in the global economy as it stands today. It would frustrate long-term and strategic economic planning at all levels, from households to states.

At the heart of the whole matter is that, in the global virtual-financial-speculative capitalism of open economies—a sophisticated system with many forward and backward linkages—all of the aforementioned crises feed off one another, making it a powerful formula for fomenting 'chaotising instability.' Prominent economists point out that the main instigating factor of global instability in the recent years in the global economy that has been created in recent years was the 'pyramid of virtual finance,' which is subject to powerful 'transformational attacks' from financial insiders and elicited the bubble-like 'successes' of the global economy in the pre-crisis period. Robert Ward, Global Forecasting Director at the London Economist Intelligence Unit, explains:

> The growth of the derivatives market was based on... their ability to bypass regulation... The last factor just raises the issue of security and stability in this segment of the financial markets, which has a very indirect relation to the real economy. After all, these hundreds of trillions of OTC derivatives correspond to only fifteen trillion in market value, which is about one third of the world stock market turnover.[62]

---

59. For example, see: <http://finance.rambler.ru/news/economics/23860239.html>.
60. *Xinhua News Agency*, 1 January 2010.
61. Sapir, Jacques (2009). "Banishment from the 'Heaven of Globalisation'", *Ekspert* 1.
62. Cited from *Ekspert* 46 (635), 24 November 2008.

Is a Strategic Exit from the Crisis Possible?

In the 1970s, Nobel laureate James Tobin, foreseeing the danger of growing global flows of deregulated short-term capital, said the right thing to do would be "to throw some sand in the wheels of our excessively efficient international money markets" by charging all foreign exchange transactions a small tax. In that case, the majority of speculative play on the difference in exchange rates and interest rates would lose commercial sense, and capital stock would return to the lending markets of the real economy.[63]

Both economists and influential politicians have repeatedly turned to this idea in periods of global crisis, as in the current case. In early September 2009, the Chairman of the British Department for Financial Services (FSA), Adair Turner, spoke of the need for a global Tobin tax. He was later supported at the G-20 summit by British Prime Minister Gordon Brown and the Finance Ministers of France and Canada.[64] In December 2009, EU member states in an official address to the IMF called for the development of a global mechanism for introducing the Tobin tax.[65] However, as before, it did not receive any decisive support. In fact, the USA and its dependent, IMF, strongly opposed the move.

As an alternative to the Tobin tax, the USA offered to tighten the regulations of the 'virtual' financial markets and companies that enact the primary turnover on these markets. It was this objective that Obama's financial reforms (debated for over two years) addressed.[66] The original version of the reform proposed transferring nearly all operations of the 'virtual finance' markets into the hands of federal regulators. The transfer was to be all-inclusive: control of risk assessment; reporting on transactions and the rating of securities by rating agencies; and the breaking up of giant banks whose collapse (like the collapse of Lehman Brothers at the beginning of the crisis) could bring the entire economy crashing down.

---

63. Tobin, James (1978). "A Proposal for International Monetary Reform", *The Eastern Economic Journal*, 3-4 July/October.

64. *<http://www.bankrt.ru/news/read/48777.html>*

65. *BBC News*, 10 December 2009.

66. *Bloomberg*, 17 June 2009.

The project met stiff resistance from the US financial community and the Republicans. This is what Nobel Prize winner Joseph Stiglitz, with a touch of irony, wrote *vis-à-vis* the debate:

> The bankers are able to make personal fortunes, even undermining the economy and causing huge losses to their own companies... If effective restrictions on derivative work using state guarantees for banks... do not disappear from the final version of the bill, common interests will win out over private ones and democracy over rich lobbyists.[67]

But limitations in the field of derivatives, contrary to the hopes of Stiglitz, gradually began to disappear from the bill. It was because of this stubborn resistance to a radical reform by the financial lobby in Congress and the Senate that the US President publicly expressed his indignation at "fat cats on Wall Street."[68] For all his protests, the bill on financial regulation was approved in a form that some analysts have openly referred to as 'castrated.' All the same, the bill does place a portion of financial companies and derivative contracts under federal oversight, as well as sets up special bodies to monitor risks in the financial system and protect the interests of consumers.

However, in the first place, a huge part of this 'virtual finance' still falls outside the scope of control, hedge fund speculation has no serious limitations, banks have not been broken up and the rating agencies are not subject to control. Secondly, in order to implement the bill, qualified personnel must still be recruited as administrators in the new regulatory regime and hundreds of new rules will have to be put in place, on the basis of which the news staff will monitor, investigate and regulate the whole process. A fierce lobbying battle has ensued in Washington to determine who will head the new regulatory authorities.[69]

Analysing the wrangle in Washington over the bill, at the debate on crisis control issues at the G-7 and G-20 summits, the leaders of competing centres of economic power (especially the EU and China) have expressed the conviction that the major US and multinational masters of 'virtual finance' have no intentions as giving up their rigid stance. The aforementioned attacks by hedge funds, rating agencies and US banks on the financial stability of the EU and the euro currency have shown

---

67. *Newspaper Vedomosti*, 8 July 2010.
68. *Bloomberg*, 15 December 2009.
69. *Newspaper Izvestiia*, 20 July 2010.

that there are just two options: either the global 'financial architecture' is changed fundamentally or all states will have to 'save themselves' on their own. In January 2010, the Governor of the Bank of England, Mervyn King said " ...to adjust the global balance of trade imbalances and prevent the threat of new crises, it is necessary to transform the G-20 into the IMF Board of Governors".[70] In March 2010, the European Commission began to formulate a mechanism that would put firm restraints on the uncontrolled hedge funds-cum-private equity groups in the EU.[71]

On 19 May 2010, the Federal Financial Supervisory Authority of Germany (*BaFin*) imposed a 'temporary ban' on high-risk stock market speculations. The ban encompassed: deals playing upon reduction of the rates of State Treasury Bonds of euro zone countries; trade in credit-default swaps; and speculative short selling of shares of the 10 leading financial institutions, including Deutsche Bank, Commerzbank and Allianz.[72] On the same day, the summit of EU Finance Ministers decided that foreign hedge funds carrying out operations in the EU must obtain a special permit; in addition, they are "prohibited to engage in financial transactions with countries and regions that do not fully meet EU requirements, including a number of offshore companies".[73]

In mid-June 2010, the Republic of Korea announced limitations on forward positioning by banks on a number of derivatives.[74] At the end of May 2010, a plan came into effect for establishing an EU fund of 750 billion euros, designed for anti-crisis measures in the 'problematic' countries in the Eurozone.[75] On 16 June 2010, it was reported that German Chancellor Angela Merkel and French President Nicolas Sarkozy, in the course of the talks in Berlin, "agreed in principle to the creation of a European Economic Government for all 27 EU member states".[76] On 12 July 2010, the President of the European Central Bank, President Jean-Claude Trichet said in an interview with the newspaper *Liberation*: "it is necessary to end the global

70. *BBC News*, 21 January 2010.
71. *Financial Times*, 10 March 2010.
72. *Deutsche Presse-Agentur*, 19 May 2010.
73. *RBC-Daily*, 19 May 2010.
74. *Bloomberg*, 6 July 2010.
75. *BBC News*, 27 May 2010.
76. *Deutsche Presse-Agentur*, 16 June 2010.

oligopoly of the three major international rating agencies Fitch, Standard & Poor's and Moody's".[77] On 13 July 2010, the Chinese Company *Dagong Global Credit Rating* became the first 'alternative' credit rating agency to publish sovereign credit ratings of the leading states. Moreover, China was ranked higher than the USA, Britain and Japan "because the budget deficit and national debt in developed countries was growing".[78]

It is noteworthy that Germany received from *Dagong* the same high rating of 'AA+' as China did on debts in national currency. It became known that China began to actively get rid of its US Treasuries in the summer of 2010, reinvesting in Japanese and European securities, including treasury bills from southern European countries. On 30 July 2010, the French insurer *Coface* announced its willingness to serve as a 'European' global ratings agency.[79] On 19 July 2010, after several statements by Federal Chancellor Angela Merkel to the effect that German taxpayers did not intend to finance the "irresponsibility of the authorities of some euro zone countries", the German Finance Minister Wolfgang Schäuble in an interview with *Der Spiegel* said: "If a company suffers a bankruptcy, creditors must accept the fact that they lose some of their money. The same should happen in bankrupt states."[80] Then a discussion ensued in the world press about the idea of establishing a special body of the EU designed to manage the problems of insurance insolvencies in the eurozone, as well as potentially control the bankruptcy procedures for EU states in crisis. The press has already given the body the telling name of 'the Berlin club'.[81]

What's Next?

Thus, against the backdrop of a multitude of updates about the start of post-crisis economic growth, there are 'individual' actions by the world's major centres of eco-financial power aimed at easing the crisis or at least preventing a "second wave"—the possibility of which is very much present in the agenda. But at the same time, there are all the more clear-cut

77. *RIA Novosti,*13 July 2010.
78. *INTERFAKS-AFI*, 13 July 2010.
79. *RBC-Daily*, 30 July 2010.
80. *Ekspert* 28 (713), 19 July 2010.
81. For example, see: *<http://economyobzor.com/ekonomika/14743-evro-podeshevel-posle-soobshheniya-v-smi-o-planax.html>*.

claims of the fundamental transformation of global economic and financial architecture at both the global and macro-regional level. There is a growing awareness all around that the 'liberal mainstream' and the global economic system built upon it and dominated by a financial speculative structure have failed miserably. There is growing recognition that the recent investments and credit boom were based on the phenomenon once called 'spoiling the coin' and that this phenomenon in transnational financial pools has only slightly abated the crisis, but has not stopped it. There is a growing realisation that, even if a solution is found and the crisis passes, it would, in all probability, still be only a prelude to the next such crisis, given the fact that the reforms put in place were merely 'cosmetic.' And, each new crisis will be more powerful and destructive than the previous one.

It is now a common knowledge that the era of ideological domination of the 'liberal mainstream' and the 'virtual finance' it has generated has resulted in the erosion of traditional business ethics and a mass transformation of the entrepreneur to profiteer in the majority of developed countries. All of the above have created a fundamentally irreversible state of instability leading to 'chaostisizing instability' in the world economy; mutual trust in all markets have been undermined and there is an acute crisis in the multi-level strategic planning of economic development. It has become clear that the economies of countries that have to a large degree 'financially' isolated themselves from the world market created a large public sector and are empowered with a wide range of government regulation measures (China, India, in part, and a number of others) and are able to weather the current crisis much better than the economies of extensively 'liberalised' countries.

Thus, China and India had almost regained their pre-crisis growth rates by early 2010.[82] Moreover, China increased its GDP growth to over 10 per cent per year by the end of 2010.[83] Furthermore, during the crisis, China was able to significantly 'turn' its national economy from increasing the share of exports in GDP to increasing the share of its domestic consumption. This was facilitated both by huge domestic government

---

82. The growth of China's GDP in the second quarter of 2010 was 10.3 per cent and India's GDP was 7.4 per cent, *Bloomberg*, 20 July 2010.

83. In 2010, China's GDP grew by 10.3 per cent, while in 2009, it grew by only 9.2 per cent, *Bloomberg*, 19 January 2011.

investments and loans[84] (issued both by the government and indirectly by state-controlled banks) and by measures to increase consumer demand among the poorest strata of the population.[85] In addition, China sharply expanded its use of foreign currency reserves to purchase productive assets abroad, becoming one of the world's largest providers of private investments.[86] As a result, we see that during the global crisis, some very powerful economic and financial centres have been established, working on different (and to some extent conflicting) economic and financial policies.

But, for all this, the situation brought about by the USA continues. As earlier noted in detail, the financial and political elite of the USA has no intention of either giving up any income from the state and private businesses that drive its global dominance in the 'virtual financial speculative structure,' or financing budget deficits with resources drawn from other countries by creating investment chaos among their global competitors (by manipulating the markets through politico-military special operations). It is with the hope of repairing the damages it caused that the USA carried out a 'cosmetic repair' of its system by employing national regulators—ultimately indicated by Obama's financial reforms. But, it continues to resolutely reject any attempts of other countries to set realistic rules for global financial regulation that would 'bind the hands' of the dominant US financial companies on virtual world financial markets. For example, in October 2010, Bernanke said that the huge amount of US$ 1.7 trillion spent by the Fed to purchase bank assets was insufficient to overcome the recession and therefore it was necessary to continue the

---

84. In 2010, the total amount of loans granted by Chinese banks to businesses and individuals in the country amounted to 7.95 trillion yaun or about US$ 1.2 trillion at the exchange rates. Moreover, China's foreign trade balance surplus on the basis of 2010 decreased to US$ 183.1 billion (from US$ 196.06 billion in 2009 and almost US$ 300 billion in 2008), *Vedomosti*, 12 January 2011.

85. "The leadership of the People's Republic of China announced a massive increase in minimum wage in China. From 30 June 2010, in nine Chinese provinces minimum wage will increase on average by 33 per cent to 600 yuan per month (approximately US$ 89.5). This increase affects no less than 100 million workers and employees of enterprises of different ownership forms—from public to private", *Xinhua News Agency*, 11 June 2010.

86. According to the analytical business portal *RIC-Finance*, by the end of 2009, 12,000 Chinese companies had invested money in 13,000 foreign companies; the total sum of the investment was US$ 247.7 billion and foreign assets held by Chinese companies exceeded US$ 1 trillion, 12 October 2010, *<http://www.2stocks.ru/upload/10/4/1286961634.pdf>*.

policy of 'quantitative easing' (i.e., continuing to issue dollars). The US Congress then approved a new programme of 'quantitative easing' for another US$ 600 billion.

'Old Europe' with its financial and economic core in Germany and France is, on the one hand, more and more openly imposing the rules governing the financial markets upon the EU, apprehending the redistribution of the European 'virtual-speculative margin' in favour of the USA.[87] On the other hand, 'Old Europe' is aggressively increasing its influence in the EU, while simultaneously reducing its core countries' liability for the state of the euro currency and the union's economy. Here one needs to remember the concept of the 'Berlin club' and the plans to form a state institution to deal with the bankruptcy of the 'European failures'—Greece, Spain and Italy. This trend was especially apparent after a number of experts and major financiers made harsh predictions *vis-à-vis* the inevitable dissolution of the eurozone and the funeral of the euro.[88] Moreover, 'Old Europe' is ready to a far greater extent than the USA to 'turn the screw' of state regulation, not only in the sphere of finance but also in the economy as a whole, including control of employment and budget deficits.

China, which maintains 'regulated openness' in its economy and finance and its powerful tools of economic management in the public sector, recorded the second highest GDP, next only to the USA in 2009 [in terms of *yuan*'s (RMB) Purchasing Power Parity].[89] It also replaced Germany as the world's first in the total scale of exports.[90] In 2010, China has further gone ahead of its major competitors for these positions. It has in recent years not only carried out active global expansion of direct investment in different

87. At the EU summit in December 2010, a resolution was adopted to make the European stability fund of 750 billion EUR a permanent institution.

88. For example, see: Harvard Professor Niall Ferguson stated the following in an interview with the German newspaper *Handelsblatt*: "The single European currency will die a slow death, and the aid package the EU has formed for Greece and the creation of a special common European fund will support financial stability only in the short term", 12 May 2010.

89. *<http://iformatsiya.ru/tabl/18-vvp-stran-mira-po-paritetu-pokupatelnoj-sposobnosti-pps.html>*.

90. *Bloomberg*, 12 January 2010.

regions of the world—Southeast Asia, Africa and Latin America[91]—but also managed a kind of expansion of the *yuan* currency zone. Thus, by mid-2011, Beijing had accumulated US$ 3.2 trillion in its foreign currency reserves.[92] Since 2008, it has signed agreements on trade and investment (paying in local currencies) with more than a dozen countries, such as Argentina, Indonesia, Belarus, Malaysia, South Korea, Hong Kong and Singapore, amounting to a total of more than 650 billion *yuan* (about US$ 150 billion in Purchasing Power Parity).[93]

At present, China is still firmly 'tied' to the USA as it continues to sterilise the huge amount of foreign dollars it buys in the form of US Treasury bonds. This means an indirect form of lending for the US government's debt and the import by USA of Chinese goods. At the beginning of 2010, China and its 'subsidiary,' Hong Kong, controlled 27 per cent of the US government debt (including US Treasuries worth US$ 940 billion)[94]; it has further increased in 2011.[95] However, the 'trade currency' relationship between China and the USA during the crisis has steadily diminished (it is noteworthy that China has already begun diversifying its foreign currency reserves in favour of Europe, that is from the dollar to the euro). We can assume that in a few years, China will pursue an active policy of converting RMB into one more world reserve currency.

This means that the world is moving towards very large (possibly 'tectonic') transformations of the global financial, trade and economic architecture. Analysis of its possible configurations requires a separate study, but it is already clear that such diverse strategic target ambitions of the aforementioned centres of economic power cannot but lead to an increased conflict between them even if, optimistically speaking, the current crisis is safely 'resolved.' At the very least, contradictions will grow

---

91. *The Financial Times* reported that the sovereign state fund, China Investment Corp (CIC) created in 2007 and primarily investing abroad, may obtain an additional US$ 200 billion from the country's foreign exchange reserves, bringing its assets to US$ 500 billion, 21 December 2009.

92. *<http://www.finmarket.ru/z/nws/news.asp?id=2258137>*.

93. *RBC-Daily*, 23 July 2010.

94. *Mag Ekspert* 2 (688), 18 January 2010.

95. By March 2011, the volume of US Treasuries in China's foreign currency reserves exceeded US$ 1 trillion, *Reuters*, 8 July 2011.

because, as we see, the world's geo-economic balance is steadily shifting away from the USA and EU to China.

These contradictions are compounded by the fact that, apart from the three major geo-economic players indicated, there are many others that are not yet able to play an independent role on a global scale, but at the same time cannot refuse participation in the game, as they are caught up in financial and trade globalisation. In this regard, statements by Brazilian Finance Minister, Guido Mantega, to the effect that the world was entering an era of financial, currency and trade wars should be noted, as well as the fact that the leadership of the leading countries of the world reacted to these statements very seriously.[96]

As a consequence, players of lower economic rank may not only be involved in the geo-economic and financial games that the major global powers will play but will also be drawn into the politico-military confrontations and secret special operations. Moreover, it cannot be considered an improbable hypothesis that the wave of Middle East revolutions in 2011 has already become the first phase of the transfer of this global economic game on to this very military and political field.[97]

According to our understanding, all this means that it is necessary for India, which has managed to weather the most acute phase of crisis, and even more so for Russia, which continues to bear very painful losses from the crisis, to very carefully prepare for the upcoming era of struggle, possibly war. As has been clearly delineated in this paper, the future geo-economic architecture, which is on the make can operate 'in all fields and by all means' unleashing a localised or even global chaos, using the instruments of finance, economy, military, politics and terrorism.

To counter these destructive trends, what is of urgent need is comprehensive monitoring of the developing situation in all 'geo-economic battlefields.' Of paramount importance too are extensive consultations with

96. For example, see: the speech of the Minister of Finance of Brazil, Guido Mantega, on 28 September 2010, in front of industry leaders in Sao Paulo (*BBC News*) on the beginning of global currency and trade wars, an interview with Mantega in the *Financial Times* on 9 January 2011 and the memorandum by Treasury Secretary, Timothy Geithner, to the G20 summit of finance ministers <http://www.fd.ru/news.htm?id=37726>

97. *op. cit.* no. 39: 130-132.

international forces that do not want to send the macro-regional or even world processes into chaos and are equally determined not to be on the losing side in the 21st century battles for global domination.

9 Globalisation of Trade and Economy

Financial Crisis and its Implications on Energy Markets

Sunjoy Joshi

'Energy Security,' 'Sustainability' and 'Climate Change' have formed the grist of national and international policy documents for several years now. However, it often makes more sense to try and appreciate them today as broad signifiers rather than phrases with any well-defined meaning. Over the years, the terms have undergone a gradual metamorphosis as they have gone on accreting new layers of meaning with each passing crisis. The consequence being that all three today occupy a common yet keenly contested discursive space that lies at the intersection of various conflicting and contradictory narratives. As we witness the shift in the global balance of power, it is bound to exacerbate the tensions between these conflicting narratives, tensions which will be the key to defining global relationships in the emerging world.

This paper looks at the energy situation of countries like India and China to identify the resource pressures under which their national policies will need to necessarily operate. It should be fairly obvious that the limited room to manoeuvre available for domestic policy makers who are expected to deliver solutions, will more and more define the stand that many similar countries will be forced to take in international forums, notwithstanding any global consensus (or the lack of it) over issues of Climate Change and Trade. At the same time, the shift in power that is accompanying the growth of the new economies will make the possibility of any real consensus ever more difficult.

The Road up to the Economic Crisis and Its Aftermath

When the oil shock of 1974 forced the world to look at Energy Security, the meaning of the term was circumscribed within two broad sweeping concerns—reliability of supplies and their cost. Energy Security was predominantly a supply side concern limited to tying up reliable sources of energy at affordable prices. The first oil shock brought into the limelight the bleak outlook on resources, highlighted by the Club of Rome. What began as the ideas of a fringe group soon captured a wider audience until the discourse of scarcity got gradually mainstreamed through the Brundtland Report—Our Common Future.[1] Sustainability issues now came to be tagged on to the hitherto limited space circumscribed by Energy Security. In many ways thus, the Rio Earth Summit, which brought environmental concerns centre stage, marked the climax of this narrative.

However, paradoxically enough, the second half of the Nineties was simultaneously seeing the perspective shift from the consumer to the producer. Extreme volatility on the downside has made predictability of demand and faltering returns on investment the foremost threats to Energy Security. The constraint was no longer availability of resources, but continuing investor confidence that alone could ensure supplies. Demand uncertainty emerged as the biggest threat to long term sustainability of supply. The accompanying counter narrative was that technology could indefinitely continue to find resources and deliver solutions provided markets were allowed to perform. Sustainability of supply, the counter narrative argued, was a mere corollary to growth and development addressed via technologies that led to "Ecological Modernisation"[2] in robust self-regulated markets that automatically created the right incentives for this process.[3]

The 21st century announced the arrival of China on the global arena, India following a fair distance behind. The world suddenly awakened to the clamour of two and a half billion new aspirations, seeking *nirvana* in the

1. *Report of the World Commission on Environment and Development: Our Common Future*, UN Documents, 1987, <*http://www.undocuments.net/wced-ocf.htm*>.
2. Eckersley, R. (2004). *Green State: Rethinking Democracy and Sovereignty*. Cambridge, MA: MIT Press.
3. See Bernstein, S. (2001). *The Compromise of Liberal Environmentalism*. New York: Columbia University Press.

techno-miracles of the new century. The ensuing coal-fired growth of the emerging economies was only symptomatic of their hunger for resources. It revived the worst nightmares fuelled by the Club of Rome, bringing resource poverty and climate change back into focus in the debate on energy security.

The threat to sustainability now came to be articulated as the possible disastrous impact of the emerging economies on the global resource situation. However, with the world economy ticking away at its fastest pace in years, Economic Growth and Development were still assumed to be perpetual motion machines fired by little save the fertile imaginations of the infallible bankers of Wall Street. Inevitably, the larger issue of the un-sustainability of the Growth Machine of the developed world remained relegated as a secondary concern.

The narrative was not very different from the discourse on sustainability as espoused in the Brundtland Report, which even as it had recognised "that some consume the earth's resources at a pace that would leave little room for future generations"[4] strangely enough, had gone on to point fingers not at the Organisation for Economic Cooperation and Development (OECD) economies but at sub-Saharan Africa as it referred to droughts, floods and all manner of natural disasters as entirely man-made threats resulting from the sins of over-cultivation and deforestation. More significantly, these disasters were most likely to affect the impoverished in poor nations. It is not too difficult to draw parallels with the manner in which the Climate Change alarmists repeated similar claims highlighting the fate that awaited the most vulnerable as a result of global warming. The solutions therefore, as pointed out in Copenhagen and Durban, lay in actions by the emerging world.

And then disaster struck. Actually, the crisis of 2008 itself was no unforeseen Black Swan event—as early as 2004 people within the banking system had begun expressing the fear that the world had got onto a roller coaster it would be unable to get off until it crashed.[5] The crash, when it did come, also triggered some of the most aggressive and

---

4. *op. cit.* no.1
5. See Roach, Stephen (2005). *Original Sin*. 25 April, *<http://www.morganstanley.com/views/gef/archive/2005/20050425-Mon.html>*

coordinated interventions across the developed world. Yet, in spite of all the interventions, the year 2009 saw the first real decline in global Gross Domestic Product (GDP) since 1946.

As the crisis continues to take its toll, Energy Security has garnered yet another dimension: the rhetoric of climate change has come to be discretely tempered by far more pragmatic concerns about continued economic growth and more importantly the creation of jobs in faltering economies. As energy prices become critical in the creation and sustenance of jobs everywhere, including the OECD, policy enthusiasm for stringent carbon control measures that could impact energy costs finds political support not too easy to come by. Yet again, policy makers across the globe are left grappling with the multiple and often-contradictory meanings inherent in the terms Development, Energy Security and Sustainability as they grope for solutions in a crisis that threatens power structures both within and between nations.

There is some evidence to show that besides the net fall in emissions forced by de-growth in the OECD, the effect of the economic crisis has on the whole, not been very positive for global efforts to combat climate change. Following the slowdown, in countries like China and India that registered increasing energy consumption, the rate of increase seems to have outpaced the growth in the GDP. This is hardly surprising as the increase largely came from more infrastructure spending, which would be highly energy intensive. At the same time, in 2011, the European Union (EU) has shown a surprising appetite for US coal which ensured that the decline in its emissions (2.8%) has fallen behind the decline in its energy consumption (3.1%).[6]

The political posturing behind the competing claims and counter claims through what are often outright trade and control negotiations masquerading as negotiations for 'saving the planet,' the rhetoric that attempts to label the 'good guys' and the 'bad,' is really beyond the scope of this paper. What this paper attempts to do is to take a bottom up view from the perspective of a country like India and examine the options available to policy makers. Once these are understood, we may be better placed to

6. *BP (British Petroleum) Statistical Review* 2012.

hazard a guess as to the position these countries may be found taking in global negotiations.

Impact on Energy Markets

Post 2009, if anything was more significant than the decline in the global GDP, it was the fact that this decline was highly uneven, masking islands of continued growth. Economic powerhouses, like India and China, even while slowing down considerably, have continued to see enviable growth in their national GDP.

The year 2010 did initially surprise by showing signs of an early recovery. It seemed the interventions had indeed worked. Unemployment in the Eurozone seemed to have peaked at 10 per cent. But then systemic fatigue inevitably overtook the overdose of steroids, unleashed as stimulus packages to revive credit growth in economies paralysed by deep distrust. High fiscal deficits in Europe now usher in an era of spending cuts that threaten to curtail growth. Counter cyclical spending sparked sovereign debt troubles. What began with Greece threatens to engulf more and more of the OECD economies. However, distress in the OECD has only served to further show case the trend already in evidence during the first half of this decade, *viz.*, OECD growth may already have peaked. It could be some time, if ever, before these economies regain earlier levels of growth. And yet, as Europe lags, Asia continues to lead the shift in the centre of gravity of the world economy: a shift that has now been more than a decade in the making.

As the world economy heads into what is a possible second dip, the energy consumption patterns observed during 2008-09 serve as illustrative indicators of the trends. In spite of major deceleration in the Indian economy, and the cooling down of the Chinese economy, across the range of the dominant energy commodities: fossil fuels such as oil, gas and coal, energy consumption trend lines through 2011 endorse the fact that Asian consumers are set to emerge more and more as the price makers rather than the price takers. In more ways than one, the year 2009 marked a watershed, with the USA seeing its primary energy consumption decline from 2,320 metric million tonnes of oil equivalent (mmtoe) in

2008 to 2,206 mmtoe in 2009.[7] The USA thus registered a 4.9 per cent decline in energy consumption, while the EU saw an even greater decline of 5.8 per cent. However, in spite of the not so insignificant drop in the consumption of these countries, global consumption fell by a mere 0.88 per cent that year. China and India saw their energy consumption increase by 8.2 per cent and 9.3 per cent, respectively. The year 2009 saw Chinese consumption overtake that of the USA to become the world's largest energy consumer. With Japan's energy consumption declining by 8 per cent, 2009 also saw India overtake Japan as the world's fourth largest energy consumer.

Following the crisis, had China and India mirrored global trends, the world's consumption of primary energy would have fallen by 4 per cent rather than the 0.88 per cent actually recorded. Before the crisis, the years 2002 to 2007 had already seen 85 per cent of all incremental oil demand coming from emerging markets. It was on the back of this demand that trade in speculative paper had caused crude prices to spike up to $148 a barrel (bbl) in June 2008. Little wonder then that India and China came to be blamed for everything from global warming to Hurricane Katrina to the next energy crisis.

Thus, the recession may in fact have provided a necessary reality check. Between 2008 and 2009, global oil consumption declined by 1.7 per cent to 84 million barrels per day (mbpd). Crude oil prices collapsed to below $35 per bbl in December 2008 until the 6 mbpd of OPEC spare capacity came in handy to help prices climb back over $80 per bbl.

The false dawn of 2010 did see energy consumption across the world surge again by 5.5 per cent, but hopes were short lived. If 2011 showed anything, it was that the crisis was never really over. As Stephen Roach summed up "as the global economy..... (goes) from crisis to crisis...the cure has become part of the disease".[8] In spite of a 3.1 per cent decline in the EU, 2011 saw global consumption increase by 2.5 per cent. More importantly, buoyed by the shale gas boom, the USA has shown definite signs of disassociating from trends across the Atlantic; the US energy consumption declined by marginal 0.3 per cent.

7. Energy consumption figures are taken from *BP Statistical Review 2012*.

8. Roach, Stephen (2012). "Macro Malpractice", *Project Syndicate*. 20 September. <*http://www.project-syndicate.org/commentary/federal-reserve-quantitative-easing-ecb-emerging-economies-by-stephen-s--roach*>.

The spurt in gas consumption notwithstanding, the US in 2011 remains the world's largest consumer of oil at 834 million tonnes; China follows with a distant 462 million. In 2009, even as oil consumption shrank in all but 20 countries across the globe, China, Saudi Arabia and India between them still consumed an incremental 1 mbpd. The good news is that with shale gas production ramping up in the USA, markets globally seem fairly complacent that no major supply issues are likely to emerge. BP's ill fortunes in the Gulf of Mexico and the ensuing threat of tighter regulatory and environmental monitoring of oil and gas developments have done little to shake that belief. Even as the Middle East exploded into civil unrest following the Jasmine revolution, the regime collapsed in Libya, and post-Fukushima Japan prepared to shut down its nuclear establishment: supply disruptions seemed remote.

Today, the policy impetus across the OECD and Asian emerging economies as well as the shape of their growth charts are increasingly getting out of sync. The shale gas boom in the USA may only make Asian suppliers turn evermore to markets in Asia. The first signs were already evident as the 'Asian premium' that used to be charged by OPEC producers traditionally from Asian buyers had, by March 2010, become an 'Asian discount.' This premium had averaged about $1.2/bbl since 1988. However, in March 2010, Saudi Arabia sold Arab Light crude to Asia at $6.37/bbl less than it charged European buyers. Kuwait and Iraq followed suit.[9] The oscillation between premium and discount notwithstanding, Russia, so far dependent on Western markets, in December 2009 opened up a potential 300,000 barrels per day (bopd) export route to East Asia through its new terminal at Kozmino near Nakhodka.[10]

How Long: King Coal?

Traditionally, China and India have been dependent on coal to fuel most of their energy needs. With the third and fourth largest reserves respectively in the world, the share of coal in the fuel basket of China is

---

9. Petroleum Intelligence Weekly, quoted in *The* Wall Street Journal dated 25 May 2010, <*http://online.wsj.com/article/SB10001424052748703341904575266913913683300.html*>

10. Stanton, Chris (2010). "Russia Threatens Asian Premium", *The National, 13* February, <*http://www.thenational.ae/business/energy/russia-threatens-asian-premium*>.

over 70 per cent whereas India draws 52 per cent of its energy from coal. Access to cheap sources of domestic supply in both countries has been the primary reason for this high dependence, which has given both countries a measure of energy independence, which they could not have otherwise had.

Fuelled by a massive demand for power to energise a rapidly growing manufacturing and infrastructure base, coal demand is likely to see a continuing surge in both countries. However, in spite of substantial domestic reserves, both countries are facing shortages in domestic supplies because of constraints in production as well as bottlenecks in transportation. Both are finding it increasingly attractive to rely on coal imports to fuel their more rapidly developing coastal areas. This is even as China's share of global coal production jumped from 40 per cent in 2005 to touch 50 per cent by 2022. India's coal production, which had been growing more or less steadily at 5.0 to 8.0 per cent annually until 2009, has subsequently faltered. Consequently its share in global coal production has marginally declined from 8.05 per cent in 2009 to 7.64 per cent in 2011. Saddled with problems in obtaining environmental clearances as well as inability to acquire land for mining, the annual growth in domestic coal production has fallen to a bare 2.5 per cent.

The net consequence has been that both India and China have become the biggest importers of coal. China also consumed half of all the coal in the world in 2011. Demand for coal is fuelled by the rapid expansion in coal-fired generation capacity in both countries. The skewed energy mix is apparent as 79 per cent of China's and 68 per cent of India's electricity fed into the grids comes from coal. Already in 2009, the two countries accounted for 22 per cent of the total global trade in coal. Needless to say, movements in global coal prices in the coming years are therefore going to be increasingly determined by what happens to demand for the commodity in these two countries.

In 2010, 52 per cent of India's generation capacity was coal based. More importantly, it contributed over two-third of all the power fed into the grid. Given low plant load factors, the contribution of renewable energy (other than hydro) was 3.7 per cent even though it made up for nearly 10 per cent of the installed capacity. Hydro contributed a 15 per cent share of power to the grid compared to its 23 per cent share as installed capacity. It is therefore not difficult to see why coal is bound to remain the backbone of the power sector for several years to come.[11]

Over the next two decades, China and India, between them, could require additional imports of close to a billion tons: 660 million for China and 300 million for India. That represents 80 per cent of all the incremental demand for coal in the world. The logical question arises, from where would India seek to acquire these growing imports? On the supply side, the only significant increases in exportable coal would probably be from Australia, Mozambique, Botswana, Colombia and Russia. These, too, may potentially be limited to roughly 300 million tonnes.

What this mismatch does to international coal prices can only be guessed. Besides international competition for securing supplies and the price risks involved, inadequate growth in the infrastructure to handle coal imports will meanwhile continue to play the spoilsport. Therefore, assured supply would continue to remain a persistent problem.

Of the roughly 100 billion tonnes of proved reserves India has, the extractable half has an ash content as high as 45 per cent. Current levels of coal production, however, do still give India enough reserves for the next hundred years or so. However, given India's extreme energy poverty, a per capita power capacity as low as 80 watts per person, a fourfold increase in generation becomes non-optional. What this translates in terms of actual generation comes close to 3250 terawatt (TWh) of electricity over the next decade.[12] The big question is what fuels are going to be used to fire this huge capacity. Nuclear as well as renewable energy while seeing a steady growth in net capacity addition are not seen to be making a very significant dent in the net share of fuels in the energy basket over the next two decades. Events in Japan have also put brakes on any policy enthusiasm for nuclear plants, which are going to face increasing local resistance. This puts the onus of basic energy poverty alleviation targets for growth on fossil fuels, and that too largely on coal.

---

11. Planning Commission (2006). *Integrated Energy Policy: Report of the Expert Committee.* New Delhi: Government of India. p.27

12. See Gupta, Rajan, Harihar Shankar and Sunjoy Joshi, "Development, Energy Security and Climate Security: India's Converging Goals," *<http://cnls.lanl.gov/~rajan/Gupta_orf_writeup_v9.pdf>*.

At current rates of growth, it may be possible to attain a coal production of 1.4 billion tonnes per annum, which with increasing efficiency could just feed about 300 gigawatt (GW) of coal-based power plants. However, having reached these coal production capacities, the available coal reserves would have declined to just about 35 years. This could act as an automatic peak beyond which further addition in coal-based capacities would come with great difficulty and only on the back of enhanced coal imports. Thus, if domestic coal reserves were to limit the expansion of coal-fired capacity in India, the country's CO_2 emissions are unlikely to increase beyond 4.5 billion tonnes, which would still be a very modest 3 tonnes per capita.[13]

The Game Changer: Non-conventional Gas

Meanwhile, the most significant development in the last few years has been the phenomenal growth of non-conventional gas. The USA, which had been eyeing increasing liquefied natural gas (LNG) imports in 2006, has now become self-sufficient in natural gas, thanks to developments in shale gas. Gas production in the USA saw a 25 per cent surge as the share of gas in the energy basket rose from 24.2 per cent to 27.6 per cent from 2005 to 2011. The immediate impact has been that Henry Hub prices in 2012 fell below $2.5 per million British thermal unit (mmBtu), giving the USA the benefit of highly discounted energy prices. The reverberations of the shale gas boom in the USA are now being felt across the world.

As shale production grew in the USA, LNG intended for the US is available across the Atlantic. Spot gas prices in Europe have begun to be influenced by Henry Hub price movements. As early as 2009, this had created a big differential between available spot prices and the longer-term oil indexed prices of gas being supplied by Russia. Ironically, enough, since Russia's European gas contracts followed crude prices with a six to nine months lag, gas prices in Europe reached their highest level ever in the beginning of 2009 in a contra movement to crude prices. The result was that European buyers, already smarting from the slowdown, frantically

13. Gupta, Rajan, Harihar Shankar and Sunjoy Joshi (2011). "Development, Energy Security and Climate Security: India's Converging Goals", in Sunjoy Joshi and Marlies Linke (eds.), *Sustainable Development and Climate Change*. New Delhi: Observer Research Foundation and Academic Foundation.

scoured for alternative sources. Gazprom subsequently had to renegotiate minimum contracted volumes and introduce an element of spot prices to be able to retain market share. According to the *BP Statistical Review 2012*, the economic slowdown saw gas consumption in Europe declined by 6.5 per cent from 490 billion cubic meters (bcm) to 460 bcm between 2008 and 2009. They recovered to earlier levels in 2010 only to fall as much as 10 per cent in 2011 to 448 bcm, a decline far greater than the 3.1 per cent fall in its energy consumption. It is cheap coal from the USA that has been substituting gas in the EU, resulting that in spite of falling total energy consumption, coal consumption has increased by 3.6 per cent.

A slowing Europe in the throes of a crisis rediscovered its appetite for cheaper coal from the USA now available across the Atlantic. Thus even before the first LNG export terminals appeared in the USA, shale gas exports have already begun: not as gas but as coal to Europe, showing the inherent inter-connectedness of energy markets. So, even as European gas consumption continues to fall, the EU has seen coal consumption rise for two successive years in 2010 and 2011. This can certainly not be good news for votaries of clean energy in the EU.

Figure 9.1

Natural Gas Prices

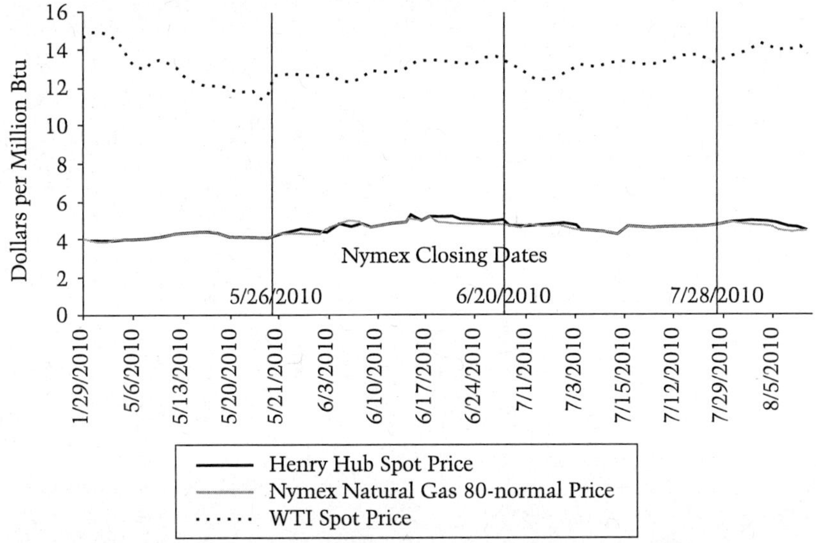

Source: USD Energy Information Administration (EIA), Natural Gas Weekly Update,19 August 2010.

The appearance of the shale boom almost on cue with the Financial Crisis thus completely altered the dynamics of global gas markets. Unconventional gas includes not just shale gas but also Coal Bed Methane as well as tight gas: the last denoting conventional gas reserves locked in reservoirs having very low permeability making it traditionally very expensive to produce the resources until advances in technology such as horizontal drilling and fracturing have made these resources extractable and viable. It is difficult to put a figure on exactly how much of non-conventional gas resources remains locked in the world. Estimates have tended to vary widely as not only the reserves have not been proven but also because reserves in the ground may not necessarily translate into an extractable resource. The pace of extraction will consequently depend on factors such as gas prices, costs and the pace of regulatory and policy frameworks.

Table 9.1

Estimate of Unconventional Gas Reserves[14]

Region	*Coal Bed Methane (Tcf)*	*Shale Gas (Tcf)*	*Tight-Sand Gas (Tcf)*	*Total (Tcf)*
North America	3,017	3,842	1,371	8,228
Latin America	39	2,117	1,293	3,448
Western Europe	157	510	353	1,019
Central and Eastern Europe	118	39	78	235
Former Soviet Union	3,957	627	901	5,485
Middle East and North Africa	0	2,548	823	3,370
Sub-Saharan Africa	39	274	784	1,097
Centrally planned Asia and China	1,215	3,528	353	5,094
Pacific (Organisation for Economic Cooperation and Development)	470	2,313	705	3,487
Other Asia Pacific	0	314	549	862
South Asia	39	0	196	235
World	9,051	16,112	7,406	32,560

While the above figures are guesstimates made on the basis of geological comparisons, it is estimated by *IHS Energy* that the US shale gas reserves would be sufficient to last 100 years of supply at current rates

14. Holditch, S.A. (2006). "Tight Gas Sands", *SPE Paper* 103356, *Distinguished Author Series* 2006. Data after Rogner, H.H. (1996). *An Assessment of World Hydrocarbon Resources*, May. ILASA, WP-96-26, Luxemburg, Austria, <*www.spe.org/jpt/print/archives/2006/06/JPT 2006_06_DA_series.pdf*>.

of consumption.[15] A Massachusetts Institute of Technology (MIT) study[16] released in 2010 places the current mean projection of recoverable shale gas resource at approximately 650 trillion cubic feet (Tcf), with low and high projections of 420 Tcf and 870 Tcf, respectively.

Low Henry Hub prices are already playing a spoiler mounting pressure for export of gas from the USA. Wood Mackenzie has projected that by 2020 nearly 70 per cent of all gas in the USA could come from unconventional sources. According to estimates by J.P. Morgan, European shale gas could be sufficient to displace the equivalent of about 20 million tons a year of LNG by 2015, and about 60 million tons a year by 2020. The US shale gas could grow by 2015 to a similar scale as the entire global LNG market currently and has already demonstrated its ability to displace significant LNG volumes.

The study by MIT quoted above only states the obvious when it says that natural gas will play an increasing role in the US energy mix in the next several decades contributing increasingly to electricity generation. In 2010 and 2011, while energy consumption in the USA declined by 0.4 per cent, the increasing share of gas brought about a 1.8 per cent decline in its CO_2 emissions. Natural gas being the obvious fuel of choice for replacing the several coal-fired power plants that have outrun their economic cycle, the next decade could see a greater shift in transport fuels as well. This is most likely to happen first with private passenger transport in the USA. On a net energy basis, gas contributes just half the carbon emission compared to coal. Therefore, natural gas for the USA presents the easiest and most viable option to address both emission control and affordable energy.

The question on everyone's mind today is whether a similar shale gale would sweep across Europe and China leading to a global over-supply of natural gas. While chances of any massive global oversupply are remote, continuing recession is mounting pressure for delinking gas prices from traditional crude indexation.[17] However, over the next few years, China can

---

15. Ryan, Jane Van (2010). "Natural Gas 'Shale Gale'", *Energy Tomorrow Blog*, 15 March, <*http://blog.energytomorrow.org/2010/03/natural-gas-shale-gale.html*>.

16. Connors, Stephen R. *et al. (2010). The Future of Natural Gas*. Cambridge, MA: MIT, <*http://web.mit.edu/mitei/research/studies/report-natural-gas.pdf*>.

17. "IEA sees gas glut until 2015, rising coal role", <*http://www.reuters.com/article/idUSLA022008*>.

be expected to move rapidly to tap its own considerable shale gas reserves. Its second offer for 20 shale blocks concluded in October 2012 with 152 bids.[18] The overhang will most likely continue to depress LNG and impact coal prices to the benefit of Asian countries. Eventually, LNG prices will be highly dependent on gas markets such as China, India and Japan.

The US example in fact shows how market-based models of energy governance have the potential to fuel innovation. So far, except for the USA, unconventional gas resources had been largely ignored. While Europe may also see shale gas development progress within the next five years, India may continue to lag because of retrograde policy frameworks. The country's unmet gas demand continues to be the consequence of poor infrastructure and severely restrictive markets. This has impacted its ability to import gas through cross-country pipelines or as LNG and also curtailed the expansion of gas networks across the country. Underdeveloped and government-controlled gas markets continue to hamper the growth of investments both for domestic production and for necessary infrastructure to facilitate imports as either LNG or trans-national piped gas.

China and India were late entrants in international gas markets, setting up their first LNG terminals almost simultaneously in 2004. The share of gas in the overall energy mix is far below OECD countries. The share of gas in China's energy basket while growing rapidly just about climbed to 4.5 per cent in 2011. India, which on the back of new production from the East Coast in 2009 had climbed beyond 10 per cent, is today facing imminent decline in domestic production. It is estimated that policy, infrastructure and market constraints could slow the development of shale gas in India for at least another 10 years. However, as the USA and Europe and then China unlock their shale potential, countries such as India are going to be better placed to take advantage of even conventional gas markets.

18. "China says 83 companies make bids in second shale gas tender", *Reuters*, 25 October 2012, *<http://in.reuters.com/article/2012/10/25/china-shale-tender-idINL3E8LP1R220121025>*.

Figure 9.2

Relative Share of Natural Gas in the Energy Mix

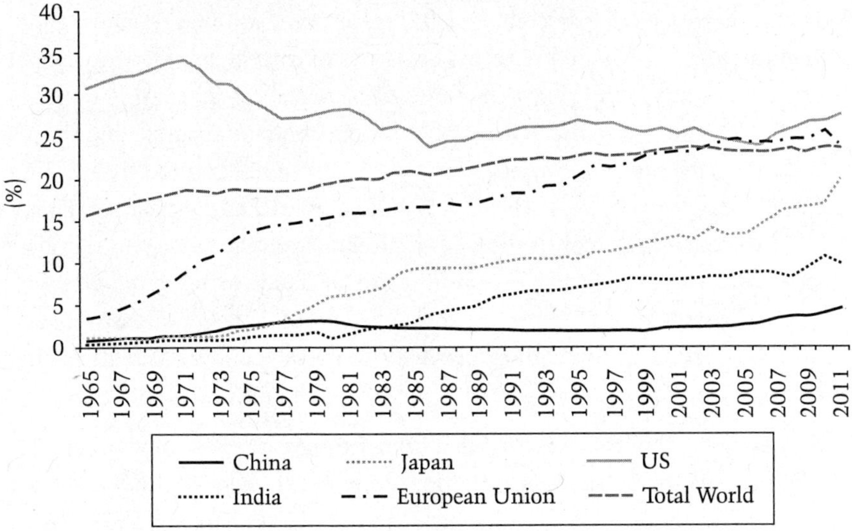

Source: *BP Statistical Review of World Energy, 2012.*

To meet commitments made in the Copenhagen declaration of achieving up to 40 per cent reduction in the carbon intensity of its GDP, the National Energy Administration (NEA) had unveiled plans to cut China's excessive dependence on coal and reduce SO_2 emissions by 7.8 million tonnes and CO_2 emissions by 1.2 billion tonnes. The NEA estimates that gas consumption by 2015 would reach 260 bcm making for 8 per cent of China's energy needs.[19] The thrust to use more and more natural gas has been a part of the Chinese policy. Acknowledging pressures to clean up its air, China's 2020 Plan, laid out in its National Energy Policy and Strategy Report (2004), spoke of promoting the use of natural gas as a clean alternative to coal and reiterated the target spelt out in the 10th Five Year Plan of raising the contribution of natural gas to the energy basket to 10 per cent by 2020. Whether China's target of achieving a 10 per cent share for natural gas may or may not be reached, gas demand can be expected to continue to grow at 10 per cent or more year on year.

19. <*http://english.peopledaily.com.cn/90001/90778/90862/7076933.html*>.

Even historically, the increasing share of natural gas in the energy mix has been the single largest contributor to lowering the carbon intensity of energy use across the world. In the USA with gas more or less consistently providing between 25 per cent and 35 per cent of all energy since 1965, carbon intensity (measured in terms of tonnes of carbon dioxide emitted per tonne of oil equivalent energy) has ranged between 2.7 and 2.9. Countries like the UK and Germany with high coal dependence through the 1960s eventually saw the carbon intensity of energy use decline from 3.5 to levels at par with the USA with the rising share of natural gas (see Figure 9.2). With fossil fuels continuing to dominate over the next two decades, the trends in the emerging economies are unlikely to be very different. Barring efficiency gains brought in through pro-active policy measures, any significant decline in the carbon intensity of these economies is also going to come largely through fuel substitution of coal by natural gas.

Post the economic crisis, even as natural gas consumption in the OECD declined by 3.1 per cent (Europe alone registered a decline of almost 6 per cent), China's consumption grew by 9.4 per cent to touch 88.7 bcm in 2009. Interestingly, in spite of rapid growth, the share of natural gas in China's total fuel mix still remains a mere 4.50 per cent in 2011 (the global average is 24 per cent). However, by 2009, with gas still commanding a modest 3.67 per cent overall share of the energy mix, China had already overtaken the gas consumption of countries like Japan (87.4 bcm) and the UK (86.5 bcm).[20] On the back of production of domestic gas from its new east coast discoveries, India saw consumption jump of 26 per cent to 52 bcm in one single year (2009), increasing the share of natural gas in the fuel mix to almost 10 per cent from 8.4 per cent a year ago. The promise, however, has been short lived with 2011 marked by declining domestic production in the face of a combination of geological problems, contractual disputes and spats over gas pricing between contractors and the government.

So far, the biggest constraint that has stalled the growth of gas in both China and India has been the limited availability of gas. Paradoxically, enough early attempts in the 1980s to tune in to global energy shifts and promote the use of natural gas ended up in policies that artificially

---

20. Source for figures: *BP Statistical Review of World Energy 2010 and 2012.*

depressed gas prices. Both countries through the 1980s kept well head prices artificially low to promote use of natural gas by the fertiliser industry. Once in place, the political economy of agriculture ensured that prices were allowed to move only for selected sectors leading to very complex pricing practices. It is not merely that different users paid different prices, the same users could pay different prices depending on the source of gas. By a strange irony, therefore, initial attempts to promote the use of gas ended up trapping producers and consumers into artificially low price regimes. Once in place, these served as a disincentive for the induction of technology as well as investments in greater domestic production. Consequently, domestic markets failed to integrate with international markets. Controlled pricing regimes made it risky for companies to invest in infrastructure for gas imports as also its extensive distribution. Thus, besides curtailing investments in the exploration and production of domestic resources, this resulted in poor infrastructure to tie up long-term gas supplies and make for the shift to natural gas that was in evidence across the world. Both countries have over the years been making progressive attempts to make domestic prices more closely aligned with international markets. As these attempts gather steam, not only the share of gas in the energy basket is bound to rise but also the attractiveness of both China and India as burgeoning gas markets is bound to increase.

Meanwhile, softening gas prices post-2008 are also creating conditions conducive to price reforms in China and India as they juggle policies and relax price controls to access an energy resource that has since been trading at significant discount to crude. India and China raised prices for domestic gas almost simultaneously in May-June 2010. While India nearly doubled the price of gas being produced by state-owned companies to bring them at par with private producers, China raised gas prices by 25 per cent. Over the coming years, given the resource constraints faced by both the countries, the march towards market prices will probably be inexorable. Given the upheaval in international gas markets, with the cry against oil indexed gas prices getting shriller by the day, it is no longer a question of if, but rather how long it will be before China and India fully integrate their gas markets with the world.

What this means for gas producers across Russia and Central Asia is yet to be seen. With incremental growth in demand and more open and transparent pricing regimes, one can anticipate an increasing interest in supply lines from Central Asia as well as southern and eastern Russia. The next few years may, therefore, see the pipedreams of yester years become real. Even at the height of the 2008 boom in oil and gas prices, as a pragmatic EU hesitated sanctions in the wake of the Georgian conflict, Russia seeking to demonstrate its independence from a single market expressed its resolve to diversify eastwards with the ESPO (East Siberia Pacific Ocean Pipeline). Central Asian producers simultaneously leveraged both Europe and China to extract higher gas prices from Gazprom. It is hardly a coincidence that if August 2007 saw work start on the Central Asian Gas Pipeline (CAGP) linking Turkmenistan-Uzbekistan-Kazakhstan and China to supply 30 bcm of gas to China, November 2007 had Gazprom promising, first Turkmenistan and then Uzbekistan, prices at par with Europe for their gas.

The CAGP is already a reality with the first section consisting of two 650 km pipelines, being commissioned in December 2009.[21] Beginning at the Turkmen-Uzbek border city Gedaim, it is meant to transport gas from China National Petroleum Corporation's (CNPC's) gas fields on the right bank of the Amu Darya river in Turkmenistan through central Uzbekistan and southern Kazakhstan before reaching Horgos in China's Xinjiang Uygur Autonomous region. From Horgos onward, the 8,700 km Second West East Pipeline, on which work started in 2008, will cross 14 states linking domestic gas fields in the Pearl River and the Yangtze River delta to end in Hongkong. By the end of 2013, this could supply 30 bcm of gas from Central Asia.[22]

India's distrust of Pakistan as well as pricing and transit fee disputes have long stalled the much negotiated India-Pakistan-Iran (IPI) Pipeline. As with its counterpart from Turkmenistan (the TAPI), both projects have been the subject of a fair amount of diplomatic shuttling back and forth between the partner countries. However, even as India, unsure of whether to play ball with a pariah Iran, continued to dither over the IPI, Pakistan desperate for gas has gone ahead and inked the agreement. Even as construction on

21. "Flow of Natural has from Central Asia", *<http://www.cnpc.com.cn/en/press/Features/Flow_of_natural_gas_from_Central_Asia_.htm>*.

22. "Central Asia-China Gas Pipeline", *<http://www.cnpc.com.cn/en/aboutcnpc/ourbusinesses/naturalgaspipelines/Central_Asia□China_Gas_Pipeline_2.htm>*.

the project is yet to begin, the Pakistan Minister for Petroleum and Natural Resources recently announced that Iranian gas can be expected to flow into Pakistan by December 2014.[23]

So far, a major sticking point in both projects, IPI and TAPI, had been the price. However, in May 2012 Pakistan, Afghanistan, India and Turkmenistan signed the Gas Sale and Purchase Agreement for the TAPI. The pipeline will carry 90 million metric standard cubic meter per day (mmscmd) of gas with Pakistan and India availing of 38 mmscmd each.[24] With substantial new domestic gas in India coming from new East Coast discoveries in 2009, the immediate pressure for transnational pipelines coming to India had eased somewhat. But successes in domestic exploration have not kept pace. Meanwhile, the momentary surge in gas production has created far greater gas dependency. With ever rising demand and the existing fields setting into decline, India is already hard pressed to scour for gas imports either as LNG or piped gas or both. With Pakistan already having inked a deal, it will not be long before Iranian gas makes its way close to India's borders. Acknowledging that even Iran cannot be consigned to its pariah status in perpetuity, it is a matter of open speculation as to how long will it take commercial imperatives make the push into India a matter of course.

Conclusion

Countries like India even as they move rapidly to upscale their poverty alleviation programmes will have to greatly expand employment generation in the secondary and tertiary sectors of the economy in the next few years. While proper planning and efficiency measures will certainly help in reducing energy demand, the energy intensity of the emerging pattern of growth itself cannot be wished away.

High international coal prices, constraints on domestic coal production and its transport, civil society pressures for clean air (more than international calls for carbon cuts) and comparatively more attractive

---

23. "Iranian Gas will Start Flowing from December 2014: Dr Asim Hussain", *The Express Tribune*, 4 September 2012, *<http://tribune.com.pk/story/430894/iranian-gas-will-start-flowing-from-december-2014-dr-asim-hussain/>*.

24. "TAPI Pipeline Gas Sale Agreement Signed", *The Hindu*, 23 May 2012, *<http://www.thehindu.com/business/Economy/article3449588.ece>*.

gas prices in the short run will work in tandem to create the conditions for these economies to shift into being far more gas dependent than they are at present. Over the next two decades, the largest cuts in emissions will result not so much from new technologies but rather from efficiency gains and fuel switching within the fossil fuel space. Natural gas is more and more going to emerge as the fuel of choice. Even if they rapidly move to unlock their own conventional and non-conventional gas potential, the growth in demand will be too high to keep pace with local production. As this happens, we can foresee major shifts in global inter-dependence, which can be expected to re-define global geo-politics.

The coming years are therefore likely to see different national alignments as regional priorities getting re-defined and Asian countries increasingly deal and transact with their neighbours. Of course Asian energy markets will need to mature before greater interconnectedness makes price integration a possibility. Yet the future does hold the promise for far more nuanced and complex patterns of cross-dependence. Countries like India and China have few options but to seek a far more assertive role in Middle East as well as in Central Asia. However, rather than leading to increased or hostile competition for resources, the way forward will be through increasing market integration.

Meanwhile, as international negotiations continue to lose their way over the most optimal interventions (emanating from top down approaches that go on building ever more complex emission control models), national policies will continue to meander through the path of least resistance using far more pragmatic bottom up approaches.

10 Geo-Climatic Concepts as Instruments in Global Governance, Business and Ideology

Vera Sorokina

Despite the fact that it has been a subject of primary interest to mankind for centuries, the climate of the earth remains an under-investigated science and the weather, to date, is still seldom predicted precisely. All that can be thought of as well established is that the world's climate has cyclically changed many times during the Earth's geological history and that global warming and cooling (including the 'glacial periods' on a planetary scale) has occurred tens and hundreds of millions of years before the appearance of mankind. Currently, climate scientists identify at least four groups of cycles that affect climate:

- 'extra-long' cycles lasting 150-300 million years, correlated with the solar system's orbital period around the nucleus of our galaxy;
- 'long' cycles correlated with the dynamics of the surface (lithosphere) plate movements of the crust (tens of millions of years);
- 'short' cycles caused by fluctuations of the Earth's rotational axis (lasting 93,000; 41,000; and 25,750 years);
- 'ultra-short' cycles correlated with periods of solar activity (11 or 22 years cycles).

The nature of climactic changes associated with planetary cycles is also influenced by many other factors, such as the thermal inertia of the oceans or volcanic activity and, after the appearance of life on Earth, influence on the climate of the Earth's biosphere, etc.

As relatively accurate systematic meteorological observations began only about 200 years ago, the amount of accumulated scientific data on climate is completely insufficient to predict climate change in the long term. Therefore, responsible scientists are extremely cautious in their approach to answering the question on weather and to what extent it is possible that human activity can impact on processes of such a scale as the global climate.

Climate Change as an Issue in International Cooperation

In the last quarter of the 20th century, human impact on global climate began to be actively discussed at the international level. Moreover, the initiators of this discussion were not disturbed either by the shortage of scientific facts or the absence of proof for the concepts put forward. All doubts were interpreted in favour of the hypotheses that anthropogenic influences affect the atmosphere of the planet and its climate as a whole.

The Concept of Global Warming

The development of 'climatic' anthropogenic hypotheses began with the discussion of human impact on the environment. In 1972, the first International UN Conference on the Human Environment (the first 'Earth Summit') was held in Stockholm on the initiative of the USA and with the participation of representatives from 113 countries. The conference adopted a concept that had been proposed slightly earlier in 'The Limits to Growth: A Report for the Club of Rome' by Donella and Dennis Meadows as the basis of the new global environmental policy.

According to Meadows' model, the rapid growth of the Earth's population and the need for a sharp increase in food production as well as the growth of industrial production will cause long-term exhaustion of agricultural land, depletion of the majority of non-renewable mineral resources and large-scale environmental pollution in the coming decades. All of these threaten mankind with global catastrophes as early as the beginning of the 21st century. Critics of the model pointed out that it does not take into account the diversity of trends and the pace of development in different countries; ignores the ability of social systems to respond to the threats of change in industrial, environmental and population policy; and is clearly neo-Malthusian in nature (right up to the appeals to 'decisively stop population growth').

Despite the criticism, since 1972 (when the first 'Earth Summit' was held and the UN Environment Programme [UNEP] was created), state agencies and organisations aimed at solving environmental problems such as environmental ministries and departments began to be introduced. Ecology became a part of international policy and diplomacy and norms of environmental law have begun to develop.

A new environmental outlook became a part of global processes. In 1975, American climatologist, Wallace Broecker first used the term 'global warming' in the magazine, *Science*. His article was titled *Climate Change: Are We on the Brink of a Pronounced Global Warming?* Broecker proposed contemplating the change in trend from the gradual decline in global temperatures (which has been occurring since the 1940s) to the increase in temperatures. Moreover, not only did he label the possible effects of human influence on the climate as the term 'global warming,' but he also said that a 0.8 degree celsius rise in temperature over the 20th century was caused by the increasing concentration of carbon dioxide (CO_2) in the atmosphere.

Thus the main culprit for the global rise in temperature across the globe came to be identified. In July 1988, after a speech in the US Senate by climatologist James Hansen that was widely publicised in the media, the term 'global warming' came into common usage. Moreover, Hansen emphasised the existence of a cause and effect relationship between the greenhouse effect and the observed warming.

The creation of the Intergovernmental Panel on Climate Change (IPCC) in 1988 and the signing in 1992 of the UN Framework Convention on Climate Change (UNFCCC) made the term 'climate change' widespread within the scientific and global political community. It refers to climate change directly or indirectly caused by human activity that alters the composition of the world's atmosphere and is superimposed upon natural climate fluctuations observed over comparable time periods.

The Fight for the Ozone Layer

The phenomenon known as 'ozone holes' was the first globally recognised ecological problem. These are a localised drop in the concentration of ozone in the Earth's ozone layer. This is the layer that protects the Earth from the direct effect of ultraviolet rays of the sun, which are harmful to life.

In 1985, British experts discovered that during the Antarctic spring, the content of ozone in the atmosphere (especially over Antarctica) is substantially reduced. They remembered the hypothesis made back in 1974 by the American scientists, Mario Molina and Sherwood Rowland that the depletion of the ozone layer may be caused by the impact of CFCs (chloro-fluorocarbons and bromo-fluorocarbons) on the atmosphere. At that time, CFCs were widely used as cooling agents in refrigerators and air conditioners as foaming agents for plastics, in aerosols, etc.

Three years later, in 1977, representatives from 32 countries developed the first Plan of Action for the Protection of the Ozone Layer at a meeting in Washington. The USA, Sweden, Norway and Canada were the first to ban the use of CFCs in aerosols. In March 1985, the Vienna Convention for the Protection of the Ozone Layer was adopted. Its signatory countries proposed to take measures to reduce the negative impact on the ozone layer, to conduct systematic research on the ways for its preservation and to create an international structure to coordinate the protection of the layer.

In 1987, more than 36 countries signed the Montreal Protocol on Substances that Deplete the Ozone Layer. This protocol now determined specific measures for the reduction or elimination of the production, consumption, import and export of ozone-threatening substances, as well as the timing of their withdrawal from economic circulation. In an unprecedented show of awareness and cooperation, the world community voluntarily adopted measures to restrict the use of CFCs and then their complete withdrawal from production without waiting for sound scientific evidence.

At the same time, in the course of the 'anti-CFC' campaign, the American scientists, Rowland and Molina and the Dutch chemist, Paul Crutzen were awarded the Nobel Prize in 1995, thus crediting their hypothesis with the status of scientific truth. From 1990 to 1999, the list of banned ozone-depleting substances was expanded to 96, and the number of countries who had joined the Protocol rose to almost 200. Virtually all countries ceased operations with the banned substances that had allegedly destroyed the ozone layer.

Later, when the hype around CFCs had died down, the voices of sceptical scientists began to be heard. It turned out that the Nobel laureates used only laboratory models to justify their hypothesis and did not take into account the natural processes that regulate the concentration of ozone in the stratosphere. It was also shown that the reduced concentration of ozone levels observed in different regions of the world is regularly associated with natural fluctuations, rather than with anthropogenic factors.

In this connection, Russian scientist, Grigory Kruchenitsky, Head of the Laboratory on Ozone Monitoring at the Central Aerological Observatory, referred to the Montreal Protocol as "a document without a scientific basis, a grand scam, and outlined by financial goals".[1] The famous Russian geographer and member of the Russian Academy of Sciences, Andrey Kapitsa, also emphasised that the decrease and increase of ozone concentrations in the stratosphere is a natural "oscillation process".[2]

Indeed, in 1998, the concentration of stratospheric ozone over Antarctica 'suddenly' returned to the 'pre-Montreal' level and then began to increase. Although the theory of the impact of CFCs on ozone hole formation was destroyed, the ban on the production of CFCs was not abandoned. The winners were producers of CFC-free refrigerants, primarily the US companies. Only 10 years after the Montreal Protocol, the production of new refrigeration compressors in the USA rose by 60 per cent. From the global replacement of CFC refrigeration equipment with other cooling agents, the world's chemical companies earned tens of billions of dollars.

In Russia, which produced approximately 60 per cent of the world's CFCs and was the biggest US competitor in this area, the CFC industry has been completely destroyed as a result of the implementation of the Montreal Protocol. Also, according to Grigory Kruchenitsky, "...the money that was allocated for the modification of chemical production went to the destruction of the chemical sector of the state defense industry".[3]

1. Sinitsyna, T. (2007). "Ozone Holes or Ozone Fraud?", *RIA Novosti*, 14 September.
2. Moldavanov, D. (1998). "Vestnik and Vedomosti", 23 October <*http://www.aircon.ru/useful/details.php?item_num=501*>
3. *op. cit.* no.1.

The Climate Aspect in the Concept of Sustainable Development

In the next phase, the climate aspect found its place in the concept of sustainable development. In 1983, the UN established the World Commission on Environment and Development. Four years later, the Commission warned in a report, 'Our Common Future' that humanity must make many changes in its economic activity and way of life, or else it would face many problems born of a sharp deterioration of the environment. The Commission, named the Brundtland Commission after its Chairman, the former Prime Minister of Norway, who, calling for a "new era of environmentally friendly economic development," declared: "Humanity has the ability to make development sustainable to ensure that it meets the needs of the present without compromising the ability of future generations to meet their own needs".[4]

In June 1992, the UN Conference on Environment and Development was held in Rio de Janeiro. It consolidated the 'concept of sustainable development' presented in the Club of Rome reports, beginning with the aforementioned report by Meadows and developed by the Brundtland Commission as a new model for the development of a civilization, "satisfying the needs of the present and not compromising the ability of future generations to meet their needs".[5]

The Conference also adopted the Declaration on Environment and Development, Convention on Climate Change and Biodiversity, and the Declaration on Forest Resources and Desertification, as well as the Agenda for the 21st Century—a programme of how to make development sustainable from the social, economic and environmental points of view. Among the Agenda for the 21st Century, proposal was to control the growth of the planet's population, called "a sustainable balance between consumption, population, and the Earth's life-supporting capacity".[6]

---

4. Agenda for the 21st Century and Other Documents of the Conference in Rio de Janiero in Summary (1993). Geneva: Center for Our Common Future.
5. Report of the World Commission on Environment and Development (MKOCP) (1989), "Our Common Future". Moscow: Progress.
6. *op. cit.* no. 4.

Greenhouse Gases and Emissions Trading

The next step is the Kyoto Protocol. This is an international document on limiting and reducing emissions of greenhouse gases (GHGs), which was adopted in Kyoto, Japan, in December 1997. The Protocol defined the obligations of countries to limit and reduce anthropogenic emissions of gases that cause the greenhouse effect and global warming. Its significant feature was that it first applied the mechanisms of international trade for greenhouse gas emission quotas.

However, in 2001 the USA, which accounted for more than 36.3 per cent of greenhouse gas emissions, announced its withdrawal from the Protocol. The central argument for the withdrawal, presented by President George W. Bush, was that the data given in the agreement were based on "incomplete state of scientific knowledge [about] of the causes of and solutions to global warming".[7]

Russia, whose share of world greenhouse gas emissions in that period was about 17 per cent, approved the Kyoto Protocol in 2005 without any preconditions. It must be kept in mind that, as a country in the extreme north, it obviously needs to use a far greater amount of gas and oil for heating (and hence produces significant emissions of CO_2). It must also be noted that the terms of Russia's inclusion in the agreement do not take into account the fact that the vast Russian forests consume hundreds of millions of tons of CO_2 per year and thus release huge amounts of oxygen into the atmosphere. Russia could have demanded compensation for this and used the funds for financing for forest regeneration measures. But this did not happen.

Thus, even if scientific ambiguity is factored out, the Kyoto Protocol in its present form is extremely unfair to Russia. For this reason, it was assessed extremely negatively by Russian experts. Russian President Vladimir Putin's advisor, Andrey Illarionov, called the agreement "an ecological holocaust for Russia" in an interview with the British Daily Telegraph in 2004.[8]

---

7. Bush, George W. (2001). "Text of a Letter from the President to Senators Hagel, Helms, Craig, and Roberts", Office of the Press Secretary, 13 March.

8. *Novaya Gazeta* 37: 27-30, May 2004.

Subsequent 'Climate Summits': From Failure to Failure

At the 2002 Summit in Johannesburg (South Africa), the 10-year results of "movement towards sustainable development" (after the Rio Summit) was reviewed. These results have been disappointing in all respects. More countries in the world have become poorer (with a few exceptions such as China). The average income gap between the poorest and the richest has doubled. Although the threat of ozone depletion has 'naturally' gone off the agenda, the 'threat of global warming' has been actively placed on the agenda.

Already at the summit in Johannesburg, it became clear that the majority of countries interpret the concept of sustainable development in an entirely new way—based on the principle of 'every man for himself.' Developing countries announced that they would pursue sustainable development through economic growth and trade with the maximum use of their competitive advantages. They also demanded that the USA, Canada, Europe and Japan (where 17% of the world's population consumes 70% of total resources) free developing countries of their debts, open access to the markets of developed countries, and increase aid and investment.

Developed countries proposed a shift from bilateral agreements to agreements with major multinational corporations. About 200 transnational corporations participating in the summit, including Dupont, Toyota, British Petroleum, BMW, and others, said they were ready to implement programmes in poor countries to develop 'environmentally friendly infrastructure' and 'green technologies.' But the proposal carried a condition: privatise the energy and water supplies of poor countries for the benefit of transnational corporations. The majority of poor countries refused and the summit ended in failure.

In December 2009, the Copenhagen Summit, upon which there were great hopes, also failed miserably because it was known well before hand that its main task would be to conclude a new convention on reduction in harmful emissions to replace the Kyoto Protocol expiring in 2012. Even before the opening ceremony of the summit, it became known that the positions of developed and developing countries on this issue were fundamentally contrary to each other.

Developed countries proposed to base a new version of the Protocol, which limited the permissible global warming to less than 2 degrees. Developing countries (including China) demanded more stringent restrictions—not more than 1.5 degrees. They also added the condition that developed countries would have to pay for environmental programmes in developing countries. China demanded that Western countries importing Chinese goods pay for quotas on the emission of greenhouse gases produced by Chinese enterprises involved in export. It was supported by the Asia-Pacific Economic Cooperation (APEC) members.

These positions could not be reconciled, in part, because of the scandal that arose around the draft agreement developed by representatives of the USA, Great Britain and Denmark. In this draft, developed countries could produce nearly twice the emissions of developing countries; moreover, it was proposed to transfer monitoring of the finances allocated for the fight against climate change from the UN to the World Bank, which is, as is well known, controlled by the developed countries.

The reaction of countries not involved in the draft (The Group of 77, consisting of developing countries led by China) was of course negative. For the adoption of the final UN summit document, the unanimous decision of the 193 participants of the summit was required. But since most countries opposed the text, it was not put to a vote, but was merely 'taken into consideration.' In connection with this, European Commission President, Jose Manuel Barroso, not hiding his disappointment, was forced to admit that "this accord is better than no accord. This was a positive step but clearly below our ambition." German Chancellor, Angela Merkel gave a similar assessment, noting that "the only alternative to the agreement could be failure".[9]

In contrast to these two politically correct statements by high-ranking officials, the guru of the worldwide 'green' movement, James Lovelock, has been more outspoken, noting at the end of the summit: "I have a feeling that climate change may be an issue as severe as a war. It may be necessary to put democracy on hold for a while".[10]

9. "Developing Countries Strongly Condemned the Climate Agreement", *RIA Novosti, Ecology*, 19 December 2009.

10. Klein, Naomi (2010). "A New Climate Movement in Bolivia", *The Nation*, 21 April.

It is notable that a whole series of scandals developed around the failed Copenhagen Summit. Firstly, before the summit, information about a multi-billion dollar tax fraud in Denmark emerged in world media around the sale of quotas on greenhouse gases. The second scandal, dubbed 'Climategate,' arose due to the publication of 10 years' worth of extensive, compromising scientific correspondence on the Internet, as well as documents on global warming. It turned out that the Climate Research Unit (CRU) at the University of East Anglia deliberately suppressed facts that refute the anthropogenic nature of global warming. It was the assessments of the CRU at the University of East Anglia that were officially used in the calculation of global temperatures over the land area. Thus, the documentary evidence presented by the hackers' concocted reasons to create the belief that anthropogenic theory about global warming to a large degree was falsification of facts.

Simultaneously, 140 climate scientists from different countries have approached UN Secretary General, Ban Ki-moon with the demand to provide scientific evidence that changes to the Earth's climate are caused by human activity, i.e., have an anthropogenic nature (and are "not normal variations caused by solar cycles, ocean currents, changes in the Earth's orbit, and other natural phenomena"), before taking any hasty action.[11] Finally, one more effective nuance to the atmosphere of the Copenhagen Summit was given by the scandal around the prediction of the melting of the Himalayan glaciers—no earlier or later than by 2035.

This prediction was made as early as in 2007 by the authoritative UN IPCC. Such an obviously unfounded prediction was the basis of the documentary by US Vice President, Al Gore, 'An Inconvenient Truth' about the dangers of global warming. The film was widely advertised and was awarded an Oscar. Also in 2007, the IPCC, its Chairman Rajendra Pachauri and Al Gore were awarded the Nobel Prize for their work that identified and disseminated a large body of knowledge about climate change by human activities and pointing out the measures needed to counteract such change.

However, the four leading glaciologists decisively and conclusively refuted the catastrophic prognosis in the influential journal *Science*.

11. Petrov, A. (2010). "Global Warming: A Conspiracy of Money Grubbers", *Free Press*, 31 September, <*http://svpressa.ru/world/article/29712*>.

Because of the large public response, the UN was forced to start verification of the IPCC in relation to the promulgation of such a gross 'mistake.' The IPCC had to admit that a key thesis for substantiation of global warming was taken from an interview with an Indian scientist in 1999, who later admitted that his arguments were based on assumptions rather than on scientific facts. The organisation's reputation was severely damaged, and the career of Rajendra Pachauri was put in jeopardy, as was partially the theme of global warming itself.

The signing of a new agreement to replace the Kyoto Protocol, previously scheduled for December 2010 in Cancun (Mexico), was again postponed. Russia, Canada and Japan, who had been dutifully fulfilling their obligations to reduce emissions, opposed the extension of the protocol. They stated that developing countries already produce more emissions than developed ones and that the Kyoto Protocol did not take this into account at all.

In contrast, developing countries (India, China, the Latin American bloc, the small island states) believe that a 'second period' of—or a reprieve for—the Kyoto Protocol is vital. They insist that rich countries have already thrown huge amounts of greenhouse gases into the atmosphere (since the Industrial Revolution of the 18th century), and therefore poor countries should have a legitimate chance to develop their industries without reducing emissions.

New Ecological Ideology and Religion

In the sphere of international agreements, 'global environmental policy' may have met with apparent difficulties because of contradictions between developed and developing countries—but the theme is captivating the public consciousness at an increasing rate. Today, both environmental threats that actually exist and those that are far-fetched are being used to create new global ideologies aimed at fundamental changes in human psychology.

James Lovelock and the Gaia Theory (The Gaia Hypothesis)

Among the many ideas that underlie the ideological basis of environmental movements, a special place is occupied by James Lovelock's hypothesis (theory) of *Gaia* (Earth). This British scholar who advised NASA on its research programme on the moon and planets in the early 1970s came to the conclusion that the Earth is a self-regulating biological system that can maintain a comfortable climate and chemical composition for the organisms inhabiting it. (It is noteworthy that as early as in the 1930s, similar ideas were developed in the 'theory of the noosphere' by the greatest Soviet geochemist and philosopher, Vladimir Vernadsky.)

But then Lovelock veered away from a fully scientific hypothesis, that the planet maintains its own homeostasis, to the assumption that the earth itself is a living creature. This was reflected in his naming the 'theory' after the Greek Earth goddess (the figurative and mythological name *Gaia* was suggested to the author by the famous English writer William Golding). Gradually, the scientific trappings of Lovelock's hypothesis were replaced by a spectacular myth. The author predicted that the living planet, striving for self-preservation, would be forced to negatively respond to human interference in the environment. This is reflected in the names of his six books: the first was titled *Gaia: A New Look at Life on Earth* and another was called *The Revenge of Gaia*. So, in 2006, Lovelock again argued that climate change would come under control... if we reduce greenhouse gas emissions. In his last book, *The Vanishing Face of Gaia* (2009), the 90-year-old Lovelock mocked those who "try to save the Earth." The planet can take care of itself: it was the people living on it that needed to be saved... and urgently.

But does it need to be saved? Lovelock is convinced that "to expect that sustainable development or 'business as usual' can adequately respond to the environmental crisis is like to hope that the victim of lung cancer will be cured if he stops smoking. The earth is ill with a fever caused by the number of people."[12] The reason for environmental problems is not so much the amount of emissions as the number of people.

What is *Gaia*'s future? According to Lovelock, the first is the total death of both the planet and humanity. The second is that Mother Earth will get rid of its 'tumor' in the form of humanity and remain alone (*The Revenge of Gaia*). Finally, humanity will become a healthy nervous system

12. Lovelock, James (2006). *The Revenge of Gaia: Why the Earth is Fighting Back and How We Can Still Save Humanity*. Santa Barbara, CA: Allen Lane.

of the planet, bringing itself into harmony with Mother Earth. Of course, Lovelock himself personally no longer has any hope for the last scenario. His idea is popular both in fiction and in Hollywood. The Gaia theory was first embodied in a series of novels by Isaac Asimov. The plot of James Cameron's film *Avatar* has the same idea: the biosphere super-organism of the planet *Pandora* is the living soul *Eywa* (*Eywa* acts to keep the ecosystem of *Pandora* in perfect equilibrium).

Having the status of an 'independent scholar,' Lovelock is not only a recognised guru of the 'greens,' but has a very practical impact on attitudes to the climate issue. For example, it was Lovelock in 1966, with an electronic detector, who detected the presence of CFCs—in the atmosphere, which played an important role in the development of the theory of the ozone layer, and later the greenhouse effect. In 2001, the *Gaia* hypothesis was recognised *de facto* by the international scientific community. At the final declaration of the international climate change conference in Amsterdam, the phenomenon of climate change was defined as proposed by Lovelock earlier: "The Earth behaves as a single, self-regulating system, consisting of physical, chemical, biological, and human components".[13]

Radical and Moderate Anti-anthropocentric Environmental Movements

The *Gaia* theory has given rise to a number of environmental sects and movements that proclaim a 'non-anthropocentric' model of existence on this planet. The ideology of these sects asserts that human place in the ecosystem cannot and should not be different from the place of a plant, animal or virus, and anthropocentrism is seen as a negative worldview that is discriminatory in relation to nature.

Two major trends in the ideology of environmental protection that stand in opposition to anthropocentrism are ecocentrism and biocentrism. They differ only in that biocentrism places above all the interests of the individual (fauna or flora) and ecocentrism the interests of the ecosystem. Biocentrism, as it were, brings the value system of liberal democracy to the animal world. The supporters of radical biocentrism are represented by 'liberators' of animals (they free laboratory animals intended for

13. Lovelock, James (2009). "The Revenge of Gaia", *Ecological Postmodern*, 17 January, <*http://ecocrisis.wordpress.com/2009/01/17/1111/*>.

experiments and release the animals from kennels and zoos 'in the name of freedom'), as well as supporters of the global 'vegetarianisation' of humanity. From the standpoint of ecocentrism, the rights of any individual can and should be violated if they threaten a species or ecosystem. The logic of ecocentrism is the logic of nature.

However, both biocentrism and ecocentrism indicate that man, his life and his interests by themselves cannot be considered the measure of value. Individual human life has no greater value than the life of an individual bear or a ferret. Based on this logic, they conclude: "there are too many people on Earth" and both human life and human progress are not significant values.

The next step in the development of biocentrism was 'Deep Ecology.' The term was introduced in the early 1970s by Norwegian philosopher, Arne Naas, aiming to fundamentally (deeply) change views on environmental and social issues. For this, according to Naas, an essential ideological reorientation of civilisation is needed. Namely, self-awareness as being a part of the Earth and a part of a whole will cause a person to act in the name of life and to defend its non-humanoid forms. Deep Ecology proposes working with awareness through 'self-identification with others.' This is a question of psychotherapy, or as Naas calls it, social therapy. To restore the 'ecumenical relations with the outside world,' supporters of Deep Ecology are turning to Eastern spiritual traditions and ancient pagan rituals and rites. For this purpose, the so-called Council of All Beings was created, which helps people to speak on behalf of other life forms. It is no accident that one of the most important principles of Deep Ecology is to preserve wildlife intact. Thus, 'depth' offers a way to escape from the world and from its social conflicts.

Obviously, the variants of anti-anthropocentrism described are to a large degree focused on the renunciation of progress—in essence, on the secondary archaisation of mankind and human degradation as such. So it is not by chance that the American scholar and professor of English at City University of New York, Anne Gardiner, in her article *Human sacrifice at the altar of Gaia* has called the *Gaia* theory and 'Deep Ecology' two "handmaidens of the Culture of Death".[14]

---

14. Gardiner, Anne Barbeau (2008). "Human Sacrifice on the Altar of Gaia", *New Oxford Reviews*, June.

Climate Initiatives for the Third World and the Developed West

Six months after the Copenhagen Summit, Bolivian President Evo Morales called the People's World Conference on Climate Change and Mother Earth's Rights. Morales invited "social movements and defenders of Mother Earth, scientists, teachers, lawyers, and government"[15] to his anti-Copenhagen summit in Bolivian Cochabamba. At the conference, Morales promulgated the concept of the 'Good Life,' which accused the capitalist system of causing the climate troubles and the existing crisis "with its unbridled industrial development".[16]

What is the solution to the environmental impasse to which capitalism has lead humanity, as seen by Morales? It calls for the abandonment of the urban madness, "to reassess the communal way of life..." once lived by "the [American] Indian peoples" and to combat climate change by restoring the traditions of indigenous people and to create a lifestyle that does not depend on non-renewable energy sources, but is based on a harmonious relationship between man and nature. What are proposed here is regression, stagnation and rejection of development—in full accord with the 'deep ecologists'—as a way to deal with "the excesses of consumer society and mindless technological progress". To who is it proposed? The entire world?

But developed countries have no intentions of abandoning the achievements of a 'consumer society' and the benefits offered by progress. For example, the consumer movement LOHAS (Lifestyle of Health and Sustainability) is rapidly growing in these countries. Not only prices but also values are important for LOHAS. Moreover, these values include product quality, safety for oneself and one's health, and even some measure of social justice. Thus, a follower of the ideology of LOHAS does not go to coffeehouses that serve coffee, peasants who actually grow the coffee beans are paid a pittance, that is, adherents of LOHAS try to combine their health and their pleasure with localised social responsibility.

The majority of current Western 'eco-activists' have views that are not far from the views of LOHAS. No longer do they preach 'austerity in the

15. Klein, Naomi (2010). "A New Climate Movement in Bolivia", *The Nation*, 21 April.
16. "The Concept of 'a Good Life'—Bolivia's Point of View." Article in English distributed by the Bolivian delegation at the UN in April 2010, <*http://www.proza.ru/2010/10/18/1596*>.

name of ecology' and are not concerned with protest demonstrations. They argue that 'the 'green' idea does not pose a threat to economic growth; to the contrary, 'green' products and technologies have become the engines of development for 'a new industry.' 'Green' technologies refer to, among other things, the most efficient use of resources, the transformation of global energy and its transition to the expanded use of renewable energy sources. Eco-activists propose to avoid damaging nature by carrying out simple sensible rules (conservation of water and energy, recycling materials, sorting and recycling waste, etc.), but at the same time, 'living with pleasure.' Thus, the militant asceticism of early ecologists has been replaced by the 'enlightened hedonism' of the 'new green' or 'eco-sexual' (their slogan is "Being green is not just trendy—it is terribly sexy!").

Conclusion

In conclusion, it should be noted that the environmental initiatives (of which only a small part has been noted) are aimed at denigration of the role of man and human development. They have skilfully shifted the issue from the sphere of high priorities, replacing them with far-fetched, often mythologised environmental priorities. In the most radical and progressive variants of environmentalism, an idea is being put forward, which is, in essence, a call for secondary archaisation and anthropological regression. Moreover, Western countries try to impose these ideas of regression as an inescapable norm upon developing countries, yet preach for themselves 'gentle environmentalism,' 'enlightened hedonism' and moderate consumption. It is obvious that these double standard notions will lead to a sharpening of the contradictions in the world and, above all, the contradictions between developed and developing countries.

It is no less obvious that these contradictory trends—economic, socio-cultural, military and political—will make the world all the less sustainable and secure.

11 The Migration Process in Russia

Integration or Enclavisation?

Marina Volchkova

Migration is one of today's most pressing problems. Massive flows of people from underdeveloped economies (Southern countries) are streaming into the prosperous countries of the 'Northern Ring' (Northern countries) in search of a better life. These flows have reached such a size that some researchers describe the changes associated with them as an 'actual revolution.' According to the International Organisation for Migration (IOM), the migration figure was 214 million people in 2010, representing 3.1 per cent of the world's population.

In the not so distant past, the migration process in the former Soviet Union was of a controlled and planned nature. Large masses of workers migrated within the country for seasonal work or to work at large construction projects. Besides, migrant skilled workers took up permanent residence in a given region in order to operate large industrial plants. After the collapse of the USSR, voluntary mass migratory movements began. They were triggered by acute trouble—ethnic conflict broke out in a number of regions of the former USSR and people fled from the combat zones. In some of the new republics, people of Russian origin were forcefully expelled. The closure of the Soviet industrial circuit led many people who had been deprived of work to leave their place of residence in search of livelihood.

The law 'On entry into the Russian Federation' was passed in Russia in 1993 in order to regulate the voluntary migration of citizens, and the country became a part of international migration routes, quickly becoming one of the largest immigration centres in the eastern hemisphere.

According to the World Bank, Russia was ranked second in the world after the USA in terms of the scale of migration since 2005. Around 38.4 million immigrants entered the US in 2005 and more than 12 million migrants come to the Russian Federation annually.[1] Russia holds the second place in the list of top 'migration corridors'. The list includes the following routes between Mexico-US, Russia-Ukraine and *vice versa*, Bangladesh-India, Turkey-Germany, Kazakhstan-Russia and *vice versa*. Mexico-US corridor is used by approximately 10.3 million migrants annually, and a total of 12.8 million migrants move through the Russia-Ukraine and Russia-Kazakhstan corridors in both directions.[2] Countries that receive large numbers of migrants and countries through which they pass face several challenges.

In this paper, these challenges are examined using Russia as the main theme. The general migration situation in Russia is characterised as follows:

- Steady population decline: Russia, like many developed countries in the North, needs foreign labour force due to its demographic crisis;
- Russia's lack of a targeted immigration policy: While admitting millions of migrants, Russia so far has not developed a policy for their adaptation and integration;
- The growth of illicit (illegal) labour migration, primarily from the Central Asian republics and China: The number has grown steadily, insofar as it suits both employers, who use them as cheap labour, and a certain section of the local authorities, not to mention the migrants themselves (who do not have to pay taxes);
- Increase in crime: According to the Interior Ministry, illegal migrants are markedly worsening the crime situation in the country;
- Deterioration of the sanitary and epidemiological situation: Migrants, as shown by both worldwide and Russian experience, often become disseminators of infectious diseases;
- The emergence of ethnic tensions.

---

1. World Bank (2008). Migration and Remittances Factbook.
2. Sergeer, M. (2008). "Russia: A Magnet for Migrants", *Nezarisimaya gazeta*, 21 March.

The Demographic Situation in Russia and the Problem of Labour Migration

In 1992, the death rate in Russia exceeded the birth rate for the first time since 1944. Subsequently, the continuing decline of the Russian population was partly offset by immigration. Primarily, these were Russians, displaced in large numbers from the breakaway Soviet borderlands—the Caucasus, Central Asia and the Baltics. For 15 years, from 1992 to 2007, immigration 'compensated' for the natural loss of 4.3 million people (without this substitution, the natural decline of Russia's population would have exceeded 11 million).

Since 2003, increased substitution for the natural decline of the population has occurred on account of migrants (Figure 11.1).

Figure 11.1

Substitution for Natural Population Decline by Net Migration

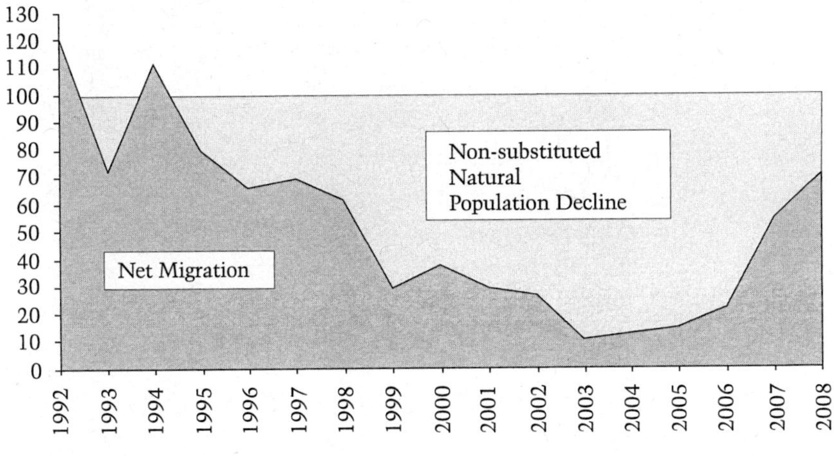

Source: *http://www.demographia.ru/articles-*

In subsequent years, an increase in net migration and a decrease in the natural decline led to a slowdown in population decline. In 2008, 71.0 per cent of the natural decline was replaced by net migration (in 2007, 54.9 per cent and in 2006, 22.5 per cent). In 2009, for the first time in many years, a minimal growth in population, rather than decline was recorded. In 2009, 1,764,164 people were born and 2,013,590 died. The natural population decline, was 249,426 people. However, net migration in the same year equalled 272,726 people. Thus, the overall increase in the population of Russia amounted to 23,300 people.

This trend has even provided some politicians with grounds to cautiously claim a 'demographic turning point for the better.' However, all serious-minded demographers warn that a further decline in the birth rate lies ahead. According to Programme Director of the Independent Institute for Social Policy, Natalia Zubarevich, Russia will face a new demographic low in late 2012, and therefore the deficit of working population will have to be compensated for once again by migrants.[3] At this time, the numerically smaller generation born in the 1990s will begin to work and will have reached childbearing age (in the years following the collapse of the USSR, the birth rate in Russia was very low). The situation is compounded by the fact that the numerically large post-war generation will retire at the same time. Thus, according to estimates of the Ministry of Economic Development and Trade, by 2015, the total number of citizens in Russia will decrease from the current 89.8 to 77.2 million people.

A World Bank report issued on 24 March 2010, stated that Russia can expect the problem of an acute labour shortage. It is predicted that in the next 20 years, Russia will need more than 12 million immigrants to compensate for the reduction in labour force.[4] The majority of Russian demographers are even more pessimistic. According to them, the natural decline in the working-age population could reach 19 million people prior to 2026, and in the coming two decades, about 25 million immigrants will be required. These developments place on the agenda the need for continued import of migrant labour.

Until recently, there were two conflicting opinions on this issue. According to the first, the country cannot do without guest workers due to the demographic crisis. Proponents of the other approach argue that given the potential political, religious and ethnic consequences, it is better not to admit migrants or at least to severely restrict their number. Reputable and popular demographers in Russia hold that mass migration

3. Ibid.
4. *RIA Novosti*, 24 March 2010.

is necessary. They describe the situation in the Russian labour market as "unprecedented, and if nothing is done—catastrophic".[5]

According to the Director of the Centre for the Study of Forced Migration in the (CIS), Zhanna Zaionchkovskaya:

> An alternative to this immigration scenario could be the shrinkage of Russia's populated area to the south-western sector of the European part of the country. Stagnation and then decline of the eastern regions (including the Urals) up to the loss of territory, the partial scrolling back of production, and cuts to pensions and other social programs. Thus, for Russia the issue of immigration is simultaneously also the fate of its territory and its continuity.[6]

At the same time, Zaionchkovskaya believes that complete substitution for the natural decline of Russia's working-age population on account of the inflow of immigrants is unlikely. "The Russian economy in the period under consideration will inevitably operate in conditions of a labour-scarce labour market".[7] Truth be told, labour shortages threaten almost all developed countries. On the global market of immigrant labour, Russia will have to compete for workers with the USA and European Union (EU) countries; their birth rate is the same as in Russia, and they expect to attract one million migrants per year. Countries that supply migrants (Latin American countries, Indonesia and China) regularly send labour forces to the population deficit countries of the 'Northern Ring.'

It is predicted that birth rates in 'immigrant supplier countries' will decline to 1.85 children per woman by 2050, that is, there too the birth rate will be lower than necessary for reproduction.[8] This means that in the near future, Russia's rivals will try to 'redirect' the flow of migrants from Commonwealth of Independent States (CIS) countries at least partially. Moreover, this process has already begun. Due to Russia's inconsistent migration policy, a partial reorientation of migration from the CIS to other countries is taking place. For example, residents of Moldova and Ukraine

5. Grafova, L. (2010). "You'd Better Come to Us: How Does the Demographic Low Threaten Us?", *Rossiiskaya Gazeta*. 30 June.

6. Zaionchkovskaya, Zh. (2010). "Migration: This is the Fate of Russia", *Rossiiskaya Gazeta*, 30 June.

7. Ibid.

8. Vishnevsky, A. (2003). "Great Sparsely-Populated Power, Russia-2013: High Death Rate and Low Fertility Rate", *Russia in Global Politics*, July-September.

are increasingly going to work in Spain, Italy and Portugal. The flow of migrants from CIS countries to Russia has decreased by 15 per cent in 2009.

The main argument of opponents of large-scale migration is that the process would be accompanied by irreversible changes, as a result of which Russia will cease to be the Russia that it is. Such fears are not unfounded. To date, the flow of 'Russian immigrants' from the former Soviet republics has already dried up. The programme of 'Voluntary Resettlement of Compatriots Living Abroad to the Russian Federation' from 2006 was a hopeless failure. The total number of people who came to Russia through the government repatriation programme was 21,213,[9] though Moscow had counted on the arrival of an estimated 3-3.5 million ethnic Russians from the former Soviet republics and about the same number of representatives of these new 'titular' nations—that is, those who had already studied in Soviet schools, speak Russian well, and who are by and large similar to Russians by mentality and culture.

The flow of migrants coming to Russia today is already largely non-Russian. According to the Federal Migration Service of the Russian Federation (FMS RF), about 13 million foreign citizens entered Russia in 2009; about 70 per cent of these immigrants came from CIS countries and 30 per cent from further abroad. Proponents of large-scale migration recognise that this process may lead to a significant change in the ethno-sectarian balance of the country. As pointed out by Anatoly Vishnevsky:

> With a high degree of probability, towards the middle of the 21st century migrants and their descendants will constitute greater than one-third of the country, in the second half of the century they may exceed half its population, and by the end of the century, the descendants of today's Russians will already have become the minority. [However, in his opinion], this is by no means a specifically Russian situation: there are many other countries in the 'Northern Ring' (European countries, the US, Canada, and Japan) in a similar situation.[10]

9. *RIA Novosti*, 3 July 2010.
10. Vishnevsky, A. (2000). *Replacement Migration: Is a Solution to Declining and Ageing Populations*. New York: United Nations.

Problems in the Integration of Migrants

Whatever be the dispute between supporters and opponents of large-scale migration, the fact is that millions of migrants do enter Russia every year. The question is how to help them adapt to the culture and traditions of Russian life.

In Soviet times, the model for coexistence of different peoples was based on shared ideology. It was assumed that Soviet citizens did not identify themselves on sectarian or ethnic grounds, but on the concept of the 'Soviet Man' and the communist ideology. After the collapse of the USSR, when the Soviet identity was fractured, the argument that the "time of great ideologies had passed" gained wide circulation in both Russia and the West. Therefore, a number of experts advised Russia to follow the approaches of 'civilised countries' on the issue of integration of various ethnic elements into a single society.

By and large, there are two approaches. The first is the assimilation or the "melting pot," where the various ethno-cultural and ethno-confessional elements join the host culture that receives them. The second is the multicultural model, where the basic cultural differences of migrants are preserved.

Models of Integration of Diverse Ethnic Elements

Model Based on Common Ideology (USSR)	Assimilation Melting Pot (USA)	Multi-Culturality (Canada, Great Britain, Germany)

The problem is that both these recipes have proved to be unpalatable. The USA went in for the assimilation model; the immigrants from different countries were expected to 'melt' into the American identity, and come to uphold a 'single standard.' But this process began to 'bog down' as soon as the flow of immigrants increased.

Each year, up to one million illegal immigrants enter the USA from Mexico alone. According to various estimates, there are a total of 10-12 million illegal and semi-legal immigrants in the country. They tend to live in isolated enclaves, they do not want to obtain legal grounds for their stay in the country (as then they would have to pay taxes) and they do not learn English. Legal Hispanic immigrants have even demanded that Spanish be given the status of an official language. Samuel Huntington in his book *Who Are We?: The Challenges to America's National Identity* has raised the alarm about the growing disintegration of the American society. According to him, ignoring growing Hispanic immigration could mean the disintegration of society "into two cultures (Anglo and Hispanic) and two languages".[11]

In recent years, American experts have noted a worsening of the 'segmental' nature of the assimilation of immigrants, i.e., newly arrived migrants group up with their countrymen and avoid mingling with the local population. This recipe for integration is aptly called a 'mixed salad."

The French model of assimilation has faced resistance from Muslims, who defend their Islamic identity at the expense of the national identity. Riots in Paris suburbs in 2005 and 2007 staged by second-generation immigrants—the children of Moroccans, Egyptians and Algerians who came to France in the 1950s—indicated that the problem is very acute.

Canada was first to choose the 'multicultural' model of integration—in many ways to soothe the sting of Francophone Quebec separatism. English and French languages were given equal status and the Law on Multiculturalism was adopted. However, this model, initially touted by liberals in Western countries as positive (the UK officially chose the course of multiculturalism in 1997 and Germany followed in 1998), has lost its credibility.

On 5 February 2011, British Prime Minister, David Cameron, speaking at a Munich security conference, acknowledged that the policy of multiculturalism had failed. According to Cameron, tolerance of and non-interference in the affairs of those who reject Western values had not proved justifiable. According to him, 'muscular liberalism' in which national identity was formed, even at the expense of democracy, equal

11. Huntington, S. (2004). *Who Are We? The Challenges to America's National Identity.* Moscow: Tranzitkniga.

rights, the rule of law, and freedom of speech, was necessary. He offered to stop funding those organisations, which do not support Western values.[12]

In Germany too, the failure of multiculturalism is an open fact. The first sign came in autumn 2010 with the publication of a scandalous book by Thilo Sarrazin, entitled *Germany Does Away With Itself*. The author writes: "...the birth rate among the Arabs and Turks is two to three times higher than that of the local population. And the vast majority of them cannot and do not want to integrate..." While the officials were quick to condemn Sarrazin's book, polls showed that almost 60 per cent of the population of Germany supported the position of the author. A little later on 18 October 2010, Chancellor Angela Merkel, speaking at a conference of the youth organisation of the Christian Democratic Union in Potsdam, ruefully noted, "... And of course, the approach [to build] a multicultural [society] and to live side by side and to enjoy each other... has failed, completely failed".[13]

Following Angela Merkel and David Cameron, French President Nicolas Sarkozy did not mince words when he spoke about the failure of multiculturalism. "We don't want a society in which communities co-exist alongside each other. If you come to France, you agree to base yourself in a single community, the national community. If you don't accept that, you don't come to France,"[14] stressed the President.

Thus, both the Western models—assimilation and multiculturalism—no longer meet today's challenges. However, Russian ethno-sociologists still continue to debate which of these models is better for Russia. On 14 February 2011, measures to strengthen inter-ethnic harmony were discussed at a meeting of the Russian Federation State Council devoted to National Policy. It was recommended that the experience of Western countries in "developing several ethnic groups in the same state" and "co-existence as a state of two or more languages" be taken into account. At the same meeting, it was suggested not to abandon the USSR's experiment in creating a single entity—the Soviet people.

---

12. <*Lenta.ru*>, 5 February 2011.
13. *BBC*, 17 October 2010.
14. <*InoSMI.ru*>, 11 February 2011.

We can only point out that in Russia, there is still no coherent model to integrate diverse ethnic groups into a common society. Consequently, some strange 'grassroots initiatives' are being attempted, which tend to push the country towards 'enclavisation.' For example, in May 2008, Co-chairman of the Council of Muftis of Russia, Nafigullah Ashirov, proposed the creation of ghettos for ethnic minorities in major cities. These ghettos, in the opinion of Ashirov, should possess entirely autonomous infrastructure—shops, schools, kindergartens, etc. In 2010, he also proposed the establishment of an Islamic enclave in South Butovo (the outskirts of Moscow) with an Islamic militia to maintain order. He later said that the specified area was too small because "Muslims are so numerous in Moscow today that they would occupy a whole district" (in Moscow there are 10 districts and 15 million inhabitants).

Although experts also caution Moscow against taking the course of Paris or Berlin with their 'suburb syndrome' (settlement of migrants in the outskirts), there are entire areas in the capital where migrant communities of a particular nationality have already settled down. As a result, the percentage of the non-Russian population in these areas is becoming much higher than the city average. For example, in Dorogomilovo District, Ukrainian migrants make up to 35.1 per cent of the population. In Izmailovo, the proportion of the non-Russian population has reached 35.9 per cent. This is where more than half of all the Chinese people in Moscow and more than a third of the Vietnamese have settled down.

According to sociologists, there is a numerical parameter for the 'threshold of tolerance of conflict.' If the proportion of migrants in a society crosses 10 per cent or 15 per cent, it will inevitably face outbreaks of xenophobia.[15] However, some specialists are quick to allay such fears, pointing out that Moscow from the very outset has been a cosmopolitan city, 'melting pot' for immigrants. But psychologist Victor Ponomarenko contradicts the second view, pointing out how the names of the streets in Moscow tell a different story: "...Maroseika is Maloroseika (i.e., Ukrainians

15. Kozlov, V.I. (1987). *Immigrants and Ethno-Racial Problems in Britain*. Moscow: Nauka.

lived there), Large and Small Georgian streets speak for themselves, Tartars lived on Ordynka... Time passes and Moscow assimilates them all".[16]

Nonetheless, the problem of potential enclavisation still worries Muscovites. According to surveys, 57 per cent of the capital's residents do not approve of 'guest workers' and only about 40 per cent just about tolerate their presence. But Muscovites are united in opposing the creation of separate districts for migrants, such as China Town. How can enclavisation be prevented? Thus far, the originators of adaptation programmes have found no 'breakthrough' or any acceptable techniques. What are commonly heard are calls to 'improve immigration policy' and 'establish conditions.' Generally they offer to organise folk dance festivals, national food festivals, etc. To help migrants who often arrive in Russia without knowing the Russian language, various kinds of instruction booklets are published, in which useful phone numbers and addresses can be found, as well as advice on finding a job, an apartment, etc.

Moscow officials formulated what they called a Muscovite Code—a set of rules that would help newcomers adapt to unfamiliar surroundings. It is supposed to explain what can be done within the framework of 'Russian culture and traditions' and what should not be done. For example, "do not cook barbecue on the balcony, do not walk around the city in national costume, speak in Russian...."[17] Experts have pointed out that the code cannot be called a successful initiative, as it does not mention any benefit; it only helps to provoke anti-Russian and anti-Moscow sentiments. It is this absence of a well-thought-out policy that causes all the major problems already mentioned. Russia has not yet come up with a model for ethnic relations, which is coherent and convincing for the entire population.

Negative Factors Caused by the Migration Process

Experts acknowledge that mechanisms for the full integration of migrants into the already existing socio-cultural relations have not been developed. As a result, the movements of many millions of migrants pose a

---

16. Polukhin, D. (2007). "Half of all of Moscow's Chinese live in Izmailovo", 28 February, <*www.kp.ru/daily*>.

17. BBC Russia, 16 June 2010.

threat of destabilisation. Listed below are the negative factors elicited by the migration process.

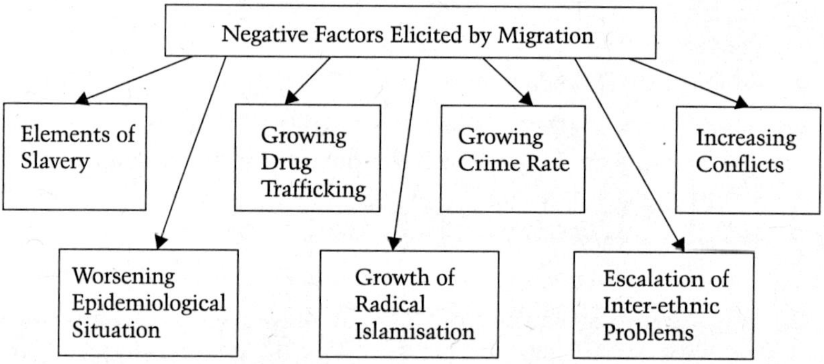

Factor No. 1: There is a demand for archaic forms of social relations that just cannot work in a modernised country. We are talking about what would amount to slavery. Under the pressure of life circumstances (even starvation), illegal migrants are forced to agree to the status of slaves to get jobs.

The Russian quota in 2010 for foreign labour force was about 2 million people. But the actual number of illegal immigrants that entered Russia that year was close to 10 million. Primarily, these were from CIS countries. President of the National Assembly of Specialists in the Field of Labour and Social Policy, Nikolai Volgin, admits "Russia is currently unable to control the number of illegal immigrants".[18]

In Russia, as in the rest of the world, illegal labour migration has led to labour market segmentation and isolation of the types of work in which migrant populations are primarily engaged. Above all, this is a dirty, dangerous work that requires no qualifications or high-intensity work. Migrants are often involved in the criminal sector of the economy (in unregistered firms, production of counterfeit goods, etc.). They are ready for hard work with low salaries (at home their wages are several times lower). Guests from abroad settle anywhere, often live in dilapidated houses, basements and garages in unsanitary conditions. For example, in May

18. *Newsru.com*, 29 January 2010.

2011, an entire city of illegal immigrants was discovered in east Moscow in the Kosino-Ukhtomsky district—immigrants from Uzbekistan and Tajikistan had built about two dozen dugouts and were connected to each other via tunnels.[19]

Migrants throng daily to an informal/illegal labour exchange ('slave markets') in search of work. Employers come and pick up the required number of migrants who do what ever job they are told to do. Here's how a reporter, disguised as a worker going through the hiring process, describes it: "In an old jersey with a tag around my neck, I join the rows of poorly dressed, sullen guest workers... It seems as if the entire former Soviet Union is crowding here. Each is labeled with a sign: 'inexpensive repairs,' 'ceilings', 'plasterer and tile layer,' 'carpentry'.... Closer to 8 am, 'buyers' begin to walk along the rows. They look over the 'slaves.' They feel their muscles. They all but look in their mouths, like horses."[20]

Usually, the hirers take away the passports, thus putting a stamp on their slavery status. In June 2008, the following fact came to light. Several Azerbaijanis forced about 50 Uzbeks to work for free, intimidating and beating them for any infraction.[21] In July 2008, police freed 77 Vietnamese in Moscow who had worked in the shop for sewing children's clothes. They had not been paid and their passports had been taken away.[22] In 2010, an illegal clothing manufacturing unit was found in suburban Noginsk. Children 11-17 years old, as also citizens from Kyrgyzstan, were working there. As is the case the world over, prostitution is a part and parcel of illegal immigration. According to the media, about 80,000 girls of so called 'easy virtue' walk the streets of Moscow.[23]

The 2006 UN report on trafficking of people in the Russian Federation stresses that Russia is a country of admittance, export and transit of 'live goods.' The most common objectives of human trafficking in Russia are

19. "An Entire City of Illegal Immigrants Discovered in East Moscow", (2011). *Vesti.Ru*, 26 May.

20. Samodelova, S. (2005). "A Guest in One's Throat: How and Why Guest Workers Work in the Capital", 13 December, <*http://www.mk.ru*>.

21. Aliev, T. (2009). "Two Hundred Slaves Freed in Dagestan", *Newsland*, 15 July.

22. Ibid.

23. Mushtuk, O., "Moscow is a Center of Attraction for Migrants", *Obozprevatel*, <*www.nasledie.ru*>.

for slave labour and sexual exploitation.[24] "It is possible that now there are more slaves in the world than 200 years ago," said a representative of the Norwegian Police, Jarl Bjerke, at a police conference of Nordic countries.[25]

The Russian economist Mikhail Delyagin, a well-known patriot with conservative views, paints an alarming picture:

> Obtaining cheap labor can be considered a plus, but labor immigration also has many disadvantages. This is the deterioration of the labor market; the local population is constantly hearing from employers that they are "spoiled" because they do not want to work for the pennies hardworking immigrants agree to work for...This is the general demoralisation of society. When society is filled with people who have almost no rights and their labor is worth almost nothing, this is called a slave society. In a sense, that is what Russia is today.[26]

Factor No. 2: There has been an increase in conflict between various ethnic groups of migrants. In Moscow, at least 100 mass brawls involving migrant workers from Tajikistan, Azerbaijan, Kyrgyzstan and Kazakhstan took place in 2010, causing the death of 72 people. Some say such fights occur almost every week. If a few years ago the causes of mass brawls were economic competition and the struggle for territory, then the reason now is religious and ethnic hatred.

Factor No. 3: Ethnic clashes between migrant groups and indigenous populations. In July 2006, local residents in Salsk (Rostov region) demanded the eviction of Dagestanis living in Salsk region. In November 2006, Azerbaijanis living in the village Kharagun in the Trans-Baikal Krai were expelled. The most salient incident occurred in September 2006. In the course of fighting in the Russian city of Kondopoga, natives of Chechnya and Dagestan killed two Russians. Riots ensued. The next day, the rally participants demanded authorities evict all illegal immigrants from the city, largely from the Caucasus and Central Asia. The riots in Kondopoga lasted several days and the authorities had to use Special Weapons and Tactics (SWAT) teams (Special Police Units) and to immediately remove about 60 Caucasians.

---

24. *<www.un.org/russian/news/>*.

25. Radio Voice of Russia, 24 March 2010.

26. Delyagin, M. (2009). "Migration: To Be Or Not To Be?", 4 December, *<www.job.ru>*.

A truly momentous event took place in Moscow on 11 December 2010. After the death of Spartacus soccer team fan Yegor Sviridov in a brawl with Caucasians, about 5,000 football fans and nationalist-minded youth gathered for an unsanctioned rally in the city centre at the Manezhnaya Square. The crowd chanted nationalist slogans: "Do in the khaches (expatriates from the Caucasus)!" and "Russia for Russians!" In response, the Caucasians agreed by Internet to hold a retaliatory rally on 15 December 2010. Consequently, the event turned into a riot and about 1,200 people were arrested. Attempts were also made to organise rallies in other Russian cities.

According to the survey by the All-Russian Public Opinion Research Centre (VCIOM), the presence of migrants causes a sense of unease to 54 per cent of respondents in some regions; we cannot exclude the possibility of this feeling of animosity to erupting into riots.

Factor No. 4: Currency export from Russia. Migrant workers are often blamed for sending a significant portion of their earnings to their families back home, thereby exporting currency from Russia. The Head of the Federal Migration Service of Russia, Konstantin Romodanovsky, speaking in September 2006 at the UN headquarters, called the migrants a "threat to the country's national security." According to him, foreign workers send more than $10 billion out of Russia per year.[27]

It is worth noting that remittances from migrant workers are an important source of revenue for the countries from which they come. According to the World Bank, the volume of remittances in 2008 accounted for 49 per cent of the Tajik, 30 per cent of the Moldovan, 27 per cent of the Kyrgyz and 13 per cent of the Uzbek Gross Domestic Product (GDP).[28]

But transactions, carried out with the help of the widespread Muslim value transfer system, the 'hawala,' remain outside the focus of the World Bank (WB). The basis of this archaic system is based on trust. There are no boundaries, taxes or controls. Through the 'hawala office' at Cherkizovsky Market in Moscow alone (before it was closed), transfers of 14 billion roubles (about $550 million) were made from January 2006 to October

27. Kharchenko, A. (2006). "The FMS Called Migrants a Threat to National Security", *Kommersant*, 18 September.

28. Ibid.

2008. The WB estimates the volume of money transfers from Russia (by both formal and informal channels) reached $12-15 billion dollars in 2008.[29]

Factor No. 5: Increase of drug trade activity. The routes of narco supplies coincide with migratory flows. Deputy Director of the Federal Drug Control Service of Russia, Oleg Safonov, has said, "half of the cargo exported from Afghanistan enters Russia. And the remaining 50% is divided between the Balkan and Southern Route."[30] More than 90 per cent of heroin is delivered by drug couriers from Tajikistan, which is the main corridor from Afghanistan to Europe. Over 80 per cent of those involved in drug trafficking are Tajiks and Kyrgyz citizens. They usually arrive under the pretence of labour migration. More than 1,500 foreign nationals were convicted in Russia for bulk sale of drugs in 2009. Almost all of them were citizens of Central Asian countries.

Factor No. 6: The deterioration of the sanitary-epidemiological situation. Throughout the world, it is a recognised fact that migratory movements contribute to the transfer and spread of infectious diseases. For example, in the spring of 2010, three cases of polio carried in from Tajikistan were reported in Russia (two from children who arrived from Dushanbe and one from a 19-year-old youth). According to health officials in Moscow, "up to 15 per cent of migrants suffer from infectious diseases".[31] According to the Federal Research and Methodological Centre for the Prevention and Control of HIV/AIDS, 9,337 HIV-positive foreign nationals were identified in the period from 1987 to 2007.

Factor No. 7: Ethnic and religious radicalism is entering Russia with the migrants. Hizb ut-Tahrir and Tablighi Jamaat have become active in the Volga region. "Their goal is to create chaos in the country," says the Secretary of the Spiritual Board of Muslims of the Samara region, Minahmet Sagirov. According to him, "amid the large-scale labor migration from the Central Asian states, radical Islamist agents are coming into the

---

29. *op. cit.* no.1.

30. "UFSKN: Half of the Afghan Drug Traffic Enters Russia", *VolgaInform*, 21 May 2010.

31. "Foreign Labor is Under Strict Control. Head of the FMS K. Romodanovsky Spoke at the Round Table Held in the Duma about the Tasks Before the FMS RF", 14 January 2008, <*www.fms.cov.ru*>.

region and creating a highly secret network of organisations for political propaganda and to discredit our [spiritual] authorities."

In Russia, representatives of Tablighi Jamaat began proselytising in the mid-1990s in the Tatar villages of Tyumen region. Then, on the advice of the Supreme Mufti, Talgat Tajuddin, local Muslims drove them out. In 2004, Tablighi agents began to return in the guise of employees of different companies. According to experts, the main task of the Tablighi agents was to prepare the ground for more radical organisations and the recruitment of Muslims for terrorist acts. According to researcher Alex Aleksiev, "after joining a Tablighi Jamaat cell in the local mosque, the most active newcomers are invited for four months of further training in Pakistan, where they meet with representatives of terrorist groups that collaborate with Tablighi Jamaat and receive the offer to undertake military training..."[32] The Secretary of the Spiritual Board of Muslims of the Samara region, Minahmet Sagirov, said that "amid large-scale labor migration from the Central Asian states radical Islamist agents come into the region and creates a highly secret network of cells consisting of five members for organisation of political propaganda and to discredit our [spiritual] authorities."[33]

The never-ending series of scandals that began with the appearance of Tablighi Jamaat in the Volga region ended with a decision by the Supreme Court. On 7 May 2009, Russia's Supreme Court recognised Tablighi Jamaat as an extremist organisation and banned its activities in the country.

Preliminary Findings

Studies conducted in Russia suggest that the problem of adapting migrants still has not been completely resolved. The indigenous population of the country generally tolerate their presence only because they provide cheap labour, but have no intentions of accepting them as Russians. Neither do migrants have any desire to merge with the indigenous population, or 'melt' into the Russian socio-cultural environment; they create their own space, essentially, ethnic enclaves with a comfortable environment familiar

32. Aleksiev, A. (2003). "Tablighi Jamaat: An Unseen Legion of Jihadists", *Otechestvennye zapiski* 5.
33. Bondarenko, A. (2005). "Hizb ut-Tahrir has Arrived in Samara", *Interfax*, 20 May.

to them. They seem willing to pay for this cultural isolation with social exclusion.

The massive influx of migrants, which partially solves the shortage of working-age population caused by the serious demographic situation in Russia, has lead to dangerous trends. There is an increase in ethnic conflict and social tensions. It must be remembered that the destruction of the Soviet identity led to an awakening of the 'demons' of national and regional separatism in Russia. National separatists are eager to secede from Russia, for example, Tatarstan and the North Caucasus republics. They want the areas in West Siberia and in the far East to unite as separate Republics and subsequently leave Russia.

One can only hope that Russia will be able to work out a formula of interethnic relations in the coming years that will first allow it to absorb the flow of migration while at the same time enable it to maintain its own civilisational identity and, second, strengthen the relationship between its indigenous people and the immigrants and eliminate centrifugal tendencies. But all this requires extensive research and no less extensive, costly and decisive actions.

Conclusion

In connection with the aggregate of immigration problems in the world, renowned sociologist, Immanuel Wallerstein, predicts a new revolutionary situation. He maintains that, in the short term, there will be an increase in right-wing movements demanding limitations on the influx of immigrants, while at the same time one can expect the burgeoning of migration to the 'Northern Ring.' In the medium term, a statistically significant group of migrant families (often including families of the second generation)—low-paid, not socially integrated and almost certainly deprived of political rights—will be the lowest layer of the working class in countries of the developed North. According to him, if this happens, then the situation that Europe found itself in before 1848 will be repeated—the presence of a lower class concentrated in the city, this time clearly defined by ethnicity, without rights, yet with great claims on society. It is this situation that led to the appearance of the first apparition about which Marx and Engels expounded, says Wallerstein.[34]

Obviously, the problems of migration in the world are generally not resolved either by practical processes or scientific methods. Migrant flows (both legal and illegal) are inherently destabilising factors. Study of migration in the world has presented enough factual material but there appears to be an inadequacy among policy makers, which limits them to come out with mere conceptual generalisations. In short, what the rapid development of the processes of global migration requires is intensive work to understand the current problems and then find ways to solve them.

34. Wallerstein, Immanuel (2004). "The End of the World as We Know It", in *Social Science for the Twenty-First Century.* University of Minnesota Press. 18 July, *<http://www.2015.ru>*.

12 Migration in the 21st Century

Perspectives and Challenges

Vivan Sharan

An interesting dilemma confronts human civilisation in this post-modern age. From the dawn of time, human beings have constantly been moving from place to place and, in what can be called the first known immigration, the earliest man wandered out of Eastern Africa well over 100,000 years back. Today, with civilisation standing at a crossroad and given the background of globalisation, policymakers (especially in the West) need to re-examine their immigration policies and decide whether increased global migratory movements should be promoted or contained.

Mobility across wide regions and geographic entities allows us to search for greener pastures. The 'search for something better' still remains the fundamental reason for most people to move from place to place. This migration, which can be both within state boundaries or from state to state, is as embedded in the societal psyche as any other natural social phenomenon has been.

The paper focuses on voluntary migration of people. This entails deliberately omitting the past migratory process of forced labour, mainly for two reasons. First, ever since the forced African migration to provide labour in America, there have been no significant movements on a large scale in a short period of time. Second, this paper attempts to stay away from moral concerns behind migratory patterns, of both the sending and the receiving country, because this would be a theme for an altogether different set of analyses from the subject under study in this paper.

Today, we find ourselves at the dawn of a new global era, with nations facing non-traditional human security issues such as those associated with energy, food, demographics and environment. How we respond to such challenges is ultimately going to shape our future. The paper discusses the reasons for and patterns of migration and analyses the traditional and non-traditional concerns that migrants, employers and states have while dealing with the issue of geographic mobility. It then presents opinions on solutions for the new century.

Human mobility has a much more important role to play in this globalised world than policy makers acknowledge. To confront the aforementioned non-traditional security threats, global policy needs to be oriented to greater freedom of movement across boundaries in a kind of human arbitrage in consonance with modern day financial markets. This in turn will create efficiencies of human capital—a much needed medicine for current global imbalances.

Why Move?

There are essentially three reasons why people move; psychological factors, socioeconomic factors and political factors. These together form a complicated matrix of influences that determine why migratory flows are the way they are today.

Psychological factors are relevant today because personal preferences are increasingly motivating people to move place to place. These choices are formed as a result of both exogenous and endogenous factors. The common consensus about 'migration psychology' is that the decision-making process is of primary importance in the voluntary movement of an individual group of people.[1] This may seem obvious at the outset, but it is a crucial issue that cannot be omitted from an analysis such as this paper.

The decision-making process relies upon both external and internal constraints, and might not always lead to maximisation of utility. For instance, according to the behavioural theory, the relative 'instability of intentions' in comparison to attitudes has often resulted in direct attitudinal influences on behaviour. Thus migration cannot be looked at as a purely utility driven process.[2] And, indeed, we do find that there has been

1. Fawcett, J.T. (1986). "Migration Intentions and Behavior", *Population and Environment*.
2. Liska, A.E. (1984). "A Critical Examination of the Causal structure of the Fishbein/Ajzen Attitude-Behavior Model", *Social Psychology Quarterly* 47(1): 61-74.

a moderation in migratory patterns over the past few decades. Increasingly, humans have made themselves comfortable wherever they are, with labour market conditions significantly shaping their lifestyles.

Second, labour economists have for long studied the socio-economic factors behind movements. The oldest school of thought suggests that people move out in search of better income.[3] Sir John Hicks argued that "differences in net economic advantages, chiefly differences in wages are the main causes of migration." That is, wage differentials form the basis for the related decision-making process. This is, however, a narrow and incomplete insight into human preferences. Although migration today is sometimes driven by relative wage differentials, it is not a necessary condition. The rapid urbanisation in the developing world in countries like India, China and Brazil is testament to this desire to exploit wage differentials between urban and rural areas. All the same, migrating rural workers often find that they would have gained higher utility value if they had not moved at all. Besides, uncertainty leads to less than optimal utility gains.

A newer stream of thought suggests that relative economic disparity is the main driver of migration.[4] That is, members of a relatively more deprived group might prefer to move to an area of relatively less deprived group even if this means that absolute income is lower after the shift. This theory is also complementary to the behavioural aspects of migration. It accounts for the dynamics within the family in a unique way, suggesting that migration is not necessarily an assertion of independence by the younger generations in a family, but rather a form of resource optimisation.[5]

Another new tendency that gives an additional dimension to this discussion is the 'new media' and the 'web 2.0.' It has been argued that a characteristic of mass communication as we know it today has extended

---

3. See, Sjaastad, L.A. (1962). "The Costs and Returns of Human Migration", *Journal of Political Economy* 70(5): 80-93.
4. See, Stark, Oded and E.J. Tayloy (1989). "Relative Deprivation and International Migration", *Demography* 26(1): 1-14.
5. One can consider the case of a typical student who travels away from family to get education and then goes on to seek jobs in a more opportune environment, and then returns some of his/her earnings in the form of remittances, thereby optimising the utility gained by the family as a whole.

the availability of information across space and time.[6] That is, through the use of modern technology, new technical media is able to bring information to masses who are possibly far removed in both the dimensions (in space due to physical distance from the point of origin, and in time due to time lag between production and dissemination of the information from the point of origin). Eminent media scholar, John Thompson has written that "by enabling individuals to communicate across extended stretches of space and time, the use of technical media enables individuals to transcend the spatial and temporal boundaries characteristic of face to face interaction. At the same time, it enables individuals to reorder the spatial and temporal features of social organisation, and to use these reordered features as a means of pursuing their objectives."

The decoupling of space and time has led to interesting consequences for related decision making. Human beings no longer look at their immediate neighbours to compare existing relative disparities. The concept of 'despatialised simultaneity' denotes an impulse that must lead to a paradigm shift in the way man perceives the world through the lens of space and time.[7] That is, the concept of 'now' has been delineated from the point of origin or locale, giving us an objective view of time and histories rather than a subjective one. Thus, there has developed a sort of 'mediated rationality' in the decision-making process.

The third and perhaps the most controversial reason for migration is political environment. Of course, whether or not the claim of political asylum seekers is always legitimate is another matter—one that causes great concern in many countries, especially in Europe, the haven for many asylum seekers. An oppressive political environment can take various forms. Brutal oppression can be brought about by political uncertainties and feudalistic institutions. Through the course of human history, human rights violations by government controlled institutions have repeatedly found their counterpoint in the form of dissident groups who choose to

---

6. Thompson, John (1995). *The Media and Modernity: A Social Theory of the Media.* Cambridge: Cambridge University Press.

7. Gibbons, Michael, Camille Limoges, Helga Nowotny, Simon Schwartzman, Peter Scott and Martin Trow (1994). *The New Production of Knowledge.* London: Sage Publications Ltd.

use aggressive tactics to overthrow the oppressors. Civil war scenarios that result from this are perhaps the greatest and the fastest movers of a mass of people across borders, apart from a direct war between two or more states.

Whether to term conflict-induced movements as voluntary or not is a mere technicality. What is important is that the decision to move is part of a behavioural process of decision making, in which the constraints that dictate the movement are beneficial in some way. Analysing all the existing theories that explain why people move, this behavioural undercurrent in all of them is hard to ignore.

Who Moves?

Perhaps the most prominent pattern of movement is that people tend to move from areas of lower development to relatively better developed areas. That is, people tend to move to places with better living standards than the place of origin; hence, the difference between human development at the chosen destination and at the place of origin tends to be significant (three quarter of international movers move to countries which are higher on the Human Development Index than the country of origin).[8] This coincides with what is termed "in search for something better" in the previous section.

The second major pattern of movement is that most of it happens within a state rather than to other states. The 2009 Human Development Report of the United Nations Development Programme (UNDP) estimates that there are about 740 million internal migrants in the world, compared to 214 million international migrants. The reasons for this are twofold: first, it is clear that it is more expensive to travel to far off countries than within state boundaries and second, existing policy restrictions are stringent. A behavioural reason could also be contributing to this pattern—people are less keen to make a decision to move to a completely different socio-cultural environment from the place of origin if the incentive is not strong enough.

8. United Nations Development Programme (2009). *Human Development Report.*

The third and perhaps the most intuitive migration pattern is the veritable normal distribution[9] based on the probability of migration plotted against per capita income. According to the Human Development Report (2009), people with the least per capita income are also the least mobile. This is a paradox, since the people who have the most to gain from moving to a more developed region are highly immobile, and are condemned to make a living in less than optimal environments. This is a welfare-reducing phenomenon in the context of the global economy and one which needs closer examination by policy makers. As per capita income increases, so does mobility, though only up to a point; thereafter it decreases again. The probability of migration peaks at an estimated per capita income of close to US $15,000. However, according to the World Bank (WB) indicators, no African country has a per capita income above this and the Human Development Report states that only 3 per cent of Africans live in a country that is different (income-wise) from their country of origin.

This last pattern of the profile of people who move is helpful to understand why there is such a policy bias among the receiving countries towards highly skilled labour. The H1-B visa issued by the United States is a good example of this bias towards highly skilled immigrants. Regulations require that applicants should only apply for "specialist occupations" that require a high degree of skill—both theoretical and practical. Receiving countries clearly do not want an influx of poor unskilled migrants, and this marks a big policy shift from pre-1970s policy, whereby the United States and Western Europe opened their borders to a considerable amount of low-skilled labour migrants. The changing dynamics of global trade and sharp jumps in commodity prices (especially energy) led to change of policies across the developed world after a highly liberalised framework post Second World War.[10] The implications of this in the context of the globalised world are discussed in the next section.

9. The most common probability distribution in statistics.

10. The United States instituted its 'Bracero' Programme in 1942 to accept 4.6 million Mexican farm labourers which, ended in 1964, and Western European countries that heavily depended on cheap unskilled labour through their guest worker programmes also ceased recruitment after the Organization of the Petroleum Exporting Countries (OPEC) oil shocks in the early 1970s.

Globalisation, Business Cycles and the Migrant

One of the founding fathers of development economics, Simon Kuznets, proposed that all countries follow a predestined inequity cycle in the process of economic growth. The cycle begins with high economic inequality in society, when physical capital is the main mechanism of growth, and those who save and invest in this are better off than the rest. As the development cycle continues and economic growth increases, there is then a trickle down effect, due to investment in the economy by those who have benefited in the initial phase of the cycle. As a result, economic inequality decreases steadily and this whole cycle, which leads to transformation from developing to developed economy, is illustrated in the shape of an inverted U. This is known as the Kuznets curve, and in the case of the American economy, Kuznets noted that the peak of economic inequality was reached in 1890 and thereafter started to decline and stabilised after 1920.

However, Kuznets conclusions on the American economy have failed to hold true after the OPEC oil supply shocks of the 1970s. This period of time, when the famous 'Nixon Shocks' led to the discontinuation of gold-backed currency, was also a period when the American economy was battling with inflation led by a spike in energy prices and unemployment at the same time. This 'stagflation' led to reversal of the Kuznets curve as inequality once again started increasing. This has also been termed the 'great U turn' by economists,[11] and many of the erstwhile OECD countries also followed this trajectory in terms of increasing economic inequality. The 2009 UNDP Report highlights that the United States is ranked third on the list of countries with the highest inequalities. The poorest 10 per cent of the American population have 1.9 per cent of the share of total income and expenditure, while the richest 10 per cent have close to 30 per cent share.[12]

For policy makers in the West, it is increasingly difficult to justify this increasing inequity between the rich and the poor in their countries. This

---

11. Alderson, Arthur S. and Francois Nielson (2002). "Globalisation and the Great U Turn: Income Inequality Trends in 16 OECD Countries", *American Journal of Sociology* 107(5): 1244-99.

12. *Business Week*, 16 October 2009.

has resulted in finger pointing at the usual suspect—immigration. Although in terms of percentage of the world population, international migration has been stable at close to 3 per cent over the past few decades[13]; the overall volume of immigration has been increasing due to the population explosion that the world has undergone during the same time. The USA has been the recipient of the largest number of immigrants for many years now, and in between 1990 and 2000, it received about a third of the world's immigrants.[14] A large proportion of the immigrants are from Mexico, and most immigrate illegally by crossing over the border into the southern states like California and Texas (and then further diffusing to other parts). Studies have suggested that undocumented immigrants' financial resources, capacity to obtain formal jobs and access to healthcare are all predictably lesser than those of legal immigrants.[15]

At the outset, it would not be counterintuitive to assume that influx of unskilled immigrants can cause a skew in the income pattern (i.e., inequality) of the labour in the receiving country, though there is perhaps no empirical way to establish causality. A recent study has suggested that in the case of low-skilled Mexicans immigrating to the USA, the extra supply of labour is absorbed by changes in skill intensity within narrow industries, without significant impact on the overall wages (except in the case of the existing uneducated/drop out workforce).[16] Furthermore, since the strict policy regimes in place in most of the developed world have clearly favoured highly skilled immigrants for over four decades,[17] the argument can be reversed because the turn in the inequity curve has occurred simultaneously, even though it should have further stabilised due to implementation of biased policies towards letting in the highly skilled immigrants. In the current world scenario dominated by free market and

13. United Nations Development Programme (2009). *Human Development Report.*

14. US Census Bureau (2003). *The Foreign-Born Population: 2000.* Washington, DC.

15. Nandi, Arijit, Sandro Galea, Gerald Lopez, Vijay Nandi, Stacey Strongarone and Danielle C. Ompad, (2008). "Access to and Use of Health Services Among Undocumented Mexican Immigrants in a US Urban Area", *American Journal of Public Health* 98(2): 2011-20.

16. Card, David and Ethan G. Lewis (2007). "*The Diffusion of Mexican Immigrants During the 1990s: Explanations and Impacts*", *Working Paper* No. 11552. National Bureau of Economic Research.

17. Castles, Stephen (2002). "Migration and Community Formation under Conditions of Globalisation", *International Migration Review* 36(4): 1143-68.

neo-liberal ideologies, globalisation has made nations truly interdependent: the countries that are not sufficiently integrated in the globalised market framework of shared risk and increased trade are left on the periphery. There is constant political rhetoric voiced by the developed world about increased cooperation, free trade etc., and yet there is a reversal of liberal immigration agenda post Second World War.

Joseph Schumpeter coined the phrase 'creative destruction' back in 1942, referring to the destruction of old technologies by new, better technologies, thereby promoting human progress and innovation.[18] The actualisation of this process has brought human civilisation to the point that it is at right now. It has predicted the way companies and industries operate within the new paradigm of globalisation, where they have to be at the competitive edge in order to survive. The consequence of this has been the rapid introduction of technologies in formerly labour-intensive processes such as manufacturing. This in turn has resulted in a sectoral shift in the demand side for labour-intensive jobs and immigrants (from manufacturing to services). Countries in the West no longer require low-skilled workers in droves in order to work in factories and mills, and the emphasis for employment growth has now shifted to the service sector. This has further incentivised policy makers in the West to adopt stringent policies that favour only the highly skilled workers.

Another product of creative destruction has been the increasing emphasis on productivity. For example, the 2007-2008 global financial crises demanded a lot of changes in the productivity and efficiency with which private sector companies in the Western world operate. The companies that were able to make the appropriate changes have survived and are probably much more efficient, closer to operating according to an optimal utility framework than before. This emphasis on productivity has meant that the workers who are not absolutely essential are without jobs in the West. In such a situation, migration of workers across borders, if there were no barriers, would mean a movement from low-productivity areas to

18. Schumpeter, Joseph (1942). *Capitalism, Socialism and Democracy*. New York: Harper and Row.

high-productivity areas in a kind of labour arbitrage. This would improve labour productivity and overall efficiency in the global economy.[19]

As for the question of whether only the receiving countries would gain or whether there would be mutual gains between the sending and receiving countries, it would be useful to remember that most of the gains from migration would largely be caught by the migrants themselves, which would be shared with their families in the form of remittances. There would be no clear winners or losers, as the welfare gains would be observed in a global context rather than a regional context.

Migration and Non-Traditional Threats

Demographic threats are one of the more pronounced non-traditional threats to global welfare. While the threat represents itself as overpopulation (putting a strain on resources) in the developing world, it is the lack of population growth that is a threat to advanced developed countries. According to a recent study, the median age of the population of the world is projected to increase from 26.6 years in 2000 to 37.3 years in 2050.[20] This 'acceleration' in ageing is set to affect the developed world in an adverse way. The remarkable gains of life expectancy (from about 70 years to 78 years in the United States and even higher in the case of Japan over the past half century, according to the WB indicators) and simultaneously declining natality in the developed world have resulted in unforeseen consequences for social welfare.

In countries like Germany and Japan, peak populations have already been reached, as the decline in births have more than offset the increases in longevity.[21] Without a growing workforce (of young people), there has emerged a serious need for immigrant workers. Germany has already benefitted from liberalised immigration policies in the 1960s (due to shortage of labour during the German "economic miracle") and this in fact justifies the European Union (EU) migration policy towards member

19. Hanson, Gordon H. (2008). "*The Economic Consequences of the International Migration of Labour*", *Working Paper* No. 14490. UCSD and NBER.

20. Lutz, Wolfgang, Warren Sanderson and Sergei Scherbov (2008). "The Coming Acceleration of Global Population Ageing", *Nature* 451: 716-9, February.

21. Cooper, Richard N. (2008). "Global Imbalances: Globalisation, Demography and Sustainability", *The Journal of Economic Perspectives* 22(3): 93-112.

states.[22] Most of the migration to Germany has taken place from countries within Europe such as Turkey and Poland and not from countries that are relatively much worse off in the Human Development Index.

Figure 12.1

The Cumulative Probabilities of Reaching a Proportion 60+ of one-third or more for the World and Selected World Regions by Calendar Year

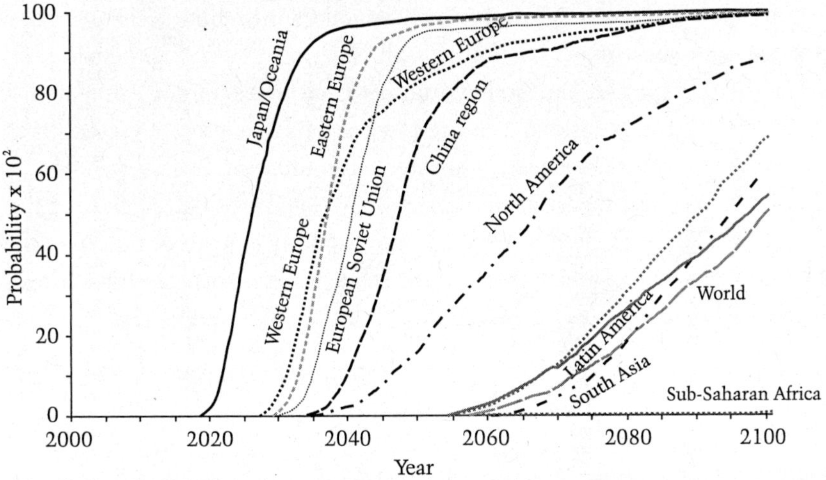

Source: See footnote no. 20.

The second big non-traditional threat is in the form of environmental challenges. It is no secret that climate change has lead to a rise in the global surface temperature and global mean sea level. Although there is a lack of evidence to support the claim that climate change has already lead to a shift in migratory patterns[23], this can be put down to the fact that the effects of climate change have not been very severe up till now, and may not be for another decade. The Stern Review Report on Climate Change predicts, conservatively, that there is a very real potential for additional mass migration of 150-200 million people by 2050.[24] The report observes

22. European Union free movement of workers principles require that all member state citizens have the right to solicit and obtain work in Germany free from discrimination on the basis of citizenship according to the Treaty on European Union Article 39.

23. Salehyan, Idean (2005). *Refugees, Climate Change and Instability.* San Diego, CA: University of California.

24. Stern, Nicholas (2007). *The Economics of Climate Change: The Stern Review.* Cambridge University Press.

that "climate change will lead to hundreds of millions more people without sufficient water or food to survive or threatened by dangerous floods and increased disease". Furthermore, severe drought and flood risks are already changing migratory patterns.[25] Low lying flood-prone high-density areas like those in Bangladesh are especially under threat from rising sea levels.

Under this sort of scenario, both regional and international migration are surely going to be important and people will increasingly start to incorporate climate change and its consequences into their decision-making process. The question, 'why move?' will be given a fourth dimension, and we are of the opinion that policy makers need to be suitably prepared for humanitarian interventions and the integration of 'climate refugees' in the future. Furthermore, resource shortages are additional concerns that are likely to affect the decision-making process of individuals contemplating migration. The unabated rise in commodity and food prices seems to be a long-term trend going forward, and fresh water shortages have already caused significant shifts in migratory patterns around the world.[26]

Conclusion

The narrative of human evolution can be traced through the perspective of migration. From over 150,000 years ago when the earliest man started his journey out of erstwhile Ethiopia, to the migration from the Iberian peninsula to the colonies in the Americas, and to the great African migration of slaves, the human odysseys and sweeping socio-economic transformations have greatly been influenced by the migratory phenomenon. It is only in the last few decades that the slowdown of migration (in terms of percentage of the world population) has occurred, along with the spread of globalisation.

The majority of international migration takes place between countries that are either linked geographically, such as the USA and Mexico or are sufficiently close to each other, and between countries that share other

25. Black, R., D. Coppard, D. Kniveton, A. Murata and R. Skeldon (2008). "Demographics and Climate Change: Future Trends and their Policy Implications for Migration", *Working Paper* (T-27). Development Research Centre on Migration, Globalisation and Poverty, University of Sussex.

26. Widgren, J. (1990). "*International Migration and Regional Stability*", *International Affairs* 66(4): 749-66.

established socio-political/socio-economic linkages, such as the member nations of the EU. In both cases, labour tends to flow from relatively low-productivity to high-productivity areas, enhancing overall global welfare. With existing imbalances caused by structural mismatches wreaking havoc in the global economy, it is the perfect time for policymakers to reform immigration policies—especially in the developed world.

A lot goes on behind the decision to migrate. The human decision-making process is pivotal to understanding the dynamics of where people move and why. This cerebral process has been greatly influenced by the new media, and that people now make decisions with a 'mediated rationality.' The implication of this is that migrants are increasingly aware of the prevailing environments both in their point of origin and destination. Voluntary movements by people searching for 'something better' are increasingly sieved through the perceptive realities of the migrant, which are in turn increasingly shaped by factors such as the new media.

Need-based migration is sure to increase in the coming years, given the increasing lack of resources, impact of climate change and other non-traditional threats. This is going to lead to unpredictable consequences, whereby certain nations are going to feel greater sustained immigration pressures than others. The paper highlights the fact that this need-based migration should be treated as a global burden rather than a local one to enhance global welfare. Countries should promote the process of multilateral dialogue on this issue and resolve themselves to sharing the burden when the time comes. The recent global financial crisis has provided a blueprint for the modalities of cooperation on financial/fiscal issues. Such multilateral cooperation and experience sharing could be a worthwhile example to follow, with emphasis on resolving issues of mass, need-based migrations to combat non-traditional threats and to increase global labour efficiencies.

Part III
India-Russia and the World

13 Models of Global Hegemony and their Influence on the World Order

Sergey Kurginyan

When discussing proposals for possible models of world order, such as the proposal for global hegemony under a single power as opposed to those that are more balanced and even minded, we must first find clear answers to a series of elementary, yet at the same time fundamental, questions. The first among them is the simplest and at the same time the most difficult: Why are new models needed, hegemonic or others?

Indeed, can the world really not carry on growing within the framework of the existing model that has facilitated the development of mankind throughout centuries? Has this model begun to fail and stopped responding to new challenges and threats? Only if this was the case, would it be necessary to modify the existing model. There is no single, definitive answer to such questions. One has to admit that no new model has been invented by humanity so far. (The author's meaning of the word 'model' in this paper is 'paradigm' or a 'new grand narrative.')

The alternative paradigm that had existed, called 'communist' (or, in a gentler form, 'socialist'), has been significantly compromised not so much by its own failures, as by the collapse of the USSR. More time and tremendous effort, both intellectual and political, are required to reach an answer so that we, that is, those responsible for the collapse of the USSR, can grasp the deeper meaning of what happened and develop something new on the basis of this awareness.

Fascism can hardly be called a new alternative paradigm, no matter what its modernised versions are. This would be impossible, first and foremost, because in the way of such a concept stands an insurmountable moral, existential and even metaphysical barrier. It would be unthinkable to call something that has a direct relation to 'Absolute Evil'—the new alternative paradigm. That is not all—for fascism in its innermost essence, freed from its hypocritical mask, has historically been proven anathema to our new world. Fascism hates history and despises newness. Of course, the neo- or neo-neo-fascists will brazenly argue that one must accept this new paradigm because the previous one is now too old and tired to be of any use. But this would be just another of its lies, neither the first nor the last.

In fact, it is not fascism, in its new guise, destined to be a new paradigm substituting the one formed out of the wreckage of the world that came into being after the French Revolution of 1789, although the formation of this world began three centuries earlier. No, it is not fascism that will replace this great paradigm, which is called the 'Modern' project or the "epoch of modernity" and is based on the ideas of progress and humanism inspired by the great slogan "Liberty, Equality, Fraternity".

Fascism can only oppose the Modern project with the fundamentalist Counter-Modern in the form of strategic alternative. But we cannot assume that the Counter-Modern is a new paradigm, or a new historical proposal for humanity. It is no more than an effort to turn the wheel of history back to return to a Pre-Modern, Pre-Enlightenment epoch—an epoch of the new Middle Ages or something even more archaic. But if it is not fascism that manifests a new 'something' coming to replace the essentials of the Modern project, then what is it.

Maybe, this role should be delegated to the so-called Post-Modern, a model actively promoted by certain Western elites? But post-modernism too is neither a new paradigm nor a new grand narrative (despite the fact that it was post-modernists who began to talk about grand narratives). Why not? There are many reasons. The post-modernists (not the cultural figures, but the politicians and philosophers with this orientation) deny the validity of all projects, including what they call the "Human" project. These philosophers and politicians are engaged not in building a new grand narrative, but in criticising all the grand narratives as such. The objective of post-modernism is certainly not in any way to build a new edifice for any world order designed to replace the edifice of the collapsed world order. Post-modernists do not want to build a new edifice. They are busy developing an entirely different approach—an approach based on how they can settle down upon the ruins of a collapsed edifice, totally refusing to build anything at all.

It seems humanity will tend to find such a scenario abhorrent. In any case, this scenario has nothing to do with what we are discussing—that is, to any of the possible new world orders. Rather, this scenario can be called the basic scenario for 'disorder' and the rejection of order as such. But not everybody will be ready to reject an already existing social and economic setup all at once. Hence, those who do not reject it will dictate something to the rest. What is it? And why, with such a deficit of new models, is it impossible to prolong the life of the existing model, that same Modern project, whose fate even today hangs by a very thin thread?

There are many reasons demanding very rapid transition from Modern to something new. One simple reason which, to the author's regret, politically very incorrect reason is that the world, which we like to believe is the 'West' and its leader as ever is the US, cannot maintain its hegemon playing by the rules proposed by the Modern project. It is worth remiding, that this 'Western' world imposed these rules on the rest of the world, calling them 'absolute' and 'sacred.' It has taken upon the mission of implementing Modernist rules, presuming that it still had to bear what the champion of British imperialism, Rudyard Kipling, so outrageously called the 'white man's burden'.

Over the course of two centuries (four, if we add the Pre-Modern epoch), the West controlled the world with the rules they put forth, etched on the stone tablets of the Modern project. Now it cannot do that. It has become clear that, in order to move fast along the path of Modernism, we must constantly feed its furnace with a particular fuel, and this fuel is none other than 'non-modernised human material'. This human material can be drawn only from the depths of traditional society.

That is what the most successfully modernising major Asian countries, India and China, are engaged in. Fuel for development of the Modern project is very much there and they know where to find this much sought after 'material.' In the West, such as in Russia, there is no such material. Without it, the Modern project in the West is beginning to stall. What this stalling implies is that China and India are beginning to grow faster than the USA and Europe. Leaving aside Europe, which will have to deal with its numerous problems for a long time and which still cannot be called a fully formed super-state of the new type, we will examine what it implies for the only real western superpower, the USA. We will consider it without any prejudice, unemotionally and objectively.

The global economic crisis demonstrated that the USA cannot weather the world race, as long as this race is carried out according to Modernist rules. A lot of numbers can be presented as evidence, but sufficient for the purpose here are some few well-known ones cited below.

According to various estimates, the USA produces 18-24 per cent of the global Gross Domestic Product (GDP) and consumes 28-36 per cent. Even if we take the minimal gap between what it consumes and produces, this is a gap of 4 per cent, which represents an increase in US debt by more than US$ 2 trillion a year. If we take the extreme figures—18 per cent production and 36 per cent consumption—then the US debt figure reaches US$ 10 trillion a year. (We are speaking of the accrual of implicit and explicit debts.)

But even with a minimum accrued debt at 4 per cent of global GDP per year (this is the most complementary of all possible estimates), the USA would have to declare itself bankrupt over the course of the next decade, having accumulated US$ 20 trillion of debt (in fact, even more). At the end of April 2010, the US Federal Reserve Chairman, Ben Bernanke, had publicly stated that a further increase in the US national debt was unacceptable because it was becoming impossible to service it. It is not only impossible to give it back, but also to service the debt. And, according to the International Monetary Fund (IMF) forecast (June 2011), in five year's time, China will overtake the USA by the sheer size of its GDP, calculated on the basis of the Yuan's Purchasing Power Parity.

So, when we speak of the game being played according to the rules of the Modern project, then the USA (and not only the USA) must recognise that, having won for a long time by these rules, they are beginning to lose by them. Would it appear that there is something unusual and bad in this? Humanity has always had different leaders at various stages. Within the Modern project framework, the leadership has also changed. For example, it was transferred from the British Empire to the USA and this was far from painless. Why should it not pass the baton of world leadership to someone else? Why would the world not continue to live according to the same Modern model, but with a different leader who would also once become tired and step down?

But first of all, unlike a sports competition, the baton of world leadership is rarely passed on sportingly from one country to another. If it were passed on smoothly, then perhaps at some point, the leader would have become Germany, not Great Britain. It is to avoid this situation that at least one World War—the first—was unleashed. This happens to be the basic common practice for the transfer of the baton in the Modernist world.

Hilferding, and Lenin after him, called this method "the law of uneven development" under imperialism. At the present stage, the transfer of the baton, according to the principle stemming from this law, would mean a third world war between the USA and China. Moreover, the former would be playing the role of the old imperialist country as Great Britain did in 1914 and China the role of the new imperialist country, similar to the one played by Germany in 1914.

This 'Third World War' would unfold on the lines of the First, rather than the Second World War, because the Second one had been fought over a strong ideological scheme. When talking about the possibility of the future war, we are not speaking of a conflict of ideologies, but a conflict of interest, the much vaunted 'place under the sun'.

There are many reputable experts, both American and European, who claim that this Third World War is not far off and that the USA has only up to 2017 to win such a war. For a long time, some of these estimates, such as the estimates of Paul Wolfowitz and his private group B-2,[1] were not discussed in the press. Now, gradually they are beginning to be discussed and the files are coming out of the 'top secret' shelves. But suppose everybody wants some other solution and rejects the very notion of a war, knowing that it will be a nuclear war, what could be the solution?

---

1. See, for example, the interview of Giulietto Chiesa, Member of the European Parliament with the Internet portal *rosbalt.ru* at the international media-club "Format A3" meeting on 21 February 2011. Chiesa refers to the "Project for the new American century", paper published in the USA in 1998, which claims that China will be the largest threat to the US security in 2017, <*http://www.rosbalt.ru/ukraina/2011/02/21/821655.html*>.

Could the USA agree to cede its position according to the Modernist rules? Let us see what the price of losing would be. Had the USA foreseen such a threat of this loss immediately after the production-consumption gap had begun to increase, everything would have been fine. The country could have agreed to step down from the highly favoured first place to a second place, reformed its economic policy and then tried to make an economic breakthrough and return to the first place.

But in order to avoid the perceived ignominy of the 'second place', which would not have been that painful, the USA began the game of dollar manipulation. First was the Jamaica agreement, turning currencies into market commodities, and then the build up of the foreign exchange game and the attempt to block the risks involved by the creation of new financial instruments called derivatives.

We have gradually come to a situation in which the annual gross world product was not much above US$ 50 trillion and the total amount of derivatives amounting to nearly US$ 4000 trillion or US$ 4 quadrillion, according to the Bank for International Settlements in Basel (sometimes called the 'Bank of Banks'). The volume of virtual finances thus exceeded real finances by almost 80 times.

This is what led to the global crisis. The fire of this crisis was extinguished with empty pieces of printed paper—massive currency emission. Real product did not increase. The 'bubble' that was purportedly burst in 2008 has begun to inflate again and a new crisis looms ahead. And nothing else can be done until one of the two things are done: either revert to Modernist rules following which the USA must lose or change the rules. The latter can be done only by replacing the existing world order (a.k.a. Modern) by some 'new grand narrative'—a new order or a new disorder.

The USA can now not agree to let the rules set by the Modern project work because if these rules are allowed to work, then, as the time for the breakthrough is already lost, the US step down would not be from the first to the second place, but to the fourth or fifth place with a disastrous effect on American prosperity. It would destabilise the political and social life of the country and will have unpredictable consequences for both the USA and the world.

It is impossible to prolong the existing order for a long time. One will soon witness a blatant non-compliance to the rules of the game, not because someone is defiant, but because sooner or later the rules will collapse and, what is worse, no one knows exactly when that collapse will happen. They could collapse at any moment or they could survive for several more years.

A well-known European expert told the author:

> It's not that we do not like to ride in the American car, but that we do not know how much longer it can go on—when the wheels will begin to fall off and the gas tank blow up. We would like to jump out of the car before it happens, but we do not know how to do this. We are afraid to think about it and at the same time think only of this.

So, what can the USA do if it cannot and does not want to give up the garland of primacy and at the same time cannot and does not want to win the world game by Modernist rules? The option for them is to abolish them and create new rules by which they can begin to win or to abolish all the rules for a time. It is for this reason that the problem of "controlled chaos" is becoming so serious today, and it is the problem of a new world disorder (disorder, not order).

In this regard, we all need to honestly answer the question—for whom and why is this disorder, chaos, instability, etc., needed in today's world. As yet, answers to this question have been so elusive and made to sound so serene that they are hardly believable. It is necessary to make one important reservation. When an official political actor says at an official event that he needs stability here and there, then it is not idiocy and not a crime, but an absolutely necessary and permissible statement, but has zero substance. It is about such statements that Charles-Maurice de Talleyrand once said, language was given to man to conceal his thoughts. By man, this great diplomat was of course referring to diplomats. Let the diplomats use language to conceal their thoughts at official functions. This is normal.

What is unacceptable is when people outside the official framework who have taken upon themselves the hard work of discovering the truth use language to conceal the truth. This is personally unacceptable to the author. It is unacceptable morally, epistemologically and existentially. The establishment of this position is especially necessary today, as it is time to gather together all those for whom 'the Lie' is unacceptable. If we let the moment pass, something irreparable may occur. We would never forgive ourselves if we did not do all that we could at the necessary moment.

So who really needs instability? Let us assume that we have an enemy. We are at war with our enemy. We are clearly not interested in stability on enemy territory. In fact we want the opposite. Let us now complicate the example slightly. There is now our competitor. We are not at war with our competitor, but in competition. Are we always interested in the stability of our competitor's field of operation? To speak honestly, we are almost never interested in its stability.

Does this mean that we will always and by all means undermine the stability of our competitor? Of course not. If we are law-abiding businessmen, then we will not use unlawful means to undermine the stability of a company with which we compete. But if we can do this using legal means and if it suits our interests, of course we will do so. Otherwise, we are not a law-abiding businessman, but a good Samaritan.

But are there many law-abiding businessmen in today's world? Especially, for a business that is risky and done on a large-scale? Of course there are still law-abiding businesses left, but not very many. The rest, as analysis of the global crisis has shown, are entirely ready to act outside the law, sometimes to minimise risk with a breach and sometimes taking risks. This type of business, which is gaining more strength, should be considered separately.

We engage in a certain kind of competition with our competitor, which has been described by scholars and practitioners as economic war. Long ago, George Soros described financial warfare in detail.[2] The famous scholar, Daniel Yergin, who has an impeccable academic reputation, long ago described energy warfare in detail.[3] The list of the types of economic warfare is long. Do those who conduct such wars need to ensure the stability of their enemy? It is obvious that, to the contrary, they need to ensure its instability by all means possible, and these stratagems, as we know, need a wide range of funds.

2. Soros, George (2001). *The Alchemy of Finance*. Moscow: INFRA-M.
3. Ergin, Daniel (1999). *The Prize: The Epic Quest for Oil, Money, and Power*. Moscow: DeNovo.

This is what differentiates economic warfare from economic competition. Oil competition involves a struggle for the reduction of costs and the increase of profitability. Oil warfare involves sabotage of the competitor's oil pipelines or the organisation of tribal wars on the territory through which the pipelines pass. We all know how exactly oil, gas and other wars are conducted. They have been described in detail. From these descriptions, it is incontestable that instability is very much needed and that very many people do not shun the most dirty and bloody means to ensure this instability. These people certainly do not always fall into the 'axis of evil' category. It is not evil, but profit that attracts them. As they say: "its nothing personal. It's just business".

So far, only respectable businesses that use disrespectable funds in a particular type of competition have been discussed. It is very important to stipulate that, besides them, there are completely disrespectable businesses, but they are very large and powerful, such as the global drug corporate. According to experts' estimates, revenues from drug trafficking are between US$ 600 billion to US$ 1 trillion per year.

Prior to the deployment of the US-led international coalition troops in Afghanistan in 2001, drug production in Afghanistan was 185 tons per year. The revenue from its sale was about US$ 3 billion a year. After the invasion, drug production increased by more than 40 times. According to official figures of the UN Office on Drugs and Crime (UNODC), the income from the sale of drugs produced in Afghanistan has risen to US$ 100-110 billion. Experts are well aware that we are talking about the income of rather highly centralised drug corporation, rather than the income of numerous minor, unrelated drug dealers.

Meanwhile, the Afghan drug corporation, although one of the largest, is by no means the only one. The aggregate earnings of the global drug cartel that controls Afghanistan, Colombia, Burma and other drug-producing regions range from US$ 600 to US$ 1000 billion a year. Of course, this mega-drug cartel is not a pyramid controlled from a single centre, but a network system. However, this network system has a fairly high level of covert centralisation. Does this system need stability in their field of operation? Of course not—it needs instability. This is obvious from the nature of the trade itself.

Experts know that large-scale drug trafficking is carried out to a significant degree on the basis of bartering 'weapons for drugs'. Weapon barons visit disadvantaged regions where warring tribes, groups and clans require arms. They exchange these weapons for drugs. The higher the degree of conflict in a disadvantaged area, the demand for weapons is more and hence more drugs can be received in exchange for weapons. Accordingly, the weapons barons have an interest in keeping the conflicts maximally high. They use various types of terrorist groups to control conflicts.

Thus, apart from the direct interests of drug lords in increasing instability and the lack of prosperity (the higher the instability and lack of prosperity, the more drugs are produced and consumed), there is also this drug-weapons-terrorism demand for instability. We are well aware that the actors in this arena are drug-weapons-terrorism consortia that are related to one or another elite clan in the security forces to a significant degree. It is not national interests that begin to play a decisive role here, but the interests of these clans, which by their very nature, are more inclined to trans-nationalisation.

As we see, the demand for volatility is huge because the consortia under discussion not only reap huge profits, but also invest the money they receive in different areas, particularly in activities directly or indirectly related to politics. A number of experts believe that the blood money from such structures is particularly useful in a situation of the current global financial crisis. The extent to which this crisis is connected with the legalisation of such huge amount of black money has been discussed at many fora.

Finally, there is a large-scale, although implicit, demand for instability by those who seek a new world order, or the new world orders under the hegemony of a single individual country, an 'alliance of the leading world powers' (such as G-2, otherwise known as 'Chimerica'), or on other foundations. It is an issue that has been much discussed by experts. Some of them are scared by such a possibility, while others believe that only under such an order can future global catastrophes be avoided.

As to the new world disorder (a.k.a. controlled, manageable chaos), it has begun to be discussed fairly recently but very actively, clearly in connection with the failure of attempts to create a particular kind of world order. The idea of controlled chaos is very simple. If we cannot rule by means of order, yet want to, we can exercise control by means of disorder. In fact, we rule others as long as we are the best of the lot—the most attractive and the most successful.

If others begin to develop quicker than us, we have two options. First, we develop faster. Then, we will preserve the greatest appeal and even if others develop, we will continue to control them. However, that is if we can develop faster. What if we cannot grow faster or if we begin to develop more slowly? Then the only way to continue to rule over others is to stop the development of those 'others' and even facilitate their degradation. Only thus, on the backdrop of the rapid deterioration of the situation of others and the slow deterioration of our own situation, we continue to control others.

In this situation, there arises a natural and extremely powerful demand for instability and the power to ensure that instability. Let us assume that this instability is promoted by radical Islam that is hostile to us. If we have a very strong need for instability, even though it is hostile to us, we will strive to make friends with it and to control it, because what is important for us in such a situation is to destabilise the major, fast-growing countries and to hinder their development or to reverse it. Radical Islam does not scare us, insofar as it has absolutely no wish to develop. Its ideal is not development at all, but the return of the Middle Ages in a new garb.

To make friends with radical Islam in 2010 after we have been fighting it since 2001 is possible only by presenting radical Islam with new opportunities in some regions, such as in the Middle East, in Northern Africa or in the Middle Asia. Providing such opportunities is only possible by betraying someone. In general, it is clear who that someone is: above all, it is the former allies and previously powerful elite of those countries that had decided to take the path of a Modern project (at different speeds and with different costs). The events that unfolded since the beginning of 2011, for some reason called the 'Arab Spring' are more than convincing in their illustration of this 'betrayal'.

Russia is not ready to discuss a scenario of controlled chaos, because it is concerned that this controlled chaos will also be created on its own territory. In conclusion, several classes of actors who create the demand for global and regional instability are noted below:

- The first class of actors—those who strive for the military or political destabilisation of their opponent.
- The second class of actors—conventional business structures involved in unconventional competition (economic warfare).
- The third class of actors—unconventional business structures (narcotics, arms, terrorism, etc.).
- The fourth class of actors—forces that place a stake on controlled chaos for world order.

All these four classes of actors are linked; they do not exist as 'things in themselves'. Thus, there is a huge demand for global and regional instability. This instability is not a result of mere errors committed by well-meaning actors who yearn for stability. This instability is also not the result of the machinations of isolated, relatively weak 'forces of evil.'

It is a consequence of the realisation of the large-scale demand from very serious and varied forces. Only by taking into account this demand, can we discuss the prospects of a G-2; the prospects of a unipolar American hegemony; and the prospects of building peace on the basis of a paradoxical alliance between the USA and radical Islam and peace based on even more complex configurations arising, for example, out of the special role of alliances between Pakistan and Saudi Arabia, Saudi Arabia and the USA, the USA and China, and China and Pakistan. The circle in the figure is a closed one.

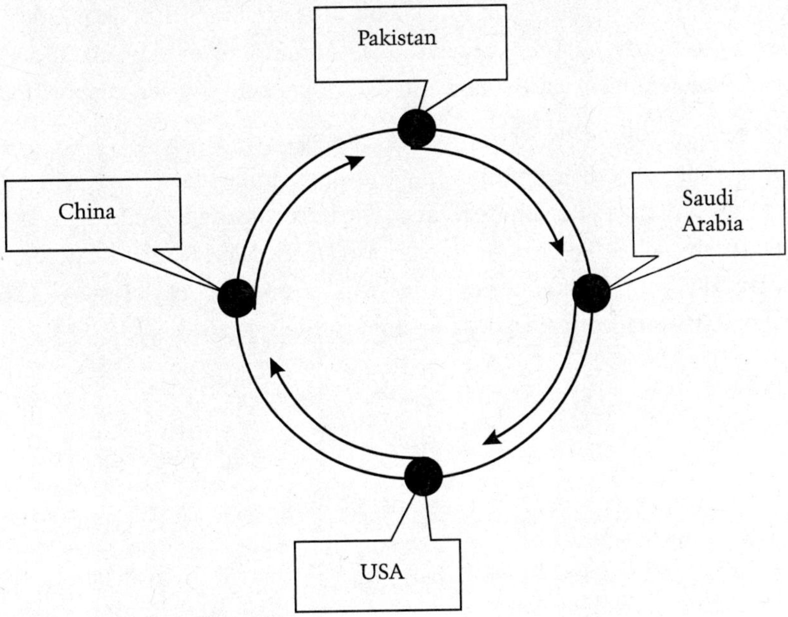

A careful and impartial consideration of similar configurations (combined with an analysis of the prospects of the course called "controlled chaos" and with the crisis of the grounds for micro-projects) can provide more data for practical policy than an analysis of the compromises and conflicts between the USA and China, which are unfolding before our eyes. In the end, it was no accident that not only Henry Kissinger, who has long been called the "chief lobbyist for the Chinese", not only came out in support of a G-2, but also his irreconcilable rival, Zbigniew Brzezinski, who has always aimed at building an alliance between the USA and radical Islamism.

The big game has just started. Our countries must be very careful in considering both its subtle structure and its logic, without ever succumbing to the temptation to demonise anyone. The world and humanity must find positive ways out of the current impasse. But these solutions will not emerge by themselves. In order to find them, we must look fearlessly at the situation in its entirety. We must look at what might be the political philosophy underlying the negative development of events discussed above, and what forces, groups and interests that may provide support for advancing this philosophy.

Only then, through genuine and thorough joint efforts, we will be able to resist the most dangerous trends that have already become apparent in the framework of the current demolition of the world order structure. Otherwise, our people and our countries will become victims of the global processes that we failed to diagnose in time in their entirety.

14 Emerging Patterns of International Hegemony and their Implications for the World Order

G2 or a New Cold War?

M. Rasgotra

A prominent thread in the discourse on international relations has been the idea of one or more states seeking to establish their hegemony in the world. Most recently, this idea has been given the form of an emerging G2, which refers to the possibility of a world order dominated and controlled by the USA and China.

Having emerged from a relatively simpler period when the world was made up of self-contained, essentially patriarchal states, the concept of global/international hegemony originated as a part of the state centric geopolitical discourse.

In today's world however, there are a host of different and new factors at play—modern technologies are empowering even relatively small states, while, at the same time, globalisation is eroding the salience of the individual state and empowering sub-state actors. In some sense, borders are becoming less relevant and other identities, ethnic, sectarian, etc., are assuming significance.

Equally, a series of economy-related developments have seen the relative decline of the West in comparison with new, emerging economies like China, Southeast Asia and India among others. This trend has had the effect of pluralising the international power patterns.

In this increasingly complex background, we can see a number of parallel developments—the growth in absolute numbers of the world population, the changing demographies in different regions, the growing urbanisation (along with the nature of much of this urbanisation today)—challenging the traditional structures and paradigms.

Each of these challenges is impacting upon the way societies and nations are ordered, perhaps even in ways not too well understood at the present time. The core trend, however, that is becoming visible is that it will increasingly be difficult for any single power or even a small grouping of states to embark upon a coherent, cohesive project of hegemony. Equally, given the increasing interdependence of states, it is becoming difficult for states or blocs of states to enter into lengthy conflictual relationships.

Historical Development

World War II and the End of European Hegemony

The world has been in a state of dynamic transition since the end of World War II and the world we see today is the outcome of those processes that began in 1945. For a great many years prior to World War II, power and control over much of the rest of the World had, for a variety of reasons, been consolidated in the North Atlantic states of Western Europe—mainly Great Britain. This consolidation of the British Empire was followed by three broadly parallel trends—the consolidation of American economic power, the unification and rapid industrialisation of Germany and the rise of Japan. The World Wars essentially marked the tussle between these powers to achieve a dominant position in the world. By the time the Second World War ended, Germany and Japan had been defeated and much of Europe lay devastated. Great Britain, though victorious, was completely exhausted. At that point, only America emerged relatively unscathed.

The Consolidation of Two Power Blocs and the Cold War

However, although it emerged into the most advantageous position, America was not unchallenged in the world. The Soviet Union, though much enervated by the war, managed to establish its hold over the countries of Eastern Europe. Thus, the war ended the European hegemony over the world and the world then split into two major camps opposed to one another; one led by the USA and the other by the USSR.

Both of these blocs were built upon radically differing ideologies. Beyond the political divide, there was a divergence in socio-economic pathways. In terms of motivation, however, the desire to proselytise their belief system and core values was eclipsed by a far more potent driver—an almost paranoid fear of the Other. In fact, the Cold War itself was less a hegemonic episode than a struggle to contain the Other's hegemony.

Liberation of Colonies

Another factor that we need to consider was the liberation, over a period of 20 years, of what were the colonies of Britain, Germany, USA, Portugal and Spain. In 1945, the UN had 45 members. Today, it has 193 members. This wave of liberation of nations across the world represents the final dismantling of the European hegemony and marked a shift in the global power dynamic—away from Western Europe.

More than the creation of a host of big and small nations, the lasting legacy of this process of liberation was due to the fact that it was often the result of protracted national liberation struggles. These movements were often modernising in nature and they created identities that people could adopt and a desire to achieve and consolidate their independence. This shift in the locus of political power also reflected the fundamental shifts that were occurring in all socioeconomic areas. Effectively, this huge fragmentation of power created a serious impediment for future attempts to establish hegemony.

Non-Aligned Movement

With the liberation process emerged a new movement called the Non-Aligned Movement (NAM). In a sense, this movement embodied the desire of a large number of the newly independent nations to resist being corralled into the Cold War Blocs that were consolidating at this very point in time.

Equally, the NAM represented a nascent desire to craft an ideological alternative, to both Communism and Capitalism, which would be more appropriate to the needs of the developing world.

As it turned out, the NAM was powerless in terms of economic or military power, but had considerable political influence on the world in general. While this movement has receded in relevance, there is no reason to suppose that the essential germ of opposition to hegemonic control will be weakened.

The Dynamics Today and the Rise of Asia

The world has not stopped changing. The dynamic transition continues and changes are sweeping the global scene. This transition is driven or manifested in several unfolding trends. The most visible trend on the global stage has been the rise of Asia. The dissolution of the Soviet Union itself was another vital element in this transition. This event temporarily weakened Russia and also created a number of new states in Asia. These developments were followed, after some years, by the re-emergence of a strong Russia.

The strong emergence on the global stage of a very dynamic China in economic and military terms has been followed by the comparatively slow rise of India. Japan, too is now assuming a larger political and unspoken military role in the region.

The most critical development is essentially the rise of China as an economic and military power. China was first an economic-industrial power. The Chinese Communist Party used the money from China's economic development for the growth of China's military power.

There is also the delayed rise of India as an economic power. India also has ambitions to become a military power and to be counted among the great powers.

The fundamental reality of today's world is that the economic, political and even military weight has shifted from the Euro-Atlantic region to the Asia-Pacific region.

Underlying Processes

Many of the changes that we have observed are underpinned by certain global trends. One of these very fundamental trends is the way in which the world's population is changing. Firstly, in absolute terms, the world's population has grown from around 3 billion at the end of World War II to around 7 billion. This has created a large number of challenges—in terms of food, water, livelihoods, environment, etc.

However, serious as this growth in numbers is, there is an even greater transition—taking place below the surface—the populations of much of the developed world are ageing while those of the less developed world constitute a youth bulge and are entering the employment. This has aggravated the problems these nations traditionally faced.

The response from states like America and Europe has been to try to offshore many of the lower end jobs to emerging economies. To match this, states like China and India have been trying to adopt a process of accelerated, capitalist development. As a result, there has been a serious shift of economic activity from the developed world towards these emerging economies.

These broad trends influence or affect, in different ways, some of the major world power contenders.

The United States

The USA for example, has acquired a stronger Asian role in the last couple of decades. It is present everywhere in the Asian mainland, Asian seas, etc. This broad footprint creates the impression of the USA as a hegemon. However, in reality, because of its involvement in wars in Iraq and Afghanistan, and a recession hit economy, it cannot impose its will and in critical situations is compelled to act in alliance partnership with regional actors.

The other powers—China, Russia, India and Japan—are even less capable of exercising hegemony.

Russia

Russia in its imperial period as well as in the Soviet era had made substantial inroads into adjoining areas and greatly expanded the territories under its control. Following the Afghan war, however, a number of internal challenges led to the collapse of the Soviet empire. For a period, Russia appeared vulnerable, but over time, it made a strong recovery and began a phase of consolidation. In time, Russia started leveraging its huge energy resources and began to position itself as a critical energy supplier for the future. In the process also, Russia has begun to exercise its new strength towards re-establishing its dominance in its immediate vicinity. Russia also takes a diplomatic position that is often at odds with the USA and with Europe.

Russia's most engaging dynamic is its evolving relationship with China. The long history of animosity between the two powers is now being exacerbated by the very real fears of a virtual take-over of Russia's East by Chinese migrants. However, at the same time, Russia is emerging as China's largest energy supplier.

China

At a cursory glance, China has a huge economy, vast territories and the world's largest population. Thus, there are very real fears that it might emerge as a global hegemon. However, if we look carefully, China does not have an easy path ahead of it.

China's population is concentrated in the coastal and inland provinces in the eastern half and beyond this, vast areas in the West are mainly sparsely populated desert terrain. Moreover, the populations here differ from the majority *Han* population and often belong to different religions. Within the Chinese heartland, there is a serious developmental divide—the coastal regions are far more prosperous than the more inland regions.

The economic miracle of China over the last 30 years basically sought to condense the process of industrialisation. This process has given rise to socio-economic tensions, widespread inequalities—individual/regional, land dispossessions, rising expectations and aspirations for an even better life and more individual freedom. All of these tend to challenge the state and the ruling Communist Party.

Militarily, while China does have a coastline, its sway over the seas beyond its shores is contested by a host of ethnically distinct and historically suspicious neighbours and in the larger Pacific Ocean, it faces the formidable naval power of the USA.

At another level, we must remember that China's cities have experienced war—in living memory. These memories were encased in policy by the Communist Party regime for its own purposes; while they generated nationalism, they also left a residue of anti-war sentiment. Precisely, the factors that spurred its economic rise are now driving consumerism and aspirations within China; these are creating a layer of vested interest in avoiding major conflict and the consequent disruptions.

Effectively then, much though China might want to be a hegemon, it does not really have the wherewithal, the geo-strategic vantage, will to war and perhaps even, the need.

India's Role on the World Scene

In point of time, India entered the global stage as a significant power much after China. India's rise is anchored in its very young demographic shapes combined with the existence of a large pool of technically skilled, English speaking manpower. This enabled India to leap over the phase of industrialisation and directly enter the global services sector as a major player.

Once its economic liberalisation and integration with the world economy were in place, India began to be taken far more seriously than before. This obvious economic weight combined with the collapse of its one time ally, the Soviet Union, gave India the opportunity to revisit its patterns of foreign engagement and led to a closer embrace of the Western models.

India has made tremendous progress in all domains. However, it remains essentially a developing nation since the majority of its population still continues to live at a subsistence level and income disparities keep growing. Its foreign policy has apparently made a u-turn from the pro-Soviet Union to a pro-US stance. However, there are certain constants —India has always prized its independence of action and it places a great premium on its core value of pluralism and democracy. In its foreign policy, it will remain opposed to military alliances and military intervention and will always have a preference for softer, consensus-based options. At the same time, given India's fundamental value system, it will display a preference for democratic/plural dispositions. Similarly, it will tend to oppose aggregation on sectarian/religious basis.

Thus, for example, while India cooperates with China on global issues like environment and energy security and engages in trade and economic activity with China, it strongly opposes Chinese strong arm tactics towards India or any other country. India's foreign and security policies are free of any hegemonic impulses, and while it is slowly developing its economic and military strengths, its soft power accounts even more for its growing role and influence in world affairs.

Japan

Japan rose from the ashes of World War II and found itself bound inextricably by the conditionalities imposed by the post War Order and its alliance with the USA. In the circumstances, the Japanese adopted a policy of leveraging their manpower and its skills towards becoming a manufacturing super power, predicated massively upon exports. In a short span, Japan emerged as the world's second largest economy. Its peculiar predicament was aptly captured in the description "an economic giant and a military pygmy".

However, that stance is undergoing a change. Japan is faced with a sometimes-hostile relationship with North Korea and China. Moreover, there is a growing sense that the relationship with the USA has had its ups and downs and thus, the American security umbrella may not suffice or it may not be available when really needed. Therefore, Japan has lately begun to adopt more overt military postures to defend itself. Japan is beginning to emerge as a serious military and naval power.

Europe

There is the evolutionary process in Europe. While the sheer economic weight of its constituents has allowed much of Western Europe to carry its prosperity into the contemporary period, in absolute terms, Europe without its empires and with a noticeably ageing population has long been on a declining trajectory. Nevertheless, the European Union (EU) is an important economic and political bloc, with a large market and labour sources, even as it contends with problems created by the Eastwards expansion and migrations.

Europe, today, remains caught up in the tension between integration and enlargement. Of course, part of this Eastwards drive is politically inspired—in particular—by the imperatives (after the collapse of the Soviet Union) of the US–European project to contain a possible resurgence of Russia.

But Europe is still a work in progress and it also faces a number of internal challenges like the ageing of population and the imperfect assimilation of migrants into the European value system. Therefore, Europe today does not exercise the kind of military effect on global developments as the Europe of old did.

Analysis

A number of new situations arise from this complex set of processes at play.

First, as the emerging economies gather strength, they are becoming more assertive politically too. Second, as their own needs rise and as resources dwindle globally, the new emerging economies are entering into active competition with the developed world for resources. Third, with large population and with widespread and accelerated developmental processes, pressure is mounting on the global environment leading to palpable change in the earth's climate. Weather conditions in different regions are already becoming increasingly unpredictable.

The result of these major transformations, however, will not be scarcity-driven wars, but the evolution of new challenges and processes. These processes will demand greater cooperative action on scales unimaginable even for the largest of states. It is this fact, and not just good intentions, that will reduce the possibility of major conflicts and attempts to impose hegemony.

The main actors on the global stage are themselves being transformed at the same time as powerful new actors appear on that same stage. With the change in economic weight and with the demographic changes taking place across the world, a new balance will need to be forged.

Additionally, a number of non-state actors have entered the scene. Some multinational corporations have businesses larger than the Gross Domestic Product (GDP) of many states. Then, there are individuals and groups that are becoming empowered in ever new ways and are sometimes challenging the *status quo*. Humanity as a whole is being confronted by a host of unprecedented challenges. These will curtail the abilities of individual states to act singly for human security and for the further advancement of human civilisation.

Interdependant Economies

In this situation, another element has entered; economic globalisation has resulted in the close interdependence of all these major countries, other countries and the regional groupings in the world. Take for instance, the Chinese economy and the American economy, the two countries could be possible focal points of the world's division into two centres of power. However, while they might well compete, diverge or even enter into low-level localised conflicts, their economies are so embedded in each other that there is no real scope for any major conflict between these countries.

Globalisation Leads to a Wider Distribution of Power

One of the results of globalisation is that it leads to a wider distribution of power in the global system. The main protagonists will always tend to engage in a complex web of cooperation and competition so that there will be a constantly shifting drama of blocs and groupings. Thus, due to this distribution of power over the five major countries with their affiliates, their partners, friends, associates and the regional groupings, there is no danger of China and the USA coming together to form a G2 and exerting joint hegemonic power over the rest of the world.

Shifting Alliances: Economic and Security Groupings

As time progressed, in the so-called Third World and in Europe also, a new pattern emerged: of groupings of countries for economic and development purposes and for exerting their influence on world developments. This can be seen from the growth of the Association of Southeast Asian Nations (ASEAN) in the East, the EU and the coming together of some Latin American countries and the beginnings of the South Asian Association for Regional Cooperation (SAARC) process in South Asia. The SAARC process has been sluggish and even Europe's evolution is not yet complete. ASEAN has gathered some cohesion and strength.

In parallel, several security and political groupings like the SCO (Shanghai Co-operation Organisation) and BRICS (Brazil, Russia, India, China and South Africa) have emerged to try to push collaborative or synchronised challenges that might be beyond a single nation's capabilities.

Competition plus Cooperation

While there is no real danger either of hegemony or conflict, there is every possibility of each country trying to win associates or friends in their respective regions for greater political influence, though not dominance. India, for example, has very good relations with the USA, Japan and Russia. It has a difficult relationship with China due to the border problems. There is also a sense of rivalry between the two Asian powers. China is trying to expand and exert political presence and influence in the South Asian region. This is resented by India now, but in the long run, India will realise that this is a normal process. Similarly, as India rises economically and militarily, it will begin to exert influence in China's periphery. Russia has a developing relationship with Europe and the USA. It has a decent but evolving relationship with Japan. It has a relationship of cooperation, competition and suspicion with China. China has a relationship of rivalry with the USA. It is trying to woo India while also trying to restrain and constrain India and is trying to reduce India's influence in its own periphery. China's relationships with the USA, Russia and India and the way they shape will determine the question of Asian stability, peace and harmony.

In a decade or more, a kind of Asian equilibrium will emerge. So, this will be a period of ups and downs, small disturbances here and there and a process of readjustments. There is no likelihood of major conflicts. But the process of readjustments among the five powers will go on for one to two decades.

Conclusion

Thus, there is also no real possibility of a cold war either and hopefully a world of peace and harmony will emerge before too long.

States, governments and societies need to move their thinking beyond the earlier discourse and begin taking cognisance of the new emerging realities. While the geopolitical discourse has remained anchored in the Cold War, the world has moved on. This discourse, therefore, needs to be updated to enable us to take care of these emerging challenges.

15 The System of Multilateral Intergovernmental Organisations as a Mechanism for Dominance and Control by the 'Strong'

Yury Byaly

Multilateral Organisations: Formation of the System

Post 17th century, with the global emergence of numerous countries that cooperated militarily, politically and economically, the practice of bilateral negotiations and agreements became insufficient for ensuring the sustainability of co-existence among nations. There arose the need to create conciliation mechanisms to discuss multinational issues and for decision making. After numerous attempts with various degrees of success, the Westphalian system,[1] founded three and a half centuries ago in Europe, was chosen as the first such mechanism and, in a sense, the model for future multilateral organisations (MOs), including the United Nations (UN). Nonetheless, until the early 20th century, an effective and permanent MO was an exception rather than the rule.

World War I gave a powerful impetus for the creation of multilateral institutions. However, the League of Nations, established in 1920 and intended to provide a global security system, turned out to be an inefficient body, failing to ensure effective sanctions against Japan when it attacked Manchuria in 1931 or Italy when it attacked Ethiopia. Nor could it prevent the internationalisation of the Spanish Civil War. By 1940, the League of Nations was no longer involved in resolving international security issues.[2]

---

1. The Westphalian system of international relations was established by European nations in 1648 after the 30 years' war. The principles of observing national sovereignty and respect for international law were laid down.
2. *Encyclopedia Collier* (2000). Open Society.

The global recognition of the disastrous military, political and economic effects of World War II led to the establishment in 1945 of global MOs like the UN, the International Monetary Fund (IMF) and the World Bank (WB), as also the General Agreement on Tariffs and Trade (GATT)—later the World Trade Organization (WTO).[3] At the same time, a number of MOs in specialised fields were created or transformed into global entities (e.g., the League of Arab States (LAS) and the International Criminal Police Organisation—Interpol).[4]

The next impetus to form a modern multilateral system was provided by the disintegration of the colonial system that brought about the need to resolve many regional conflicts among the newly emerged states (especially in post-colonial Africa). During this period, regional MOs in the field of political and economic cooperation began to crop up, such as the Organisation of African Unity (later the African Union—AU), the Organisation of the Islamic Conference (OIC), the Economic Community of West African States (ECOWAS) and Economic Community Central African States (ECCAS), etc.

During the Cold War, most of the regional security problems were resolved, one way or another, by the two rival superpowers (the USA and the USSR), within the UN, through the confrontation of politico-military blocs: the North Atlantic Treaty Organisation (NATO) and the Warsaw Pact, or by the influence of one of the superpowers in their semi-formal

3. The UN was established on 24 October 1945, on the initiative of the USSR, the USA, Great Britain and China with the aim to maintain international peace and security on the basis of equal rights and self-rule of nations and just settlement of international disputes by peaceful means (Current International Law, 3 Volumes. V. 1. M., 1999, 1-2). The WB was established on 1 July 1944, to provide loans to states in need of financial resources to carry out effective economic policy. The IMF was established on 27 December 1945, to lend credit to countries with a balance of payments deficit, stabilisation of exchange rates and promotion of foreign exchange and trade cooperation. GATT was signed on 30 October 1947, for the provision of a Most Favored Nation trade regime (it was transformed into the WTO in 1995).

4. The LAS is a regional organisation of Arab states. It was established on 22 March 1945, by Egypt, Iraq, Syria, Jordan, Lebanon, Saudi Arabia and Yemen and currently has 22 members. The Interpol was created in 1919 and ceased to function in 1938, insofar as its headquarters were located in occupied Austria. It was reconstituted in 1946 and its current Charter was adopted in 1956. Interpol's main task is to coordinate the activities of countries in their fight against crime.

or informal 'zone of responsibility.'[5] During this period, given the inability of global economic MOs (the IMF, World Bank, WTO) to ensure the development of the world's 'economic periphery,' MOs were formed in all regions to ensure economic cooperation among the participants. Among them the salient ones are: the Association of Southeast Asian Nations—ASEAN; the Latin American Economic Union—*Mercosur* (Argentina, Brazil, Uruguay, Paraguay, Venezuela); the South Asian Association for Regional Cooperation—SAARC (India, Pakistan, Nepal, Bangladesh, etc.); the Organisation of Eastern Caribbean States—OECS (Antigua, Dominica, Grenada, etc.); the Cooperation Council for the Arab States of the Gulf (Saudi Arabia, Oman, UAE, Bahrain, Kuwait, Qatar); and the *Andean* Community (Bolivia, Colombia, Ecuador Peru), etc.

At the same time, a number of MOs for resolving humanitarian problems (the Red Cross and Red Crescent, Doctors Without Borders, and others) were formed and the existing bodies' objectives and membership expanded.[6] In the process described above, ultimately the basic, 'standard mechanism' for the formation and functioning of multilateral organisations was worked out. As a rule, an MO was created as a permanent association on the basis of an international agreement (in the form of a charter or Statute) in which its scope, objectives, procedures, subject matter and procedures were defined, as also the mechanisms for decision making on specific issues. At the same time, in the majority of MOs, regardless of their statutory mechanisms for decision-making (consensus, majority voting, etc.), these decisions were not mandatory but were in the nature of recommendations even for the member countries, but more so for countries not included in the organisation.

---

5. The question of the post-war superpowers' 'zones of responsibility' began to be resolved with the Yalta (February 1945) and the Potsdam (July 1945) Conferences. Thus, Yugoslavia, Albania, Bulgaria and Romania fell within the zone of Soviet responsibility. Coming up against the hard line of the USA and Britain, the USSR relinquished claims to spread its influence to Iran and Turkey, however, insisted on preservation of its 'zone of responsibility' in Poland and Czechoslovakia.
6. The international organisations, Red Cross and Red Crescent, obtained legal status in 1949, when the Geneva Conventions was adopted. In 1965 at the 20th International Convention in Vienna, the basic principles of the organisation were formulated: humanity, impartiality, neutrality, independence, voluntary service, unity, and universality. The international non-governmental organisation (NGO), Doctors Without Borders was created in 1971 in Paris by a group of French doctors and journalists to provide help to victims of armed conflicts and natural disasters.

The only exception is the UN, in which decisions taken by the Security Council are binding for both member states and the few remaining non-member countries. For example, Yugoslavia was pronounced as "a nation in a state of collapse" after Slovenia and Croatia declared independence in 1991 and was excluded from the UN, but the Security Council resolutions specifying the political and military demands for Yugoslavia were mandatory.[7]

Multilateral Organisations: The Internal Mechanisms of Domination

There exist MOs that set exclusive prerogatives for a few founding members upon their formation. Thus, in the UN, the five permanent members of the Security Council have the exclusive right of veto. In the IMF, the ability of a country or groups of countries to influence decision making is determined by the country's/group's quotas—that is, their share of financial contributions to the Fund's equity shares capital.[8] This is a formalised, simpler and more transparent mechanism for dominance.

Figure 15.1

Formalised Statuary Dominance of a Participating Country in a Particular MO

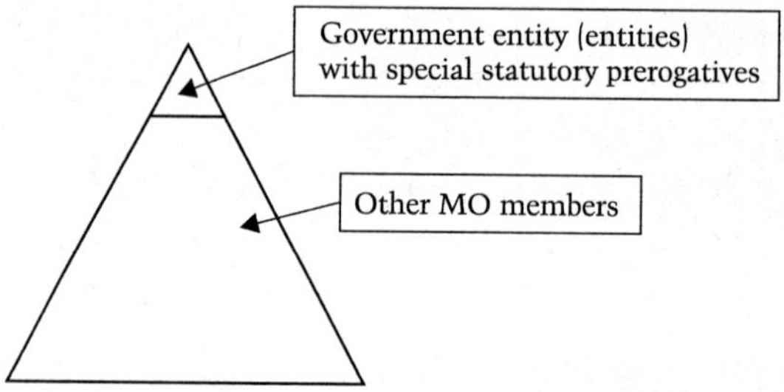

7. In July 1992, the NATO began patrolling the waters of the Adriatic Sea in support of United Nations Security Council (UNSC) resolutions No. 713 and No. 757, introducing an arms embargo and other sanctions against the former Yugoslavia. On 25 May 1993, the UNSC adopted resolution No. 827, approving the Charter for the International Tribunal for the former Yugoslavia. On 15 December 1995, the UNSC resolution No. 1031 was adopted giving IFOR (Implementation Force of the Peace Agreement in Bosnia and Herzegovina) a mandate to maintain peace and, if necessary, to enforce peace. On 23 September 1998, UNSC resolution No. 1199 dictated that Belgrade cease hostilities, withdraw Special Forces from Kosovo, start a dialogue with the Kosova Albanians, and ensure conditions for the return of refugees.

8. *<http://www.imf.org/external/>*.

The principle of formal equality between members has been incorporated into the Charters and Statutes of a majority of MOs. Nonetheless, mechanisms for informal leadership are manifested to some degree in such MOs, allowing for the substantial dominance of individual members or their groups in determining priorities and in the development and implementation of resolutions.

For this, the 'strong' players most frequently use both the weak members' various dependencies on them (including investment, credit, technological, military, political and other dependencies) and the 'donor' mechanisms, where the 'strong' players finance the activities of the MO beyond their obligations set forth in its Charter (Figure 15.2), their aim being to make the MO serve their own self-interests.

Figure 15.2

Informal Dominance of 'Strong' MO Participants

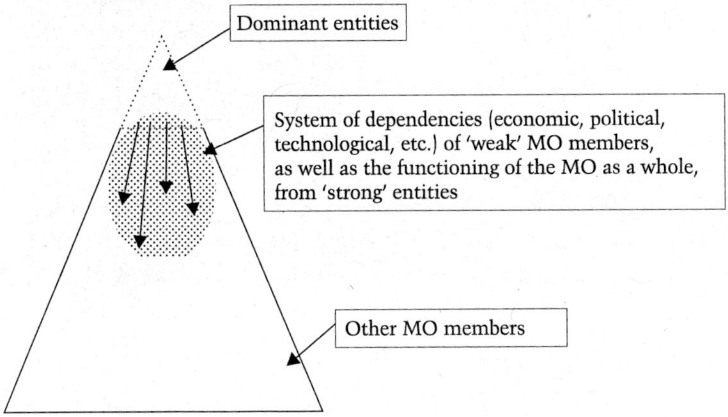

Thus, in the history of the UN, there have been numerous cases in which the 'superpowers'—the USA and the USSR—used their influence over 'dependent' members of the UN and non-permanent Security Council members to make the 'necessary' decisions. Currently, countries such as Germany, Japan and a number of others that are not among the Security Council's permanent members have a growing influence on the larger UN decisions in various areas on account of their expanding economic relations with many UN member countries, as well as on account of targeted funding of a number of UN projects in excess of the statutory requirements.[9]

Saudi Arabia, despite the mandatory equality among members in the OIC, attempts to dominate by taking advantage of the following factors: the placement of the OIC headquarters on its territory (Jeddah); the world-wide Muslim pilgrimage to the 'original' Islamic holy sites; many Saudi charities' informal influence in the Islamic world; position of dominance on the world oil market; lobbying for Islamic interests in the West through financial means; and a system of informal influence by the Saudi elite to increase its influence in the OIC.[10]

In this context, it is very difficult for a group of 'weak' MO members to get their own interests accommodated and to have a role in coordinating the actions, thus disenabling them from effectively opposing the 'strong' when decisions are taken by the MO. They react to this situation by trying to 'sabotage' and block the decisions from being implemented. It is for this reason that many of the MOs the world over function on paper only.

New Trends in Dominance in the System of Multilateral Organisations in the Post-Bipolar World

Prior to the collapse of the Soviet Union, the policies of countries within the Western and Eastern blocs and the MOs in which these countries participated were to a large extent determined by the clear dominance of the two 'superpowers,' but with the fall of the Soviet Union, there have been radical changes in the global system of the organisations.

Firstly, several MOs have begun to assume a more important status and functions, besides expanding their geographic zones of influence, responsibility and scope of activities. That is, by default, they gained a dominating position.

---

9. For example, in the late December 2006, the UN General Assembly adopted a resolution on financing the budget for 2007-2009 in the capacity of US$ 2 billion. The USA's share of funding for the UN budget was 22 per cent, Japan's 16.6 per cent, followed by Germany and Great Britain (*RBC Daily*, 6 February 2007).
10. See, for example: <*http://i-r-p.ru/page/stream-nb/index-9774.html*>.

Figure 15.3

Dominance of a Strong MO on Account of Intercepting Functions

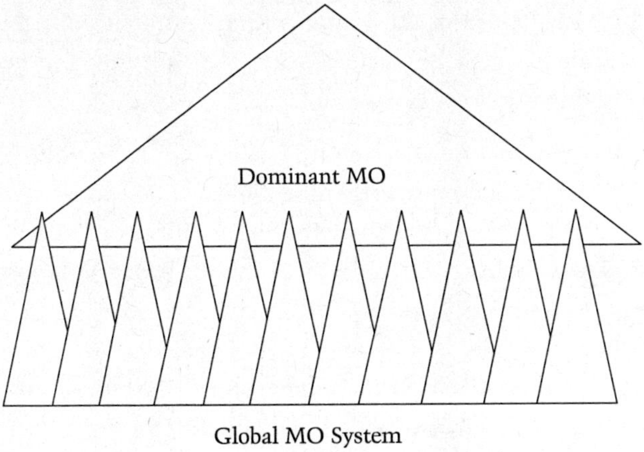

The most striking example is that of the NATO, which at first *de facto* (in the first Iraq war and in Yugoslavia) and then *de jure* (at the NATO Anniversary Summit in April 1999) assumed the core functions of the Security Council and peace-keeping forces. It incorporated into its purview the right to use force without UN Security Council sanctions, even outside the member states' territories of the alliance.[11]

Secondly, a kind of 'vacuum' crept into many of the organisations' will to dominate, a will which had previously enabled the imposition of coordinated decisions or resolutions. Because of this 'vacuum,' the competition between the participants within MOs for leadership as well as for building a hierarchy of priorities has dramatically escalated. For example, there is growing competition for leadership in the OIC between Saudi Arabia, Iran and Turkey. In the LAS, there has long been an intense

11. Arbitrarily interpreting the UNSC resolution No. 678 of 29 November 1990, which demanded Iraq withdraw its troops from occupied Kuwait before 15 January 1991, an international coalition led by the USA went to war against Iraq in the Persian Gulf on 17 January 1991, <*http://daccess-dds-ny.un.org/doc/RESOLUTION/GEN/NR0/575/28/IMG/NR057528.pdf*?OpenElement>. On 24 March 1999, NATO troops began an intervention in Yugoslavia without sanction from the UNSC (Luc Rosenzweig. "L'OTAN a reçu l'ordre de bombarder la Yougoslavie." Le Monde. 25 March 1999). At the Washington Summit on 24 April 1999, the use of military force outside the territory of the NATO member countries was included into the number of the alliance's statuary authorisations (e.g., see: The Alliance's Strategic Concept, 24 April 2011, <*http://www.nato.int/*>).

competition for leadership between Saudi Arabia, Egypt and Libya. The competition between the Saudi Crown Prince (now King) Abdullah and the former Head of Libya, Muammar Gaddafi took on a most acute character. For example, on the eve of the Iraq War that commenced in 2003, Gaddafi positioned himself with Baghdad at the LAS Summit and accused Saudi Arabia of serving the West.[12]

Thirdly, a wide field of competition appeared between various MOs active in similar or overlapping fields. This occurred because the majority of the countries are participating members of several MOs. The indivisibility and the inter-relatedness of the fields of regulation of the MOs (with profiles) predetermined the kind of 'intersection' of interests of these MOs-member countries in different areas of regulation. This spelt a high probability of collision between incongruous charters (statutes) and the norms of various MOs in 'overlapping' regulatory spheres.

It is in these areas of conflict that opportunities arise for the 'strong' to increase their influence on decision making and the implementation of resolutions by interpreting the bylaws and resolutions to their interests and benefit. This increases the scope for domination.

Figure 15.4

Dominance through Management of Conflicts in Norms of Various MOs in the Zone of Intersection in their Spheres of Regulation

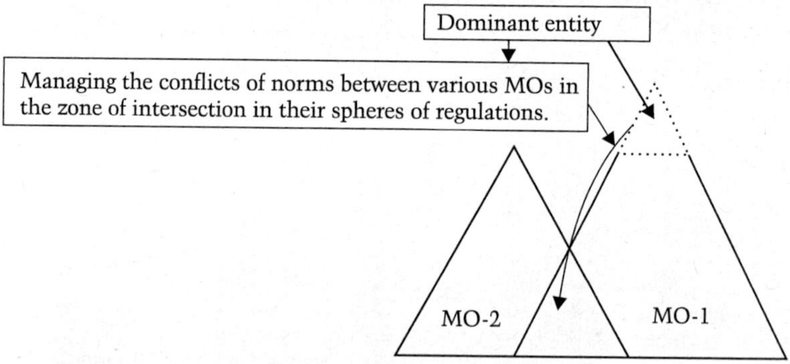

12. See, for example: Myers, S.L. (2003). "Hussein is Urged by Arab Emirates to Give Up Power", *The New York Times*, 1 March.

Thus, during the global financial economic crisis, the 'strong' countries in Europe, having failed to come to an agreement with the USA through the IMF and the G20 summits on the issue of the global limit for speculation in financial markets, began to restrict financial speculation in the economic space of the European Union (EU). For example, seeking to stop speculation on the stock market, the German financial regulator, Ba Fin, banned unsecured transactions with state bonds within the Eurozone, credit-default swaps and shares of the 10 largest financial institutions in the country on the rationale that there was 'extreme volatility' of debt securities in euro-area countries.[13]

An even more striking example was witnessed during the conflict in Libya in the spring and the summer of 2011. The main onus of investigations into human rights violations during the conflict fell on the UN International Court of Justice (ICJ), as well as on MOs such as Amnesty International and Human Rights Watch. An inquiry commission, which Gaddafi repeatedly invited to Libya, was not sent by the ICJ. The Human Rights Watch investigation into the number of fatalities and the wounded in the attacks by Gaddafi's troops in Misurata completely refuted rebel statements about the shelling of civilians and there being thousands of fatalities among women and children.[14] An investigation by Amnesty International too completely refuted rebel statements about mass rape by soldiers.[15]

And yet, Head of the International Criminal Court (ICC), Luis Moreno-Ocampo, issued international arrest warrants for Gaddafi and his closest associates solely on the basis of rebel claims, all under the biddings of interested members of the Security Council.[16] It is obvious that the contradiction between the MOs' bylaws relating to and the resolutions on incidents described above would lead to a severe weakening of the effectiveness of these MOs in their 'overlapping' spheres of activity. This means the undermining of the ability of member countries to realise their interests with the help of these MOs.

---

13. *RBC Daily*, 20 May 2010.
14. *Boston Globe*, 14 April 2011.
15. *Corriere della Sera*, 25 June 2011.
16. *AFP*, 27 June 2011.

The following scenarios illustrating the weakening of MOs have been the most typical in the 'post-bipolar' epoch:

- A game by the member countries of several MOs to identify their priorities on an *ad hoc* basis within these organisations. For example, Turkey, positioned at the intersection of interests between the OIC and NATO, strongly supported the NATO operation in Yugoslavia (as did the vast majority of the Islamic world). But Turkey unambiguously sabotaged the NATO operation in Iraq (as a member of the OIC).[17] The former Soviet republics of Central Asia often torpedo regulatory initiatives by Russia and also the initiatives of each other, referring to the various statutory restrictions of different MOs. This happens because they are simultaneously members of the OIC, the Shanghai Cooperation Organisation (the SCO) and the Collective Security Treaty Organisation (CSTO).[18]
- Serious difficulties arise in developing sustainable policies for countries caught in the intersection of the regulatory spheres of several multilateral organisations to which they are affiliated or intend to enter. For example, these problems constantly occur in Persian Gulf countries that are 'at an intersection' between their membership to OIC and the LAS, on the one hand, and on

---

17. Turkey was among the 18 NATO countries that participated in the military invasion onto the territory of Yugoslavia, which began on 24 March 1999. Moreover, in an interview with an American television channel, President Demirel said that for over half a century Kosovo had been part of the Ottoman Empire (Interview with Turkish President Suleyman Demirel, PBS 22 April 1999, *<http://www.pbs.org/newshour/bb/europe/jan-june99/demirel_4-22.html>*. But on 1 March 2003, the Turkish Parliament rejected the possibility of coalition lead by the USA using the country's territory for an attack on the Iraqi territory (Filkins, D. (2003). "Turkish Deputies Refuse to Accept American Troops", *The New York Times*, 2 March).

18. At the time, the Collective Security Treaty Organization (CSTO) was established in 2002 (comprising Russia, Belarus, Kazakhstan, Armenia, Kyrgyzstan, Tajikistan and Uzbekistan), there already was a group in the region for the coordination of economic and military issues (the SCO), which includes Russia, China, Kazakhstan, Kyrgyzstan, Tajikistan and Uzbekistan. However, in the SCO's mechanism, members have no obligation to ensure their mutual security, which in the context of the growing likelihood of military, terrorist and political destabilisation in Central Asia was important for a number of former Soviet states. It was in this capacity that the CSTO led by Russia arose, which is often seen as an alternative to the SCO led by China (for example, see: Miller, L. (2010). "Fear and Loathing in Central Asia", *Foreign Policy*, 5 August).

the other, in the Cooperation Council for the Arab States of the Gulf as also with the OPEC, the oil cartel group. Former Soviet republics meet with serious difficulties in reconciling the rules of economic policy between the Eurasian Economic Community (EEC) that they have created and the rules of the WTO.[19]

- Member countries of several 'multilaterals' often attempt to weaken the capability and the international role of MOs that have mechanisms that are not in their interest and are more of a burden to them. For example, Libya is a member of the League, but when it came into conflict over policy with Saudi Arabia, it began to torpedo the initiatives of the League's African countries who were also members of the AU, the composition of which 'overlaps' with that of the LAS.[20] The LAS endorsed the EU proposal to join the Mediterranean Union it had established and ultimately obtained an observer status.[21] However, the initiator of its establishment and the informal leader of the AU, Muammar Gaddafi, did not allow the African countries to join the Mediterranean Union and demanded that the EU not interfere in the affairs of the continent.[22]

The expansion and increasing complexity of the global system of MOs, whose activities conflict or overlap in the global economic, military, political and humanitarian fields, are gradually leading to chaotic functioning in almost all spheres of their statutory responsibilities. This

---

19. Moldova is an associate member of Eurasian Economic Community (EAEC); moreover, the conditions of its membership in the WTO do not coincide with the customs regulations of the EAEC. Similar problems await Kazakhstan after its proposed entry into the WTO in 2012. Experts believe that the "environment" in the Russian led Customs Union economic regime will inevitably complicate the trade relations of the WTO countries within the Commonwealth of Independent States (CIS) and will create external economic problems for Russia-Belarus and the EAEC. In the case of Russian accession to the WTO, all these alliances will be virtually meaningless.

20. The AU was established in 2001 as a regional organisation of 52 African states with the objectives of dialogue with the international community from a unified position, the protection of the sovereignty and territorial integrity of member states, promotion of peace and security on the continent, and the resolution of regional conflicts, *<http://www.africa-union.org/Official_documents/Treaties_Conventions_fr/Acte%20Constitutif.pdf>*.

21. *Le Point*, 3 November 2008.

22. *The Daily Telegraph*, 10 July 2008

automatically reduces the activity of the vast majority of MOs that are part of the global system of multilateral institutions.

Figure 15.5

Reduction of Activity of Elements in the Global MO System through Chaotisation of their Activities in the Conflicting Intersections between their Spheres of Regulation

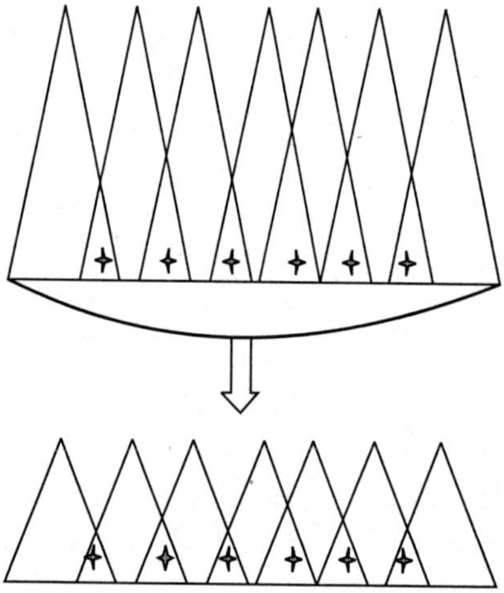

For example, the SAARC[23] was practically inoperative as a result of an unflagging conflict between its two most powerful members. The main problem with this MO is the severe disagreements between India and Pakistan on many sensitive issues, including territorial disputes, the division of the waters of the Indus River, Pakistan's role in terrorist activity in India, the rivalry between the countries for influence in Afghanistan, etc.[24]

Secondly, the trends described automatically increase the role and influence on global processes of large states (entities) and, concomitantly, the MOs formed by them: these states are able to 'force through' their own interests and achieve their objectives even if they are in conflict with the

23. The SAARC was established in December 1985, comprising Bangladesh, Bhutan, Maldives, Nepal, Pakistan, India and Sri Lanka. Afghanistan joined SAARC in April 2007.

24. For example, see: Zamaraeva, N.A., "Pakistan and the 2010 SAARC Summit," *Middle East Institute*, *<http://www.iimes.ru/rus/stat/2010/03-05-10b.htm>*.

processes of the existing MO system. The most striking example is the USA, which since the terrorist attacks in New York and Washington on 11 September 2001, has been overriding the UN, the Islamic Conference and the LAS and spearheaded NATO's wars in Iraq and Afghanistan.[25]

Thirdly, this allows these large entities to increase their influence at both the local and the global level through mechanisms, resulting in conflicts of interest and further chaos in the global MO system. Thereby, they manage to build up a position of dominance in the regions involved.

Figure 15.6

Dominance Due to 'Controlled Chaotisation' of the Global MO System

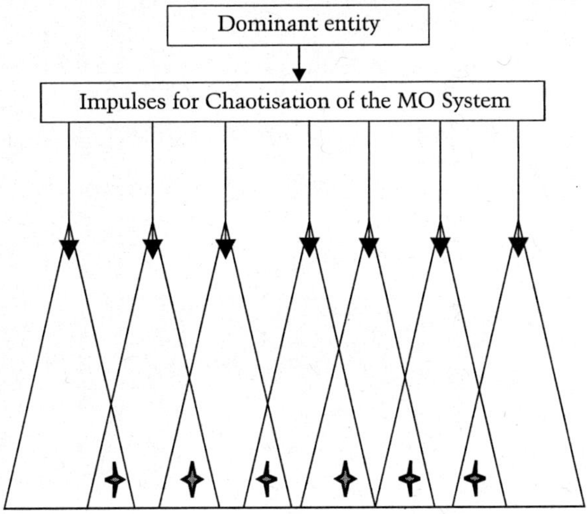

25. Both military operations were launched by NATO member countries without the agreement of the UNSC and in violation of its Charter. The military operation in Afghanistan began on 7 October 2001. Only on 29 December 2001, did the UNSC adopted resolution No. 1386 on the establishment of the International Security Assistance Force (ISAF) in Afghanistan (placed under NATO control from 2003), *<http://www.un.org/russian/documen/scresol/res2001/res1386.htm>*. The invasion of the military coalition of NATO countries into Iraq began on 20 March 2003. The UNSC resolution No. 1483 of 22 May 2003, retroactively justified this invasion, welcoming the creation of the Provisional Ruling Council of Iraq and the UN Mission for post-war reconstruction of the country, *<http://www.un.org/russian/documen/scresol/res2003/res1483.htm>*.

For example, the Chinese initiative to establish a Free Trade Zone (FTZ) with the ASEAN[26] met with stiff opposition from the USA and came to a peak when discussions began for the inclusion of the US allies, Japan and South Korea in the FTZ. As a counter measure, the USA first started to strengthen the MO it dominated—the Asia-Pacific Economic Cooperation (APEC) Forum—and then tried to create an alternative MO with a working name of the North ASEAN, comprising the USA, Japan, Russia, Canada and South Korea. This idea was formulated at the American Brookings Institution.[27]

This weakening of the world's formal and transparent MOs is creating conditions highly suited for an increase in the secret activities of non-formalised and non-transparent MOs, which to some degree are usually connected to the world's powerful governmental entities.

Figure 15.7

Dominance on Account of Attacks on the Global MO System with the Help of Subordinate ('Auxiliary') Non-transparent Entities

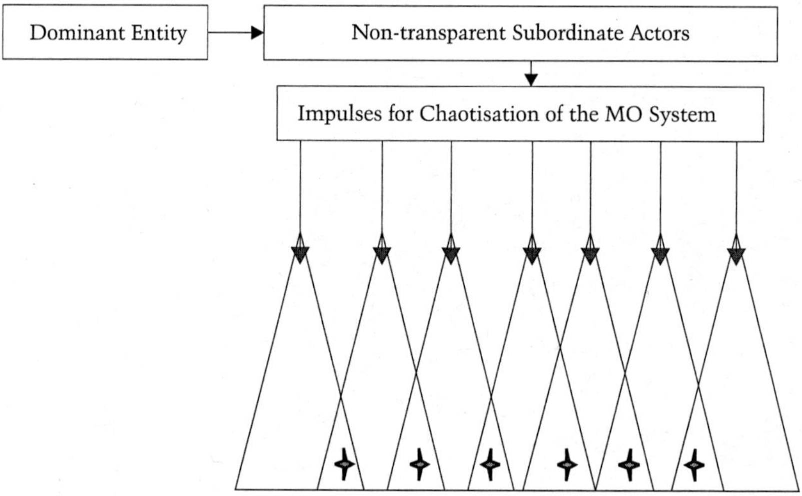

26. On 1 January 2010, an FTZ between China and ASEAN was officially opened, with a population of 1.9 billion, a GDP of over $6 trillion, and an external commodity turnover of more than $4.5 trillion, <*http://russian.china.org.cn/business/txt/2010-01/02/content_19169848.htm*>. Following the China-ASEAN FTZ, it is expected that in 2011 there will be an FTZ between South Korea and ASEAN, and a year later, a Japan-ASEAN FTZ. As they develop, these three FTZs could be united into one large FTZ in the format of '10+3,' promoting the eventual formation of an East Asian Economic Community, <*http://www.russchinatrade.ru/ru/news/2010-01-01-freetrade*>.

27. <*http://www.brookings.edu/cnaps.aspx*>.

Widely discussed examples of this variety are some state intelligence services' linkages with terrorist organisations, as well as to the international drugs and arms runners, in their fight with geopolitical adversaries. A striking example is the acknowledgement of Zbigniew Brzezinski in an interview in the French magazine *Le Nouvel Observateur* that US President Jimmy Carter had signed a secret directive to aid the Afghan Mujahedeen on 3 July 1979, that is, six months before the Soviet military contingent's entry into Afghanistan.[28] According to numerous reports, the intelligence services of a number of NATO countries actually encouraged the cultivation and processing of the opium poppy in Afghanistan, resisting UN efforts to combat drugs proliferation.[29] Another recent example is the use of 'non-transparent' organisations in 'economic warfare.' According to reports in the world media in spring 2010, at a secret meeting in early February 2010, 18 US groups involved in hedge fund deals had developed a plan for a combined speculative attack on Euro currency.[30]

Crises and the World System of Multilateral Organisations

The global economic crisis, intensifying the global struggle for national and bloc interests far beyond the confines of the real economy (including military, political and other accounts), had a profound destabilising effect on global organisations. The wave of 'revolutions' that erupted in 2011 in countries dominated by Islamic population further stirred

28. "Les révélations d'un ancien conseiller de Carter: Oui, la CIA est entrée en Afghanistan avant les Russes...", (1998). *Le Nouvel Observateur*, Janvier 15-21.

29. For example, see the allegations of the encouragement of drug production against the President of Afghanistan, Hamid Karazi, as well as the Pentagon and the British military, put forward by former US State Department Coordinator for Counternarcotics in Afghanistan, Thomas Schweich, (Schweich, T. (2008). "Is Afghanistan a Narco-State?" *The New York Times*, 27 July) and the *New York Times* article about the drug trafficking of the Afghan President's brother, A.V. Karzai and his long cooperation with the CIA, (Filkins, D., M. Mazzetti and J. Risen (2009). "Brother of Afghan Leader Said to Be Paid by CIA", *The New York Times*, 27 October).

30. On 9 February 2010, the heads of the largest US hedge funds (including SAC Capital Advisors and Soros Fund Management) discussed at a secret meeting the prospects of a speculative attack on the euro with the aim of lowering its rate to the level of the dollar. The US Department of Justice has begun an investigation into this matter and sent the funds participating in this meeting a letter with a 'strong recommendation' not to destroy any documents or electronic communications concerning their euro transactions (The *Wall Street Journal*, 26 February 2010).

up and complicated both the multitude of global conflicts and internal contradictions in various MOs and aggravated the chaotic state (and, hence, the weakening) of the MO system at all levels, thereby increasing the 'capacity for dominance' by the strongest players in the global MO system, besides widening the range of their 'mechanisms of domination.'

One of the very telling conflict processes connected with the current 'revolutions' in the Islamic world was the rift in a number of key MOs on issues revolving around these 'revolutionary events.' For the first time since the inter-bloc rivalry of the Cold War between the USA and the USSR, the UN and its Security Council became an arena for violent conflict. Both the wording of the UNSC Resolution No. 1973 on Libya (a mandate with extremely dangerous ambiguity) and the nature of action 'in the execution' of this resolution divided the Security Council and the UN as a whole.[31] No less dramatic a conflict was laid bare in the UNSC in the beginning of June 2011 while discussing the draft resolution on Syria, introduced by Great Britain and France.

Back in May, Russian President Dmitry Medvedev had announced that Russia would refuse to adopt the resolution on Syria. On 8 June and 9 June, 2011, this position was once again confirmed by Russia's official representatives at the Ministry of Foreign Affairs and the UN.[32] These conflicts were ground enough for some analysts to talk about the imminent conclusion of the 'UN epoch.'

The LAS also has not escaped sharp divisions. The Security Council meeting that adopted Resolutions No. 1970 and No. 1973 against the government of Muammar Gaddafi was convened citing the supposedly unanimous demand at the LAS meeting for intervention in Libya, but the meeting had been attended by only 11 of the League 22 members. At first, the proposal to appeal was supported by only seven members, the six Gulf monarchies and Egypt represented by the League Secretary General, Amr Moussa. After the debate, nine members supported the resolution, but two countries, Algeria and Syria, still voted 'Nay.'[33] Moreover, just three days after the adoption of the UNSC Resolution No. 1973 (and the start of the

31. lenta.ru, 25 May 2011.

32. Interfax, 09 June 2011.

33. *Asia Times Online*, 30 March 2011.

coalition's bombing of Gaddafi's forces), Amr Moussa said that the allied operation in Libya did not "meet the stated objectives" of the resolution.[34]

Another proof of the discord within the LAS was a wave of accusations against Qatar in the media of many member states of the OIC and the LAS during the 'Arab revolutions.' They claimed that the Emir's policy and false propaganda on the TV channel *Al-Jazeera* instigated at the behest of the USA, Great Britain and 'world Zionism' had provoked incidents of armed violence. This was followed by publications in the Arab media and on the Internet directly accusing Qatar, claiming that the opposition groups, which participated in the campaign to overthrow Egyptian President, Hosni Mubarak, received training in the Qatari capital Doha under American and Israeli instructors.[35] Some experts said that the policies adopted by a number of Arab countries in the current wave of 'Arab revolutions' raised doubts about there being any sense in the continued existence of the LAS.

Also, very revealing is the imminent division in one of the most important MOs in today's world, the OPEC, the cartel that dominates the global oil business. Despite the fact that Qatar, Kuwait, and the United Arab Emirates (UAE) urged that the envoy from the National Transitional Council from Benghazi be accepted as the legitimate representative of Libya at the OPEC summit on 8 June 2011, the majority of OPEC members agreed to negotiate only with representatives of the official Libyan authorities from Tripoli, that is, the Gaddafi Government.[36] The OPEC meeting on 8 June 2011, was an extremely contentious one and concluded with the rejection of Saudi Arabia's proposal to increase the cartel's oil production quota.[37] Then the world media, citing the Arabic newspaper *Al-Hayat*, published in London, reported that Saudi Arabia, ignoring the decision of OPEC, intended to increase its oil production from 8.8 million to 10 million bbls/day from July.[38] It also commented that this conflict situation made the very existence of OPEC meaningless.

---

34. CNN, 21 March 2011.
35. *<http://www.vesti.ru/050311>*.
36. ITAR-TASS, 24 May 2011.
37. *<http://www.elitetrader.ru/index.php?newsid=123747>*.
38. *Bloomberg*, 10 June 2011.

Even more indicative of the situation is the growing schism in as powerful a MO as NATO. For example, for the first time in many years, an important member of NATO, Germany, abstained from voting for the approval of the 'Libyan' Resolution No. 1973 of the UNSC, openly siding with Russia and China's stand. The Head of the German Ministry of Foreign Affairs, Guido Westerwelle, announced that Germany would not participate in a military action against Libya.[39] On 9 June 2011, US Secretary of Defense, Robert Gates, lambasted NATO's European members during a speech in Brussels, saying that their desire to shift the burden of financing and execution of the alliance's military operations to the USA called into question the very existence of NATO.[40] Such situations of conflict are also occurring in the major international economic MOs, the IMF and the EU.

In the process of electing a new head of the IMF after the resignation of scandal tainted Dominique Strauss Kahn, there was an immediate polarisation of positions. Leaders of the major developing countries (China, India, Russia, Brazil, South Africa, etc.) stressed that the tradition, formed after the creation of the IMF that the Head of the World Bank must be an American and the Head of the IMF a European, not only was undemocratic and contrary to its Charter, but also does not correspond to the new realities in the distribution of positions in the global economy. The Finance Ministers of Brazil (Guido Mantega) and South Africa (Pravin Gordhan) held firmly that the highest post in the IMF cannot and should not be reserved for a European.[41] The Governor of the Central Bank of China, Zhou Xiaochuan, demanded changes in the IMF management to "reflect changes in the global economy structure" and to "better represent" the emerging markets.[42]

Furthermore, a joint communiqué of the participating countries in BRICS (Brazil, Russia, India, China and South Africa) stressed that the new Head of the IMF should not be a European, and that he "should not only be a strongly qualified person with [a] solid technical background and acumen,

39. *<http://www.fondsk.ru/news/2011/03/18/>*.

40. For example, see: *The Guardian*, 10 June 2011.

41. *<http://www.bfm.ru/articles/2011/05/19/>*.

42. *Diario del Pueblo*, 24 May 2011.

but also a person [who] is committed to continuing the process of change and reform of the institution so as to adapt it to the new realities of the world economy".[43]

Severe differences troubled the EU between the fall of 2010 and the spring of 2011 on the question of 'saving' the economies of fringe European countries, especially Greece. In fact, we are speaking about whether the economic leaders of Europe, especially Germany, are ready to pay a lot and indefinitely to preserve the EU in its present form or if they would prefer a new European norm where the EU controls the state defaults of outsiders and the transition of their economies to external control, i.e., by the EU.[44] Otherwise, an extreme option would need to be initiated, a 'civilised divorce' of the EU as a MO and its most 'hopeless' economic outsiders (starting with Greece, but obviously not ending with it). This would mean the exit of these outsiders from the Eurozone and a return to national currencies and economic autonomy.[45] Thus, it is not for nothing that some experts assess the current processes in the Eurozone to be symptoms of its imminent 'disintegration.'

Finally, the continuing military and political crisis of 'revolutions' in countries dominated by an Islamic population has brought to life a new type of MO: 'semi-formal' international entities that claim the right to speak on behalf of the international community regarding local conflicts in place of organisations such as the UN. The most striking example is the so-called 'Contact Group on Libya'. All the Foreign Ministers of NATO countries, Qatar and the UAE, as well as the UN Secretary General were at the Conference on Libya that was convened on 29 March 2011 in London and decided on holding a summit to discuss the implementation of the UNSC Resolution No. 1973. But Russia, China and representatives of the AU were not invited. The official part of the Conference was devoted to examining questions about how to remove Gaddafi from power and how the opposition in Benghazi should hold talks with the leaders of the Libyan tribes about the country's future. The 'Contact Group on Libya' was also established at the Conference session, a body with an uncertain status and

43. *Rebelion*, 31 May 2011.

44. *The Financial Times*, 30 May 2011.

45. *Ekspert Magazine*, No. 22, 6 June 2011.

composition, declared a "political complement" to the NATO war machine for the implementation of Resolution No. 1973.

But on the sidelines of the London Conference, US Secretary of State Hillary Clinton, British Prime Minister David Cameron and British Foreign Secretary William Hague discussed an entirely different matter with a Special Envoy sent by the opposition in Benghazi, Gaddafi's former Minister of National Planning, Mahmoud Jibril, who was officially 'absent' at the Conference. They thrashed out the plan for the future of Libya, including the selection of acceptable candidates for the new government, the allocation of funds from the assets of the National Oil Company and the Investment Fund of Libya, frozen in the USA, to the National Transitional Council in Benghazi, as well as 'other means' of assisting the opposition. The 'means of assistance' were immediately revealed by Susan Rice, the US Special Envoy to the UN, who said that the US offer did not exclude the supply of weapons to Benghazi, which explicitly contradicts the UN arms embargo and all international norms.[46]

Subsequent events have shown that this MO contrary to initial claims of the London 'constituent conference' had, right at the start of the first meeting of the Contact Group in the Qatari capital Doha, contacted Benghazi but not Tripoli; it had claimed that NATO instructors and men of the Special Forces were, in defiance of the UNSC, surreptitiously participating in a ground operation against the forces of Gaddafi, besides providing funds and arms.[47]

We emphasise that this is a completely new phenomenon in the field of international MOs. Previously, such as in the case of the Contact Group on the former Yugoslavia, both the opposing sides as also the other parties at least participated in the negotiation process, staying firmly within the formal structures of the UN. The facts delineated above prove the following:

What is happening today is a serious breakdown of the global regulation structure. The statutory equality among MOs' members, as well as the formal equality of various global MOs in the context of conflicts

46. *<http://www.rian.ru/arab_analytics/20110329/359044864.html>.*

47. For example, see: *Figaro*, 29 June 2011, *<http://www.rosbalt.ru/main/2011/04/16/840140.html; http://www.ng.ru/world/2011-06-02/1_livia.html>.*

between 'overlapping' mandates and the lack of a legitimate 'dominant will' (especially in the context of crisis-level conflict of interest) is further undermining the MOs' efficient functioning, and one cannot but help see the coming collapse of many organisations. This includes even those MOs that are officially considered competent in fulfilling their obligation, which is to regulate the global and macro-regional processes in the spheres of politics, economics and security.

On the one hand, this increases the scope for dominance by 'strong' participants both within individual MOs and in the global MO system. At the same time, this also leads to changes in numerous crisis processes in the world in an essentially 'unregulated' regime. Moreover, a new 'space of opportunities' is created for dominance by self-proclaimed 'regulation coalitions' and 'contact groups' that are essentially independent from the global and macro-regional MOs and their regulatory mandates. Often, the actions of such groups contradict their self-proclaimed aims and instead increase chaos in the spheres they allegedly 'regulate.'

We emphasise that the post-bipolar 'global reformatting of the world order' is only the beginning: its mechanisms will inevitably lead to both 'natural' and man-made crises on various scales, affecting all aspects of human life and international relations without exception (socio-economic, military, political, ideological, psychological, socio-cultural, etc.). The current situation, the absence of distinct "poles" of global influence and responsibility, will continue for quite a while during the ongoing unfolding of the 'crisis of world re-ordering.' Hence, given the scenario of 'chaotic plurality' in the global MO system, the situation will be used as an opportunity for dominance by the most powerful actors of various types: the state, the self-proclaimed and non-transparent entities. Moreover, their dominance will take place in the absence of universally recognised, legitimate and sustainable mandates and mechanisms for resolving disputes and conflicts, thus increasing global chaos.

One can conclude that the present situation examined in this paper calls for an in-depth analysis, comprehensive discussion and a systemic response from all world forces interested in curbing global chaos.

16 The Middle East

An Era of Reconfiguration

Vladimir Novikov

The Middle East, which has long been one of the most serious 'hot spots' in the world, has recently become a region of global political reconfiguration. For scrutinising the key factors behind this process, we need to note the following facts.

The terrorist attacks in New York and Washington and the subsequent open US military intervention in Afghanistan and Iraq have significantly changed the format of relations between the USA and the Islamic world and have created a number of new local and global 'centres of conflict.' The development of these centres has led to the appearance of new trends in relations between the West as a whole (most significantly, the USA) and Israel.

Against this backdrop, fundamental transformations in the domestic and foreign policy of Turkey have begun, which at first were at a low key but then developed rapidly. The emerging contours of the Middle Eastern 'regrouping of forces' are certainly not definitive. New circumstances could always emerge that would significantly change one or another parameter of the process. However, there is reason to document the current alignment of positions and give an overview of the major trends in political change in the region.

New Dimensions in American-Israeli Relations

The main constant in the Middle East situation over the past few decades has been the Arab-Israeli conflict. In this context, there have been major transformations related to US-Israeli relations in the past years. These relations seemed quite unshakable until recently. Their roots go back to the time of the Cold War, which decisively determined the basic alignments and alliances in the region. There was Israel which played the role of the "unsinkable US aircraft carrier" in the Middle East. There were the secular Arab regimes, the majority of which were oriented towards the Soviet Union (probably, with the exception of Anwar Sadat's regime in Egypt). Standing alone was the Shah's Iran, which firstly was a bearer of non-Arab Persian identity and secondly was generally oriented towards an alliance with the West and Israel.

But in those same years of the Cold War, there existed Arab regimes that were non-secular and anti-Soviet. For example, Saudi Arabia was extremely anti-Israel and at the same time extremely anti-Soviet. Saudi King Faisal, as his biographers testify, believed that *Zionism* and Communism both played against the Arab world, strictly distributing roles among themselves. *Zionism* directly opposes the Arab (and wider Islamic) world, and Communism offers Arabs its protection in exchange for the abandonment of Islamic principles and the adoption of a "godless ideology".[1] At the same time, Faisal justified the ideological principles of his alliance with the United States as follows: United States was not a Western-style democracy, but a country that based its policy on a belief in God (even if it was the Protestant denomination of Christianity rather than Islam).[2]

Thus, during the time of the Cold War, some of the Arab elite had already built an alliance with the USA, all the while flaunting their anti-Israeli positions. But some influential elite groups in the USA also wanted such an alliance for various reasons (energy security, interest in capital inflows from oil monarchies to the USA—the political pragmatics of using the potential of Islam for their own purposes).

During the period of Soviet troops' deployment in Afghanistan in 1979-1989, the alliance of some American elites with the religious and monarchical Arab regimes (above all, the Saudi regime) reached its peak, as if sanctified by the struggle against the 'common enemy' the USSR and 'godless communism.' But even in this period, US-Israeli relations, which were extremely close, began to 'test the limits' of the US-Islamic alliance that has been mentioned.

---

1. Vasiliev, A.M. (2010). *King Faisal, Individual, Epoch, Belief*. 363.
2. Ibid.: 360.

The collapse of the USSR and the end of the Cold War led to questions being raised about Israel's status as the 'unsinkable US aircraft carrier' in the Middle East. The Russian Federation is not the USSR. Its interests in the Arab world clearly do not have the same 'Soviet scale' and indeed Russian capabilities are much more modest than Soviet ones were. Moreover, in the early post-Soviet years, Russia demonstrably turned away from its Arab allies of yesteryears. The connection of Arab countries in the region with Russia was greatly weakened and ceased to be a decisive factor influencing the course of events in the Middle East.

In this situation, the significance of Israel for the USA as an undeniable strategic ally in the Middle East has been steadily declining. Moreover, Israel has in some degree became a hindrance for the USA in realising new opportunities in the Middle East that have opened after the collapse of the USSR (the development of relations with 'the Arabs abandoned by the Soviets,' etc.). The problems that arose from the US tilt towards Arabs have made its relations with Israel, with all the reservations, one of the leitmotifs of the Clinton Presidency.

Of course, huge inertia existed that hindered and still hinders any radical transformation of US-Israeli relations. In particular, there exist strong lobbies both in the USA and in Israel, for whom the strategic relationship between Washington and Tel Aviv is their 'political bread and butter' and the key condition of their political survival. In Israel itself, few have illusions about the safety of their state without US support.

The presidency of George W. Bush witnessed new US-Israeli rapprochement (once again, with many reservations). The Bush administration began a confrontation with radical Islam (i.e., the 'war on terror'). For Israel, in a state of conflict with its Islamic surroundings, it was almost the perfect formula for strategic cooperation. However, early in George W. Bush's second term, some influential members of the US administration had already begun to send signals that the USA was prepared, under certain conditions, to find a compromise with radical Islam. For example, the then Secretary of State, Condoleezza Rice stated during her speech at the American University in Cairo in the summer of 2005 that the US efforts to establish stability in the Middle East to the detriment of democracy were to no avail. In Rice's words, "...now, we are taking a different course... We are supporting the democratic aspirations of all people. It is time to abandon the excuses that are made to avoid the hard work of democracy."[3]

What is the 'hard work of democracy' in regard to the Middle East? To allow a full-fledged political democracy in countries like Egypt means to legitimise politically the radical Islamist forces in Israel's neighbourhood, such as the Muslim Brotherhood in Egypt, or even those that are no strangers to Al Qaeda. Therefore, Rice's talking point on "excuses that are made to avoid the hard work of democracy" is a clear signal that the USA is willing to sacrifice the interests of Israel for the sake of better relations with Islam, even with the baggage of its rather radical forms.

When Barack Obama came to power, the US-Israeli relations almost immediately cooled. On his path to power, Obama declared that he fundamentally rejected the policies of the previous administration. If Bush had fought against Islam, then by that very logic, Obama should make peace with it. Obama's famous Cairo speech delivered on 4 June 2009, became a kind of policy statement for this reconciliation.[4] But in order to make peace after a long war, the party interested in reconciliation must be ready for sizable and demonstrative concessions to its opponent (in the language of past eras: 'to pay an indemnity'). The most obvious US concessions to Islam would be:

- withdrawal of troops from Iraq;
- withdrawal from Afghanistan and integration of the 'moderate' part of the Taliban into the government; and
- pressurising Israel in the interests of the Islamic world.

At the same, it is clear that the withdrawal of troops from Iraq and Afghanistan "without losing face" would be a very complicated and unconventional procedure, if only because it is categorically unacceptable for the Obama administration that this withdrawal be seen as a demonstration of America's defeat in the Islamic world and a re-enactment

3. Quote at *<http://www.expert.ru/printissues/expert/2005/24/24ex-pov3/>*.
4. *<http://www.whitehouse.gov/the-press-office/remarks-president-cairo-university-6-04-09>*.

of the 'Vietnam syndrome'.[5] In the strategic bargaining of the USA with the Islamic world, Israel has become a key 'bargaining chip' and relations with it can be used to pay an 'indemnity.'

On 18 September, 2009, an interview with President Carter's former National Security Advisor, Zbigniew Brzezinski, was posted on the Internet publication *The Daily Beast*. One topic touched upon during the interview was a possible Israeli air strike on Iranian nuclear facilities:

> Brzezinski: We are not exactly impotent little babies. They have to fly over our airspace in Iraq. Are we just going to sit there and watch?"
>
> DB: What if they fly over anyway?
>
> Brzezinski: Well, we have to be serious about denying them that right. That means a denial where you aren't just saying it. If they fly over, you go up and confront them. They have the choice of turning back or not...[6]

For some, Brzezinski is the 'the Gray Cardinal of global government,' and for others, he is 'simply a retired person.' But he is neither. He is a very informed person with elite connections close to the Obama team. His statement about the US willingness to shoot down Israeli aircraft flying to bomb Iran may represent his private point of view. Nonetheless, one cannot deny the fact that it reflects the position of certain circles of the American elite and the government. In case Brzezinski speaks on behalf of these 'certain circles,' he may be exaggerating their resolve to go so far (shoot down planes, etc). However, he signalled to the Israelis that their attack on Iran would not be supported and that the expression of this decision would be extremely harsh.

And after all, this signal was heard in Tehran as well, where it could not but be understood unambiguously: the Americans will block any military strike on Iran, and therefore it is possible to behave quite freely *vis-à-vis* Israel. Thus, Brzezinski probably sent this strict anti-Israeli message on behalf of influential American groups. But the matter is not limited to this. On 15 April 2010, the President of the World Jewish Congress, Ronald Lauder, sent an open letter to Obama, which was

---

5. Vietnam Syndrome is the common name of a series of moral and psychological repercussions of the US defeat in the Vietnam War, which caused a deep crisis in American domestic and foreign policy.

6. "How Obama Flubbed His Missile Message", *The Daily Beast*, 18 September 2010, *<http://www.thedailybeast.com/blogs-and-stories/2009-09-18/how-obama-flubbed-his-missile-message/>*.

published in the newspapers *The Wall Street Journal* and *The Washington Post*.

The letter reads as follows:

> Our concern grows to alarm as we consider some disturbing questions. Why does the thrust of this Administration's Middle East rhetoric seem to blame Israel for the lack of movement on peace talks? After all, it is the Palestinians, not Israel, who refuse to negotiate... Every American President who has tried to broker a peace agreement has collided with that Palestinian intransigence, sooner or later. Recall President Clinton's anguish when his peace proposals were bluntly rejected by the Palestinians in 2000. Settlements were not the key issue then. They are not the key issue now... In that spirit I submit, most respectfully, that it is time to end our public feud with Israel and to confront the real challenges that we face together.[7]

Lauder is not only the President of the World Jewish Congress, but also a highly influential representative of the American Jewish community and a major multinational businessman, who is very cautious in his statements. If he uses such strong language as "it is time to end our public feud with Israel," it means that the US-Israeli relations are truly experiencing severe problems.

There is enough evidence that these problems exist. On 2 June 2010, the former Director of Intelligence Assessment in the Office of the Secretary of Defense, Anthony Cordesman, published an article with the very indicative title 'Israel as a Strategic Liability?' on the website of the Center for Strategic and International Studies. Cordesman writes that the USA is not abandoning Israel because of its existing moral and political commitments. However, these commitments do not justify the actions of the Israeli government, which are turning Tel Aviv into a burden for Washington. Therefore, the American commitment to Israel does not mean that the USA must support its Israeli friends when the Israelis do not try to make peace with their neighbours. According to Cordesman, Israel must understand that not only the US has obligations to it, but that it has obligations to the USA;[8] that is, Cordesman has said openly that the

---

7. *<http://www.worldjewishcongress.org/en/main/showNews/id/9264>*.
8. *<http://csis.org/publication/israel-strategic-liability>*.

confrontation between Israel and its Arab neighbours interferes with the US policy in the Middle East.

On 27 June 2010, the Israeli newspaper *Haaretz* reported that the Israeli Ambassador to the USA, Michael Oren, during a briefing at the Ministry of Foreign Affairs dedicated to the 6 July meeting between Barack Obama and Benjamin Netanyahu, described the situation in US-Israeli relations as a tectonic shift, in the course of which, Israel and the USA are drifting away from one another like two continents.[9] Oren's first career was as a writer and historian. But he is also an official who is obliged to weigh every word, even those said within a closed circles. Moreover, Oren's statement on a tectonic shift in the US-Israeli relations has been cited by representatives of the well-respected Israeli press.

On 5 July 2010, a columnist in the British *The Guardian*, Chris McGraw, addressed the topic of US-Israeli relations in his article 'US questions its unwavering support for Israel.' McGraw noted that Netanyahu's persistence in construction of Israeli settlements is seen in Washington as a lack of real interest in establishing a Palestinian state and a factor that increases hostility towards the USA from the Islamic world.[10] Next, McGraw gives a series of statements by US politicians who were dissatisfied with Israeli policy. For example, in early 2010, Obama stated that a resolution to the Israeli-Palestinian conflict is of vital interest to US national security. Vice-President Joe Biden met privately with Israeli Prime Minister Netanyahu and told him how Israel's policy poses a threat to American troops in Afghanistan and Iraq. Senior American military officials, including General David Petraeus, have identified the policies of Israel in Palestine as an obstacle in resolving the Afghan and Iraqi conflicts.[11]

Thus, the deterioration in US-Israeli relations is obvious. How far it will go and whether Israel and its allies in the USA can stop this 'tectonic shift' is for now an open question. But the above facts suggest that an influential part of the American elite wants to make Israel a 'bargaining

9. *<http://www.haaretz.com/print-edition/news/envoy-to-u-s-michael-oren-denies-saying-israel-u-s-drifting-apart-1.298471>.*
10. *<http://www.guardian.co.uk/world/2010/jul/05/us-israel-support>.*
11. Ibid.

chip' in a larger US strategy game. It can be the case that we are talking about not only a reconciliation with the Islamic world, but also the implementation of the strategy that has been conventionally referred to as 'Brzezinski's concept.' The essence of this concept is an American alliance with radical Islam to be used, as an instrument in the execution of the US policy.

A classic example of the application of 'Brzezinski's concept' was the late 1970s to early 1980s policy in Afghanistan, when the administration of Gerald Ford and Ronald Reagan implemented a large-scale programme of assistance to the Afghan *mujahedeen* against the USSR. It was Brzezinski who was the author of this programme.[12] However, the use of radical Islam as an instrument to combat a geopolitical competitor (in this case, the USSR) was not an invention on the part of Brzezinski or his followers. It was an extension of Britain's traditional use of radical Islam as an instrument to contain the 'Red Bear,' as the USSR was then called. For example, it is known that Wahhabi Islam was instrumental in Great Britain's fight against the Ottoman Empire.[13] If in this case, we are speaking of America implementing a parallel strategy, then the only question that arises is: against whom does it plan to use this 'Islamic weapon.' A separate study is of course necessary to answer this question.

Here we will note the following: the chill in US-Israeli relations and the attempts by the Obama administration to once again resort to an alliance with Islam cannot but elicit the corresponding reaction in the Islamic world. If the USA makes peace with Islam and is even willing to give the 'go ahead' to a certain radicalisation of Islam, then the question of who will become the leader of the Islamic world is on the agenda. This question cannot fail to initiate a process of realignment in the Islamic world. There is a significant part of the Arab world that has long played with the idea of re-creating the world *Caliphate*. There is radicalised Iran. But its radicalism is Shiite, which is not compatible with the principal sentiments of the Sunni Muslim *Ummah*, although in recent years, Iran

12. For example, see: Brzezinski's interview with the daily newspaper, *Le Nouvel Observateur*, No. 1732, 15-21 January 1998, 76.

13. The activities of the British Government Agent, H. St. John Philby, who actively patronised the Saudi's Wahhabi dynasty, are well-known (for example, see: A.M. Vasiliev, *History of Saudi Arabia*, M: 1982).

has been trying to gain a position in the Sunni world (in particular, through patronage of Palestinian *Hamas*).

And there is Turkey, which until recently was considered a kind of bastion of secularism and even anti-Islamism within the region. However, in June 2010, after the incident with the *Freedom Flotilla*,[14] Turkey began to accelerate its turn towards Islamism in its foreign policy.

Is Turkey's New Course the End of Kemalism?

The 'Freedom Flotilla' incident is hardly a 'passing episode.' The incident, defiant and provocative in form and content, essentially means a punctuated break in the Israeli-Turkish alliance. This alliance was based, firstly, on relations between Turkey and the Arab world that historically have been uneasy and, secondly, on the secular nature of the Turkish state, which was continuously emphasised by the authorities. The westernised secular character of Turkey and its rigid opposition to radical Islam is the legacy of the post-*Ottoman* policy of Kemal Ataturk, which became the political basis of the Turkish state.[15] However, in recent years, having failed to ensure the entry of Turkey into the European Union (EU), which would have meant a higher degree of 'Europeanisation' of the country, Kemalism abruptly surrendered its positions. It was the blocking of Turkey's EU accession that was, perhaps, the main reason for the political success of the Islamic Justice and Development Party, headed by Tayyip Erdogan and Abdullah Gul.[16]

---

14. This refers to the incident between the so-called 'Freedom Flotilla' (an international convoy that tried to break through the naval blockade of the Gaza Strip) and the Israeli authorities on the night of 30-31 May 2010. An inspection team of the Israeli authorities was attacked by activists from the 'fleet' on board, the *Mavi Marmara* and force was used in response. Nine activists from the *Flotilla* were killed and 30 wounded, and 10-15 Israeli soldiers were also wounded. The ships in the convoy were escorted to the port of Ashdod. The incident with the *Freedom Flotilla* became an occasion for a major international scandal and the marked aggravation of relations between Israel and Turkey.

15. Kemalism is a political doctrine formulated by the founder of the modern Turkish State, Kemal Ataturk. The essence of the doctrine can be reduced to the full secularisation of the Turkish State and Society and its Europeanization. For Kemal and Kemalism, see: A. Zhevakhov Ataturk, (M:2008).

16. *The New York Times* columnist Thomas Friedman writes on the EU's reluctance to expand at the expense of Turkey as a cause for the "Islamic Reversal" in Turkey, *<http://www.nytimes.com/2010/06/16/opinion/16friedman.html>*.

If the Kemalist era is truly coming to an end in Turkey, there arises the question of new orientations for its foreign and domestic policy. In the 'Freedom Flotilla' incident, Turkey essentially acted as the official protector of *Hamas*. Some observers (for example, *The New York Times* columnist Thomas Friedman) have even called its present government 'Islamic'.[17] Friedman names three reasons that drive the current Turkish government to pursue a new policy: the EU's reluctance to expand at the expense of Turkey, the 'leadership vacuum' in the Middle East and the weakness of the secular opposition.[18]

We note that the topic of 'Turkey and *Hamas*' deserves a separate analysis. Some experts argue that an alliance has recently been formed between Turkey's ruling Justice and Development Party and the *Hamas* movement, and that Ankara has essentially offered itself to Hamas as a strategic partner rather than Tehran. These same experts believe that the Hamas movement has already allegedly decided to shift priorities from Iran to Turkey, which also facilitates a Turkish-Syrian dialogue.[19] At the same time, according to data from the same sources, Turkey considers *Hamas* rather than *Fatah* to be the power capable of leading a Palestinian state. Moreover, Hamas' acceptance of Turkey's patronage would ostensibly lead to the recognition of Israel by Hamas within the 1967 borders, allowing Hamas to lift the blockade on Gaza in the short term, as well as unlock a lot of money from Arab sponsors.[20] It is further alleged that all of the above is causing resistance to the Iranian lobby within *Hamas*, which is 'tied' to the supply of Iranian weapons, among other things.[21]

It is possible that the above are exaggerated expert assessments. However, the meeting of Turkish Minister of Foreign Affairs, Ahmet Davutoglu, and the Political Leader of Hamas, Khalid Meshaal, on 19 July 2010, shows that officials in Ankara are essentially flaunting their dialogue with *Hamas*. At this meeting, Davutoglu and Meshaal discussed efforts to restore the unity of the Palestinian people and the peace process in the

17. *<http://www.nytimes.com/2010/06/16/opinion/16friedman.html>*.

18. Ibid.

19. Kirsanov, E.E., "Hamas: Choosing the Path of Development", *<http://www.iimes.ru/rus/frame_stat.html>*.

20. Ibid.

21. Ibid.

Middle East. Moreover, the Head of the Turkish Ministry of Foreign Affairs expressed the need to do everything possible to lift the blockade of the Gaza Strip and emphasised that Turkey continues to wait for an apology from Israel for the deaths of Turkish nationals on board the *Mavi Marmara*.[22]

If Turkey, as shown above, is trying to 'buy' Hamas from Iran, then we are essentially speaking about the transformation of Hamas into a tool of Turkish politics—a tool that can be used both to blackmail the West ("If you will not accept us into the EU, we will become 'bad' and make friends with Hamas") and as a strategy for achieving the aims of Ankara in the Islamic world.

As for the possibility of 'buying' *Hamas* from Iran, this tactic is quite logical. If Turkey becomes Islamised, it simply must get its 'stake' in the enterprise called 'Islamic radicalism.' There are significant 'equity packages' that already belong to Turkey's competitors: the Arabs, Iranians and Pakistanis.

However, one can see that the Turkish game is more subtle and complex. On the one hand, Ankara truly can try to 'buy' some Islamic radicals from Tehran. On the other hand, in a number of respects, Turkey is playing a new game with Iran as well. The purpose of this game is a compromise or even a tactical alliance with its historical Persian antagonist. In support of this statement there is, for example, the emergence in May 2010 of a joint Turkish-Brazilian initiative to provide Iran with low-enriched uranium for the development of its medical programme. Essentially, Turkey and Brazil are seeking to become a guarantor for the world community that Iran is 'nuclearly unarmed'. But at the same time, this proposal means an attempt to take the issue of non-proliferation of nuclear technology out from under the exclusive control of the 'five' permanent members of UN Security Council (UNSC). This in turn creates the risk of further dismantling the non-proliferation system.

However, recently Turkey has become a kind of mediator between Iran and the outside world not only in the 'nuclear' sphere, but also in other

22. *<http://www.newsru.co.il/mideast/20jul2010/ahnet8012.html>*.

areas, including the transit of Iranian gas to Europe.[23] Some experts believe that in exchange, the Turkish government has the right to require reciprocal preferences from Tehran (including supplying energy resources)[24], and that Turkey's next requirement could be a 'fee' from European countries interested in cooperating with Iran in the form of softening their positions on the issue of Turkish membership in the EU.[25]

Another area in Turkey's recent foreign policy activity is the expansion of cooperation with Arab countries. We note that this Arab policy is rather problematic for Ankara. Relations between the Arabs and Turks have been very complicated since the early period of the Ottoman Empire. But the new Turkey of Erdogan and Gul is actively building a new relationship with the Arab world.

Turkey and Arab Countries: A New Dialogue

In May 2010, Saudi Arabia and Turkey signed an agreement for military and technical cooperation (including the training of military personnel). This is, in fact, the first document on military cooperation between the two countries. The agreement was signed in Ankara by the Saudi Assistant Minister of Defense and Aviation, Prince Khalid bin Sultan bin Abdul Aziz, and the Chief of the Turkish General Staff, Ilker Basbug.[26]

We note that Prince Khalid is the son of the Crown Prince of the Saudi Kingdom, Sultan bin Abdul Aziz, who is the country's Minister of Defence. The Prince often acts as the Defence Minister in place of his father.[27] At a press conference in Ankara, Prince Khalid noted "deep brotherly relations" between the two countries and also pointed out that the signed agreement "lays an important foundation for expanding bilateral military ties and is... a strong incentive for further development of the partnership".[28]

---

23. Thus, on 20 January 2009, Turkish Prime Minister Erdogan announced that without Iran's participation in the Nabucco project, there would not be sufficient amount of gas for the project. At the same time, Erdogan criticised all opponents of the Iranian participants in the project *<http://evrazia.org/news/6952>*.

24. Dzhakar, A.A., "On Turkey's Foreign Policy Activity in the Middle East." *<http://www.iimes.ru/rus/frame_stat.html>*.

25. Ibid.

26. *<http://www.rian.ru/world/20100525/238302619.html>*.

27. Ibid.

28. Ibid.

Saudi Arabia has long been the official leader of the Sunni Islamic world and ardently guards its status. Therefore, the rapprochement of Riyadh and Ankara is a 'symbolic' rapprochement. Saudi Arabia is showing that it is ready to deal with an Islamised Turkey. Another matter is how far Saudi Arabia would be willing to go in these relations if Ankara clearly signals its claims to leadership of a future *caliphate* (and this is a real possibility). In addition, the current rapprochement between Ankara and Tehran is unlikely to please Saudi Arabia.

On 12 June 2010, the *London Times* reported that Saudi Arabia is ready to provide Israel with an 'air corridor' to carry out attacks against Iranian nuclear facilities. A source in the Saudi government stated that the Saudi Air Defense and Air Force will "look the other way" if Israeli planes fly over its territory.[29] According to *The Times*, the main targets of the Israeli Air Force may be the uranium enrichment facilities in Natanz and Qom, the gas storage development unit in Isfahan and the heavy-water reactor in Arak; a secondary target may be the light water reactor in Bushehr.[30] At the same time, *The Times* points out that while the relationship between Israel and Saudi Arabia is strained, relations between Riyadh and Tehran are hostile.[31]

Thus, there are clear signs that Saudi Arabia is ready to support Iran's enemies (even Israel) in order to stop its nuclear programme. It cannot be ruled out that the Iranian issue will be one of the stumbling blocks to building a Turkish-Saudi alliance.

Other 'Vectors of Activity' in Turkey's 'New Policy'

Turkey's activities for building new relations in the Islamic world are not limited to Iran and Saudi Arabia. For example, at the Fifth Turkish-Arab Economic Forum held in June 2010 in Istanbul, Turkish Minister of Foreign Affairs, Ahmet Davutoglu, announced the intention of Turkey, Syria, Jordan and Lebanon to establish a Free Trade Zone (FTZ) and a visa-free regime. In addition to this, Davutoglu made a few 'policy' statements in his speech.

---

29. <*http://www.timesonline.co.uk/tol/news/world/middle_east/article7148555.ece*>.
30. Ibid.
31. Ibid.

The Minister said "...one after another, the walls erected in the minds of the Turks and Arabs are breaking down", and stressed that "among the Turkic and Arab countries the most ambitious dialogue on the planet will be established". Davutoglu named the 'policy of pressure on Palestine' as the main threat to security in the region and further stated that Turkish-Arab and Turkish-Iranian relations are complementary to each other.[32] Business representatives did not lag behind the Foreign Minister. For example, the Head of the Union of Chambers and Commodity Exchanges of Turkey (TOBB), Rifat Hisarciklioglu, stated "the Arab world... has a special place in the heart of the Turkish business world".[33]

Some responses to the aforementioned talking points from the representatives of the Arab world are notable. Libyan Foreign Minister, Moussa Koussa said at the forum that "without the intervention of the Ottoman Empire, today there would not be an Arab state in North Africa, and therefore there is no reason to be surprised by the current role of Turkey". He added that there is a "blood alliance" between the Turks and the Arabs.[34] The Head of the Libyan Ministry of Foreign Affairs is unlikely to have forgotten that it was Arab separatism that was one of the main reasons for the collapse of the Ottoman Empire, and he cannot be unaware of ethnic differences between Turks and Arabs. So his phrase "blood alliance" can only refer to the Ottoman Empire as a *caliphate* in the past; that is, in this passage Koussa speaks of the signs of Turkey's neo-*caliphate* and neo-*Ottoman* turn and indicates that Libya endorses this reversal.

Is there any clear basis for this? Certainly there is. Here, it is especially important that Moussa Koussa directly addressed Davutoglu, who was present at the Forum and has long been one of the highest placed ideologues of neo-*Ottomanism*.[35] Moreover, Davutoglu published a policy book in 2001, *Strategic Depth: Turkey's International Position*, which

32. *op. cit.* no.24.

33. Ibid.

34. Ibid.

35. At the end of 2009, Turkish Foreign Minister, Ahmet Davutoglu, said in his statement: "on problems with neighbors" that Turkey today is on the path to realisation of the policy of neo-*Ottomanism*, according to which Ankara has the historical right to reinstate its influence over those regions of Eurasia and Africa that were part of or fell under the complete subjugation of the Ottoman Empire, <*http://osinform.ru/20387-yeduard-abramyan-perspektivy-armyano-tureckogo.html*>.

claimed that Turkey's cooperation with Israel undermines the credibility of Ankara in the Arab world and that the objective of joining the EU is becoming all the more elusive. From this, the conclusion is drawn that Turkey should develop an independent strategy for the Middle East, taking into account the international reality.[36]

As we can see, the new 'independent Middle East Strategy of Turkey' already includes the revitalisation of the theme of 'pan-Islamic solidarity' and even flirts with radical Islam. Another matter is that, on Ankara's path towards this transformation in foreign and domestic policy, a number of serious problems cannot fail to rise. First, the conflicts between Turkey and the Arab world, as well as between Turkey and Iran, go back centuries and are unlikely to be strategically dropped in what is historically a short period of time. Second, in Turkey, there is a significant segment of the elite (primarily those connected to the military and military-industrial complex) for whom the Islamisation of Turkish domestic politics means a direct threat because it is the army that has always been the chief defender of the secular nature of the Turkish state and national politics against Islamic influences—the 'Islamic parties' will never forget this. Third, the transition to the position of the 'leader of the Islamic world' is problematic for Turkey also because in the Islamic world there exists a fair amount of public doubt in the real ability of the Turks to integrate '"into the higher truths' of the Islamic faith and way of life".

Thus, the new foreign policy of Turkey that is replacing Kemalism must fill neo-*Ottomanism* with new content (we note that many influential Turkish intellectuals, and not only the current Head of the country's Ministry of Foreign Affairs, have called this policy 'neo-Ottoman').[37] The question arises: what will this content be? Historically, the Ottoman Empire was a complex symbiosis of nations and cultures. Neo-*Ottomanism* simply cannot avoid addressing one of the two basic identities for integration. We emphasise that these are difficult and controversial to combine with one another.

36. Gadzhiev, A.K., "On the Question of Some Specific Features of Turkey's Foreign Policy Concept in the Middle East, <*http://www.iimes.ru/rus/stat/2010/19-06-10a.htm*>.

37. Ibid.

The first is the pan-Islamic (*caliphate*) identity mentioned above, for which the historical example of the Ottoman Empire is an almost implicit model. After all, *Ottoman* Turkey was the formal leader of the Islamic world and the *Ottoman* Sultan held the title of *Caliph*. The second identity is the pan-Turkic one, which drops the *caliphate* aspirations of Ankara that are of particular concern to its Muslim competitors (both Sunni and Shiite) and limits Turkey's patronage ambitions to quite extensive, but still not fully Islamic 'Turkic' world. What's more, placing a stake on pan-Turkic identity as a means of achieving its 'neo-*Ottoman*' goal is the most attractive idea for the Turkish military, which understands that it has no place in an Islamic Turkey. Wider Turkish political and financial circles are also ready to support this idea, fearing the unpredictable outcome of a struggle for 'caliphate leadership' in the Islamic world, which is extremely radicalised and prone to conflicts.

Let us note that even in the early 1990s Turkey had begun interweaving the theme of pan-Turkic solidarity into its foreign policy post Soviet collapse. The First Summit of Turkic-Speaking Countries was held in 1992 in Ankara. In essence, Ankara offered itself to former Soviet Turkic republics as a new 'big brother' instead of Moscow. This policy essentially failed, primarily because the elites of the Central Asian Republics were disappointed with both the Turks' excessive interest in securing the resources of the region and with the fact that the Turkish technologies proposed in exchange for these resources were no more modern than those of the Soviets. As a result, the 'pan-Turkic' theme in the politics of Turkey gradually faded until the middle of the last decade. But it began to revive once again in 2006 when the Summit of Heads of Turkic-Speaking States in Antalya announced promising prospects in a joint development of the 'Turkic world'.[38] Moreover, this line was confirmed at the 9th Summit of Heads of Turkic-Speaking States in the autumn of 2009.[39] This allows us to assume that Turkish politics will fluctuate between a pro-Western course, Islamism and pan-Turkism for some time.

What's more, we cannot deny the possibility that a portion of the Turkish elites will perceive the new 'Islamic policy' (including flirtation

38. Ibid.

39. <*http://www.altyn-orda.kz/kazpressreview/ix-sammit-glav-tyurkskix-gosudarstv/*>.

with radical Islam through various types of *Freedom Flotilla*) only as a kind of 'tactical blackmail' of the West. However, such tactics are steadily changing mass attitudes in Turkish society, and at the next phase, these changes may become irreversible. Already, the majority of citizens are well aware that their country will not be accepted into the EU in the foreseeable future. Recognition of this has led to the fact that many Turks are becoming either supporters of Islamisation or adherents of the pan-Turkic project.

The final collapse of Turkish Kemalism, if it happens, will inevitably be a turning point for the entire Middle East. Post-Kemalist Turkey (the most powerful country in the region militarily, politically, economically and demographically) will be transformed either into a major source of Islamic radicalisation or a factor in the 'Pan-Turkic threat' for a considerable number of its neighbours. Moreover, if the pan-Turkic vector triumphs in Turkey, we cannot rule out the consolidation of its Arab neighbours around a common platform of 'Islamic solidarity against the Turk menace.'

In conclusion, we note that the crack in relations between Israel and the USA and the new policy in Turkey are clear signs of the beginning of a large-scale reconfiguration in the Middle East region. The willingness of the current US administration to move away from strategic support of Israel has already provoked the growth of radicalisation in the Middle East region, including the growth of '*caliphate* ambitions' in Turkey and its Arab neighbours. In losing its secular type of governance and breaking its alliance with Israel, Turkey is fundamentally altering the entire reality of the Middle East on account of the additional 'driving' activities of political Islam among other reasons. At the same time, both an 'Islamised' Turkey embarking on securing the 'right to the *caliphate*' from its Arab neighbours and a 'pan-Turkic' Turkey opposing a regional 'peace with Islam' cannot fail to be perceived as a strategic challenge throughout the entire Middle East.

Furthermore, Turkey's neighbours cannot ignore the fact that this 'strategic choice' by Turkey is unlikely to be fully peaceful and bloodless (especially in view of the unsolved Kurdish problem),[40] and will most likely

40. Turkey has faced the problem of Kurdish separatism for decades. In recent years, Ankara has been very closely monitoring developments in neighbouring Iraq, where the Kurds have essentially created their own quasi-state. It is the fear of Kurdish separatism (the Kurds live in contiguous territories of Turkey, Iraq, Iran and Syria) that led to the conflict between the USA and Turkey in 2002-03, when Ankara in fact opposed American intervention in Iraq.

have a destabilising effect far beyond the Turkish national borders. The processes enumerated seem to aggravate the old problems in the Middle East and to create a new set of problems.

Thus, we can expect an acute aggravation of the Arab-Israeli and Iranian-Israeli conflict, with the addition of a Turkish-Israeli conflict. This will lead to a deepening of Israel's military and political isolation in the region, and consequently to an increase in the likelihood of its response to the excesses that accompany this isolation by means of 'force.'

This process will fail to increase the overall level of conflict in the Middle East. One cannot write off the possibility that, at some stage in the intensification of the conflict, one of the parties will decide to go to war or even to use unconventional weapons.

Once again we emphasise the specifics of the Middle East: they are such that destabilisation in the region is almost immediately reflected in the global economic, social, political and military stability (through energy supply, transactions with 'oil' money, the solidarity of the Islamic *Ummah*, etc.). If war breaks out in the Middle East, or even worse, if unconventional weapons are used, the world could very quickly end up on the verge of a global nuclear disaster.

17 Elusive Peace in the Middle East

The Intractable Nature of the Israel-Palestine Conflict

Ajish P. Joy

The Arab-Israeli conflict is not the largest or the bloodiest one in today's world by any yardstick. Compared to many other conflicts, it is not huge either in terms of the territory involved or in terms of the casualties. However, the conflict zone is considered to be one of the most inflammable global hotspots and is often described as the 'root cause of instability' and 'obstacle to security,' especially, in the Middle East. Beyond doubt, it remains the most enduring international conflict of our times. The term 'Arab-Israeli conflict' encompasses a fairly large number of major and minor conflicts, differences of opinion and disagreements between Israel and the Arab world.[1] Of late, it has ceased to be an exclusive Arab-Israeli affair, as non-Arab states like Iran and Turkey have taken up the issue forcefully. This paper will focus on the most important aspect of this conflict—the Palestinian struggle for statehood. The attempt is to examine the reasons behind the enduring nature of the conflict and to explain why this conflict will remain intractable in the foreseeable future.

The Palestinian conflict is at once territorial, religious and ideological. It is a story that has been repeated a million times—about a very small territory to which two separate groups stake claim with both groups believing that their claim is stronger. After Theodore Herzl, father of modern political Zionism, espoused the necessity for the Jews to have their own homeland—preferably in Palestine—due to increasing episodes of anti-Semitism in Europe, there was a sizeable movement of Jews from various parts of Europe to Palestine. This influx of Jewish population called

1. Twenty out of the 22 members of the Arab League do not recognise Israel.

aliyah, which gained momentum in the beginning of the 20th century, soon led to conflict between the Jews and the Arabs living in Palestine. The Arabs "sought instinctively to retain the Arab and Muslim character of the region and to maintain their position as its rightful inhabitants; the Zionists sought radically to change the *status quo*, buy as much land as possible, settle on it and eventually turn an Arab-populated country into a Jewish homeland".[2] The Jewish endeavour found support from the British government in the form of the Balfour Declaration (1917),[3] which promised help in the establishment of "a national home for the Jewish people in Palestine". The declaration offered only "civil and religious rights" for the Arabs who formed a majority in the region. This promise received a firm legal footing when Britain was given the mandate to govern Palestine by the League of Nations. The text of the mandate put Britain in charge of "the establishment in Palestine of a national home for the Jewish people" and recognised "the historical connection of the Jewish people with Palestine". Over the course of the next three decades, Jews from several parts of the world who were suffering persecution and who yearned for a Jewish homeland moved into Palestine. Hitler's Holocaust in which millions of Jews were killed provided sufficient moral justification for the exodus to the Palestine region.

With the conflict between Jews and the Arabs worsening, the UN intervened to find a solution. On 29 November 1947, the UN General Assembly (by a vote of 33 to 13, with 10 abstentions) passed Resolution 181 calling for the division of the Palestinian territories into two states—one for the Jews and one for the Arabs.[4] According to the plan, the Jewish state was to receive around 56 per cent of the mandate territories and Jerusalem was to be administered by the UN. Thus, Resolution 181 and the clauses in the mandate for Palestine constituted the legal basis for the creation of the state of Israel. The partition plan was perceived as unjust by

2. Morris, Benny (2001). *Righteous Victims: A History of the Zionist-Arab Conflict, 1881-2001*. New York: Vintage Books. p.49.
3. Full text of the declaration can be accessed from *The Times Archive*, 9 November 1917, *<http://archive.timesonline.co.uk/tol/viewArticle.arc?articleId=ARCHIVE-The_Times-1917-11-09-07-010&pageId=ARCHIVE-The_Times-1917-11-09-07>*.
4. UN General Assembly Resolution 181 (II). Future government of Palestine, *<http://domino.un.org/UNISPAL.NSF/0/7f0af2bd897689b785256c330061d253?OpenDocument>*.

the Palestinians, but it accorded legal sanctity for the establishment of the Jewish state.

The partition plan was rejected by the Arab states and the Arab Higher Committee of Palestine, which declared that it would "persist in rejection to the partition and in refusal to recognise UNO resolution".[5] The Resolution led to the breakout of a civil war between the Jewish and the Arab forces, which ended with considerable territorial gains for the Jews. On 14 May 1948, the day before the British Mandate was due to expire, Israeli leader David Ben-Gurion declared the formal establishment of the state of Israel. This was followed by an attack on Israel by the armies of Egypt, Iraq, Jordan, Lebanon and Syria. The hostilities ended in 1949 with terms favourable to Israel, as it increased its possessions by roughly one-third of what Resolution 181 envisaged. "The ceasefire lines in place in the beginning of 1949 left Israel in control of much of the territory that the UN had allocated for an Arab state in Palestine. Israel understandably defended its expansion by recalling that it was the Palestinians and other Arabs who had rejected partition and started the fighting."[6] Interestingly, Egypt and Jordan had no qualms in keeping the Gaza Strip and West Bank, respectively, under their control following the armistice agreements. After the six-day war in 1967, Israel took control of the West Bank and Gaza Strip as well.

Today, more than 62 years after the establishment of the state of Israel, in spite of several peace plans and processes, the conflict remains unresolved and no workable solution is visible on the horizon. There are several reasons for the intractable nature of the conflict. Some of them have been historical—as old as the conflict itself—while a number of new roadblocks have been emerging making the solution even more difficult. Most prominent among the historical reasons are the right of return of the Palestinian refugees, the status of Jerusalem and the issue of borders and settlements.

---

5. "UN Palestine Commission: Communication Ss30nc from the Representative of the Arab Higher Committee for Palestine", *<http://domino.un.org/pdfs/AAC216.pdf>*

6. *Tessler*, Mark A. (1994). *A History of the Israeli-Palestinian Conflict*. Bloomington, IN: Indiana University Press. p.273.

Right of Return

The right of return of the Palestinian refugees continues to be one of the most obdurate roadblocks to the solution of the conflict. It was one of the main reasons for the collapse of the Camp David talks in 2000. According to United Nations Relief and Works Agency (UNRWA) for Palestine Refugees in the Near East, a Palestinian refugee is one who "resided in Palestine for at least two years prior to May 1948, lost his home and his means of livelihood as a result of the war of 1948–1949, and now lives in the Gaza Strip, the West Bank, Jordan, Syria or Lebanon".[7] The number of such refugees was approximately 700,000. However, the Palestinian refugees have been accorded multi-generational status, which means that the off-springs of these refugees will retain the status. At present, the number of Palestinian refugees is estimated to be 4.7 million according to UNRWA, a significant number compared to the population of Israel.

The legal basis for the right of return, according to the Palestinians, can be found in the UN General Assembly Resolution 194, which says that "the refugees wishing to return to their homes and live at peace with their neighbours should be permitted to do so at the earliest practicable date, and that compensation should be paid for the property of those choosing not to return". However, these resolutions, unlike the Security Council resolutions, are non-enforceable. The mutual exclusiveness of the Israeli and Palestinian positions *vis-à-vis* the refugee problem makes it all the more intractable. For generations of Palestinians, the right of return is sacrosanct and their leadership has carefully and skilfully nurtured it as a dream and a beacon of hope. The right of return got "organically intertwined with an emergent sense of identity and to the national right to self-determination".[8] As a result, it has become too difficult an issue to give any concession and no Palestinian leader—not even Yasir Arafat—could sign on a document that diluted the right of return.

---

7. Shavit, Uriya and Jalal Bana, "Everything you wanted to know about the right to return but were too afraid to ask", *<http://www.mideastweb.org/refugees3.htm>*.
8. Hassassian, Manuel (2001). "The Political Refugee Problem in the Light of Peace Process", in Joseph Ginat and Edward Perkins (eds), *The Palestinian Refugees: Old Problems—New Solutions*. Norman: University of Oklahoma Press. p.60.

For the Israelis too, the right of return is an issue on which no compromise can be made. As long as the two-state solution is deemed the answer for the Palestinian problem, Israel will never permit the refugees to return to Israel proper and it expects the Palestinian leadership to sort out the matter by allowing resettlement within the borders of the newly formed Palestinian state. At best, Israel will accept a few thousand refugees as a symbolic gesture and expect the matter to be closed forever. Some compromise like permitting the Palestinian refugees to take up citizenships in their respective host countries, facilitating their emigration to countries willing to accept them (like Canada, Norway or Australia) and providing them with a compensation package with contributions from the international community are still doing rounds in Israel. Unless a national consensus is evolved, none of the Israeli leaders will be able to accept the right of return, which will spell the end of Israel as a Jewish majority state. The issue might be revisited in the event of the creation of a bi-national state—a possibility which will be discussed later on in this paper.

Jerusalem

The status of Jerusalem is also similar to the refugee imbroglio. Here, the issue transcends mere territorial claims and becomes a highly emotive religious one, making it all the more difficult to solve. There is not so much controversy regarding West Jerusalem, which Israel annexed in 1948. However, East Jerusalem, which was occupied by Israel in 1967 in the aftermath of the six-day war, remains an unresolved issue. So far, almost every prominent Israeli politician sticks to the position that Jerusalem cannot be divided. The Basic Law (1980)[9] on Jerusalem states that "Jerusalem, complete and united, is the capital of Israel". However, this Jerusalem Law was deemed null and void by the UN Security Council (UNSC) Resolution 478 of August 1980.[10]

All the Israeli leaders from the first Prime Minister David Ben Gurion to the incumbent Benjamin Netanyahu have stood firmly by the policy of an undivided Jerusalem. The only one instance in which an Israeli

---

9. Basic Law: Jerusalem, Capital of Israel, <*http://www.knesset.gov.il/laws/special/eng/basic10_eng.htm*>.

10. UNSC Resolution 478 (1980) of 20 August 1980, <*http://unispal.un.org/UNISPAL.NSF/0/DDE590C6FF232007852560DF0065FDDB*>.

leader appeared to be willing to negotiate on Jerusalem was during the Camp David talks in 2000. At Camp David, Israeli Prime Minister, Ehud Barak entertained proposals of granting Palestinians "sovereignty over the Muslim and Christian quarters of the Old City, but only a loosely defined "permanent custodianship" over the Haram al-Sharif".[11] However, after the collapse of the Camp David talks, Israel has shown no intention of giving up East Jerusalem territory. In fact, with the ascendance of the right-wing political groups in Israel, positions have hardened. It was perhaps no coincidence that in March 2010, when the US Vice President Joe Biden was in Israel, the Israeli Interior Ministry announced it would build 1,600 new housing units in East Jerusalem.[12] This was followed by the demolition of at least three Palestinian homes in East Jerusalem in July. The demolitions marked the end of a year-long unofficial moratorium.[13] The 10-month-long Israeli moratorium on construction activities in the occupied territories ended on 26 September 2010. The Palestinian negotiators and leaders stridently demanded that the ban on all construction outside the Green Line, including the settlement blocs, should be extended.[14] Israel argued that no moratorium of any kind in East Jerusalem was unacceptable. However, one interesting break from this traditional intransigent stance was visible just before the Netanyahu-Abbas talks in Washington on 2 September. Labour leader and Defense Minister, Yehud Barak, in an interview to the *Haaretz* made an unprecedented offer: "West Jerusalem and 12 Jewish neighbourhoods that are home to 200,000 residents will be ours. The Arab neighbourhoods in which close to a quarter million Palestinians live will be theirs. There will be a special regime in place along with agreed upon arrangements in the Old City, the Mount of Olives and the City of

---

11. Agha, Hussein and Robert Malley (2001). "Camp David: The Tragedy of Errors", *The New York Review of Books*, 9 August.

12. Bronner, Ethan (2010). "As Biden Visits, Israel Unveils Plans for New Settlements", *The New York Times*, 9 March, *<http://www.nytimes.com/2010/03/10/world/middleeast/10biden.html>*.

13. Sherwood, Harriet (2010). "Palestinian Homes Bulldozed as Israeli Freeze on Demolitions Appears to End", *The Guardian*, 14 July, *<http://www.guardian.co.uk/world/2010/jul/13/palestinian-homes-bulldozed-israeli>*.

14. Eldar, Akiva (2010). "Palestinians to U.S.: Israeli Settlement Freeze Must Include East Jerusalem", *Haaretz*, 26 August, *<http://www.haaretz.com/print-edition/news/palestinians-tell-u-s-israeli-settlement-freeze-must-include-east-jerusalem-1.310242>*.

David."[15] Barak has meanwhile split the Labour Party and formed a new Independence (*Sia'at Ha'Atzma'ut*) Party with the support of four (Labour) *Knesset* members. Labour party has walked out of the coalition and this makes Barak's support crucial for Netanyahu government. However, it remains to be seen whether Barak's offer on Jerusalem will lead to some positive development in the peace process.

One of the oldest solutions for Jerusalem, i.e., giving it the status of 'Corpus Separatum' (separate entity) under international control (first mooted in the UN General Assembly Resolution 181), looks a very remote possibility now. But it must be kept in mind that the idea is still alive and no major world power so far has recognised Jerusalem as the capital of Israel, and nearly all the foreign embassies in Israel are located in Tel Aviv, not in Jerusalem.

As far as the Palestinians are concerned, they have more or less given up on the claims to West Jerusalem. But they insist on Israeli withdrawal from all portions of East Jerusalem (occupied since 1967), which is to serve as the capital of the future Palestinian state. Even if Israel, as part of a peace deal, agrees to give up parts of East Jerusalem, the sovereign control of the Temple Mount/*Haram al-Sharif* can be a potential deal-breaker. This is an issue steeped in emotion and history where both sides will be unwilling to make any meaningful concessions. The place is the *sanctum sanctorum* of Judaism as the Wailing Wall in the Temple Mount is the only standing relic of the Second Temple. For Muslims, *Haram al-Sharif* is the third holiest site since it is believed that Prophet Mohammed ascended to heaven from here. Therefore, both sides have never been able to reach even a broad agreement on the status of Temple Mount/*Haram al-Sharif*. During the Camp David talks, Prime Minister Barak and Chairman Arafat had discussions about splitting the sovereign rights over the territory—the concept of vertical/ horizontal sovereignty—a condition in which Israel will retain sovereignty beneath the ground at the Temple Mount, while Palestinians will have sovereign control over everything above ground. This proposal too failed to win approval. Until the two sides can find an amicable plan on dividing the city and its holy sites, the chances of solving the conflict remains slim.

---

15. Shavit, Ari (2010). "Barak to Haaretz: Israel ready to cede parts of Jerusalem in peace deal", *Haaretz*, 1 September, <*http://www.haaretz.com/print-edition/news/barak-to-haaretz-israel-ready-to-cede-parts-of-jerusalem-in-peace-deal-1.311356*>.

Borders and Settlements

The state of Israel has never declared its boundaries, and therefore determining the borders between Israel and the future Palestinian state constitutes another major roadblock to the solution of the crisis. Israel has border disputes with Syria and Lebanon as well. The Palestinian side demands that Israel give up all the territories in the West Bank and Gaza, which it occupied in 1967. This corresponds to the Green line—the armistice line drawn at the end of hostilities in 1949. When the Armistice Agreement was signed in 1949, Israel ended up controlling 78 per cent of the Mandate Palestine territories.[16] Compared to the issues of Jerusalem and refugees, the border issue appears to be more amenable to a solution. There have been several proposals about land-swaps, since Israel needs to retain some portions of the West Bank in order to keep a number of large Jewish settlements within its borders. To compensate for the territory ceded by the Palestinians, offers were made to give them land from Israel proper. Gaza ceases to be an issue as far as borders and settlements are concerned because in 2005, under Ariel Sharon's Prime Ministership, Israel unilaterally withdrew from the strip and removed all the settler blocks.

The Israeli settlements in the West Bank and East Jerusalem present a graver threat to the peace process than the border issue *per se*. Presently, there are about 430,000 settlers in the West Bank and East Jerusalem, and according to most estimates, these settlements cover almost 40 per cent of the West Bank territory. In all the peace negotiations, the Israeli government has indicated that it would annex large settlements like Ariel, Modiin Illit, Maale Adumim, Givat Ze'ev and Gush Etzion.[17] However, apart from these larger settlements blocks, there are also small settlements and outposts and it will test the resolve of the Israeli government if it decides to dismantle those too. The settlers are gaining political savvy and there are many political groups as well as lobbies espousing their cause. Some commentators argue that Israel had successfully evicted the Jewish settlers from Gaza in 2005 and therefore settling them in the West Bank

16. Gavron, Daniel (2008). *Holy Land Mosaic: Stories of Cooperation and Coexistence between Israelis and Palestinians.* Maryland: Rowman and Littlefield Publishers. p.94.

17. Hasson, Nir (2010). "Israel Planning 50,000 Housing Units in East Jerusalem", *Haaretz*, 11 March, <*http://www.haaretz.com/print-edition/news/israel-planning-50-000-housing-units-in-east-jerusalem-1.264620*>.

is possible. However, they overlook the fact that Gaza had no religious connotation as far as the Jews are concerned, while the West Bank is the biblical territory of Judea and Samaria. Similarly, the number of settlers to be evicted from the West Bank is considerably higher than the numbers in Gaza. Again, it was Ariel Sharon who as the Prime Minister oversaw the Gaza disengagement plan and the current leadership lacks the stature to pull off a similar feat in the West Bank. One should also take into account the increasing instances of Israeli soldiers refusing to obey orders regarding dismantling settlements or eviction of settlers from the West Bank. Such events are sure to weigh in the mind of the Israeli leadership while negotiating for a withdrawal from the West Bank. Israel is also worried about the security situation in its eastern border after withdrawal from the West Bank and as a result, will insist on establishing 'defensible borders' through a number of measures like total demilitarisation of the Palestinian state, as also Israeli presence on the border between the West Bank and Jordan.

Apart from the traditional bottlenecks identified as the final status issues, there are also other problems that seriously undermine the possibility of a rapprochement between Israelis and Palestinians. The following sections will address a few such issues, such as Israel's preference for *status quo*, its gradual turn to the right, the split in Palestinian territories, the rise of political Islam and the increasing doubts about the one-state solution.

Israel's Shift to the Right and Preference for Status Quo

Israeli public opinion has been witnessing a gradual shift towards the right for more than a decade. This period has seen the decline of the Israeli left wing, the main pro-peace constituency in the country. This shift became more pronounced after the collapse of the Camp David talks (2000) between Yehud Barak and Yassir Arafat, which most Israelis believe was the benchmark in peace negotiations. This was followed by the second Palestinian *intifada*, and in its wake, Ariel Sharon of the Likud Party got elected as the Prime Minister of Israel. The move to the right gained further momentum with the US-led 'war on terror,' the rise of *Hamas*, *Hezbollah* and Iran. Under Sharon's leadership, Israel decided to move unilaterally on the Palestinian front and withdrew from the Gaza strip (2005) by forcibly evicting the reluctant settlers. Meanwhile, Israel undertook the construction of the highly controversial security/separation fence on its eastern border. The security fence, in spite of all the criticism it had to face, ensured that Israel remained by and large secure from terror attacks. Thus, the post-fence phase proved to be remarkably peaceful for the Israelis. However, while the suicide bombings nearly stopped, Israel had to face rocket attacks from Hezbollah and Hamas. In July-August 2006, this escalated into a full war between Israel and the Hezbollah in Lebanon. Similarly, when faced with rocket attacks from the Gaza Strip, Israel invaded the territory in December 2008 to January 2009. Even though these attacks led to severe criticism and international condemnation, Israel managed to put an end to the rocket attacks. Hamas acknowledged in the aftermath of Israel's 'Operation Cast Lead' in Gaza that the rocket attacks are no longer sufficient and instead, a "new emphasis on cultural resistance" is required for the Palestinian movement.[18]

Though Israel was put under a great deal of international pressure and scrutiny, the Gaza blockade has kept Israel largely safe from rocket attacks. Perhaps this was the reason, that forced Israel to forcibly block the Gaza bound *Flotilla* in the Mediterranean.[19&20] Such unilateral moves may be untenable diplomatically as well as politically in the long run; however, for the time being, Israeli citizens appear to be satisfied with the *status quo*.

The pro-right trend is evident from the results of the *Knesset* elections. In the 2009 elections, the top two parties were *Kadima* (founded by Ariel Sharon after he split from Likud) and *Likud*, the traditional right wing party. However, the most surprising performer in the elections was *Yisrael Beiteinu*—a far-right party led by the present Foreign Minister, Avigdor Lieberman. The pro-peace *Meretz* languished at the bottom of the table with just three seats, reflecting the popular mood. Moreover, the once dominant Labour party is a junior partner in the present ruling coalition led

---

18. Bronner, Ethan (2009). "Hamas Shifts from Rockets to Culture War", *The New York Times*, 23 July, <*http://www.nytimes.com/2009/07/24/world/middleeast/24gaza.html?_r=3*>.

19. Joy, Ajish P. (2010). "Attack on Flotilla: A Strategic Blunder by Israel", *ORF Analysis*, 3 June, <*http://www.observerindia.com/cms/sites/orfonline/modules/analysis/AnalysisDetail.html?cmaid=19157&mmacmaid=19158*>.

20. Horowitz, David (2010). "The Flotilla Fiasco", *The Jerusalem Post*, 1 June, <*http://www.jpost.com/ArtsAndCulture/Entertainment/Article.aspx?id=177099*>.

by *Likud* and *Yisrael Beiteinu*. It has been weakened further with the latest split led by Yehud Barak.

With relative peace prevailing, it seems that the Israelis are in no mood for changes. Meron Benvenisiti, the former Deputy Mayor of Jerusalem, identifies six reasons for the prevalence of *status quo*[21]: fragmentation of the Palestinian community and their lack of unity; mobilisation of the Jewish community in support for the occupation regime; external funding, which helps maintain the *status quo*; apparent apathy of the neighbouring states and prioritisation of bilateral and global interests; the unending peace process, which conveys the impression that *status quo* is temporary; and the silencing of all criticism as an expression of hatred and anti-Semitism. However, for an average Israeli, these are mostly abstract ideas and he is more concerned about maintaining the relative peace he is enjoying; he feels that *status quo* is the best possible option. As Shlomo Ben-Ami argues, "absorbed by their booming economy, reassured by President Barack Obama's recent commitment never to let Israel down, and convinced of their success in defeating Palestinian terrorism in the West Bank and deterring Hamas from venturing into another war, Israelis have lost any sense of urgency concerning the Palestinian problem".[22] The *Time* magazine reports that in a poll conducted in March 2010, only 8 per cent of the Israeli Jews considered the Palestinian crisis as the most urgent problem faced by the country: education, crime, national security and poverty came first.[23]

Given this public sentiment, it is well-nigh impossible for anyone in the Israeli leadership to make a bold proposal to allow concessions to the Palestinians for securing peace. Another disadvantage is the absence of a powerful and charismatic leadership. In a crisis situation, the stature of the leadership does matter. On this count, Netanyahu is no match for the Israeli leaders of yore like Menachem Begin, Yitzhak Rabin or Ariel

21. Benvenisti, Meron (2010). "The Inevitable Bi-national Regime", *Haaretz* (Opinion) in Hebrew, 22 January, translated by Zalman Amit and Daphna Levitt, *<http://www.americantaskforce.org/daily_news_article/2010/01/22/1264136400_13>*.

22. Ben-Ami, Shlomo (2010). "Phantom Middle East Peace Process", *The Korea Times*, 8 August, *<http://www.koreatimes.co.kr/www/news/opinon/2010/08/137_71069.html>*.

23. Vick, Karl (2010). "Why Israel Doesn't Care About Peace?", *Time*, 2 September, *<http://www.time.com/time/world/article/0,8599,2015602,00.html>*.

Sharon, who shaped rather than followed public opinion. As a result, the peace constituency in Israel has been weakened and depleted considerably, making *status quo* the preferred public choice in spite of the fact that international opinion is visibly hardening against Israel. This is true for the Palestinians as well. Yasser Arafat, in spite of all the allegations against him, was probably the only leader who could command loyalty of the entire Palestinian population.

West Bank-Gaza/Hamas-Fatah Split

Just as the Israelis are 'taking it easy' on the peace negotiations front, it is interesting to note that the Palestinians too are not really pressing for peace, notwithstanding customary occasional statements from the leadership. President Mahmoud Abbas's participation in the peace summit held in the USA on 2 September 2010, was largely the result of American insistence rather than any genuine desire or hope for durable peace. There are no easy explanations for this. One reason could be the *de facto* division of the Palestinian territories in West Bank and Gaza. The two regions are territorially non-contiguous and they were held together as a unit under the Palestinian Authority only by political means. But with the two regions now differing politically and ideologically, the glue that held them together no longer exists. In spite of the punishing sanctions and blockade, the Gazan population has remained by and large supportive of the Hamas government whom they elected in a democratic exercise. The West Bank meanwhile remains more liberal and secular. Its economy is also growing impressively under the leadership of the technocrat Prime Minister Salam Fayyad. The West Bank economy is more integrated with Israel, and since *Hamas* is designated as a terrorist group by major aid donors like the USA and the European Union (EU), most of the aid meant for the Palestinians ends up in the West Bank. If Gaza and the West Bank remain separate as they are today, it will be a major disincentive for the Palestinians to press hard for a state. After the Gaza *Flotilla* fiasco, Israeli Foreign Minister Lieberman spoke about an Israeli disengagement from Gaza with ultimate responsibility being handed over to the EU. The plan was to seal Gaza off "from Israel and creating an independent entity under Hamas control propped up economically by the EU. It would also be asked to secure the border with Israel and inspect ships bound for Gaza for arms."[24] This innocuous-sounding plan for Gaza will effectively create an independent Palestinian state in Gaza heavily dependent on Egypt, leaving the future of the West Bank and a viable Palestinian entity in turmoil. The plan was rejected by *Hamas* and *Fatah* as well as several European leaders.[25] Many Israelis too expressed doubts about the viability of the proposal. Lieberman later clarified that it was not a concrete plan, but an informal proposal, which was formulated at the Israeli Foreign Ministry's Political Research Council.

The peace process has little chance to succeed so long as Gaza and the West Bank stay as separate entities under separate ruling parties following fundamentally divergent ideologies and policies.

Rising Profile of Political Islam

Spread across the world with more than a billion believers, Islam's role as a global political force is on the upswing. This political face is fast becoming a rallying point for all real and perceived injustices against Muslims. This has serious implications for the Palestinian issue as well. Interestingly, the Palestinian movement was one of the most secular political movements in the Islamic world when it began. However, the long-stalled peace process, the increasing radicalisation of the Palestinian youth, the intractable nature of the problem and the sordid stories of corruption among the leadership have ensured that religion is going to play a key role in the conflict. With the Hamas victory in the Palestinian Authority elections, the transformation was evident, especially in the Gaza strip. Just as the Israeli public opinion is veering towards the right, one can discern a similar trend of radicalisation among the Palestinians. Therefore, it is not an irony that a non-Arab Shia country (Iran) and an Arab-Shia group (*Hezbollah*) are the most popular political forces in the Palestinian street today. Both Iran and *Hezbollah* adopt belligerent positions on Israel based on religious ideology. Iran, which was a marginal player in the conflict till

24. *The Irish Times* (2010). "Israel and the EU", 26 July, <*http://www.irishtimes.com/newspaper/opinion/2010/0726/1224275466887.html*>

25. Al-Naami, Saleh (2010). "Double Trouble", Al Ahram, Issue No. 1008, 22-28 July, <*http://weekly.ahram.org.eg/2010/1008/re2.htm*>.

about a decade ago, has now established itself as one of the lead actors, much to the chagrin of leading Arab countries like Egypt and Saudi Arabia.

Similarly, in a decade dominated by the 9/11 attacks, the 'war on terror,' the invasion of Afghanistan and Iraq, debates on the 'clash of civilizations' and the fading away of the unipolar moment, the Palestinian crisis has become a rallying point for several movements and groups. This is not just confined to the Middle East, but has become a part of the popular and political discourse in almost all parts of the world, especially in places where Muslims wield some influence. Just to give an example, Israel is a main talking-point in elections in Kerala—a small state in the south-western tip of India, where Muslims form nearly a quarter of the population.[26] In an era where domestic compulsions play a key role in the formulation of the foreign policy of nations, the Palestinian conflict thus gets further entrenched in places and polities across the globe. Compare this to any other movement for self-determination—for example the Kurdish one—none of them remain so vivid and active in public memory. Similarly, in the case of several other conflicts, in which hundreds of thousands of people are killed and oppressed—ranging from Congo, Rwanda, Sierra Leone, Nigeria, Liberia or Guinea—the world hardly takes notice. Noah Bernstein makes an interesting observation about the global media's bias in favour of the Palestinian conflict. He gives the example of Israel's 'Operation Cast Lead' in Gaza, which led to 926 Palestinian fatalities. In the three weeks of Israeli incursion, the event was reported 2,896 times by the media. During the same period in Congo, Joseph Kony's Lord's Resistance Army (LRA) killed 865 civilians and abducted 160 children. This event was reported just 20 times in the global media.[27]

Unfortunately, the incorporation of the Palestinian issue into the wider Islamic movement has the unpleasant effect of making its solution even more distant and difficult. It has widened the scope and the horizon of the conflict and has broad-based it, making it more unwieldy. For

26. Gopakumar, S. (2009). "Israel, a Key Poll Issue in Kerala", *The Hindu Business Line*, 8 April, <*http://www.thehindubusinessline.com/2009/04/08/stories/2009040850050400.htm*>.

27 Bernstein, Noah (2010). "A Media Eclipse: Israel-Palestine and the World's Forgotten Conflicts", *Open Democracy*, 18 March, <*http://www.opendemocracy.net/opensecurity/noah-bernstein/media-eclipse-israel-palestine-and-worlds-forgotten-conflicts*>.

example, it is now impossible for any Palestinian leader to give meaningful concessions in Jerusalem without incurring the wrath of the wider Islamic world, even if the Palestinians are willing to back those concessions. The Islamisation of the conflict has ensured that the solution should satisfy Muslims across the globe.

One-State Solution as a Road Block

Presently, the two-state model is the gold standard of the solutions to the Palestinian conflict. Since the peace process started, it has been accepted as the best possible outcome by all the key players excluding *Hamas*. The peace process at present is carried forward to achieve the two-state solution, and therefore any move to challenge the viability or possibility of the two-state solution could scuttle the peace process. However, with the two-state plan stagnating for nearly two decades now, alternative solutions are now being proposed.

The concept of a single-state solution, once widely believed to be the forte of fringe groups, has now started becoming increasingly mainstream in Israel, especially among the right-wing groups. *Likud* leader and former cabinet minister, Moshe Arens, *Knesset* Speaker, Reuven Rivlin, Uri Elitzur, a former Chairman of the Yesha Settlers Council and *Likud*'s Tzipi Hotovely the youngest member of the present *Knesset* are some of the leading advocates of the one-state solution. However, ambivalence prevails regarding the details of the one-state plan even among these supporters. For most right-wing groups, an undivided state means a state in the entire territory of Greater Israel—from Jordan to the Mediterranean—which retains its Jewish character irrespective of the present and future demographics. The supporters say that the move may take up to a generation to be completed and at the end

> the Palestinians will enjoy full personal rights, but in a country whose symbols and spirit will remain Jewish. It is at this point that the one-state right wing diverges from the binational left. The right is not talking about a neutral state of all its citizens with no identity nor about Israstine with a flag showing a crescent and a Shield of David.[28]

---

28. Sheizaf, Noam (2010). "Endgame", *Haaretz*, 15 July, *<http://www.haaretz.com/magazine/friday-supplement/endgame-1.302128>*.

For the right-wing ideologues, the annexation of the West Bank absolves Israel from international condemnation about the treatment of the Palestinians in the West Bank "because the annexation of the West Bank would grant full citizenship and voting rights to West Bank Palestinians, perhaps putting Israel out of its international isolation in a single stroke".[29] It is also interesting to note that most such plans do not envisage any role for Gaza in the new state. It gives Israel a significant demographic advantage. A single-state solution will also help Israel from an extremely difficult situation of dismantling some of the West Bank settlements—something that will carry huge financial, emotional and political costs.

After Moshe Arens articulated his views on a single-state solution, a poll conducted by the Palestinian Organization, Jerusalem Media and Communications Centre showed that the support for this concept is gaining ground among the Palestinians as well. According to the poll, around 34 per cent of respondents supported a bi-national state in all of historic Palestine over the two-state solution, which only 43.9 per cent supported.[30] The Palestinian idea of a bi-national state is of course totally different from the Israeli view. However, a difference of opinion among the Palestinians regarding the one- or two-state solution shows the real credibility-deficit faced by the official line. There are reports that even within the *Fatah* leadership, there is some amount of opposition towards the two-state solution. Some of them argue that the "two-state solution is being kept alive via artificial means and that more and more people are losing hope in its feasibility".[31] Danny Rubinstein argues that one key reason behind the increasing Palestinian willingness to be citizens of Israel is "the decline of the Palestinian nationalist movement".[32] He cites the example of the 300,000 strong Arab communities in East Jerusalem, which

29. Susser, Leslie (2010). "Is One-state Solution an Answer to Greater Israel Dreams?" Jewish Telegraphic Agency, 2 August, <*http://jta.org/news/article/2010/08/02/2740309/is-one-state-solution-an-answer-to-greater-israel-dreams*>.

30. Maan News Agency (2010). "Poll: One-state Solution Gains Ground", 21 April, <*http://www.maannews.net/eng/ViewDetails.aspx?ID=278196*>.

31. Amayreh, Khaled (2010). "Bullying Abbas into Talks", *Al Ahram*, 29 July-4 August, Issue No. 1009, <*http://weekly.ahram.org.eg/2010/1009/re1.htm*>.

32. Rubinstein, Danny (2010). "One State/Two States: Rethinking Israel and Palestine", Dissent, Summer 2010, <*http://www.dissentmagazine.org/article/?article=3254*>.

are increasingly applying for Israeli citizenship, finally realising that Israel is never going to give up its hold on any part of Jerusalem.

The one-state solution will be opposed by the Zionist groups because it will ultimately rob Israel of its Jewish nature. Also, it is highly unlikely that the Palestinians will be given equal rights in such a state. It will be almost impossible for the Jews and the Arabs to develop a common national narrative, national symbols or agree on a common history regarding the new single-state. If Israel tries to retain the Jewish nature of the state by force, the condition will be nothing less than apartheid. Therefore, the likelihood of this new state thriving peacefully is negligible. However, the one-state solution featuring prominently in the mainstream discourse can lead to more delays in the peace process.

The Palestinian issue is also a powerful tool and rallying point for citizens across the Middle Eastern states, especially in the Arab dictatorships and monarchies. Often, the issue is used to deflect attention from a range of domestic issues like lack of political reforms and inequitable distribution of wealth. While it may be preposterous to argue that the dictatorial regimes in the region promote the continuation of the conflict, it is apparent that this festering sore has provided them with a convenient refuge to tide over uncomfortable domestic situations. Most Arab countries are increasingly worried about the rising profile of Iran and its nuclear capability and, for them, Iran is a much bigger threat than Israel. In fact, they think of Israel as a bulwark against Iran's rising profile. Therefore, it curtails the will of these states to push forward with a solution to the Palestinian crisis. In fact, the Arab dictators "quite like the status quo, including the part where they get to condemn the United States for maintaining it".[33]

Similarly, the gradual decline of the power and prestige enjoyed by the United States is not helping the peace process. The beginning of the peace process coincided with the collapse of the Soviet Union and the unchallenged supremacy of American power. Israelis and Palestinians appeared to conclude a peace deal in 2000 at Camp David when the world was experiencing a rare 'unipolar moment.' Now, as the American power is

---

33. Friedman, George (2010). "Israeli-Palestinian Peace Talks, Again", *Stratfor*, 23 August, *<www.stratfor.com/.../20100823_israeli_and_palestinian_peace_talks_again>*.

in (relative) decline, there is no one to play the role of a powerful mediator who can force the two sides to conclude a deal. The situation is not helped by the fact that Iran has positioned itself as an influential actor. With its influence on *Hamas* and *Hezbollah*, Iran is sure to play a key role in the conflict and, considering the antagonistic relations between Iran and Israel, the solution appears to have been distanced further away.

Conclusion

The Palestinian crisis remains unresolved even after years of 'peace-making,' and no solution appears anywhere in the horizon. The initial years of the peace talks showed some progress, but when substantive issues reached the negotiating table, hopes for peace fizzled out. The 'final status issues' including the status of refugees, Jerusalem, borders and settlements have been kept in abeyance. Though these issues are expected to be discussed in the ongoing negotiations, because of the fundamental disagreements, painful concessions will have to be made in order to forge a peace deal. In the present circumstances, it is unlikely that such concessions will be made. The situation is further aggravated by the increasing radicalisation of the Palestinians, Israel's shift to the right, its preference for maintaining the *status quo*, the rise of political Islam, the waning influence of the United States and the complete split between Gaza and the West Bank.

More significantly, even a moderately-successful solution to these problems and the creation of a Palestinian state will not necessarily result in peace. At present, within the available territory, it is difficult to imagine a Palestinian state, which can satisfy the aspirations of the majority of Palestinians. Lack of sufficient territory for a growing population, serious problems related to territorial contiguity and the demilitarised nature of the state have the potential to destabilise a future Palestinian state and thereby further aggravate the conflict. The peace process as it progresses today is incapable of answering these issues, and it merely aims at implementing a two-state solution, hoping that peace will prevail once the Palestinian state is created. Unfortunately, as things stand today, both the creation of a Palestinian state and its peaceful coexistence with Israel remain an improbable dream.

18

Prospects of Regional Cooperation in Afghanistan

The Case of India and Pakistan

Kaustav Dhar Chakrabarti

As the coalition forces prepare to leave, diminishing international community's commitment to peace in Afghanistan, political behaviour of Afghans at this crucial juncture will be a key factor influencing the nature and outcome of the conflict in Afghanistan. In this context, it would be useful to study the manner in which the Afghans have reacted during and after the numerous invasions by foreign empires in the past. Under what conditions did they decide to give up fighting the invaders? More specific to the present era, does the Taliban's demand for the withdrawal of foreign troops as a prerequisite for negotiations echo the popular opinion embedded by history in the Afghan mass psyche? Or, will the Afghans, motivated by the desire for durable peace and security, be more amenable to their presence?

To get an insight into these dilemmas and problems, the paper examines two key issues. First, it explains how political order and stability has been determined by the incumbent regime's relations with the country's ethnically diverse people and regions. The paper will examine the changing nature of state control over the different regions and tribes over time, and the reasons for such change.

Second, it analyses the effect of international competition in its attempt to alter this delicate relationship on Afghanistan, giving centrality to the India-Pakistan rivalry. Subsequently, motivations that drive the strategies of these two countries are explained. Also explored are the prospects for reducing this rivalry, thereby opening the way for productive cooperation in Afghanistan.

I

Kabul and the Autonomous Regions

Dynastic struggles among Afghanistan's political elite and, upon victory, their relations with the country's autonomous provinces have historically determined the degree and status of the country's stability. The ability of Kandahar, in the past, and Kabul, at present, to control Afghanistan's diverse regions through a mix of patronage and coercion has shaped the country's federal character. Succession struggles were accepted by ordinary Afghans who, in turn, became recipients of largesse and were allowed to retain past practices of local politics, culture and lifestyle. This arrangement of mutual incentives served to limit political contention at the centre, insulated the provinces from 'regime change' and allowed regional communities to practice self-rule and maintain their identity.

During the stable phases of its history, especially in the pre-modern era, Afghanistan avoided state collapse and civil insurrection by limiting the number of political aspirants to hereditary elites who "saw government as their business".[1] Afghanistan's political culture restricted competition to certain elite dynastic groups. Their rule and legitimacy was established by military conquest and, once successful, was not challenged by the commoners. In fact, it was a common practice for newly crowned Amirs (rulers) to retain the services of former power brokers. Unlike the Napoleonic period of Europe, or the anti-colonial movements of Asia and Africa, which involved mass political and military mobilisation motivated by nationalism, in much of Afghanistan, there have been no such all-inclusive dynamics in the past; thus, limited resistance was faced by conquering rulers.[2] This feature of politics was accentuated by the fact that armies of the day, instead of comprising citizens, were composed of mercenaries and slaves driven by monetary incentives.

The Persian Achaemenid Empire was the first foreign dynasty to experience the largely apolitical nature of Afghans. Darius III expanded his reign to modern day Afghanistan and set up seven *satrapies*, namely, *Aria*

1. Barfield, Thomas (2010). *Afghanistan: A Cultural and Political History.* New Jersey: Princeton University Press.

2. Ibid.

(Herat), *Bactriana* (Balkh and Mazar-e-Sharif), *Margiana* (Merv), *Gandhara* (Kabul, Jalalabad, Peshawar), *Sattagydia* (Ghazni to the Indus river), *Arachosia* (Qandahar and Quetta) and *Drangiana* (Sistan).[3] The *satrapy* system was based on the principle of self-rule and allowed the local tribes to live according to their customs.[4] Though Darius faced stiff resistance from the eastern tribes and was forced to maintain strong garrisons there, much of Afghanistan accepted his rule. In fact, when Alexander invaded the region in 330 BC, the locals, especially *Bactrians*, defended the Persian incumbents, in spite of Alexander's call for their liberation.[5] Other invaders, such as Parthian, Mauryan, Gupta, Kusan, Hephthalite, Sasan, Safavid and Mughal empires shared similar experiences.

Once a ruler established legitimacy by overcoming competition from brothers and cousins, his relation with the country's powerful regions became crucial. Regions such as Herat, Mazar-e-Sharif, Kandahar and Jalalabad historically derived their identity not as Afghanistan's provinces, but rather as quasi-independent units closely associated with neighbouring empires. For much of its history, Persian (Achaemenid, Parthian, Sassanian, Safavid, Afsharid), Indian (Mauryan, Gupta and Mughal), and Central Asian (Mongol, Timurid and Uzbek) empires controlled parts of Afghanistan and often assimilated them, creating channels of trade and cultural exchanges.

Geography has greatly influenced regional distinctions. The mighty Hindu Kush mountain range, which rises in the north of Kabul separates northern Afghanistan from the south and discourages easy travel. As a result, northern regions are closer to the trans-Oxus valleys and steppes of Central Asia. For instance, the important city of Mazar-e-Sharif, shielded from the south by natural defences, is more closely integrated to Central Asia.[6] Southern Afghanistan, on the other hand, leans towards Iran and South Asia.[7] Kandahar, the most important city of southern Afghanistan, is the only major city where Pashtuns constitute a majority, and is linked with the Pashtun regions of Pakistan. In the west, the economy of Herat continues to be coupled with that of Iran.

3. Dupree, Louis (1980). *Afghanistan*. New Jersey: Princeton University Press. p.274.
4. Ibid.
5. *op.cit.* no.3: 278.
6. Ibid.
7. *op.cit.* no.1.

In addition to influencing regional autonomy, geography has also shaped the distribution of population and state control. In the West, states such as Rome had been characterised by a consistent degree of state control. These states applied uniform law and a common administration throughout their boundaries, which led to a gradual homogenisation, or 'Romanisation' of previously diverse communities. The same is not true for Afghanistan, where control and power of the state was limited to key towns, agriculture tracts and trade routes. Afghan population, therefore, were concentrated to a few centres of agriculture, interspersed with large stretches of sparsely populated regions, which effectively lay outside the authority of successive Afghan states.

Harsh terrain is not the only reason for such dispersed political control. The empires that conquered and assimilated Afghanistan were attracted not by its organic wealth and resources, but rather by the access to the greener pastures of India and Central Asia and control over the regional trade routes, besides buttressing their frontiers against attacks. Rulers of Afghanistan, therefore, consistently chose to focus on establishing control over strategic belts, leaving the rest of the country to be managed by local elites. Given that agricultural land constitutes less than 5 per cent of the country's territory, direct political control by Kabul was limited to the 'green-spots' and the roads that connected them. Such a pattern of population distribution and state control combined with the country's imposing terrain naturally favoured a decentralised political system.

Relations between Kabul and tribal leaders were crucial in maintaining order. Having confined their interests to selected areas, Afghan rulers preferred delegating power to regional elites chosen among tribal chieftains. They were rewarded with government appointments such as the Governorship of strategic cities, which gave them access to resources and placed them at an advantage over their local rivals.[8] In return, they accepted the indirect sovereignty of Kabul and, as a norm, refrained from revolting against these essentially foreign rulers.

This fundamental aspect of power structure also served to draw an indelible line between national politics and regional affairs. For instance, even though Ahmad Shah Durrani, the founder of the first independent

8. Ibid.

Afghan state, appointed his sons to important regions such as Herat and Lahore, he continued to rely on traditional leaders who "handled local administration and were practically independent".[9] This separation of powers also insulated the regions from violent changes that were common at the centre. Given the frequency of 'regime changes' in Kabul, the regional leaders simply accepted the authority of the new incumbent and rarely questioned his legitimacy.

Centralisation of the Afghan State

The two Anglo-Afghan wars, fought in 1839 and 1878, changed Afghan politics. As part of its 'forward policy,' Britain invaded Afghanistan to install a more compliant ruler to check the growth of Russia, which had come to dominate Central Asia and appeared poised to make forays into Afghanistan. The Anglo-Afghan wars led to conditions that created new political aspirants other than the traditional elite. Facing a technologically superior enemy, Afghan rulers encouraged armed resistance from previously passive subjects. Notions of safeguarding Afghan pride and defending Islam were introduced, which mobilised large sections of the society, and generated expectations for a greater role in governance after the war.

The spread of political violence from elite groups to ordinary folk (in modern day jargon, non-state actors) was aided by the introduction of gunpowder weapons such as the musket, rifle and the legendary Afghan *jezail* (musket). Gunpowder reduced the superiority of the state-owned cavalry, tilting the balance in favour of mountain tribals and the rural peasants.[10]

While earlier, Islam was projected as a motivation for outward invasions, most notably into the Indian subcontinent, resistance to British occupation introduced 'defence of Islam' as a prominent theme in domestic affairs. At the same time, Islam also served as the common cause that united the fractious tribes of the south-eastern regions.

Having become politicised by participating in '*jihad*' against the British occupation, ordinary Afghans began to pose a new security threat to their rulers, prompting a greater consolidation of the state. By the 20th century,

9. Ibid.
10. Ibid.

a centralised government, now with a fledging national bureaucracy, replaced the archaic practice of indirect rule of autonomous regions. The new, common system of administration, taxation and currency, as well as military conscription and, above all, a common feeling of hardship that they caused cut across ethnic and regional lines and helped generate a common sense of identity.

Several administrative reforms initiated by the British also contributed towards building a centralised modern nation-state. The most crucial reforms transformed the army from an old feudal cavalry-based organisation to a professional infantry-based army under the direct control of the government. Earlier, Afghan rulers fielded slave armies and relied on vassals sweetened with a large share of the state's revenues to maintain their armies and prevent subversion. Also, even tribal levies were used to meet the cost of increasing army personnel, digging deep into the state coffers, but without adding much to the military value of the slave army. The new modern national army did not have to depend on tribal chiefs, and could be ordered to fight without the lure of loot, regroup after initial setbacks and not disperse seasonally.[11] Besides raising a modern army, the British also streamlined the revenue system and imposed taxes on previously privileged classes, fattening the state coffers and strengthening the state.

Following the second Anglo-Afghan War in 1880, Abdur Rehman, the new ruler, launched a brutal campaign to consolidate power. He divided the big provinces to reduce their strength, displaced influential tribes through large-scale forced migrations, and carried out severe taxation and confiscation measures. When he met resistance, he targeted not just the regional elites, but the entire population. By the end of his rule, 'Iron Amir' as he came to be known had no rivals. Abdur Rehman's goal of ruling Afghanistan without depending on intermediaries was challenged unsuccessfully by 40 rebellions led by *Ghilzai* tribes, Turkistan and non-Sunni ethnic groups, who had previously been beyond the ambit of state control. While effective no doubt, Rehman's 'internal imperialism'[12] created a strong undercurrent of resentment, which later manifested itself through centrifugal processes such as rebellions and insurgencies.

11. Ibid.

12. *op.cit.* no.3: xix.

Period of Flux: 1901-1973

The period between the death of Abdur Rehman (1901) and the Communist Saur Revolution of 1978 witnessed tentative reigns of Amir Habibullah Khan and Amanullah Khan and a long but uneventful rule of Zahir Shah. While these rulers maintained a centralised state, in reality, they were only a shadow of the 'Iron Amir'. Kabul's control over the provinces began to wither, generating conditions conducive to state-fragmentation. The armed insurrection that began in the 1970s accelerated this process.

While Abdur Rehman consolidated political power, he made no attempts to carry out social and economic reforms. His successor, Amanullah Khan, introduced sweeping social and economic reforms. For instance, in 1923, he proposed the formulation of the nation's first Constitution, introduced new taxes, stressed on formal education for women, imposed universal conscription, abolished slavery and made changes to customs such as polygamy, child marriage and other family matters. But when faced with opposition, he failed to suppress revolts and opted for compromises. Amanullah Khan was unable to contain multiple revolts against his reformist government and was finally forced to flee and seek exile.

No doubt these measures were introduced to modernise Afghanistan and bring it at par with developments in its neighbourhood. Unfortunately, three successive wars with the British had severely weakened the Afghan state. The last of them, fought in 1919, culminated in the Treaty of Rawalpindi that declared Afghanistan as a sovereign state, thus ending the steady supply of arms and aid from Britain. Loss of external support curtailed Kabul's ability to exert its hegemony and quash internal dissension. Amanullah Khan's successors, Mohammed Nadir Shah, and his son, Zahir Shah, having learnt important lessons from his failures, preferred *status quo* and introduced fewer reforms that too confined to Kabul.

During this period of flux, the disparity between Kabul and the countryside became more acute, which further estranged the centre from the regions. The government, dominated by the new Kabul-based urban elite, grew unaffected to the sensitivities of the rural population. Much of Afghanistan's economic development, which began in the 1950s, was concentrated in Kabul. It also served as the pilot project for most modernisation drives.[13] The Kabul elite, though small in number, accrued a degree of influence disproportionate to their size and began to lobby for reforms and modernisation. However, unlike the pre-Abdur Rehman era—during which the political elite had derived their strength from tribal ties, landed estates, powerful militias and on their ability to muster the support of their cohort—their 20th century counterparts owed their allegiance to the state and the ruler, and exercised little clout among their supporters.[14]

Soviet Presence and Civil Wars: 1973 to Present

The three-decade long civil war and insurgency, which started in the 1970s, essentially reversed Abdur Rehman's centralisation by empowering the regional power-holders as 'warlords' and 'mujahedeen' commanders. They became the 21st century reincarnation of the traditional tribal elite.

The organised Afghan resistance against Soviet occupation paved the way for the return of regional powers. The anti-Soviet armed movement was initiated by the Peshawar Parties, i.e., seven Afghan political groups based in the Pakistani frontier city of Peshawar. These groups—*Khalis* faction, *Hizb-e- Islami*, *Jamiat-i-Islami*, *Islamic Union* for the Liberation of Afghanistan, National Islamic Front for Afghanistan, Afghanistan National Liberation Front and Revolutionary Islamic Movement—received generous funds from the United States and Saudi Arabia, among others, that were channelled through Pakistan. The Parties acted as a conduit between Pakistan's security agencies and religious groups, and the rebel commanders in Afghanistan.

Political leaders such as Burhanuddin Rabbani spent most of their time outside Afghanistan and failed to emerge as potential national leaders. Rebel leaders, who fought the Soviet, and Afghan government troops also remained confined to their ethnic and tribal strongholds and made little effort to expand their individual proto-states. In fact, attempts

13. For instance, Kabul welcomed the break from past and allowed its women to remove the veil and encouraged women to participate in education and professions.

14. This was done purposefully by Abdur Rehman to undercut the influence of the regional elite by including relatively weak communities such as *Muhammanzai* sardars (chiefs) and urbanised, Kabuli Tajiks into the power structure.

to move beyond traditional ethnic and tribal boundaries often resulted in internecine violence. The most notorious were the regular clashes between Ahmad Shah Massoud, the legendary Tajik commander who was based in the Panjshir Valley, and Gulbuddin Hekmatyar, commander of the *Hizb-e-Islami*.

As a result, gradually, field commanders such as Massoud, Abdul Haq and Jalaluddin Haqqani became central figures of the insurgency, thereby restoring the pre-eminence of autonomous regions. For instance, Massoud created the *Shura Nazar* (Supervisory Council), a counter-state setup in his stronghold in Panjshir, to be followed by Ismail Khan in Herat. Though both were affiliated with the *Jamiat*, their control over their respective turfs exceeded that of their leader Burhanuddin Rabbani. Likewise, Hekmatyar failed to exercise authority over commanders such as Abdul Haq and Jalaluddin Haqqani in eastern region.[15]

In spite of overarching motivations—Jihad and defence of Afghan honour—in reality, the regional orientation of the movement forced insurgent commanders to give priority to local concerns and security. Not surprisingly, after the withdrawal of Soviet forces, the incumbent President Mohammad Najibullah had to seek ceasefire accords with a large number of rebels. Between 1989 and 1992, he extended his control by distributing Soviet largesse among important power brokers throughout the country. In a couple of years, 60 per cent of former '*mujahedeen*' rebels either joined government militias or agreed to ceasefire conditions. But as the Soviet Union began to collapse, Moscow's largesse dried up and Najibullah's system of patronage withered. Seeing the central authority on its death bed, the armed militia regrouped along regional lines, thus triggering a civil war. After more than 100 years of direct control by Kabul, power dispersed to various regions.

Afghanistan was now effectively a collection of autonomous units, each fighting for superiority over the other. Ismail Khan controlled the western provinces of Herat, Badghis, Farah and Ghor; Abdul Rashid Dostum ruled the northern province of Mazar-e-Sharif; Massoud controlled Kabul and the northeast; the Nangarhar Shaura in Jalalabad controlled

15. *op. cit.* no.1: 240.

the east; and Jalaluddin Haqqani and other Pashtun leaders controlled the southern regions.[16]

The dynamics of civil war gave new forms to age-old characteristics of regional distinctions. The north, crucial for supply lines from Russia, became an important counterweight to the Pashtun-dominated south. The most prominent northern leader was Abdul Rashid Dostum, who commanded the 40,000-strong *Juzjani* militia.[17] Proximity to Russian supply lines along with the presence of powerful militia leaders led to greater stability and development in non-Pashtun regions in the north. The leaderless, fractious Pashtun militias took to lawlessness, routinely tormenting the civilian population.

Given the large number of regional players in Afghanistan during this period, no single actor could gather sufficient military power and forge alliances to claim control over the country. As a result of lack of resources and the resultant stalemate, each side began to look at neighbouring countries, including former enemies, for assistance. Neighbouring countries, in turn, started arming rival Afghan groups, making them their proxies in the new Great Game. Belligerent militias became clients of rival countries, increasing the polarisation of politics and society, and building a structural impediment against negotiations and ceasefire. It is against this backdrop that the role of India and Pakistan is examined.

II

Afghanistan, India and Pakistan

In the recent past, India and Pakistan have supported opposing Afghan factions to influence the outcome of civil wars, each with a view to see to the instalment of a friendly regime in Kabul. Over a period of time, their support to rival armed groups has assumed an ethno-regional character, accentuated regional polarity and inadvertently contributed towards state fragmentation. A brief history of the two countries' relations with Afghanistan will provide a useful background to understand their behaviour and their stakes in the civil war affected country.

16. Ibid.

17. Ibid.

India and Afghanistan

India and Afghanistan share a common history as part of the Turko-Persian Mughal Empire from 16th to 18th century. Earlier, Afghan empires routinely conquered parts of northern India and based their kingdom from Delhi. Historical linkages shaped close cultural affinity and led to both having favourable perceptions about each other, resulting in cordial relations.[18]

Geo-political factors, most decisive being the common animosity towards Pakistan, bolstered the bilateral ties. Soon after independence in 1947, India and Pakistan fought over the disputed Kashmir valley. As described in detail later, Afghanistan faced a similar disgruntlement with Pakistan over the issue of Pashtun nationalism and called for a re-negotiation of its border defined by the Durand Line. Disputes with Pakistan brought Afghanistan and India together, who signed a friendship treaty in 1950.

Bilateral ties cooled during the 10-year-long Soviet intervention in Afghanistan, which started in December 1979. Initially, New Delhi had decided to publicly condemn the intervention against a fellow non-aligned state in the United Nations.[19] However, within a month, in January 1980, the newly appointed government of Indira Gandhi tempered its criticism and adopted the stand that the intervention was carried out on the request of the Afghan government. In international forums, India made customary calls for ending the conflict. Privately, however, it was extremely critical of Soviet presence in Afghanistan and urged Moscow to extricate itself at the earliest. In fact, India was as much concerned about renewed US military aid to Pakistan for supporting Afghan rebels as about regional instability and the rise of Pakistan-based, religiously motivated rebels in the neighbourhood. To this end, Indian diplomats travelled to world capitals to

---

18. Afghans are known to most Indians as simple, large-hearted people, a perception epitomised in Nobel Laureate Rabindranath Tagore's Kabuliwala. Its inclusion in school curriculum has ensured that Afghans are well-disposed among a cross section of Indians. On the other hand, Indian culture, especially cinema and music, is extremely popular with Afghans.
19. This occurred during the interim caretaker government of Charan Singh. See: Dixit, J.N. (2000). *An Afghan Diary: Zahir Shah to Taliban*. New Delhi: Konark Publishers. p.20.

advance a regional political solution, which envisioned the exit of Soviet troops and involved Pakistan, Iran and India.[20]

Following the Soviet exit in 1989, India continued to maintain ties with President Mohammad Najibullah and provided development assistance. However, as Afghanistan descented into a civil war, following the fall of the Najibullah government, India's presence in the country ebbed and flowed.[21] New Delhi cut off ties with Kabul during Taliban's rule from 1996 to 2001. It supported anti-Taliban militias, which had retreated to northern Afghanistan under the banner of the United Islamic Front, more widely known as the Northern Alliance. The Northern Alliance comprised Tajik, Uzbek, Hazara, Turkmen and a few Pashtun militias and was led by Ahmad Shah Massoud. Besides India, they were supported by Russia and Iran.

India renewed its ties with Kabul immediately after the US invasion of Afghanistan and the defeat of the Taliban. Though the new government of Hamid Karzai was envisioned as a multi-ethnic body, it quickly came to be dominated by members of the former Northern Alliance, many of whom had earlier sought refuge in India and remained favourable towards it. After a gap of decades, India had once again emerged as an important ally in Afghanistan.

Indian assistance to Afghanistan has progressively increased since 2001. Its aid programme began with a US$ 100 million line of credit, one million tonnes of wheat to displaced Afghans and medical resources. Since then, it has committed a total of US$ 2 billion in aid, making it the largest regional donor and the fifth largest donor internationally.[22] According to the Ministry for External Affairs, India has a presence in all parts of the country and is involved in different sectors such as "hydro-electricity,

20. The new US President Ronald Regan, however, was not in favour of a political solution involving regional players, and instead opted for a more aggressive military policy of increasing support for Afghan insurgents. As stated in popular accounts of the war, the USA wanted to take revenge for the Soviet assistance to the Viet Cong during the Vietnam War. See: Roy, Arundhati (1987). *The Soviet Intervention in Afghanistan: Causes, Consequences and India's Response*. New Delhi: Associated Publishing House.

21. For instance, India remained active during the rule of Burhanuddin Rabbani. See: Sawhney, R.K., Arun Sehgal and Gurmeet Kanwal (eds) (2011). *Afghanistan: A Role for India*. New Delhi: Knowledge World.

22. The largest donor countries are United States, United Kingdom, Japan and Germany.

power transmission lines, road construction, agriculture and industry, telecommunications, information and broadcasting, education and health, which have been identified by the Afghan government as priority areas for development".[23] India has also tried to increase the quantum of bilateral trade without much success.[24] Nevertheless, India signed a Preferential Trade Agreement with Afghanistan in 2003 and identified 38 items, which were given a 100 per cent tariff concession.[25]

India is involved in several large-scale projects that are strategic owing to their scope, long gestation period, and impact on governance and nation-building. It has built the 218-km Zaranj-Delaram highway in western Afghanistan, which will connect the country to Chabahar port in Iran, and in the process nullify Afghanistan's reliance on Pakistan for access to sea. Likewise, India has also constructed a 220 kW transmission line to Kabul at a cost of US$ 111 million, which will supply power to Kabul from neighbouring countries. Reconstruction of the Parliament building in Kabul, yet to be completed, is another symbolic gesture of good will.[26]

Other important projects include food assistance of one million tonnes of high protein biscuits distributed to 1.4 million school children daily, construction of the Salma Dam in Herat province, and construction of telephone exchanges and television networks to connect the government with the population.[27]

India also provides training of civilian and military nature. The Indian Council for Cultural Relations (ICCR) offers 500 university scholarships and 500 short-term training programmes annually. Thirty Indian civil servants of Director and Deputy Secretary rank have been deputed to

---

23. Indian Embassy (Kabul), "India's Assistance Program for Afghanistan's Reconstruction", <*http://meakabul.nic.in/*> (15 July 2011).

24. This is due to Pakistan's reluctance to allow duplex traffic of goods between India and Afghanistan. While it allows the flow of goods from Afghanistan to India, the reverse traffic is not permitted. On the other hand, the high travel time associated with transport through the Chahbahar port in Iran is not feasible, given the perishable nature of agrarian goods, the primary produce of Afghanistan.

25. *op.cit.* no.21.

26. Wonacott, Peter (2009). "India Befriends Afghanistan, Irking Pakistan," *The Wall Street Journal*, 19 August.

27. *op.cit.* no.23.

various Afghan ministries as mentors to their Afghan counterparts.[28] Outside the government, a prominent Indian women empowerment Non-governmental Organisation (NGO), SEWA, conducts a programme to impart vocational education to Afghan women, especially widows.[29]

India's relations with Afghanistan are driven by three factors. First, it wants to prevent Afghanistan's revert to a 'terror sanctuary'—that is, a failed state ruled by armed militias patronised by Pakistan, which offers sanctuary logistics and training to anti-India militant groups. During the 1990s several Afghan warlords supported Kashmiri insurgents like *Lashkar-e-Tayeeba* and *al-Badr* at the behest of Pakistan. The most well-known instance of Afghan support for anti-India terrorist groups took place in December 1999 when the Indian Airlines aircraft IC 814 was hijacked in Nepal by *Harkat-ul-Mujahideen* and flown to Kandahar, where the Taliban openly supported the assailants and made impossible any attempt to storm the plane to free the 178 passengers.

Second, India views Afghanistan's stabilisation as a case to extend its influence beyond its immediate periphery. Afghanistan's significance to India can be better contextualised by locating it within its foreign policy goals. According to noted foreign policy analyst, C. Raja Mohan, India 'divides the world into three concentric circles': the immediate neighbourhood, the extended neighbourhood and the entire global stage.[30] While New Delhi aspires for global role in future, it expects to project its power into the extended neighbourhood in the immediate future. Afghanistan, as a member of the South Asian Association of Regional Cooperation (SAARC), is seen as an extension of the neighbourhood, and therefore ideally suited for New Delhi to broaden its turf. Besides, as argued by Christine Fair, enduring bilateral ties with Afghanistan helps India unhinge itself from its troubled relations with Pakistan.[31]

Third, as Afghanistan is located in the vicinity of resource-rich Central Asia, India seeks friendly ties with Kabul in order to make inroads

28. Ibid.

29. *op.cit.* no.21.

30. Mohan, C. Raja (2006). "India and the Balance of Power", *Foreign Affairs* 85(4): 17-34, July/August.

31. Fair, Christine (2010). "India in Afghanistan, Part I: Strategic Interests, Regional Concerns", *Foreign Policy*, 26 October.

into the Central Asian Republics. An example of this is the 1,735 km long Turkmenistan-Afghanistan-Pakistan-India (TAPI) pipeline project. Funded by the Asian Development Bank and approved by India's Central Cabinet in 2006, the project when operational will bring Turkmenistan's natural gas into India through Afghanistan and Pakistan, benefiting both countries.

Pakistan and Afghanistan

Afghanistan and Pakistan have never enjoyed cordial relations, even though they share the same religion and overlapping ethnicity.[32] Their ties have vacillated between apathy and open hostility, and are informed by Pakistan's inheritance of 'Frontier Politics' from Britain.

Much of Pakistan was once part of successive Afghan kingdoms. During the first half of the 19th century, Pashtun regions of modern day Khyber Pakhtunkhwa and the abutting tribal areas fell to the Sikh Empire. Sikh defeat to the British in the Second Anglo-Sikh War of 1849 brought these regions under the direct control of Britain. During the same period, Russia had reached the Amu Darya (river that marks Afghanistan's northern boundary) and began to make overtures to the Afghan emperor, sparking off an intense competition between the two powers over influence in Afghanistan, popularly known as the 'Great Game.' Britain initiated a 'forward policy' of ruling over Kabul through direct occupation, but after three costly wars, opted for a 'closed border' policy. The new strategy called for creating a multi-layered buffer zone that would safeguard Britain's colonial interests against Russian aggression. The innermost buffer comprised the directly administered North-West Frontier Province, the second buffer was made up of the autonomous tribal areas, and the outermost buffer comprised the protectorate of Afghanistan.[33] This

32. The only exception to this generalisation occurred during the Taliban rule, its relations with Pakistan too was not without its share of difficulties. Taliban refused to evict the anti-Shia Lashkar-e-Janghvi militants who had taken refuge in Afghanistan. Taliban's rigid stance on destroying the Bamiyan Buddha sculptures infuriated Pakistan, especially as it was lobbying for Taliban's acceptance in the international community. For more on Pakistan's complicated relation with the Taliban during the 1990s, read the author's interview with distinguished Taliban expert Rahimullah Yusufzai. (Chakrabarti, K.D. (2009). "Links between the Taliban and al Qaeda have Grown Stronger", *Open Democracy*, 24 November.)

33. Rubin, Barnett R. and Abubakar Siddique (2006). "Resolving the Pakistan-Afghanistan Stalemate", *United States Institute of Peace, Special Report* 176, October.

system defined Britain's policy towards Afghanistan and greatly influenced Pakistan's relations with Afghanistan-post-1947.

When Pakistan became an independent state in 1947, it inherited the Durand Line, and by extension, the buffer zones. Afghanistan was quick to point out that Britain's exit had nullified the border treaties; it demanded plebiscite in Pakistan's Pashtun regions to determine the future of Pashtunistan, the homeland for Pashtuns living east of Khyber Pass. It even refused to recognise Pakistan in the UN and deployed its armed forces along the border. Although Kabul withdrew its objection within a month, it continued to raise the issue of Pashtun irredentism at various forums.

The issue refused to die out and a point of criticality was reached when, in July 1949, Pakistan bombed an Afghan border village, prompting a furious Kabul to convene a *Loya Jirga* (Grand Council of Elders), and declared unstinting support for the Pashtunistan demand. In 1961, Pakistan broke diplomatic relations with Afghanistan and cancelled transit rights for trade, bringing the neighbour nation's economy to the brink of collapse.

Both countries have actively supported rebel groups on the other side of the border, deepening the mistrust between the two. Afghanistan gave shelter to 30,000 Baloch rebels during the 1970s and was also accused of aiding *al-Zulfiqar*, the militant splinter faction of the Pakistan People's Party, led by Murtaza Bhutto, who sought to destabilise the military regime of General Zia ul-Haq. For its part, Pakistan initiated its harassment policy by exploiting Pashtun dissatisfaction against Kabul, which arose in wake of the reformist Saur Revolution. Pakistan sought to discredit the new Communist government and supported dissidents such as Gulbuddin Hekmatyar and Ahmad Shah Massoud as early as 1975. As argued by Lawrence Ziring, Pakistan "assisted disaffected and alienated Pashtuns on the Afghan side of their mutual border, while reinforcing and providing linkages with tribal elements on their own side. Islamabad, in fact, adopted the Pashtunistan movement and reworked it to serve its own interests."[34]

Since the days of Soviet presence in Afghanistan, Pakistan has been selective in supporting rebel groups that conform to its stratagems. It favoured conservative Pashtun leaders over non-Pashtun commanders.

34. Kukreja, Veena and Mahendra Prasad Singh (eds.) (2008). *Democracy, Development and Discontent in South Asia*. New Delhi: Sage Publications.

During the civil war that followed the Soviet withdrawal, Pakistan supported eastern Pashtun (Ghilzai Pashtun) groups such as *Hizb-e-Islami*, Taliban and, in recent years, the Haqqani network led by Jalaluddin Haqqani.

After 2001, Pakistan reduced its economic assistance considerably, despite the fact that Afghanistan is the third biggest importer of Pakistani goods (bilateral trade reached US$ 1.4 billion in 2008).[35] Islamabad's contribution to Kabul's reconstruction and rehabilitation projects amounts roughly to US$ 87 million, and is focussed on health, education and communication sectors.[36]

Pakistan's Afghanistan policy is driven by its acrimonious history with Afghanistan and India. First, Pakistan seeks to balance, if not nullify, Afghanistan's episodic support to the Pashtunistan cause. Islamabad realises well that no government in Kabul, including the Taliban, has agreed to negotiate the border dispute, which remains a sensitive issue among Afghan Pashtuns. Such is the emotive appeal of ethnic solidarity that when faced with domestic criticism, Afghan leaders repeatedly espouse Pashtun nationalism inside Pakistan to deflect censure. In 2005, Hamid Karzai resumed the practice of celebrating 'Pashtunistan Day' on 31 August every year. The next year, he publicly dubbed the Durand Line a 'line of hatred,' saying that he rejected it as "it raised a wall between the two brothers."[37] Pakistan's counter move has been to aggressively promote its allies in Afghan politics and during civil wars. In fact, more critical observers of Pakistan's foreign policy argue that it would prefer that Afghanistan stayed economically fragile and politically unstable, as this would obviate any support for Pashtun separatism in the future. Pakistan's support to the Afghan Taliban and other rebel groups derives from the same logic.

Second, Pakistan is deeply sensitive about the ascendency of 'pro-India' actors in Kabul. Its foreign affairs experts and the military top brass

35. Foreign Office, Government of Pakistan, *Foreign Office Year Book 2008-09*: Islamabad: Government of Pakistan.

36. Ibid.

37. Siddiqi, Shibil (2008). *Afghanistan's Pakistan Relations: History and Geopolitics in a Regional and International Context: Implications for Canadian Foreign Policy*. Toronto: Walter and Duncan Gordon Foundation.

is convinced[38] that India nurtures close relations with Afghanistan only to create a circle of influence around Pakistan. They contend that India's aim is to create conditions for a scissor attack on both the eastern and western fronts of its neighbour country in collaboration with its Afghan allies.[39] Having learnt its lesson from the defeat in 1971 war, where it lost the Eastern wing of the nation (now Bangladesh), Islamabad is particularly apprehensive of New Delhi's intensions *vis-à-vis* Kabul. Pakistan security establishment's deeply entrenched worldview that all of its security threats are reducible to India further reinforces this alarmist perception. In this context, under-representation of the Pashtun community has made Pakistan anxious. Afghanistan's Parliament, administration and security organs—dominated as it is by former Northern Alliance members, who had received generous support from India during the war with the Taliban in the 1990s—are a matter of serious concern for Pakistan. Besides the Taliban's defeat, its exclusion from the political process, and the fractious nature of Pashtun societies in south and east Afghanistan have created a leadership vacuum, denying Pakistan the insurance of a Pashtun counterweight to the Tajik and Uzbek 'encroachment' into traditional Pashtun spheres.[40]

Lastly, the more ambitious Pakistani strategists have called for outright monopoly of influence over Afghanistan. Their argument is that Pakistan's narrow 'geo-strategic depth' leaves it vulnerable to a conventional attack by India, whose numerically superior forces could well penetrate deep into the country and split it, as it had done in the 1971 war. Given the constraints of terrain, proponents of 'strategic depth' contend that Pakistan must exploit Islamic sentiments among conservative Afghans (to be precise,

38. Civil-military relations in Pakistan are overwhelmingly dominated by the army, which has launched four coups against civilian rule. In the past three decades, the army has continued to direct the country's foreign and security policies even during periods of civilian rule. Greater analysis of civil-military relations in Pakistan can be found in Rizvi, Hasan-Askari (2000). *Military, State and Society in Pakistan*. Palgrave Macmillan. The most authoritative history of the Pakistan army is found in Nawaz Shuja (2008). *Crossed Swords: Pakistan its Army, and the Wars Within*. Karachi: Oxford University Press.

39. Pakistan's official position on India's role in Afghanistan was explained to the author by Director General of the Pakistan military's Inter-Services Public Relations. Transcript of the interview is available in Chakrabarti, K.D. (2009). *India's role in Afghanistan is encirclement of Pakistan*. Observer Research Foundation.

40. International Crisis Group (2003). "Afghanistan: The Problem of Pashtun Alienation", *Asia Report No 62*, 5 August.

Sunni, Pashtun Afghans), and not negotiate with regional players like India and Iran. The client-patron relationship will give Pakistan's armed forces the option of withdrawing to Afghanistan's rugged terrain in the event of a successful Indian invasion of Pakistan, and fight a war of attrition from there. This concept has been dismissed by several Pakistani analysts, who point out that a Punjabi-dominated army will never receive permanent refuge among the Afghans. Further, they reject with scorn the idea that their conventional army will ever be degraded to a guerrilla organisation against its historic adversary. While it is not possible to precisely gauge Rawalpindi's guiding principle, several attacks against Indian interests inside Afghanistan strongly suggest that Pakistan is unwilling to accept the healthy nature of Afghanistan-India relations in its current context. The biggest such attack targeted the Indian Embassy in Kabul on 8 October 2009, which, according to Afghan and US intelligence, was carried out by the Haqqani network at the behest of Pakistan's Inter-Services Intelligence (ISI). Likewise, a guest house frequented by Indian officials in Kabul was raided by insurgents on 26 February 2010, in which six Indians were killed.

Prospects of Cooperation

The strategic underpinnings of India-Pakistan rivalry in Afghanistan are deep and firm. That said, even as they accentuate the polarities in a third country, they also present an exciting alternative that promises to convert regional competition into cooperation and to reduce resource deficiencies in reconstruction programmes. Joint India-Pakistan nation-building teams would concurrently yield five positive outcomes: diminish ethnic and political polarities, provide necessary human resources, device mechanisms to enable India and Pakistan to verify each other's role, foster cooperation and reduce mistrust and, ultimately, provide a viable means to promote Afghanistan's neutrality.[41]

First, joint India-Pakistan teams, comprising administrators, advisors, military trainers, development experts, medical crews, bureaucrats and NGO's will facilitate dialogue between the belligerents based in the north and south of Afghanistan. As mentioned earlier, India has considerable goodwill, especially among leaders who represent northern communities.

41. These ideas were first presented by Chakrabarti, K.D. (2010). "To Build Bridges in Afghanistan, Deploy India-Pakistan Nation-Builders", *Small Wars Journal*, 30 October.

Pakistan, on the other hand, enjoys a degree of persuasive clout over Pashtun rebels based in the southern and eastern Afghanistan through covert support, ethnic and kinship ties, as well as informal ties formed in seminaries and refugee camps in the border regions. Once India and Pakistan jointly agree to relinquish the quest for monopoly over influence and, instead, cooperate to secure their respective interests concurrently, joint nation-building teams could persuade their Afghan partners to cease violence and hold negotiations. Furthermore, besides adding much needed numbers to the reconstruction effort, India and Pakistan can be counted on to remain in Afghanistan for the long haul.

Second, as the process begins to show positive results and insurgents enter the political process, India-Pakistan joint teams could be used to aid the reconciliation process. After all, even as the Taliban seek to reconcile with the 'rest-of-Afghanistan,' there are ample reasons to be sceptical about the willingness of the incumbents to make political space for their current adversaries. While Pakistani elements could encourage Pashtun rebels to hold peace dialogue, their Indian counterparts, in turn, could convince the incumbents to accommodate those insurgents who renounce violence.

As this happens, the programme will provide a system for India and Pakistan to verify claims of wrongdoing by the other. India's alleged support to Baloch insurgents and India's understanding of the extent of Pakistan's support to the Taliban are informed by history and perception, as much as by facts. Formal presence of security analysts will give policy makers additional information to make factually correct analysis and alter negative perceptions informed by past history. It will also foster confidence between agencies of the two governments. Such a change may well cascade into a less alarmist view of the other, compelling both sides to accommodate mutually beneficial policies.

The greatest service of such cooperation would be that it would contribute towards Afghanistan's neutrality, as also to a treaty whereby Afghanistan's neighbours would agree not to use Afghan soil against one another. A government that accurately represents all sections of the Afghan society will naturally refuse to be subservient to any one neighbour, be it India or Pakistan. Such an arrangement will create conditions that will limit Pakistan's penchant for exploiting militant groups as state tools. More importantly, it will help obviate Islamabad's legitimate fears, rooted in history, that India may use Afghanistan as a trump card to destabilise north-western Pakistan. Ultimately, the changed paradigm of neighbourhood relations based on cooperation will emerge, which will give Afghanistan and Pakistan enough faith to finally settle their border dispute and normalise a region that has been the stage for the longest American war of the century.

Conclusion

The cliché that Afghanistan is a 'graveyard of empires' and its 'unruly people' hard-wired to violently oppose foreign occupation is so prevalent that it continues to shape policy debates. However, this sweeping assumption belies large phases of the country's history when it enjoyed lasting stability despite the reign of foreigners in Kabul. Afghanistan's association with civil war, insurgency and its use as 'the base' (the literal translation of *Al Qaeda*) of international terrorism obscure the remarkable degree of apolitical attitude of ordinary Afghans for much of its history. Be that as it may, three Anglo-Afghan wars changed Afghans, for better or worse, into more politically conscious actors, and in the process, strengthened regional elites—both traditional and the modern 'non-state' kind—at the expense of the Centre.

The Saur Revolution exposed the state's frailty as it dismally failed to implement its reformist agenda in the countryside, where the majority of the Afghans reside. Soviet intervention of the country destroyed the little legitimacy that its client had earlier enjoyed and militarised large sections of society. Since both the state and the insurgents lacked central authority, aspiring rebels and civilians turned into local military commanders, empowering them on their home ground.

Following the Soviet Union's withdrawal and its subsequent collapse, the international community (with the exception of Pakistan) too extradited itself from what was now a devastated country with a crippled economy. In the absence of international assistance, Kabul failed to restore its control over the varied ethnic and regional militias. After years of state fragmentation, Afghanistan eventually fell victim to a vicious civil war that no one could win.

This did not stop them from striving to capture the state that they had crippled so spectacularly only a few years ago. With the Cold War over, local commanders—now firmly entrenched as 'warlords'—turned to regional state-actors for resources, military advice and diplomatic support.

Afghan belligerents—the south- and east-based Taliban, and the north- and west-based Northern Alliance—acquired the support of arch-rivals Pakistan and India, respectively. In the process, the civil conflict assumed the unenviable distinction of being both the cause and the consequence of enhanced competition between India and Pakistan. For Afghans, the bipolar nature of the conflict led to a stalemate between the warring factions and increased violence to a record level.

The dialectics between compliance and legitimacy that emerge from Afghanistan's recent history appear set to resonate once again after the US exits from the country. Despite the deployment of 30,000 troops in 2009, international forces achieved limited success, the sustainability of which hinges on continued security presence. Unfortunately, lasting security, the fundamental prerequisite to generate compliance among rebels and civilians, is not being met.[42] Foreign troops have begun to withdraw before the task of training Afghan forces to levels of self-sufficiency could be accomplished. This is evident by increased insurgent assaults on high-security complexes such as the Defence Ministry, police headquarters, military hospitals and prominent hotels. Insurgents' infiltration into the army and police cadres also points at the armed forces' lack of battle readiness.

At the moment, neither the government nor the Taliban can claim dominance. Their ability to instigate terrorist violence at a place of their choice cannot be equated with the creation of rebel proto-states, the favourable end-state sought by insurgents. The Taliban and their associates have recently made tentative forays into previously secure regions such as Herat and Takhar (northern Afghanistan). Still, the geographical spread of the insurgency is simply not matched by a corresponding increase in the degree of control exercised by it. Taliban may have the upper hand, but

42. The best analytical explanation of security as a driver for compliance in civil conflict is provided by Kalyvas, Stathis (2006). *The Logic of Violence in Civil War.* New York: Cambridge University Press.

they do not possess sufficient strength to defeat the state.[43] Clearly, neither the government nor the insurgents can claim outright victory. At the same time, there are major problems with the reconciliation process.

In such a precarious situation, the withdrawal of foreign troops generates uncertainty over the future of the Karzai regime. Its longevity depends on Karzai's ability to identify regional power-brokers and selectively distribute US largesse among them, thereby creating a patronage network to sustain his regime. This was what Najibullah had done during 1989-1992. Besides the USA, Karzai will no doubt be supported by India as well as Russia. Irrespective of its actions and public statements, the current Northern Alliance bias and Pashtun under-representation in the state apparatus will compel Pakistan to continue to safeguard its interests, which will most likely take the form of support to Afghan dissidents.

With India and Pakistan supporting opposing forces, there will be an increase in violence, leading to a stalemate that would be of no benefit to either of the countries. Pakistan, with a weak aid-dependent economy, does not have the resources to support a client-state.[44] While India's bigger economy could make a claim to sustaining a state in collaboration with others, it simply cannot get access to the land-locked country without Pakistan's acquiescence.

In conclusion, competition over monopoly of influence in Afghanistan will not yield a single winner. Cooperation, on the other hand, is a more promising option. India and Pakistan's enmity is confined to security matters. They are not economic rivals and have cooperated in projects such as TAPI. Pakistan's concerns over Pashtun irredentism and Indian 'over involvement', and India's anxieties over re-emergence of terrorist safe-havens can be met concurrently if both India and Pakistan choose to collaborate.

To end on a bright note, the idea of collaboration between two bitter rivals might appear utopian, but past experiences of cooperation between adversarial states give reasons to question the validity of this negative,

---

43. This argument is explained in detail in Chakrabarti, K.D. (2011). "Taliban's Piercing 'Spring Offensive'—Dominance or Desperation?", Observer Research Foundation, 2 July.

44. This became evident to Afghans after the Taliban failed to provide even rudimentary relief during the 3-year drought that occurred during their rule. The Taliban did not enjoy international recognition, and its biggest patron, Pakistan, could not supply enough resources to mitigate the natural disaster.

traditional judgment. The USA and Russia chose to forgo decades of rivalry and cooperated to secure nuclear weapons located in Russia and its former republics such as Ukraine, Kazakhstan and Belarus. India and Pakistan, believed to be mired in an intractable conflict of ideas and terrain, and incapable of cooperating, moved past years of daily skirmishes on the Line-of-Control in Kashmir in 2003 and, against much conventional wisdom, have succeeded in keeping the peace for almost a decade.

19 Afghanistan Quagmire

Central Asia, India and Russia

Angira Sen Sarma

Hope for peace in Afghanistan is fading away as the deadline for the international forces' departure date comes closer. The series of violent incidents in the past few years paint a gloomy future for the war torn country. Some of the attacks include the assassination of the former President and Chairman of the High Peace Council, Prof. Burhanuddin Rabbani on 20 September 2011, bomb blast at the US base in Wardak province in September 2011, attacks in Kabul on British Council (August 2011) and on the heavily guarded International Hotel (June 2011). There were other incidents—such as: the killings of President Hamid Karzai's half brother Ahmed Wali Karzai (July 2011), who was the Head of Kandahar's Provincial Council and one of the influential political figures of southern Afghanistan; Jan Muhammed (July 2011), another powerful politician and a close associate of President Karzai; and Arsala Rahmani (May 2012), who was a top member of the Peace Council—all underscoring the grim security situation in Afghanistan. Given the prevailing sociopolitical, economic and security environment in Afghanistan, the immediate and the most worrisome issue today is how capable the Government is to take over the governance of the country from the international forces once they leave Afghan soil by 2014.

The US-led coalition forces ousted the Taliban regime in 2001 but have so far failed to contain its resurgence. The grim security situation, rampant corruption, lack of development, poor economy, drug trafficking and inter-clan rivalries are some of the daunting challenges Afghanistan faces today. There has been a re-eruption of the Taliban's acts of violence, specially since 2005. Cautioning the international community about the re-emergence of Taliban, the former US Secretary of State, Condoleezza Rice stated in 2006: "Taliban has come back somewhat more organised and more capable than people would have expected".[1] The situation today has further worsened with Taliban presence increasing not only in southern and eastern parts of Afghanistan, the traditional strongholds of the Taliban, but also in northern parts. Having emerged financially stronger and 'tactically more sophisticated', the Taliban forces today are posing direct threat to the reconstruction process in Afghanistan.

This paper discusses the resultant threats faced by the five Central Asian republics (CARs), India and Russia. It also examines the possibility of cooperation among these seven concerned countries to help bring about a modicum of stability in the long troubled country. Can they come up with a regional strategy, which would initiate the process of resolving the ongoing crisis?

Central Asian Republics Facing the Direct Burden[2]

Resurgence of Taliban, a Major Security Challenge to the Region

Three of the five CARs share borders with Afghanistan. The longest border is with Tajikistan, which is about 1206 km.[3] Afghanistan has a 744 km border with Turkmenistan and a 137 km boarder with Uzbekistan.[4] Geographical proximity makes the CARs highly vulnerable to the fall out of instability in Afghanistan. The growing influence of Taliban, drug trafficking, the precarious security situation, spread of religious extremism and terrorism from Afghanistan are the prime concerns of these countries.

Since the rise of Taliban in the mid-1990s, the Central Asian region has been facing a serious security threat. The radical ideology of Taliban is a direct threat to the secular identity these infant republics have been trying to foster post-independence.[5] Moreover, Taliban has close

1. "Taliban Insurgency Stalks NATO", <*http://www.defencetalk.com/taliban-insurgency-stalks-nato-8283/*>. (16 September 2011).
2. Taken from Sen Sarma, Angira (2012). "Central Asian Republics and the Afghan Crisis", *FPRC Journal* 10(2): 202-12. New Delhi: Foreign Policy Research Centre, <*http://www.fprc.in/pdf/J-10.pdf*>.
3. <*http://www.afghanistan.org/aboutafg.html*> (12 June 2011).
4. Ibid.
5. Warikoo, K. (2011). "Introduction", in K. Warikoo (ed.), *Religion and Security in South and Central Asia*. London, New York: Routledge. p.3.

links with the extremist groups in these nations. Its support helped the Islamic Movement of Uzbekistan (IMU) to launch a series of attacks on Uzbekistan-Kyrgyzstan border in 1999 and 2000,[6] spreading panic in the region. The IMU also fought for the Taliban against the Northern Alliance forces of the slain Ahmed Shah Masood.[7] The IMU is believed to have received funds and weapons from various sources, which included opium smuggling funds from Afghanistan, the Al Qaeda, Islamic groups in Afghanistan and Pakistan, besides sponsors from the Gulf States and Saudi Arabia.[8] Juma Namangani, one of the founder members of the IMU, is said to have received US$ 26 million from Osama bin Laden.[9] Emphasising on the link between extremist groups in Central Asia and Taliban, President Islam Karimov of Uzbekistan in 2000 said: "fugitives from Uzbekistan have undergone training in Afghanistan (and Tajikistan) and have become professional militants and terrorists".[10]

A major shift in the region was noticed with the onset of the US-led war in Afghanistan post September 11. The Taliban forces were driven out of Afghanistan. The IMU supporting the Taliban also suffered a severe blow: several of its guerrillas were killed and many others fled to the neighbouring tribal areas of Pakistan.

Even after a decade of the 'Operation Enduring Freedom,' the US-led coalition forces have failed to wipe out Taliban's influence from Afghanistan. Geography links security in Central Asia directly with the Afghan situation. Peace and stability in Afghanistan is one of the determining factors for "security and ensuing sustainable development in Central Asia".[11] President Karimov, at the 2010 Summit meeting of the Shanghai Cooperation Organisation (SCO), stressed the need for peace in

---

6. Rashid, Ahmed (2002). *Jihad: The Rise of Militant Islam in Central Asia*. India: Orient Longman Private Limited, pp.164-5.
7. Ibid.: 164.
8. Ibid.: 165-66.
9. Ibid.: 166.
10. SWB (Summary of World Broadcast), "President Karimov urges Central Asia to unite against International Terrorists" SU/3934 G/1, No.1, 1 September 2000.
11. Akmalov, Shoislam (2009). "Uzbekistan's Role in Stability and Development of Afghanistan", *Policy Perspectives* 6(1), January-June, <*http://www.ips.org.pk/pakistan-and-its-neighbours/1048-uzbekistans-role-in-stability-and-development-of-afghanistan.html*>, 3 March 2011.

Afghanistan and said: "there is no need to prove that without solving the problem in Afghanistan, which has for the past 30 years been torn in war, it is impossible to talk about peace and stability in Central Asia".[12] The SCO Declaration at its Tenth Council of Heads Meeting also highlighted the fact that "continuing escalation of confrontation in Afghanistan, terrorism, drug trafficking and transnational organised crime rooted from this country remain[s] a big source of threats in the region [sic]".[13]

Instability in Afghanistan can fuel social and political tensions brewing in the region. Past experiences like the Tajik civil war (1992-1996), the Andijan incident of May 2005 and the Tulip Revolution of 2005 indicate the underlying tensions in the region. Given the CARs' experience with the Taliban regime in the 1990s, these republics today are deeply concerned about the resurgence of Taliban in Afghanistan. The CARs, as immediate neighbours, are worried about the future of their war-torn neighbour after the international forces leave the country and certain that the situation would worsen further, aggravating the prevailing tensions in the region.

Among other issues, the revival of extremist groups in the region is one of the major threats faced by these republics, exacerbated by the export of extremist ideology and terrorism from Afghanistan. Despite the setback in 2001, the IMU today has regrouped, revived and has goals that are "more ambitious".[14] The region has been witnessing the growth of other radical groups such as *Hizb-ut-Tahrir al Islami* (Islamic Party of Liberation) (HuT) and *Akramiyya*, *Hizb an-Nusra*, much to the discomfort of the regional governments. HuT has been operating in the region since the birth of these republics. The organisation has now evolved into a "major threat to [regional] stability".[15] The 2003 International Crisis Group

12. Press Service of the President of the Republic of Uzbekistan, Speech by President Karimov at SCO Summit in Tashkent (Extended Meeting), 11 June 2010, *<http://www.press-service.uz/en/news/show/vistupleniya/vyistuplenie_prezidenta_respubliki_uz_3/#>*, 7 August 2010.

13. Declaration of the Tenth Meeting of the Council of the Heads of the Member States of the Shanghai Cooperation Organization, 11 June 2010, *<http://www.sectsco.org/EN/>*, 7 August 2011.

14. Siddique, Abubakar (2010). "IMU's Evolution Branches Back to Central Asia", 6 December, *<http://www.rferl.org/content/imu_evolution_branches_back_central_asia/2240765.html>*, 12 October 2011.

15. Khamidov, Alisher (2003). "Hizb-ut Tahrir Faces Internal Split in Central Asia", *Eurasia Insight*, 20 October, *<http://www.eurasianet.org/departments/insight/articles/eav202103.shtml>*, (14 July 2009).

(ICG) report indicated that the movement first emerged in Uzbekistan in mid-1990s and eventually spread to southern Kyrgyzstan, especially after the Uzbekistan Government's repressive measures in 1997 forced many to leave the country.[16] The report added that the movement gradually extended to Tajikistan and since 2000, it has gained foothold in southern Kazakhstan and in the prisons of Turkmenistan. The CARs have declared HuT illegal. *Akramiyya* and *Hizb an-Nusra*, the breakaway factions of HuT, were established in 1996 and 1999, respectively. The series of attacks in the month of June and July 2011 against the government forces in Kazakhstan, the most stable country in the region, cast further doubts about the stability in the region. Although the Kazakh government has denied these attacks having links with terrorist outfits,[17] the incidents of violence are a wake up call for the region.

The Ferghana Valley, shared by Uzbekistan, Tajikistan and Kyrgyzstan, is located close to Afghanistan and is thus specially vulnerable to the spread of radical ideology. The Valley, having a high density of population, has been the centre of Islamic revivalism and radical groups.[18] Any unrest in the Valley would easily spread over the whole region, primarily because of its location.

Instability in Afghanistan can escalate the prevailing uncertainties in Kyrgyzstan. The fragile democracy in Kyrgyzstan and the tension between the two main ethnic groups—Kyrgyz and Uzbeks—have the potential to destabilise the region. The year 2010 was marked by violence and political unrest in Kyrgyzstan, one of the poorest countries in the region. In April 2010, the five-year rule of President Kurmanbek Bakiyev came to an end following violent protests in the country. Back in 2005, President Askar Akayev was removed from power in a similar manner. Immediately following the April 2010 incident, the country was gripped with another problem—ethnic clashes between Uzbeks and Kyrgyz at Osh and Jalalabad

16. ICG (International Crisis Group) (2003). "Radical Islam in Central Asia: Responding to Hizb ut Tahrir", ICG Asia Report No. 58, (Osh/Brussels) 30 June, *<http://www.crisisgroup.org/en/regions/asia/central-asia/058-radical-islam-in-central-asia-responding-to-hizb-ut-tahrir.aspx>*, (30 August 2011).

17. Sharip, Farkhad (2011). "Radical Islamists Step Up Militancy in West Kazakhstan", *Terrorism Monitor* 9(29), 22 July, *<http://www.jamestown.org/single/?no_cache=1&tx_ttnews%5Btt_news%5D=38214>*, (12 February 2011).

18. *op.cit.* no.5: 5.

in southern Kyrgyzstan, widening the gap between the two already polarised ethnic groups. Although the government was able to control the social unrest, the two ethnic groups continue to be suspicious of each other.

Amidst these tensions, a national referendum was held on 27 June 2010, changing the constitution from a presidential to a parliamentary system. The first parliamentary election was held on 10 October 2010, making Kyrgyzstan the first country in the region to opt for a parliamentary democracy. However, no party managed to get the required majority and, after several rounds of negotiations, Social Democratic Party of Kyrgyzstan (SDPK), *Respublika* and *Ata Zhurt* formed a coalition government in December 2010. The rivalries among the coalition partners followed and there were incidents of violence during parliament sessions among the members in April 2011, raising doubts about the future of democracy in the country. The coalition government collapsed within a year on 2 December 2011, after differences among the partners over judicial, political and economic reforms. A new coalition government was formed comprising the SDPK, *Ar Namys*, *Respublika* and *Ata-Meken* on 16 December. The country faced another political crisis in August 2012 after the coalition collapsed yet again. A new government was formed in September 2012 consisting of SDPK, Ata Meken and Ar Namys. The new Prime Minister, Zhantoro Satybaldiyev, is from the SDPK.

The socio-political instability and the poor economic conditions make the situation in Kyrgyzstan grim and could destabilise the entire region, especially the bordering countries that would face the brunt of any upheaval in Kyrgyzstan.

Drug Trafficking

The menace of drug trafficking and the nexus between narcotics trade and extremist groups have drawn the attention of the regional actors and other affected countries like Russia. Drugs emanating from Afghanistan reach Russia and Europe through the Central Asian countries. The bulk of the world's supply of opium comes from Afghanistan. According to the World Drug Report of 2010, the area under opium cultivation in Afghanistan in 2009 was 123,000 ha, mainly in the southern and western parts of the country. This accounts about 66 per cent of the world's total cultivation[19] and about 89 per cent of the global illicit opium production.[20] It is a highly lucrative source of income for the farmers who have no alternative crops to grow for their livelihood. Measures like destruction of poppy fields, seizure of opium shipments, etc., have so far failed to eradicate opium cultivation. Moreover, opium trade is a major source of funding for the extremist groups: even by a conservative estimate, the Taliban make a profit of US$ 125 million per year from the narcotics trade.[21]

The drugs trade is an additional threat to the CARs as it forms a major transit route for the Afghan narcotics trade. The route, accounting for about 25 per cent of the total Afghan heroine trade, became popular in mid-1990s.[22] The porous border, coupled with corruption, makes it difficult to check the menace in these countries. The main destination of opium trafficked through Central Asia is Russia. A small portion is also trafficked to China's Xinjiang province and then onwards to other Chinese provinces. The most frequently used route in the region is the Afghanistan-Tajikistan border.

Murat Laumulin, a noted scholar from Kazakhstan, pointing out that the 'Drugs-Crime-Radical Islamist Nexus' was a major concern for the region, says: "It is not clear the extent to which this is cause or effect but the close ties between the more violent Islamist groups and organised crime has been undeniable from the time the IMU emerged as a major drug dealing enterprise. Indeed, in this sense Central Asia and Caucasus are examples of a worldwide trend, of the increasing involvement of violent groups in organised crime, particularly the drug trade [sic]."[23] Apart from drug money financing extremist forces, these republics also have to face the burden of the increasing use of opiate by the local population, resulting in serious social and health hazards. The number of registered HIV cases has increased manifold in Central Asia. During the period 2000-2008, the

19. United Nations Office on Drugs and Crime (UNODC) (2010). *World Drug Report 2010*, New York. p.137, <*http://www.unodc.org/documents/wdr/WDR_2010/World_Drug_Report_2010_lo-res.pdf*>, 10 September 2011.

20. Ibid.: 140.

21. Ibid.: 34.

22. Ibid.: 48.

23. Laumulin, Murat T. (2007). *The Geopolitics of XXI Century in Central Asia*. Almaty: The Kazakhstan Institute for Strategic Studies. p.209.

number of cases has increased from 1,641 to 30,993.[24] Table 19.1 shows the quantity of consumption and the number of people addicted in Central Asia. The total quantity of heroine and opium consumption in Central Asia is 11 mt and 34 mt, respectively.

Table 19.1

Heroine Users and Consumption in Central Asia

Country	*Number of estimated heroine users*	*Estimated level of heroine consumption (mt)*	*Number of estimated raw opium users*	*Estimated level of opium consumption (mt)*
Tajikistan	20,300	1	4,700	3
Turkmenistan	31,200	1	1,400	1
Uzbekistan	118,600	5	13,800	8
Kyrgyzstan	25,900	1	9,600	5
Kazakhstan	86,000	3	33,000	18
Total (rounded)	282,000	11	62,500	34

Source: United Nations Office on Drugs and Crime (2010), *World Drug Report 2010*. New York, p.53. <*http://www.unodc.org/documents/wdr/WDR_2010/World_Drug_Report_2010_lo-res.pdf.*> (10 September 2011).

CARs Contribution in Afghan Reconstruction

Since stability in Afghanistan is central to stability in Central Asia, the CARs have been encouraged to engage in the reconstruction process in that country. Individually, these countries have taken small steps to help rebuild Afghanistan. For example, during the period 2006-2009, Kazakhstan provided US$ 1 million humanitarian aid to Afghanistan, scholarships to several Afghan students to study in Kazakhstan, besides providing training to Afghanistan's police and internal security service, etc.[25] It is the only country in the region to have an Assistance Programme on Reconstruction of Afghanistan. It has also built a school in Samangan province, a hospital in Bamiyan province, besides providing assistance to increase the supply of agricultural seeds. Uzbekistan has been supplying power to Afghanistan

24. *op.cit.* no.18: 53.

25. Embassy of the Republic of Kazakhstan in the United States, "Kazakhstan's Stance on Current International Issues", <*http://www.kazakhembus.com/index.php?page=foreign-policy*>, (12 October 2011).

since 2002 and has built bridges connecting Mazari-Shariff and Kabul, thereby linking the northern and eastern parts of Afghanistan.[26]

India, an Old Friend

India and Afghanistan have a long history of friendly ties, except during the four years (1996-2001) of Taliban rule. India had not given recognition to the Taliban government and had severed diplomatic ties with Kabul, but was quick to re-establish ties as soon as the Taliban was removed from power in 2001.

Why is Afghanistan important for India? Having experienced threats from Taliban ruled Afghanistan, India today is wary of its resurgence in Afghanistan. Its ascendance in Afghanistan in the mid-1990s posed security threats to India. There is ample evidence of Taliban supporting terrorism in India. The Taliban regime, besides training Kashmiri militants and fuelling militancy in the state, had set up training camps in Pakistan-occupied Kashmir and Pakistan.[27] Salient examples of its anti-India activities are the support it extended to the hijackers of the Indian aircraft IC-814 in 1999, the attacks on the Indian Embassy in Kabul in 2008 and 2009 and the attacks on Indian workers engaged in reconstruction work in Afghanistan, all indicating that India still faces threats from extremist forces of Afghanistan.

In India's strategic calculation of Afghanistan, the Pakistan factor remains significant. Sharing direct border with Afghanistan and having vital stakes in Afghanistan, Pakistan will remain an important player in the region. Pakistan was one of the three countries that had officially recognised the Taliban government. Many of the Taliban leaders and cadre members fled to Pakistan after they were driven out of Afghanistan and are still present in Pakistan's border areas. Taliban-controlled Afghanistan would serve Pakistan's activity against India, as evidenced during the four years of Taliban regime. Pakistan has opposed the presence of Indian consulates in Afghanistan. Pakistan views India's influence in Afghanistan

26. *op. cit.* no. 11.

27. Warikoo, K. (2007). "Afghanistan Factor in Kashmir Crisis", in K. Warikoo (ed.), *Afghanistan: The Challenge*. New Delhi: Pentagon Press. p.211.

as an attempt to encircle it and has therefore been trying to sabotage New Delhi's construction efforts in Afghanistan.

Economically, Afghanistan provides the shortest route for India to access the energy-rich CARs. If the Turkmenistan-Afghanistan-Pakistan-India (TAPI) pipeline sees the light of the day, India's limitations to access Central Asia will be resolved. However, among other issues, a stable and a secure Afghanistan is of vital importance if the TAPI project, the 'garland highway' (connecting India-Iran-Afghanistan, eventually extending to Central Asia) is to fructify.

India, the Largest Regional Donor

Given India's strategic and economic interests in Afghanistan, India wants to see stability returning soon to Afghanistan. It has been actively engaged in the reconstruction process in Afghanistan. The two countries have been working to "combat terrorism and build a united, democratic and pluralist Afghanistan".[28] In October 2011, both countries signed the Strategic Partnership Agreement. India was the first country with which Afghanistan signed such an agreement. India has also agreed to train personnel and provide equipment to the Afghan National Security Forces.

India's engagement in Afghanistan is based in four broad areas—infrastructure projects, humanitarian assistance, small and community-based development projects, and education capacity development.[29] India's assistance has reached US$ 1.3 billion, making it the sixth largest bilateral donor to Afghanistan,[30] as also the largest regional donor. During his May 2011 visit to Kabul, Prime Minister Manmohan Singh announced a further assistance of US$ 500 million, which will take India's total assistance to Afghanistan to about US$ 2 billion.[31] The inauguration of the 218 km Zaranj-Delaram road connecting Iran to Afghanistan in January 2009, despite facing several threats, is an example of India's commitment to

28. Ministry of External Affairs (2011). "India-Afghanistan Relations", Government of India, January, <*http://www.mea.gov.in/meaxpsite/pressrelease/2011/01/bilateralafganistan.pdf*, (17 October 2011).

29. Ibid.

30. Ibid.

31. Address by Prime Minister to the Joint Session of the Parliament of Afghanistan, 13 May 2011, <*http://www.mea.gov.in/mystart.php?id=530117626*>, (10 August 2011).

Kabul. It also constructed the transmission line from Pul-e-Khumri to Kabul and helped build a substation at Chimtala, bringing Uzbek electricity to Kabul.[32] It is also constructing the Parliament building and the Salma Dam power project in Herat.

Russia and Afghanistan: Bridging the Gap

The continuing impasse in Afghanistan is a concern for Russia too, which is carefully watching the situation in Afghanistan. The spread of Islamic extremism, terrorism and drug trafficking from Afghanistan are major threats facing Russia too. If the instability in Afghanistan spreads to the CARs, Russia's immediate neighbours, Russia's security and economic interests will also be severely undermined.[33] Russia has been the worst hit by drugs trafficked from Afghanistan. It has emerged as a "major consumer of Afghan heroine and opiates".[34] Central Asia is the main transit route for drugs trafficked to Russia. According to the World Drug Report of 2010, the number of estimated heroine users in Russia is 1,500,000; estimated level of heroine consumption is 70 mt; the number of estimated raw opium users is 160,000; and the estimated level of opium consumption is 58 mt.[35] The increased use of opium and heroine has led to various social evils in Russia, threatening the social fabric of the country.

Russia's primary goal in Afghanistan is to prevent "outright victory for the Taliban, stemming the flow of drugs out of Afghanistan, especially into Russia, and restoring a pacified and neutral Afghanistan as a buffer state between Central Asian and the Greater Middle East".[36] Despite the mistrust between the two countries, a consequence of the Soviet experience, both sides today are working to improve the bilateral ties. After a gap of 15 years, Russia reopened its embassy in Kabul in 2007. The bilateral trade in 2010 reached US$ 500 million and both sides have

32. *op.cit.* no. 28.

33. Trenin, Dmitri (2011). "Contemporary Issues in International Security: Central Asia", in Stephen J. Blank (ed.), *Central Asian Security Trends: Views from Europe and Russia*, SSI Monograph, The Strategic Studies Institute (SSI), April, pp.58-61, <*http://www.strategicstudiesinstitute.army.mil/pdffiles/PUB1063.pdf*>, 1 October 2011.

34. Ibid.: 59.

35. *op.cit.* no.19: 53.

36. *op.cit.* no.33: 60.

agreed to further strengthen economic cooperation.[37] President Karzai, in a statement during his January 2011 visit to Russia, said: "Russia is a great political, economic and military power. In the past few years our bilateral relations have significantly strengthened".[38] Calling Russia an 'important partner,' President Karzai highlighted the need for Moscow's cooperation to curb the scourge of drug trafficking.[39]

Russia in Afghanistan's Reconstruction

Russian investment in the country has increased over the years since the fall of the Taliban. Russia is also involved in the country's reconstruction process. Russian companies are engaged in the modernisation of the Naglu hydropower plant outside Kabul and for reviving the Soviet-type house-building factory in Kabul.[40] Russia has also expressed its willingness to reconstruct the Salang Tunnel linking Kabul with the Northern provinces.[41] It has also extended its support to the TAPI project. According to news reports, Putin as the Prime Minister had said that Russia is willing to "invest a half billion dollars in a power line from Tajikistan to Pakistan across Afghan territory and many more billions in a gas pipeline from Turkmenistan to India across Afghanistan and Pakistan".[42]

The two countries have strong bilateral military cooperation and Russia has supplied spare parts for the military hardware the Soviets left behind in Afghanistan, besides providing heavy armaments like tanks, helicopters and air carriers.[43] It has gifted 22,000 Kalashnikov assault rifles and 2.5 million rounds of ammunition to Afghanistan.[44] It is also engaged in imparting military training to Afghan military officers. Recently, Russia had increased the number of Afghan officers being trained in

---

37. "Afghan Leader Says Russia 'Important Partner', Seeks Closer Ties", 21 January 2011, *<http://en.rian.ru/world/20110121/162233983.html>*, (15 October 2011).
38. Ibid.
39. Ibid.
40. Igor, Bestuzhev (2011). "Afghan Army may Get Russian Helicopters", January 31, <http://english.ruvr.ru/ru/_print/42099769.html>, (10 August 2011).
41. Ibid.
42. "Russia to Return to Afghanistan", 22 January 2011, *<http://english.ruvr.ru/_pint/40804343.html>*, (15 October 2011).
43. *op.cit.* no.40.
44. Ibid.

Russia's Military Academies to 225[45], besides helping Afghanistan's law enforcement agencies.

Is Regional Cooperation the Way Out of the Present Crisis?

To rebuild Afghanistan and help the country come out of the present crisis, cooperation among the regional players is crucial. With every chance of the situation worsening after the USA starts pulling out its combat troops, it is necessary that the regional players actively cooperate to stabilise Afghanistan. India, Russia and the CARs could jointly play a greater constructive role in Afghanistan. Other important regional players, like Pakistan, Iran and China with vital stakes in Afghanistan, will have to be involved in any regional efforts to bring peace and stability in Afghanistan.

Pakistan would be one of the most important players in any regional attempt to resolve the crisis in Afghanistan. Despite tensions between the two countries, Pakistan-Afghanistan ties have been gradually improving over time. Geographical proximity and its close links with Taliban play critical role in shaping Pakistan's equation with Afghanistan. Importantly, Pakistan has always viewed Afghanistan as a strategic asset in case of a war with India[46] and will not allow its influence to wane in the nation to its west.

China, with US$ 3.5 billion investment in the Aynak copper mine, is today the largest foreign investor in Afghanistan[47] and has emerged as one of the most important stakeholders in Afghanistan. Economic interest is one of the key drivers of China's Afghan policy because the volatile situation in Afghanistan threatens the safety of Chinese investments. China is also worried that the Uyghur movement in Muslim-dominated Xinjiang Autonomous region in western China might attract support from the Taliban forces in Afghanistan. The 76 km long border between the two countries, however small, is porous enough to make China apprehensive

45. Ibid.
46. "Ganging up on India", *The Economist*, 1 July 2010, *<http://www.economist.com/node/16485368>*, (5 February 2011).
47. "As U.S. Fights, China Spends in Afghanistan", 5 July 2010, *<http://www.chinapost.com.tw/international/middle-east/2010/07/05/263320/p1/As-US.htm>*, (25 March 2011).

about the inflow of religious extremism. China thus has vital interests in seeking the settlement of the Afghan crisis.

Sharing a border of about 936 km, Iran is also deeply concerned about the deteriorating condition in Afghanistan. The growing influence of Taliban, drug trafficking and the refugee crisis threaten Iranian security too. Iran shares ethnic, religious and linguistic affinities with a few ethnic tribes of Afghanistan, such as the Hazaras and Tajiks. This affinity is also an important consideration in Iran's involvement in Afghanistan. During the Taliban rule, Iran had extended support to the Northern Alliance group (non-Pashtun) in their struggle against the Pashtun-dominated Taliban forces. After the removal of Taliban, Iran became one of the important donor countries. Iran has been engaged in various small and big projects in Afghanistan, such as building the 317 km Herat road, the Friendship Bridge connecting Milak in Iran to Zaranj in Afghanistan, etc.[48]

Cooperation among regional countries today is vital but is stymied by the differences between the various players and would not be easy to achieve, despite the urgency for such cooperation. For example, Indo-Pak differences hinder cooperation between these two important regional players. Among other issues, the two countries' equations with Taliban reflect their strong divergences. Moreover, China's presence in Afghanistan would strengthen its old ally, Pakistan, raising suspicion in India. US-Iran differences are yet another hurdle in the path of successful regional cooperation. Although Iran is a major player, the USA would try to thwart any attempt to include Tehran in resolving the crisis in Afghanistan. How far China would like to get directly involved in Afghanistan remains ambiguous.

An ideal situation would have been the regional players along with Russia and the USA working closely to restore stability in Afghanistan. The recent deterioration in US-Pakistan relations has added to the uncertainties in the region. Until all the interested players agree on a common agenda, India, Russia and the CARs, with similar concerns in Afghanistan and having enjoyed friendly ties with each other, can come forward with joint

48. Taherian, Mohammad Ebrahim (2010). "Undermining Iran's Positive Role in Afghanistan", 2 November, <*http://www.iranreview.org/content/Documents/Undermining_Iran%E2%80%99s_Positive_Role_in_Afghanistan.htm*>, 23 July 2011.

action plans. To begin with, the seven countries could jointly organise international conferences on Afghanistan, involving regional and external stakeholders to address issues of economic and security concerns in Afghanistan. At various multilateral forums, the seven countries could give voice to the urgent need for a regional approach to tackle the present situation.

In the past few years, regional players have taken initiatives to bring together the concerned parties, an example being the conference on Afghanistan held in Moscow in March 2009 under the aegis of the SCO. Other instances of such regional efforts were the three quadripartite meetings involving Tajikistan, Pakistan, Afghanistan and Russia held twice in Dushanbe (2009 and 2011) and once in Sochi in 2010. The SCO conference brought together all the stakeholders, while the quadripartite summits included only selective players, narrowing its scope.[49] The two conferences on Afghanistan held in 2011 in Istanbul and Bonn may not have come out with outstanding results, but these forums provided a common platform to identify the challenges and opportunities for discussions.[50] India, Russia and the CARs could lead the initiative to bring together more frequently all stakeholders to discuss the developments in the troubled country and try to evolve a common strategy for peace and stability.

Given the complex social and political situation, military power alone will not be able to resolve the crisis. Afghanistan needs a strong economy, firm political institutions and a social infrastructure to address the multiple challenges the country faces today.[51] Among other issues, lack of development is an important cause of discontent among the common people, which has and will continue to help Taliban to regain its support base among the masses.[52] India, Russia and the CARs are bilaterally engaged with Afghanistan in its reconstruction process. Cooperation among these countries to pull in resources for bigger reconstruction projects could

49. Sen Sarma, Angira (2012). "Central Asian Republics and the Afghan Crisis", *FPRC Journal* 10(2): 202-12. New Delhi: Foreign Policy Research Centre, *<http://www.fprc.in/pdf/J-10.pdf>*.

50. Ibid.: 20.

51. Ibid.

52. Ibid.

possibly be another way to strengthen the role of these countries in bringing Afghanistan out of the current mess.[53]

With the signing of the Strategic Partnership Agreement between the USA and Afghanistan, it is now clear that the former's presence in the country will continue post-2014. The agreement, signed on 2 May 2012, states: "...in order to strengthen security and stability in Afghanistan, contribute to regional and international peace and stability, combat al-Qaeda and its affiliates and enhance the ability of Afghanistan to deter threats against its sovereignty, security, and territorial integrity, the Parties shall continue to foster close cooperation concerning defense and security."[54]

The Chicago Summit Declaration also stated that the North Atlantic Treaty Organization (NATO) will "continue to provide strong and long-term political and practical support through our Enduring Partnership with Afghanistan. NATO is ready to work towards establishing, at the request of the Government of the Islamic Republic of Afghanistan, a new post-2014 mission of a different nature in Afghanistan, to train, advise and assist the ANSF [Afghan National Security Forces], including the Afghan Special Operations Forces."[55] For a long-term solution to the Afghan crisis, cooperation among all stakeholders, including the USA, would help in addressing the multiple challenges facing the country today. Looking at the Afghan issue from the prism of the 'great power politics' will only further complicate the situation.

53. Ibid.

54. For details see "Emerging Strategic Partnership Agreement between the United States of America and the Islamic Republic of Afghanistan", <*http://www.whitehouse.gov/sites/default/files/2012.06.01u.s.-afghanistanspasignedtext.pdf*>, 29 May 2012.

55. "Chicago Summit Declaration", 20 May 2012, <*http://www.nato.int/cps/en/natolive/official_texts_87593.htm?mode=pressrelease*>, (29 May 2012).